This is a fascinating study of the making of the Harley Psalter, an illustrated manuscript which was produced at Christ Church, Canterbury, over a period of about one hundred years, from *c.*1020–*c.*1130. The Harley Psalter was closely based on the Utrecht Psalter, the most celebrated of all Carolingian illuminated manuscripts. Through meticulous observation of the Harley Psalter, William Noel analyses how the artists and scribes worked with each other and with their manuscript exemplars in making their illustrated text. The author demonstrates that this work is best understood not as a copy of the Utrecht Psalter, but rather as one of a series of Anglo-Saxon manuscript experiments that incorporated its imagery. The Harley Psalter is undoubtedly a crucial work for understanding the development of art, script, and book making during what has been termed the 'golden age' of Anglo-Saxon art.

Cambridge Studies in Palaeography and Codicology 4

THE HARLEY PSALTER

Cambridge Studies in Palaeography and Codicology

This new series has been established to further the study of manuscripts from the middle ages to the renaissance. It will include books devoted to particular types of manuscript, their production and circulation, to individual codices of outstanding importance, and to regions, periods and scripts of especial interest to scholars. Certain volumes will be specially designed to provide students in the field with reliable introductions to central topics, and occasionally a classic contribution originally published in another language will be translated into English. The series will be of interest not only to scholars and students of medieval literature and history, but also to theologians, art historians and others working with manuscript sources.

ALREADY PUBLISHED

Manuscripts and Libraries in the Age of Charlemagne
by Bernhard Bischoff, translated by Michael Gorman

The Early Medieval Bible: its Production, Decoration and Use
edited by Richard Gameson

Cultural Interplay in the Eighth Century: the Trier Gospels and the Making of a Scriptorium at Echternach
by Nancy Netzer

The Harley Psalter
by William Noel

FORTHCOMING TITLES

The 'Miroir Historial' of Jean le Bon
by Claudine Chavannes-Mazel

Medieval English Scripts: a Handbook
by Jane Roberts

From Anglo-Saxon to Romanesque: English Manuscripts in the Eleventh Century
by Richard Gameson

THE HARLEY PSALTER

WILLIAM NOEL

University of Cambridge

Published by the Press Syndicate of the University of Cambridge
The Pitt Building, Trumpington Street, Cambridge CB2 1RP
40 West 20th Street, New York, NY 10011-4211, USA
10 Stamford Road, Oakleigh, Melbourne 3166, Australia

First published 1995

Printed in Great Britain by Redwood Books, Trowbridge, Wiltshire

A catalogue record for this book is available from the British Library

Library of Congress cataloguing in publication data

Noel, William.
The Harley Psalter / William Noel.
p. cm. – (Cambridge studies in palaeography and codicology; 4)
Based on the author's thesis (Ph.D.), Cambridge University, 1993.
Includes bibliographical references and index.
ISBN 0 521 46495 1 (hardback)
1. Harley Psalter. 2. Illumination of books and manuscripts, Anglo-Saxon. 3. Utrecht Psalter – Influence. I. Title. II. Series.
ND3357.H37N6 1996 95-955 CIP
745.6'7' 0942659 – dc20

ISBN 0 521 46495 1 hardback

In memory of my mother
Elizabeth Noel

Contents

Illustrations

Photographic Acknowledgements

Warburg Institute: figs. 1, 3, 4, 5, 7, 11, 13, 16, 19, 21, 23, 25, 28, 30, 32, 35, 37, 39, 41, 42, 43, 44, 48, 49, 50, 53, 55, 57, 59, 61, 63, 66, 69, 71, 75, 78, 81, 82, 83
Rijksuniversiteit Bibliotheek, Utrecht: figs. 2, 6, 10, 12, 15, 18, 20, 22, 24, 27, 29, 31, 34, 36, 38, 40, 47, 51, 52, 54, 56, 58, 60, 62, 67, 68, 77
The Conway Library, Courtauld Institute of Art: figs. 64, 65, 70, 72, 73, 74, 76
The British Library: figs. 79, 80
Anderson-Lovelace: fig. 46

Acknowledgements

This book has developed from a doctoral thesis which was supervised by Professor George Henderson. His lectures on medieval art at the Department of History of Art in Cambridge have been inspirational lessons in looking, and his comments on my work on Harley 603 have provoked refinements of substance and style at every stage. I have relied on the advice and friendship of Dr Rosamond McKitterick since 1986, and I would be happy to think that this book is some reward for her interest in my work. In fact it represents yet more of hers. I have also found the comments of Sandy Heslop invaluable. The time that he has spent disagreeing with me has been some of the most instructive and enjoyable that I have spent. I cannot put into words my debt to Dr Michelle Brown, unless they be the 90,000 odd that follow. To these four people I extend my heartfelt thanks. This book is inconceivable without them. I am alone responsible for the errors of fact and interpretation contained within it.

Other scholars to whom I am particularly grateful are the late Dr Peter Carter, who first introduced me to the Middle Ages; Dr Ted Powell, who tried to teach me how to argue; and Dr Paul Binski, who tried to teach me how to do it with as much art as I could muster. I am also greatly indebted to Miss Janet Backhouse and to Dr Patrick Zutshi for their valuable comments on earlier drafts of this book.

I have benefited from discussing my work with many people, in particular Dr Alain Arnould, Linda Brownrigg, Jackie Burns, Dr Sarah Foot, Dr Caroline Hull, Dr Antonia Gransden, Tim Graham, Michael Gullick, Dr Isabel Henderson, Dr Martin Kauffmann, Peter Kidd, Dr Charlotte Klonk, Dr Anne Korteweg, Dr Thomas Kren, Dr Jean Michel Massing, Margot McIlwain, Dr Scot McKendrick, Professor Nigel Morgan, Dr Michael Rosen, Dr Magnus Ryan, Kathryn Smith, Dr Patricia Stirnemann, Dr Elizabeth Teviotdale, Dr Christopher Thornhill, Nancy Turner, and Dr Tessa Webber.

I have been greatly assisted by the staff of the libraries in which I have worked. I am grateful to all the staff of the British Library Students' Room, but particularly to its supervisor, Julian Conway. Koert van der Horst, Keeper of Manuscripts at the University Library of Utrecht, was warmly welcoming in August 1991 and has been most helpful ever since. Dr Paul Taylor, Dr Elizabeth McGrath, and Dr Michael Evans of the Warburg Institute have also been extremely helpful. The time I have spent at the Warburg has been largely taken up with studying the unpublished work of Adelheid

Heimann on Harley 603. Most of the photographs of Harley used in this book are taken from the almost full-sized ones which she commissioned. She was convinced that the manuscript was the most interesting of those derived from the Utrecht Psalter, a view that I heartily endorse. I am also greatly indebted to Margaret Jocelyn, Maddie Brown and the staff of the library of the Department of History of Art, Godfrey Waller and the staff of Cambridge University Library, Trinity College Library Cambridge, the Parker Library, the Bibliothèque Municipale in Boulogne, the Bodleian Library, the Bibliothèque Nationale in Paris, the Biblioteca Apostolica Vaticana, and the Courtauld Institute of Art. I would also like to thank the staff of Cambridge University Press, and in particular Dr Katharina Brett and Alison Gilderdale, for their help in seeing the manuscript through to publication.

Throughout my undergraduate and postgraduate career I was a member of Downing College, Cambridge. Amongst the many that helped me there, I would particularly like to thank John Hopkins, and Mr and Mrs Wheeler and their colleagues. I am extremely grateful to the British Academy for the Postdoctoral Fellowship that allowed me to continue my research, and to the Department of History of Art, Cambridge University, where I hold that position.

I could not have written this book without the friendship and support of my family, and of Caryl Aitchison, Stacy Boldrick, Cecil Brown, Nicholas Brown, Susan Elderkin, Kalantha Joseph, Sylvia Stevenson, and the parents of my godchildren Emma, Hugh, and Camille.

A note on the psalm texts

When referring to the Psalms of the Harley Psalter, I cite the text in the manuscript, with all abbreviations expanded, and with modern punctuation. The Harley Psalter has an eccentric text, part Gallican, part Roman. I cite the verses as they are enumerated in the following editions: for the Roman,

> R. Weber (ed.), 'Le Psautier Romain et les autres anciens Psautiers latins', *Collectanea Biblica Latina*, 10.2, 1953;

for the Gallican,

> R. Weber and B. Fischer (eds.), *Biblia Sacra : Iuxta Vulgatam Versionem*, 2 vols., Stuttgart 1969.

I have translated my citations of the text in the Harley Psalter, and placed them in footnotes at the end of each citation. I have used the Book of Psalms in the Douai Bible as the basis for these translations, and made alterations in the light of the Harley Psalter's text, its punctuation, and its illustrations.

Introduction

Aelfric's Psalter and the Harley Psalter

In his will of AD 1003–4, Aelfric, the archbishop of Canterbury, bequeathed a pectoral cross, a ring, and a book of Psalms to Wulfstan, the archbishop of York.[1] The book of Psalms was an appropriate part of Aelfric's bequest: more than any other book of the Middle Ages, the Psalter was at the centre of both public and private worship. It was recited in its entirety at least once a week in the performance of the liturgy, and it was extensively used for personal devotions. Aelfric's ring would have been of gold. His pectoral cross might have looked like the sculpted ivory in the Metropolitan Museum of Art, New York, which has stylistic parallels with a number of English manuscripts of the first quarter of the eleventh century.[2] His Psalter may well have been made in the scriptorium of his community, Christ Church, Canterbury, which was possibly the most productive in England at that time.[3] It must have been a worthy companion to the other two treasures, and quite different from most of his books, which were bequeathed to the community of St Albans. It was probably well written and decorated, with an elaborate binding. Wulfstan, for his part, would have had high expectations of Aelfric's Psalter. Certainly he appreciated fine books: he compiled and corrected the Old English material that was added to the York Gospels, and which included three of his own homiletic tracts.[4] This book was in part written by the master scribe Eadui Basan, who

[1] Dorothy Whitelock (ed.), *Anglo-Saxon Wills*, Cambridge 1930, pp. 52–5, with notes on pp. 160–3.

[2] See J. Beckwith, *Ivory Carvings in Early Medieval England*, London, 1972, p. 51, ills. 63–4, and cat. 27; also R.H. Randall, 'An eleventh-century ivory pectoral cross', *Journal of the Warburg and Courtauld Institutes*, 25, 1962, pp. 159–71.

[3] The pioneering work on this subject is T.A.M. Bishop, 'Notes on Cambridge Manuscripts, Part VII: The early minuscule of Christ Church Canterbury', *Transactions of the Cambridge Bibliographical Society*, 3.5, 1963, pp. 413–23. T.A.M. Bishop, *English Caroline Minuscule*, Oxford, 1971, provides a wider context. Since then the bibliography has burgeoned. T.A. Heslop, 'The production of *de luxe* manuscripts and the patronage of King Cnut and Queen Emma', *Anglo-Saxon England*, 19, 1990, pp. 151–95, is a seminal article on manuscript production in the period. D.N. Dumville, *English Caroline Script and Monastic History: Studies in Benedictinism, A.D. 950–1030*, Woodbridge, 1993, esp. pp. 86–131, is the most positive assessment of the pre-eminence of the Christ Church scriptorium at this time. N. Brooks, *The Early History of the Church of Canterbury*, Leicester, 1984, pp. 255–78, discusses the contents of the texts produced in the scriptorium, and the community context surrounding them.

[4] York, Minster Library Ms. Add. 1 (E. Temple, *Anglo-Saxon Manuscripts 900–1066. A Survey of Manuscripts Illuminated in the British Isles*, vol. 2, London, 1976, cat. 61); edited in facsimile as N. Barker (ed.), *The York Gospels*, Roxburghe Club, London, 1986. See the contribution of S. Keynes, 'The additions in Old English', pp. 81–99, at pp. 81–96.

worked at Christ Church,[5] and its illustrations have been attributed to the Christ Church artist of a manuscript of Prudentius' *Psychomachia*.[6]

There were many ways of decorating a book of Psalms,[7] but none was more elaborate than that employed in the Harley Psalter, BL Harley Ms. 603 (fig. 1).[8] Since the nineteenth century, there has been little doubt that its principal exemplar was the great Utrecht Psalter, Utrecht, Rijksuniversiteit Bibliotheek Ms. 32 (fig. 2).[9] The Utrecht Psalter is generally supposed to have been made at the monastery of Hautvillers, near Rheims, around AD 830. It was one of many manuscripts brought to England in the wake of renewed political links with the continent, and then monastic reform in the tenth century.[10] The drawings in this Psalter head each Psalm, Canticle, and prayer, and run across the three columns of text. They literally depict selected verses of the following text, combining them to form visually coherent compositions. They provided the most comprehensive surviving cycle of illustrations to the Book of Psalms, and became the model for the most extensive essay in line drawing by Anglo-Saxon artists.[11] The Harley Psalter is one of the glories of Anglo-Saxon art surviving from the century before the Norman Conquest.[12] It was the work of twelve hands; two scribes, two artist-scribes, and eight artists. Three of them can be identified as working on other manuscripts made at Christ Church, and one of them wrote BL

5 For the most recent discussion of Eadui's career, see Dumville, *Caroline Script*, pp. 120–40. For a convincing interpretation of his work on the York Gospels see Heslop, 'Cnut and Emma', pp. 166–72.

6 BL Cotton Cleopatra C.viii (Temple, *Anglo-Saxon Mss.*, cat. 49). The illustrated folios are reproduced in T.H. Ohlgren, *Anglo-Saxon Textual Illustration*, Kalamazoo, 1992, pp. 473–525. See Heslop, 'Cnut and Emma', p. 167, n.45, where it is noted that the artist of fols. 4v–7v (upper illustration) of the Prudentius manuscript, was the artist of the York Gospels. Bishop, 'Notes VII', p. 421–2, ascribes the Prudentius manuscript (his art. 7) to one of the inter-related scribes of the Christ Church scriptorium (his scribe ix).

7 For a discussion of the various types of Psalter illustration see V. Leroquais, *Les psautiers manuscrits latins des bibliothèques publiques de France*, 3 vols., Mâcon, 1940–1, vol.1, pp. LXXXVI–XCIX.

8 Temple, *Anglo-Saxon Mss.*, cat. 64. Full-page reproductions of all the illustrated folios of the manuscript are to be found in Ohlgren, *Textual Illustration*, pp. 147–248.

9 Two full facsimiles are available: *Utrecht Psalter*, A collotype facsimile, 2 vols., The Palaeographical Society, 1874, and *Utrecht Psalter*, Codices Selecti Phototypice Impressi, 75, Graz, 1982–4, with a commentary volume, including a bibliography, by K. Van der Horst and J.H.A. Engelbregt. The illustrated pages of the Utrecht Psalter are reproduced in E.T. DeWald, *The Illustrations of the Utrecht Psalter*, Princeton, 1932. W. de Gray Birch, *The History, Art and Palaeography of the Manuscript Styled the Utrecht Psalter*, London, 1876, at p. 117, writes of the relationship between the Harley and Utrecht Psalters that 'no one will venture to deny that the most intimate connection between the two manuscripts exists in a very prominent and self-asserting manner'. Some have done. For example, J.A. Herbert, *Illuminated Manuscripts*, London, 1911, p. 115, envisaged a long series of successive copies intervening between Utrecht and Harley. If there is any remaining doubt, it is hoped that this book will put the matter beyond any.

10 The standard, if dated, texts of the period remain F. M. Stenton, *Anglo-Saxon England*, 3rd edn, Oxford 1971, pp. 319–93, and D. Knowles, *The Monastic Order in England*, 2nd edn, Cambridge, 1966, pp. 28–82. For links between the English church and the continent, see V. Ortenberg, *The English Church and the Continent in the Tenth and Eleventh Centuries*, Oxford, 1992. See also F.A. Rella, 'Continental manuscripts acquired for English centers in the tenth and early eleventh centuries: a preliminary checklist', *Anglia*, 98, 1980, pp. 107–16.

11 For a characterisation of the Utrecht Psalter illustrations in particular, nothing surpasses F. Wormald, *The Utrecht Psalter*, Utrecht, 1953. An analysis of each Psalm is to be found in DeWald, *Utrecht Psalter*, with additions and corrections in S. Dufrenne, *Les illustrations du Psautier d'Utrecht, sources et apport carolingien*, Paris, 1978, pp. 41–4, n.110.

12 J.M. Backhouse, D.H. Turner, and L. Webster (eds.), *The Golden Age of Anglo-Saxon Art 966–1066*, Exhib. cat., London, 1984, is a useful introduction to the art of the period, and puts it into a historical context. Temple, *Anglo-Saxon Mss.*, is a summary illustrated catalogue of the illuminated manuscripts. See also L.L. Brownrigg, 'Manuscripts containing English decoration 871–1066, catalogued and illustrated: a review', *Anglo-Saxon England*, 7, 1978, pp. 239–66.

Stowe Charter 35 in 1002 or 1003. Harley may have been started when Aelfric was archbishop, and on its fol. 2r the initial to the first psalm depicts an archbishop, wearing his pallium, prostrate before the Lord.

However, if Harley was indeed Aelfric's book of Psalms destined for Wulfstan, it is difficult to know what use either archbishop would have found for it. It stands in marked contrast to the Bosworth Psalter, of *c.* 1000, which is traditionally, but probably incorrectly, associated with another archbishop of Canterbury, St Dunstan.[13] The Bosworth Psalter is a comprehensive text, containing a Roman version of the Psalms, a calendar, a litany, and all the important texts of the Benedictine Office. The Harley Psalter may be extensively decorated, but it ends incomplete at Psalm 143, verse 11, and it has none of the auxiliary apparatus normally associated with the Psalter. At least in the form in which it has survived, the Harley Psalter is a partial and eccentric document which would certainly not have helped an archbishop in his liturgical duties, and which might well have proved frustrating in his private devotions.

It has proved frustrating also for the modern historian. While Bosworth reveals much about the liturgical practices of a monastic community at the turn of the millennium, in Harley the scholar is deprived of many of the usual methods of dating and placing, let alone understanding the purpose of a book of Psalms. As a result, there is little scholarly consensus on the origin and dates of the manuscript. Wormald considered that the Harley Psalter was made at Christ Church, Canterbury.[14] This view was substantiated by Bishop's observation that one of the scribes of Harley was a Christ Church scribe,[15] and endorsed by Backhouse.[16] Others have disagreed: James and Dodwell both thought that it was made at St Augustine's,[17] and Carver found some evidence to support their hypothesis;[18] Higgit suggested that many of the drawings may have been executed at Glastonbury, and that the manuscript may then have moved to Christ Church;[19] and Gameson has recently noted that although the manuscript was executed at Christ Church, many of its artists may have come from Winchester, and returned there after they had finished their task.[20] There is no certainty that Harley was made at Christ Church, and it is not safe to assume that it was

[13] B.L. Add. Ms. 37517 (Temple, *Anglo-Saxon Mss.*, cat. 22). P. M. Korhammer, 'The origin of the Bosworth Psalter', *Anglo-Saxon England*, 2, 1973, pp. 173–87, argues for a Christ Church, Canterbury origin for the manuscript; N.A. Orchard, 'The Bosworth Psalter and the St Augustine's Missal', in R. Sharpe (ed.), *Canterbury and the Norman Conquest*, 1995, forthcoming, argues for a St Augustine's origin. See also G.R. Wieland, *The Canterbury Hymnal*, Pontifical Institute of Medieval Studies, Toronto, 1982; H. Gneuss, *Hymnar und Hymnen im englischen Mittelalter. Studien zur Überlieferung, Glossierung und bersetzung lateinischer Hymnen in England mit einer Textausgabe der lateinisch-altenglischen Expositio Hymnorum*, Tübingen, 1968, pp. 104–5 and *passim*; E. Bishop and F. Gasquet, *The Bosworth Psalter*, London, 1908; J.M. Makothakat, *The Bosworth Psalter: A Critical Edition*, unpublished D.Phil. thesis, University of Ottawa, 1972.

[14] F. Wormald, *English Drawings of the Tenth and Eleventh Centuries*, London, 1952, p. 69.

[15] Bishop, 'Notes VII', p. 420.

[16] J.M. Backhouse, 'The making of the Harley Psalter', *British Library Journal*, 10.2, 1984, pp. 97–113, *passim*.

[17] M.R. James (ed.), *The Canterbury Psalter*, London, 1935, p. 4, n.2; C.R. Dodwell, *The Canterbury School of Illumination 1066–1200*, Cambridge, 1954, pp. 1–3.

[18] M.O.H. Carver, 'Contemporary artefacts illustrated in late Saxon manuscripts', *Archaeologia*, 108, 1986, pp. 117–45, at p. 144, n.51.

[19] J. Higgit, 'Glastonbury, Dunstan, monasticism and manuscripts', *Art History*, 2, 1979, pp. 275–90, at p. 282.

[20] R. Gameson, 'Manuscript art at Christ Church, Canterbury, in the generation after St Dunstan', in N. Ramsay, M. Sparks and T. Tatton-Brown (eds.), *St Dunstan: His Life, Times and Cult*, Woodbridge 1992, pp. 187–220, at p. 208.

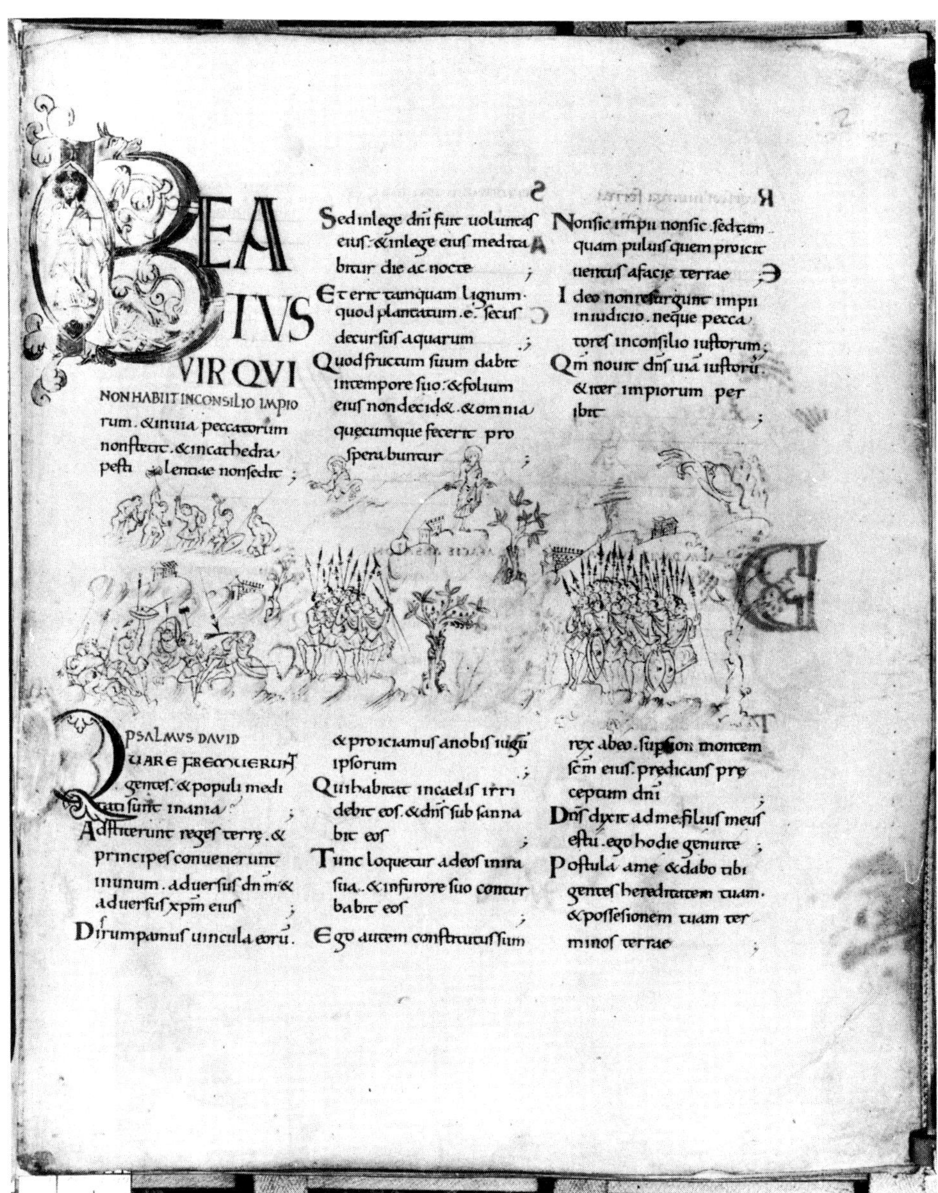

1 *The Harley Psalter, fol. 2r. The illustration to Psalm 2 is by A; the script is by scribe 1; the rubrication is by E; the display capitals and Beatus initial are by I; the initial to Psalm 2 is by J; there is a correction to the text in column a, last line,* Disrumpamus; *additions were made to the illustration by G.*

2 *The Utrecht Psalter, fol. 2r, showing the illustration to Psalm 2.*

entirely the work of the members of the scriptorium in which it was made.

Suggestions for the dates of the manuscript have also varied widely: for example, Bishop dated the work of one scribe to shortly after 1003,[21] whereas Brooks dated it to the end of the eleventh century;[22] Alexander and Kauffmann considered the presence of Eadui Basan to indicate that the manuscript was made *c.* 1015–25,[23] in contrast to Backhouse who dated the rest of the text to this time, but dated Eadui's script somewhat later,[24] while Pfaff dated all the script in the codex to the first ten years or so of the eleventh century.[25] There have been several suggestions for the patron of the Harley Psalter; the Psalter that Aelfric bequeathed to Wulfstan is but one of a range of possibilities. Backhouse considered that it was made for another archbishop of Canterbury, Aethelnoth,[26] but Hasler thought that it was begun for Aethelred the Unready, and finished for King Cnut.[27] We do not know who would have used it, nor how it would have been used.

The lack of scholarly consensus on the Harley Psalter is a measure of the state of unknowing concerning Anglo-Saxon manuscript production in the eleventh century. Much of the dissension has been caused by the fact that historians have tried to fit an interpretation of Harley into a historical framework deduced from other arguments. But the richness of the manuscript as a resource is not sufficiently appreciated if it is used merely to illustrate a historical debate. Nor are the issues surrounding it sufficiently understood for it to be used in this way with safety. The Harley Psalter merits detailed study, but to advance our understanding of it we should not begin with a patron who might have wanted it, nor with a set of historical circumstances into which it may be fitted. Rather, we should start with an analysis of how it was made, which might lead to an understanding of the circumstances of its production, and of the assumptions that lay behind the working procedure employed to make it, of the motives for its production, and, ultimately, of the patron who may have commissioned the volume.

Copying, copies, and facsimiles

The Harley Psalter is a crucial manuscript for understanding book production in England in the eleventh and twelfth centuries. It was executed over a period of more than one hundred years, and therefore offers an extraordinary opportunity to study the development of style, script, and manufacturing techniques within the confines of one volume. Moreover, it is admirably suited to an investigation of its construction. The survival of the Utrecht Psalter means that adherence to, and deviation from the

[21] Bishop, 'Notes vii', p. 420. [22] Brooks, *The Church of Canterbury*, p. 380–1, n.28.

[23] J.J.G. Alexander and C.M. Kauffmann, *English Illuminated Manuscripts 700–1500. Catalogue of the Exhibition at the Royal Library of Albert 1, 29 Sept. – 10 Nov.*, Brussels, 1973, pp. 38–9. [24] Backhouse, 'Making', p. 106.

[25] R.W. Pfaff, 'Eadui Basan: Scriptorum Princeps?', in C. Hicks (ed.), *Harlaxton Medieval Studies II: England in the Eleventh Century*, Stamford, 1992, pp. 267–83, at pp. 272–3. [26] Backhouse, 'Making', pp. 108–10.

[27] R. Hasler, 'Zu zwei Darstellungen aus der ältesten Kopie des Utrecht-Psalters, British Library, Codex Harleianus 603', *Zeitschrift für Kunstgeschichte*, 44, 1981, pp. 317–39, at pp. 320–2 and pp. 334–8.

exemplar can be noted precisely, and the decisions made concerning the manufacture of the volume can be traced in detail.

However, in studying Harley, Utrecht has caused as many problems as it has provided insights. These problems begin, not in trying to understand the differences between the two books, but rather in scholarly interpretation of Harley's fidelity to the Carolingian manuscript. Much is hidden in the familiar phrase that the Harley Psalter is the first English copy of the Utrecht Psalter. The phrase itself is the result of an accident of survival. Most books of this period were 'copies' of other books, but normally their exemplars have disappeared. Although the label 'copy' does not help us to understand the Harley Psalter any more than it does most other books, it has often been taken for an explanation of it. It is all too easy to confuse the motives that lay behind the production of the Harley Psalter with the techniques used to make it, and with the methods that the student employs in studying it. In scholarship today, Harley is used in conjunction with Utrecht, and the similarities and differences between the two books are noted. While this is undoubtedly a powerful key to interpreting the manuscript, the way that Harley is examined now has little or nothing to do with the way that it was designed to be used at the time. Did the owner of Harley really want a new manuscript for the purposes of comparing it with an old one in order to see how well the artists had copied it? If not, we must ask what it was wanted for, and whether the artists and scribes of the Harley Psalter were employing the Utrecht Psalter for reasons that might have allowed them to adapt their exemplar as well as to follow it closely. The word 'copy' does not explain the ways in which they used the exemplar, and it does not account for the reasons why they used it; if artists and scribes did follow Utrecht, we need to know how and why they did this. For example, was the sense of space created in the Utrecht Psalter something that they wished to recreate, or was it incidental to their technique, which was geared towards quite other ends? If it was the latter, it would not be relevant to judge the Harley artists by the extent to which they achieved the sense of space created in the Utrecht Psalter. It would be rather like judging William Webb Ellis by the rules of soccer:[28] the Harley Psalter was largely born of the Utrecht Psalter, just as rugby was born of soccer, but it would not be any more pertinent to accuse the Harley artists of being spatially blind than it would be to accuse a rugby player of committing handball. They may have been interested in Utrecht for quite other reasons.[29] If we can unravel these reasons, we can get close to the purpose of Harley.

The problems engendered by understanding the Harley Psalter as a copy of the Utrecht Psalter are compounded when, in later phases of its production, Harley deviates dramatically from its exemplar. Explanations for the appearance of the later quires of Harley are necessarily based upon judgements concerning its early quires.

[28] In 1823 William Webb Ellis picked up a football and ran with it over the opposing team's goal line, thereby scoring the first try.

[29] S. Dufrenne, 'Les copies anglaises du Psautier d'Utrecht', *Scriptorium*, 18, 1964, pp. 185–97, at pp. 196–7, and R. Gameson, 'The Anglo-Saxon artists of the Harley (603) Psalter', *Journal of the British Archaeological Association*, 143, 1990, pp. 29–48, *passim*, discuss the degree to which the Harley artists maintained the sense of space created in Utrecht.

Since it has been assumed that Harley was intended to be a copy of Utrecht, deviation from this goal has been understood as a radical change of intention in the programme, or in the circumstances surrounding the manufacture of the volume. Fuelled by the distressed appearance of the manuscript on the one hand, and by the drama of the Anglo-Saxon Chronicle on the other, scholars have sought to explain the manuscript by reference to events outside the scriptorium. For example, Dodwell thought that Harley was made at St Augustine's, Canterbury and that Utrecht, which he believed was at Christ Church, a stone's throw away, was only intermittently available.[30] Hasler suggested that the Utrecht Psalter was moved to Winchester, along with other artistic treasures, to save it from the ravages of the Danish army in 1010–11, and that therefore it was not available to the later artists of Harley.[31] There is nothing inherently unlikely about these suggestions. Manuscripts clearly travelled, and so did artists. The Stockholm *Codex Aureus* is a well-known example of a manuscript that was taken hostage, ransomed, and given to Christ Church.[32] But, unlike the Stockholm manuscript, there is no evidence that Harley was subjected to similar treatment. The only reason for supposing such an explanation is an inability to account for the physical state of the Psalter in any other way. Before resorting to these hypotheses, it is wise to study in detail the scribes and artists who worked on the book, and to understand the reasons for their actions. If Harley had a purpose of its own, independent of its exemplar, it would be a mistake to qualify the extent to which it is a copy of the Utrecht Psalter, and it would be a mistake to introduce *ad hoc* hypotheses to explain why it ceased to be one. This would be to work from an incorrect premise.

Rather, we might ask why the Utrecht Psalter was useful as an exemplar in the creation of Harley, why the responses to the exemplar were so different, and why a patron might have wanted a manuscript like Harley. It is not just that the hypotheses of Dodwell and Hasler leave so much unexplained, but also that they might not be necessary. The best account of the Harley Psalter surely is the one that explains the work of the scribes and artists of the book most fully, that makes the fewest auxiliary suppositions beyond the evidence available, and that is consistent with the range of possibilities in the eleventh and twelfth centuries.

The trouble with the word 'copy' is that it can be used as a verb and as a noun. As a verb, it is as useful as the verb to follow. As a noun, it gives a name to something that defines it entirely by its relationship with another thing, omitting all reference to its other characteristics, and the function it might have performed. In the eleventh century the Harley Psalter was not defined solely by its relationship with the Utrecht Psalter. We can speak of copying, a copyist, and a copy, but it is only possible to speak of following and a follower, adhering and an adherent. If words other than 'copy' are used, it is possible to articulate the techniques of manufacture employed in the book without characterising it as a whole. The word 'copy' will not be used as a verb again in this book. It will only be used as a noun to highlight its inadequacies.

30 Dodwell, *Canterbury School*, p. 3. 31 Hasler, 'Zu zwei Darstellungen', p. 322.

32 Stockholm, Royal Library, Ms. A.135 (J.J.G. Alexander, *Insular manuscripts 6th to the 9th century, A Survey of Manuscripts Illuminated in the British Isles*, vol. 1, 1978, cat. 30).

At its most extreme, 'copy' as a noun is synonymous with 'facsimile'. It has occasionally been suggested that the Harley artists set out to create a facsimile of Utrecht. Scribes and artists did make facsimiles in the medieval period. They should not be judged facsimiles by the extent to which they look like the original, for that is always relative.[33] Rather they should be judged by the presence of the intention to duplicate, for the purposes of topographical accuracy or deception, or because admiration of the original (for whatever reason) was unqualified. In certain respects some of the Harley artists and scribes imitated Utrecht, but if they had set out to make a facsimile of it, they would not have deliberately made their manuscript different from it at the same time.

Making the Harley Psalter

From the start Harley was to be different from Utrecht in some important respects, and these differences are revealing. It was to be in colour, not monochrome. Although Anglo-Saxon artists did frequently employ the technique of coloured line drawing,[34] this represents a deliberate choice on the part of the artists, and not just a natural translation into a new idiom; some line drawings made in this period were executed in only one colour, notably illustrations to a metrical calendar which are stylistically similar to the Harley Psalter.[35] It was also to be written in Caroline minuscule, and not in Rustic capitals like the Carolingian manuscript. By the time work on the Harley Psalter had started, Caroline minuscule had superceded Anglo-Saxon minuscule as the script in which Latin texts were normally written.[36] Possibly this change of script was a natural choice to make, and the Rustic capitals of Utrecht may have appeared outmoded to Anglo-Saxon scribes. However, Anglo-Saxon artists and scribes did recognise the formal qualities of Rustic capitals, and employed them, for example, in the *De laudibus sancte crucis* of Rabanus Maurus in Trinity College, Cambridge.[37] The change in drawing medium and in script betrays a willingness to experiment with the model that is also reflected in the version of the Psalter text employed. While the text of the Utrecht Psalter is Gallican, in accordance with the liturgical usage of Carolingian Francia, the Harley Psalter was initially to follow the Roman version of

[33] Compare, for example, the differences between the three photographic facsimiles of the Utrecht Psalter.

[34] For the use of multicoloured line drawing by Anglo-Saxon artists see J.J.G. Alexander, 'Some aesthetic principles in the use of colour in Anglo-Saxon art', *Anglo-Saxon England*, 4, 1975, pp. 145–54, *passim*; also R. Deshman, 'The Leofric Missal and tenth-century English art', *Anglo-Saxon England*, 6, 1977, pp. 145–73, at pp. 158–162.

[35] BL Cotton Ms. Julius A.vi (Temple, *Anglo-Saxon Mss.*, cat. 62). A similar choice to use multicoloured line drawing was made by the artists of two manuscripts of Prudentius' *Psychomachia*, BL Cotton Ms. Cleopatra C.viii (Temple *Anglo-Saxon Mss.*, cat. 49), and Cambridge, Corpus Christi College, Ms. 23 (Temple, *Anglo-Saxon Mss.*, cat. 48), while the main artist of another one, BL Add. Ms. 24199 (Temple, *Anglo-Saxon Mss.*, cat. 51) worked in monochrome.

[36] See Bishop, *Caroline Minuscule, passim*; also Dumville, *Caroline Script, passim*.

[37] Cambridge, Trinity College, Ms. B.16.3 (Temple, *Anglo-Saxon Mss.*, cat. 14). See S. Keynes, *Anglo-Saxon manuscripts and other items of related interest in the library of Trinity College, Cambridge*, Old English Newsletter *Subsidia*, vol. 18, 1992, cat. 4.

the Psalms, introduced to Canterbury from Rome by St Augustine and his colleagues.[38] But the reasons for the change are not as simple as this neat distinction between traditions would imply. In the late tenth and eleventh centuries the Gallican gradually replaced the Roman as the liturgical norm in Anglo-Saxon England, no doubt because continental practices had such a profound effect on monastic reform.[39] Even at Christ Church, where there is evidence that the Roman version lingered well into the eleventh century,[40] it is probable that a Gallican Psalter was made around the year 1000.[41] If the relative status of these two versions of the Psalms was in a period of transition, as it seems to have been, the initial decision to make a Roman Psalter is not so much an indication that Utrecht's text was unacceptable, as it is evidence that Harley was designed to be a very different book. The Utrecht Psalter is a Gallican psalter with monochrome illustrations written in Rustic capitals. The Harley Psalter started life as a Roman Psalter with coloured illustrations written in Caroline minuscule, using the Utrecht Psalter as an exemplar. Between the Utrecht Psalter and the Harley Psalter lay the English Channel and two hundred years of history, and even at the start of the campaign on Harley, the cultural distance of the two books is fully reflected in their appearance.

However, before the Harley Psalter was left unfinished in the twelfth century, the campaign on the manuscript had undergone many developments. It is not just that the Utrecht Psalter was not followed later in the programme, but also that nearly all the initial decisions concerning the making of the book, which made it different from Utrecht, were overturned. Some of its illustrations are monochrome, some of its text is Gallican, and some of the letter forms of the Utrecht Psalter are reproduced. I intend to unravel how and why this happened.

My first two chapters are concerned with how the various quires of Harley were made. Planning an illustrated manuscript could be a complicated process.[42] After the

[38] See Leroquais, *Psautiers*, vol. I, pp. XIV–XL, for the various texts of the Psalter. That the Gallican is Jerome's second revision of the Psalter is not disputed; whether his first can be equated with the Roman text we have is still apparently an open question – see D. de Bruyne, 'Le Problème du Psautier Romain', *Revue Bénédictine*, 42, 1930, pp. 101–26, who disputes his authorship, and A. Vaccari, 'I Salteri di s. Girolamo e di s. Agostino', *Scritti di erudizione e di filologia*, 1, Rome, 1952, pp. 207–55, esp. at pp. 211–21, who finds evidence to support it. Later writers have come down in favour of the different points of view, but do not seem to have added to the evidence: see, for example, E.F. Sutcliffe, 'Jerome', in G.W.H. Lampe (ed.), *The Cambridge History of the Bible Vol. 2: The West from the Fathers to the Reformation*, Cambridge, 1969, pp. 80–101, at pp. 84–5, and R. Loewe, 'The Medieval history of the Latin Vulgate', in the same volume, pp. 102–54, at p. 111. See also Weber (ed.), 'Le Psautier Romain', pp. vii–xxiii.

[39] C. and K. Sisam, *The Salisbury Psalter*, Early English Text Society, 242, 1959, pp. 47–52, discuss the introduction of the Gallican Psalter to England.

[40] BL Arundel Ms. 155 (Temple, *Anglo-Saxon Mss.*, cat. 66), is the last known Roman Psalter from Christ Church, and can be dated to 1012–23: see F. Wormald, *English Kalendars Before AD 1100*, Henry Bradshaw Society, vol. 72, 1934, pp. 169–81 for the calendar; the entry for the martyrdom of Alphege is in the original hand, the entry for his translation is a twelfth-century addition. Brooks, *The Church of Canterbury*, pp. 261–5 notes the conservatism of the Roman liturgical usage, but it might not have been confined to Christ Church; see above n.13 for the Bosworth Psalter.

[41] Dumville, *Caroline Script*, p. 108, n.127 has noted that the Gallican Psalter, Cambridge, Corpus Christi College, Ms. 411 (Temple, *Anglo-Saxon Mss.*, cat. 40), should be attributed to the Christ Church scriptorium, and should be dated to the early eleventh century.

[42] An excellent introduction to the subject is J. Vezin, 'La réalisation matérielle des manuscrits latins pendant la haut Moyen Âge', *Codicologica*, 2, 1978, pp. 15–51. The essential texts for the codicology of late Saxon

vellum had been cured and scraped, it had to be cut to size. Was the new manuscript to be the same size as the exemplar? In the case of Harley at least, it was. It then had to be ruled. But who was going to rule it, the illustrators or the scribes? How were they going to rule it, in hard point or in lead point? Was the work to be divided, and if so, how? With the majority of manuscripts these questions did not have to be thought about – in a well organised scriptorium, techniques of manufacture would be matters of everyday procedure. But in Harley, even though an exemplar was followed, it provoked considerable thought. It will be shown that scribes ruled certain quires, but that artists ruled others, that hard point was used in some quires, and lead point in others. The ruling was an important stage in the planning of any manuscript, especially a well illustrated one. Its eccentric and inconstant character in Harley is an indication that, in their attempt to make the Harley Psalter, its artists and scribes differed in their interpretations of their task. Once a particular decision is understood, such as that of the artists to follow the Utrecht Psalter layout when the scribes were writing in a script that took up less space, we can begin to appreciate the motives that lay behind production techniques.

The responses of the Harley artists to the style of Utrecht have often been examined, and it has been observed how well the Anglo-Saxon artists were able to imitate it. However, there has been no close analysis of how they did this. Whatever style is, it is in large part a product of technique, and technically there were severe limitations on the extent to which the Anglo-Saxon artists could imitate the Utrecht Psalter. For example, part of the success of Utrecht's illustrations lies in the unity given to the various elements of the composition by the impression that everything is subject to the same violent wind. This was largely achieved through an agitated impressionism that allowed wooden and stone structures to appear to be battling against a gale in the same way as the figures that crowded the landscape. In Harley by contrast, every architectural structure was executed using a straight edge. As a result, the vivifying wind of Utrecht has to be understood locally in Harley, through the draperies of the figures. Similarly, the Utrecht Psalter's coherence is largely achieved by the fact that, extraordinarily for such a *de luxe* volume, it is executed in one colour. This lends the manuscript a spatial coherence with which the dramatic use of local colour by many of the artists of Harley is at odds. This difference affected their illustrations profoundly. The closest imitator of Utrecht actually paints a stage on which his figures can perform, not a landscape in which they live. Moreover, the use of colour affected the actual process of 'recreating': it will be seen that the artists often used one colour at a time, and that, as a result, even adjacent parts of an illustration could be executed at different stages in the coloured line drawing process. The ambitious use of colour in the manuscript was not, however, the

manuscripts are N.R. Ker, *Catalogue of Manuscripts Containing Anglo-Saxon*, Oxford, 1957, esp. pp. xxiii–xxv, and Bishop, *Caroline Minuscule*, *passim*. For a general study of techniques in the making and decorating of illuminated Anglo-Saxon manuscripts see M.P. Brown, *Anglo-Saxon Manuscripts*, London, 1991, pp. 46–53. C.R. Dodwell, 'Techniques of manuscript painting in Anglo-Saxon manuscripts', *Settimane di Studio del Centro Italiano di Studi sull'Alto Medioevo*, 18, 1971, pp. 643–62, is not a reliable guide. A seminal study in the planning and execution of an illuminated manuscript in the eleventh century is that by Clemoes in P. Clemoes and C.R. Dodwell, *The Old English Illustrated Hexateuch*, Early English Manuscripts in Facsimile XVIII, Copenhagen, 1974, pp. 53–8.

most challenging aspect of the art of the Harley Psalter. In many of the illustrations, the dimensions and the proportions were also substantially altered: not only did these artists reconstruct their illustrations in terms of colour, they sometimes reorganised the interrelated motifs within them. If the focus of a particular illustration in one Psalm is in a different position to the same focus in the Utrecht Psalter, every figure in that Psalm whose gaze was directed towards that focus had to have its aspect altered accordingly. Under such circumstances, the whole illustration had to be rethought and reconstructed, rather than transposed. The fact that such alterations occur in some illustrations more than in others will only serve to demonstrate further that very real differences in attitude to the exemplar are displayed, even by those artists normally categorised as 'the copyists'. The Utrecht Psalter presented the Anglo-Saxon artists with complete scenes, but they had to make up their own images in a very complex way.

The Utrecht Psalter itself is such a tour-de-force of literal illustration that it might be possible to see close adherence to it as a result of the wish to recreate its literalism. However, we should be wary, for the same reason that we should question the desire of the Harley artists to recreate space. To demonstrate the desire to interpret the Psalm text literally, we are necessarily concerned not simply with adherence to the Utrecht Psalter by the artists, but also with deviation from it. It is by analysing the nature and extent of these deviations that the very different attitudes that the Harley artists had to their exemplars can be analysed. Given the sheer wealth of imagery in Utrecht it is not surprising that examples of omission of textually significant elements are to be found. The literacy of the artists is not to be judged by their omissions: if an artist omits a halo from an illustration, it does not mean that he could not read, just as if he omits a hand from an archer, it does not mean that he did not know what the human body looked like; these are visual symbols that would have been clear to the artist without reference to the text. Rather, it represents a failure of technique, and such failures are remarkably few. Neither is a misunderstanding of a textually significant detail evidence that the artist was illiterate; it might mean simply that he was not exercising his literate skills. If there are no examples of literate visual invention over and above those presented by Utrecht, we might begin to suspect that the artist was illiterate rather than uninterested in the text, but just one example of textual understanding in the image-making process demonstrates an interest in it and an involvement with it. Both omission and invention have to be considered when assessing the response of an artist to his exemplar, and one way of assessing this response is by comparing his images with the same images in other manuscripts.

This is why Cambridge, Trinity College, Ms. R.17.1, the 'Eadwine Psalter',[43] and Paris, BN Ms. Lat. 8846,[44] two other manuscripts which employ the Utrecht Psalter, are

[43] C.M. Kauffmann, *Romanesque Manuscripts 1066–1200, A Survey of Manuscripts Illuminated in the British Isles*, vol. 3, London, 1975, cat. 68; see also James (ed.), *The Canterbury Psalter*; also M.T. Gibson, T.A. Heslop, and R.W. Pfaff (eds.), *The Eadwine Psalter: Text, Image, and Monastic Culture in Twelfth-Century Canterbury*, Modern Humanities Research Association, vol. 14, London, 1992.

[44] N. Morgan, *Early Gothic Manuscripts (1): 1190–1250. A Survey of Manuscripts Illuminated in the British Isles*, vol. 4, London, 1982, cat. 1; H. Omont, *Psautier illustré (XIIIe S.). Reproduction des 107 miniatures du manuscrit latin 8846 de la Bibliothèque Nationale*, Paris, 1906, reproduces the illustrations. See also Leroquais, *Psautiers*, vol.2, pp. 78–91; and F. Avril and P. D. Stirnemann, *Bibliothèque Nationale, Département des Manuscrits: Manuscrits enluminés d'origine insulaire viie–xxe siècle*, Paris, 1987, pp. 45–8.

so useful. The Eadwine Psalter dates from the mid twelfth century, while the Paris manuscript was made *c.* 1200. Both were made at Christ Church, Canterbury. Dodwell has demonstrated that, for the illustrations, Paris looked to both Eadwine and Utrecht, deriving motifs from both.[45] There is no conclusive evidence that the Paris artist also looked to Harley.[46] What is remarkable is the extent to which both Paris and Harley found it necessary to reinterpret the same images. Though they frequently do this in different ways, they nevertheless reveal a similar engagement with the illustrations that they are following and a reliance upon the text. Where inventions in Harley are mentioned, the reaction of the Eadwine and Paris artists will also often be noted. It will be argued that the alterations that the Harley artists made to Utrecht very often did not involve a casual use of familiar forms, but rather that they adapted their exemplar at precisely those moments when Utrecht itself was deemed to be inadequate. In understanding the ways in which Utrecht was perceived as deficient, its attractions as an exemplar also become clearer.

In the third chapter I analyse the campaign of production through time. I discuss its sequence, the dates of the various hands, and where they might have worked on the manuscript. An analysis of the individual quires is a necessary preliminary to this entire investigation, but the issues raised in chapter 3 are too complex and involved to be integrated satisfactorily within the first two chapters. Having established how the manuscript was made, and having then placed it in a historical framework, it is possible to consider how it could differ so much from the Utrecht Psalter at certain points. This is done in four related essays in chapter 4. In the first, parallels are drawn between Harley and the Bury St Edmunds Psalter, Vatican Library, Ms. Reg. Lat. 12.[47] Building on the work of Harris and Heimann,[48] I show that the manuscript tradition most fully represented by the Bury Psalter exercised its influence on Harley from the very start of the campaign. As well as from the Utrecht Psalter, Harley's illustrations are derived from the imagery of another manuscript altogether, and therefore it makes no sense merely to consider that the artists of Harley wanted to make a copy of the Utrecht Psalter. In the second section, Harley is compared with other examples of Psalters containing the imagery of the Utrecht Psalter, notably Paris, BN Ms. Lat. 8824,[49] and the various layouts of the Harley quires are discussed in the light of practical considerations in planning the illustrated page. It will be made clear that Utrecht's layout was followed because it was considered useful in the manufacture of some of the quires, and that in others it was adapted and changed because it was considered less

[45] C.R. Dodwell, 'The final copy of the Utrecht Psalter and its relationship with the Utrecht and Eadwine Psalters', *Scriptorium*, 44.1, 1990, pp. 21–53. This study supercedes that of A. Heimann, 'The last copy of the Utrecht Psalter', *The Year 1200: A Symposium*, The Metropolitan Museum of Art, New York, 1975, pp. 313–38, where it is supposed that there was a lost model drawn on by both the Eadwine and Paris 8846 Psalters.

[46] See Dodwell, 'Final copy', pp. 29–30, n.37.

[47] Temple, *Anglo-Saxon Mss.*, cat. 84. For a technical description see A. Wilmart, *Codices Reginenses Latini*, I, Vatican, 1937, pp. 30–5. Ohlgren, *Textual Illustration*, pp. 249–97, reproduces the illustrated folios.

[48] R.M. Harris, 'The marginal drawings of the Bury St Edmunds Psalter (Rome, Vatican Library Ms. Reg. lat. 12)', unpublished D.Phil. thesis, Princeton University, 1960, esp. pp. 101–231, and pp. 553–9; A. Heimann, 'Three illustrations from the Bury St Edmunds Psalter and their prototypes. Notes on the iconography of some Anglo-Saxon drawings', *Journal of the Warburg and Courtauld Institutes*, 29, 1966, pp. 39–59.

[49] Temple, *Anglo-Saxon Mss.*, cat. 83. Edited in reduced facsimile as B. Colgrave (ed.), *The Paris Psalter*, Early English Manuscripts in Facsimile, VIII, Copenhagen, 1958.

useful; the aims of the campaign need not have fundamentally altered. In the third section, the relative importance of the images and the text in the volume are discussed. An analysis of the illustrated section of an astrological manuscript, BL Harley Ms. 2506,[50] demonstrates that the images in a manuscript can be just as important as the text to its meaning for the reader. In the case of the Harley Psalter I show that the Utrecht layout could only ever have been considered useful in the making of the Harley Psalter because of the importance of the illustrations to its meaning. In the final section, the developing character of the Harley Psalter is interpreted in the light of experience gained by the scribes and artists making the various quires of the book, and the time taken to execute them. Having tackled these matters, it is possible to ask how the Harley Psalter would have been read, and for whom it was made. These questions are addressed in chapter 5.

My argument, then, is constructed in the way that one puts together a Russian doll – from the inside out. I discuss how various quires were made, before discussing when and where they were made. Following from this I examine how it was possible for the Psalter to change its appearance so dramatically over the course of its production, and only then do I attempt to deduce its function. I will seek to demonstrate that a context for the Harley Psalter does not need to be sought in the battles of the Anglo-Saxon Chronicle, but rather that it can be found in a battle confined to the scriptorium of Christ Church, Canterbury; that Harley does not lie on some schizophrenic borderline between copy and invention, but rather that the different techniques employed by its makers can be understood and accommodated within the function that the book was supposed to perform; and that the most relevant question to ask of Harley is not why is some of it so different from the Utrecht Psalter, but rather how could the medieval reader consider that all its various sections are compatible with each other. It is hoped that this analysis will leave the reader with a better understanding of the intellectual and artistic environment that made the Harley Psalter possible.

But before entering into an interpretative account of the Harley Psalter, it is necessary to give a technical description of the manuscript.

The Harley Psalter: a technical description[51]

Physical condition

The present binding of Harley 603 is of natural pigskin and dates from some time between 7 December 1956 and 31 January 1957.[52] There are nine sewing stations in the

50 Temple, *Anglo-Saxon Mss.*, cat. 42. See also F. Saxl and H. Meier, *Catalogue of Astrological and Mythological Illuminated Manuscripts of the Latin Middle Ages III: Manuscripts in English Libraries*, 2 vols., ed. H. Bober, London, 1953, vol. 1, pp. 157–60. The illustrated section has also been usefully and extensively discussed by P. McGurk in P. McGurk, D.N. Dumville, M.R. Godden, and Ann Knock (eds.), *An Eleventh-Century Anglo-Saxon Illustrated Miscellany (British Library Cotton Tiberius B.V, Part 1)*, Early English Manuscripts in Facsimile XXI, Copenhagen, 1983, pp. 67–78.

51 A useful guide to technical terms is M.P. Brown, *Understanding Illuminated Manuscripts: A Guide to Technical Terms*, London, 1994.

stitching of each quire. The quantity of old sewing stations in the gutters of the manuscript indicates that this is at least its third binding. Originally each quire probably had seven sewing stations; this is evident from the impressions left by the sewing threads on the vellum, which are Z-shaped, indicating that the threads were twisted in an S shape.[53] On fol. 1r, and fol. 73v, there are signs of rust which are the result of discoloration by an earlier binding, and indicate that at the time of this binding the manuscript commenced at its present fol. 1, and finished at its present fol. 73.

The manuscript shows signs of careless treatment. Many of the surviving folios are in bad condition, and the first and last are particularly badly soiled, perhaps indicating that the manuscript was left unbound at some stage in its history. Stains at the top edges of the last twenty four folios, which become bigger towards the end of the book, indicate that, at some stage, the manuscript has been left in a pool of water. On fols. 35 and 44, originally blank vellum has been cut out and replaced with modern vellum. Quire 7 is in particularly bad repair, and the inner margins of the folios are rebuilt. On every folio in the first five quires there are marks running down the inner margin, at between c. 30 mm and c. 60 mm from the gutter. Inside these marks the vellum is cleaner than outside. These marks are precisely mirrored, not on folios next to each other, but on each folio's conjoint leaf.[54] This is unlikely to have occurred in the preparation of the vellum, but it indicates that at some stage in its history the manuscript was unbound and the individual bifolia kept separately, not in quires, and interleaved with some material.

Folios are wanting from the extant quires, as is evident from the following losses to the text:

after fol. 28
  Psalm 49, v.7 (after *testificabor*), Psalm 50, and the illustration for Psalm 51;
after fol. 33,
  Psalm 63 and the illustration for Psalm 64;
after fol. 45,
  Psalms 83, v.5 (after *saeculi*) to 89, v.14 (commencing *et delectati*);
after fol. 49,
  the illustration spaces and text of Psalms 98 and 99, and the illustration space for Psalm 100.

Assessing the extent to which the manuscript has been mutilated at its beginning and end is more difficult. While the Utrecht Psalter contains illustrations to the 150 Psalms, a set of canticles, the Lord's Prayer, the Creed, the *Quicunque uult*, and finally the supernumerary Psalm – *Pusillus eram*, Harley ends incomplete on fol. 73v at Psalm 143, in the middle of verse 11 (*filiorum alienorum* ...).[55] The distressed appearance of the

[52] I am grateful to Janet Backhouse for this information.

[53] I am grateful to Nancy Turner for this information.

[54] These marks are clearest on fols. 3r and 3v, and 6r and 6v, but are to be found on the other bifolia of the first five quires, without exception.

[55] In the literature other verses of Psalm 143 have frequently been cited as the last surviving in the manuscript.

manuscript might suggest that folios have been lost at the end.[56] However, Harley was never finished in the first place, because illustrations were not even begun for Psalms 68–100, and it will be argued below that there are some reasons for supposing that these would have been completed before any attempt was made to write the text after Psalm 143, verse 11. The manuscript may not have lost its last few quires. The only prefatory material in Harley is a full-page illustration of the Trinity on fol. 1r; there are no prayers, nor is there a calendar. Since Utrecht has no such material, and since Harley began by adhering so closely to the Carolingian manuscript and was never completed, it might be that prefatory material was never executed.

Size and structure

Page layout. In the eleventh century the Utrecht Psalter consisted of 92 folios.[57] Each page has a written space of *c.* 246 mm by *c.* 223 mm, and the text is laid out in three equal columns of 32 lines. The folios have been extensively trimmed. Harley's 73 untrimmed vellum folios measure 376 mm by 312 mm. The text block also laid out in three columns of 32 lines, and clearly derives from that of Utrecht, which here shows its own debt to the late antique.[58] Harley's text area varies slightly in size from quire to quire, but is consistently a few millimetres larger than Utrecht, at *c.* 248 mm by *c.* 224 mm. The outer margin measures *c.* 63 mm, the lower *c.* 78 mm, the upper *c.* 50 mm, the inner *c.* 22 mm, and the two intercolumnar margins *c.* 16 mm.

The correspondence with Utrecht originally extended to the placement of the text in relation to the margins of the page. While the folios of Utrecht are trimmed, the proportions of Harley correspond reasonably closely with the layout prescribed by the ninth-century scribe who stipulated that the height of a codex should be to the width as five is to four, that the lower margin and the outer margin should be one fifth of the height, that the upper margin should be two-thirds of that fifth, that the inner margin should be two-thirds of the upper margin, and that the margins between the columns should be the same as the inner margin.[59] Expressed as decimal fractions, the proportions desired by the scribe, and the approximate proportions of Harley, are as follows:

[56] As argued by Backhouse, 'Making', p. 98: 'This abrupt finish is almost certainly due to later mutilation rather than interruption to the original campaign of work on the book.'

[57] Van der Horst and Engelbregt, *Kommentar*, p. 53, demonstrate that the leaves at the end of the manuscript and those of the Psalter itself were both rebound separately, at least twice, before they were bound together in Cotton's Library. I am grateful to Dr Van der Horst for access to the conservator's report in August 1991, made at the time of the rebinding of the manuscript, now kept in the University Library of Utrecht, which demonstrates this quite clearly.

[58] B. Bischoff, *Latin Palaeography: Antiquity and the Middle Ages*, trans. D. Ó Cróinín and D. Ganz, Cambridge, 1990, p. 28, notes the rarity of the three-columned text before the twelfth century (giving examples in n. 70), and notes in Utrecht's case the probability of an antique model.

[59] The scribe wrote on fol. 2v of Paris, BN Ms. Lat. 11884. For a transcription of this note see E.K. Rand and L.W Jones, *The Earliest Book of Tours, with Supplementary Descriptions of Other Manuscripts of Tours*, Studies in the Script of Tours II, Cambridge, Massachusetts, 1934, pp. 87–8.

Proportion	prescribed	Harley 603
width to height	0.80	0.83
outer margin to height	0.20	0.17
lower margin to height	0.20	0.21
upper to lower margin	0.666	0.64
inner to upper margin	0.666	0.45
inner to intercol. margin	1.0	1.4

The correspondence is close except for the last two figures, and indeed the text area of Harley appears to be a little close to the gutter. Significantly it shares this characteristic with the Utrecht Psalter itself, which had an even smaller inner margin of *c.* 15 mm. The 'four-fifths' proportion of the overall size of Harley is a consequence of the desire by Anglo-Saxons to imitate a Carolingian manuscript, and while this proportion is occasionally found in the ninth century, it is very infrequent in the eleventh.[60]

Gatherings. Apart from the leaves added when the manuscript was in Sir Robert Cotton's collection,[61] the Utrecht Psalter's folios are arranged in the following manner:

1^{10} lacking 10, $2–11^{8}$, 12^{4} lacking 1

Folios are missing from Harley, and the original quire arrangement is not clear from the present binding. After fols. 28 and 33 in quire 5, and fol. 49 in quire 8, it is clear that only one leaf was needed in each case to accommodate the missing text. This allows the fifth quire to be plausibly reconstructed as a regular one of eight leaves. After fol. 45 it is probable that four more leaves were needed, and that quire 7 was also a quire of 8, while fols. 46 and 47 belonged to quire 8.[62] Fols. 48 and 49 of quire 8 were conjoint, as they still are, and since only one extra leaf was required between fols. 49 and 50, this quire had to have a singleton. I propose that the manuscript comprised the following:

1^{8}, 2^{10} lacking 9, 3^{2}, $4–7^{8}$, 8^{6} lacking 5, $9-11^{8}$

At first sight there is little connection between the gatherings of Utrecht and those of Harley reconstructed above: the first quire of Harley for example, is a regular quire of eight leaves. However it will be suggested in this book that the gatherings of Utrecht profoundly affected the course of the production of the Harley Psalter, and that the Utrecht Psalter was disbound to facilitate this production. Appendix 2 is a parallel collation of the Harley Psalter – as I have reconstructed it – and the Utrecht.[63]

[60] Statistics for the sizes of manuscripts can be found in J.P. Gumbert, 'The sizes of manuscripts: some statistics and notes' in A.R.A. Croiset van Uchelen (ed.), *Hellinga: Festschrift/Feestbundel/Mélanges*, Amsterdam, 1980, pp. 277–88; see esp. pp. 278–80, and p. 288, n.8. [61] See above, p. 16, n.57.

[62] The text that is missing after fol. 45 in Harley takes up 7 1/2 pages (ie. 3 3/4 folios) of Utrecht. The scribe of this part of Harley could condense or expand the spacing of his text as compared to Utrecht but overall, if four folios are missing at this point, this scribe's section of text took up 29 folios, and the equivalent in Utrecht 30. It is therefore unlikely that the missing section of text in Harley took up only 3 folios. Moreover, this would leave fol. 46 as the eighth folio in a regular quire, but it could not have been conjoint with the first folio of this quire, the present fol. 42, because both have hair side rectos. [63] Appendix 2 is to be found on p. 214.

The hands at work: a list of attributions

Here follows a list of the hands found in the Harley Psalter. They are listed in the order in which they worked on the manuscript. The same information is given in tabulated form in Appendix 1 on p. 207. Working out the sequence of work in the manuscript is one of the aims of this study, and my final conclusions are put forward in chapter 4, pp. 183ff. The attributions that follow will be substantiated in the course of the book. They are extensively based on Wormald's attributions for the hands of the artists,[64] and Bishop's, for the hands of the scribes.

A (artist)	Identified and labelled by Wormald. Responsible for arranging the vellum, ruling the folios, and illustrating the Psalms in quire 1, and for ruling and illustrating folios 9r, 10v, 11r, 11v, 16r and 16v in quire 2.
1 (scribe)	Identified by Bishop as distinct from scribe D2.[65] Responsible for the main text of fols. 2r–27v,[66] and fols. 54r, column a line 24–73v. Also responsible for arranging the vellum and the ruling of quires 10 and 11, and fol. 15v in quire 2.
B (artist)	Identified and labelled by Wormald. Responsible for arranging the vellum, ruling the folios, and illustrating the Psalms in quires 3 and 4, and for ruling and illustrating folios 12r, 15r and 17r of quire 2.
C (artist)	Identified and labelled by Wormald. Backhouse has questioned his separate identity from artist A.[67] He was responsible for ruling and illustrating fols. 13 and 14.
D2 (artist-scribe)	Identified and labelled as artist D by Wormald, and as responsible for the illustrations in quire 9. The scribe of fols. 50r–54r column a, line 23 inclusive was identified by Bishop.[68] I identify these two hands with each other, and attribute the arrangement of the vellum and the ruling of this quire to the same person. He was also responsible for the

[64] Wormald, *English Drawings*, pp. 69–70.

[65] T.A.M. Bishop, 'Notes on Cambridge Manuscripts Part v: Mss. connected with St Augustine's Canterbury, continued', *Transactions of the Cambridge Bibliographical Society*, 3.1, 1959, pp. 93–5, at p. 94, n.1. Contrary to his opinion at that time, fols. 50–3 are not a quire.

[66] In the literature this hand is frequently stated to have begun his work on fol. 1. There is no text on fol. 1 (but rather the illustration of the Trinity on the recto, and of Psalm 1 on the verso), unless one includes the text inscribed on the book of the *Beatus uir*, and this appears to be the work of artist A; see below, chapter 1, p. 57.

[67] Backhouse, 'Making', p. 99.

[68] See above, n. 65. In Bishop, 'Notes vii', p. 423, he is scribe xviii. The extent of his work is unclear from the literature. Bishop, 'Notes vii', p. 420, states that scribe D2 ends his text on fol. 54v, column a, line 23; the true extent of his work is given on p. 423. The confusion has spread: D.H. Wright, *The Vespasian Psalter: British Museum, Cotton Vespasian A.I*, Early English Manuscripts in Facsimile xiv, Copenhagen, 1967, p. 42, n.4, is grateful for the suggestion of Bishop that the first hand wrote fols. 2–27 and 50–54r/a/23, but this seems to be a misunderstanding. Alexander and Kauffmann, *English Illuminated Mss.*, p. 38, and Temple, *Anglo-Saxon Mss.*, p. 82, claim that the hands change at fol. 54r/a/20. Backhouse *et al.*, *Golden Age*, p. 75, note that one scribe was responsible for fols. 1–27 and 50–73. Pfaff, 'Eadui Basan', p. 272, notes that this scribe ends his work in the middle of fol. 54v.

verse capitals, *tituli*, and Psalm initials, fols. 50r–54r/a/23. He originally executed the initial to Psalm 101 on fol. 50r, but this was later erased and replaced by artist I. I refer to this artist-scribe as 'scribe D2', when discussing his text, and as 'artist D2', when discussing his illustrations.

F (artist) — Identified and labelled by Wormald. He was responsible for all the illustrations that head Psalms in quires 10 and 11, and for one illustration that does not, at the bottom of fol. 59r.

E (artist-scribe) — Identified and labelled by Wormald. He was responsible for completing the illustration on fol. 15r, executing that on fol. 15v, and adding illustrations on blank vellum on fols. 53r, 58v, 61r, 61v, 62v, 67r, 70r, 70v, and 72v. He was identified as the main rubricator of the manuscript by Duffey.[69] This rubricator was responsible for the *tituli* and verse capitals to scribe 1's text, and for the Psalm division to Psalm 17, verse 26, on fol. 9v.

I (artist) — Responsible for the Trinity illustration on fol. 1r, the *Beatus* initial on fol. 2r, and the initial to Psalm 101 on fol. 50r. He was also responsible for the display capitals to Psalm 1 on fol. 2r.[70]

J (artist) — Responsible for the initials to the text of scribe 1, with the exception of the *Beatus* initial.

Eadui Basan (scribe) — Identified as the scribe of fols. 28r–49v by Bishop.[71] He was responsible for the arrangement of the vellum and the ruling of these folios, quires 5–8. He was also responsible for the *tituli* to his Psalms, for their Psalm divisions, and for the lead point underdrawing of their initials. He was probably also responsible for corrections to scribe 1's text, and for adding Psalm divisions at the following places: Psalm 9, verse 20 (fol. 5v), Psalm 36, verse 27 (fol. 21v), Psalm 67, middle of verse 20 (fol. 35v), Psalm 68, verse 17 (fol. 36v), Psalm 77, verse 36 (fol. 42v), Psalm 103, verse 25 (fol. 52r), Psalm 104, verse 23 (fol. 53r), Psalm 105, verse 32 (fol. 54r), Psalm 106, verse 25 (fol. 55r), Psalm 138, verse 11 (fol. 71r), Psalm 143, verse 9 (fol. 73v).

G (artist) — Identified by Wormald, and labelled by Gameson.[72] Responsible for illustrating fol. 28, and adding an illustration to fol. 17v. Gameson noted that he was responsible for a number of

[69] J.E. Duffey, 'The inventive group of illustrations in the Harley Psalter (British Museum Ms. Harley 603)', unpublished D.Phil. thesis, University of California, Berkeley, 1977, pp. 209–10.

[70] Wormald, *English Drawings*, p. 70, attributes the drawing of the Trinity hand E. This attribution is accepted by Duffey, 'Inventive group', p. 209, who also attributes the *Beatus* initial to this hand, but Gameson, 'Anglo-Saxon artists', p. 33, is right to question it.

[71] Bishop, *Caroline Minuscule*, p. 22.

[72] Gameson, 'Anglo-Saxon artists', p. 30.

	additions to other artists' work.[73] I attribute more additions to his hand. He was also responsible for the initial to Psalm 48 on fol. 28r.
H (artist)	Identified by Wormald, as responsible for illustrations on fols. 29r–35r. He was also responsible for the initials to Psalm 51, 53, and 57, on fols. 29r, 29v, and 31v. Labelled artist R by Gameson.[74]

The preparation of the page

Arrangement of the membrane. The arrangement of the membrane in Harley is not consistent. In quires 1, 2, 4 and 9 hair side faces flesh with the hair side on the outside of the quire. Quire 3 is a bifolium, and the hair side is on the outside. Independent evidence will be presented to suggest that artists prepared the folios of these quires. In quires 5–8 and 10–11 hair side faces hair, again with the hair side on the outside of the quire. Scribes prepared the folios of these quires.

Pricking. Utrecht's pricking no longer survives, because the manuscript has been trimmed. The pricking marks in Harley are still visible, 13–19 mm from the outer edge, 5 mm–20 mm from the top, and 2 mm–28 mm from the bottom of the folios, varying from quire to quire. There is no pricking at the inner margins. The pricks at the outer margins are from 6.5 mm–9 mm apart on any given folio.

Even though there is no pricking on the inner margins, the usual practice in this manuscript seems to have been that leaves were pricked a quire at a time after folding: indents are to be found on the rectos, and rises on the versos. The pricking pattern is normally constant within each quire, although in quire 2 the bifolium 12/15 was pricked separately. Frequent repricking was necessary, and this manifests itself in a variety of ways. On fol. 17 there are two sets of pricking marks. In quire 4 the first four folios were pricked together, and then the last four – the fifth leaf of this quire being heavily pricked. As well as this, the last three folios of this quire (fols. 25–27) were pricked again, with the result that fols. 25 and 26 have two sets of pricking marks, and fol. 27, only the second set. In quire 11 the last four folios were repricked: the pricking of the lower edge is noticeably different here to that on preceding folios in this quire – three pricks are to be seen for each lower inter-columnar margin, not two. Further anomalies present themselves: in quire 9 the last folio has the largest prick marks and therefore this was pricked again, while in quire 1 it seems possible that the sheets were rearranged after pricking – not only does fol. 8 have larger holes than fol. 7, but fol. 6 has larger holes than fol. 5.

[73] Ibid., pp. 33–4, and especially the appendix on pp. 43–4.

[74] R. Gameson, in P. Beal and J. Griffiths (eds.), 'The Romanesque Artist of the Harley Psalter', *English Manuscript Studies 1100–1700*, 4, 1993, pp. 24–61. Gameson presumably terms this artist 'R' because he considers him to be 'Romanesque'. The other artists are not judged on the basis of their style. The difference between A and G is bigger than the difference between G and H, and the space of time between them may have been as large. The term Romanesque is hard to define, and artist H is not a classic example of the style.

Ruling. Utrecht has 65 ruled lines per folio, and they are equally spaced. On an unillustrated folio, 32 lines of text were written, and the text occurs on every other line, taking up the whole of the height of the line. This meant that the Rustic capitals were bounded at their top and bottom by a ruled line, and this must have helped the scribe keep his letters at a consistent height. Normally, the text was written down the page on lines 2,4,6 to line 64. However, if an illustration was to be inserted, the scribe could restart the next Psalm on a line with an odd number, and end the text to that page on line 65. The ruling is uniform throughout, with no care taken to avoid the illustration spaces.

The ruling in Harley is truly extraordinary, and changes from quire to quire, and even from folio to folio. It will be shown that the ruling does not fall easily into our understanding of manuscript production in the eleventh century. Two traits that all quires have in common are particularly important. The first is that even those quires that are ruled in hard point are ruled on both sides of the folio, separately. Grooves are to be found on every single recto and verso in the manuscript. Ridges are occasionally seen, but these refer to the ruling patterns on the other side of any given folio, which, in all but the last two quires, were always different. The second is that the ruling is extremely faint. Diagrams of the ruling pattern on certain folios are found in the illustrations and are referred to in the text.

The ruling patterns in Harley are crucial in their implications, and their importance in understanding the working procedures of artists and scribes cannot be over-estimated. Ruling practice can be discerned with the help of analysis of scribal and artistic working procedure, and, in turn, the ruling will shed light on this procedure.

The contents of the manuscript

The script of the main text. Utrecht's text is written in Rustic capitals, while that in Harley is in English Caroline minuscule. Because the minuscule took up far less space than the Rustic capitals of Utrecht, it proved to be very difficult to achieve a felicitous physical relationship between script and illustration, while adhering to the format of the Utrecht Psalter, without the script appearing 'stretched'. The various attempts at solving this problem will be seen to be largely responsible for the changing character of the book. There has been confusion over both the nature of the Harley text, and the division of scribal hands, and though the two matters are connected, this is not at all clear in the literature.

That three scribes are responsible for Harley's main text is clear. The script of scribes 1 and D2 is very similar, and both used a dark, nearly black ink. The ductus of scribe D2 is more refined than that of scribe 1, and differences can be observed in details of letter form (compare figs. 3 and 4). While scribe D2 normally employed the 'figure 2' 'r' after 'o', scribe 1 never did;[75] scribe D2 used has a more extended head stroke to 'a' than scribe 1. The first line of each of scribe D2's Psalms is written in Uncials that closely

[75] The 'figure 2' 'r' of *confitebor*, Psalm 41, verse 6 on fol. 24v/b/19, is a later correction, using a different ink, and extending beyond the margins of the column, to which scribe 1 adheres closely at this point.

3 *The Harley Psalter, fol. 63v. A script detail, lines 1–8. The main script is by scribe 1; the rubrication is by E; the initial is by J.*

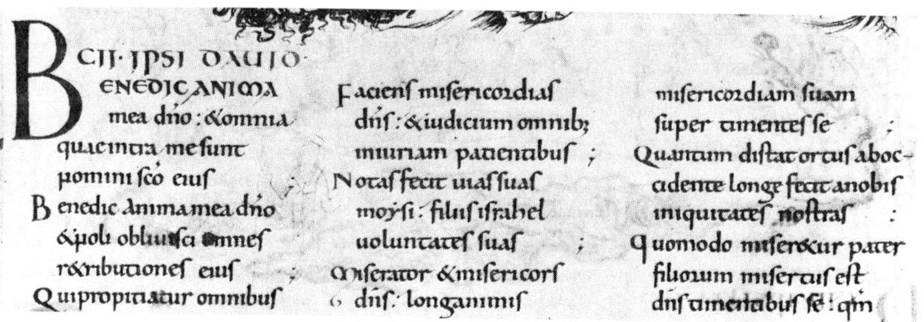

4 *The Harley Psalter, fol. 51r. A script detail, lines 1–8. The script, the rubrication, and the initial are by D2.*

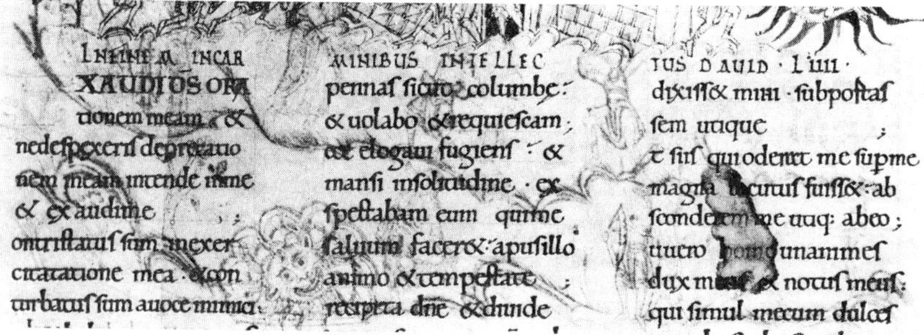

5 *The Harley Psalter, fol. 32r. A script detail, lines 1–8. The script, the rubrication, and the lead point sketch for the initial are by Eadui Basan.*

reflect those of Utrecht, while the first line of scribe 1's Psalms are written in a hybrid with Uncial and Rustic capital elements. Scribe D2's script is consistently of a very high standard, but that of scribe 1 becomes increasingly careless in its ductus. With the lapse in ductus some letter forms alter, in particular the use of '3-g' becomes more evident in his work from fol. 54r/a/24 onwards. However, there is no need to divide the hands in Harley 603 further, and characteristics of scribe 1's script later on in the manuscript can be observed in his earlier section.[76] The script of Eadui Basan is altogether different (fig. 5). It is executed in a brown ink, it is more rounded in aspect, and it is more calligraphic:

wedges are consistently applied to ascenders, and flat feet are given to the minims. Particularly distinctive individual letter forms are the tall 'rt' ligature, the closed 'ct' ligature, the relatively frequent use of 'oc' 'a' after 'r', the frequent use of a straight backed 'e' to which a calligraphic hook is occasionally added, and a rounded 'g' in which the tail starts at right angles to the base of the bow. He retains the elaborate treatment of the first line of each psalm, influenced like scribe 1 by the Uncials in Utrecht, but modified by his own style of writing in capitals.[77]

The script of scribes 1 and D2 is of a type that has been associated with the first efforts in English Caroline minuscule by the scribes of Christ Church, and dating from around the year 1000, since Bishop wrote his seminal article on the subject in 1963.[78] Indeed Bishop discerned the hand of scribe D2 in three other places, including BL Stowe Charter 35, which can be dated to *c.* 1002/3.[79] This type of English Caroline is generally considered rather earlier than the work of Eadui, who was writing at his best around *c.* 1018.[80] However, Dumville has recently questioned important aspects of Bishop's analysis including his identification of scribe D2 with the scribe of BL Stowe Charter 35 which was itself important in establishing the Christ Church origin of his stemma of inter-related hands.[81] The questions of origin and date posed by the three hands will be analysed in detail in chapter 3.

The content of the main text. The Utrecht Psalter follows the Gallican version of the Psalms. Harley's text is more complicated. It follows the Roman version of the Psalms, except for Psalm 100 to Psalm 105 up to the middle of verse 24, where it follows the Gallican.[82] this Gallican text takes up fols. 50r–54r column a, line 23 inclusive. From this it should be completely clear, as only Duffey has noted,[83] that the Gallican text coincides precisely with the work of scribe D2, which also ends on fol. 54r, column a, line 23. While other texts have occasional readings in the Gallican when they are essentially Roman, and vice versa, I know of no parallels in the main text of any other

76 There is, for example, a clear '3-g' form on fol. 26v/b/12, *regis*.

77 See Heslop, 'Cnut and Emma', pp. 166–7.

78 Bishop, 'Notes VII', *passim*.

79 Ibid., p. 420. The other two texts are B.L. Harley Ms. 1117 (ii), and BL Royal Ms. 7.c.iv. Bishop dated Stowe Charter 35 to 1003, but see below, chapter 3, p. 136.

80 See Bishop, *Caroline Minuscule*, p. 22. BL Stowe Charter 38 contains the date 1018.

81 Dumville, *Caroline Script*, pp. 86–110 and esp. pp. 109–10.

82 Wormald, *English Drawings*, p. 69, terms the Harley manuscript Gallican, while Dodwell, *Canterbury School*, p. 3, states that it is Roman. There have been other variations on this theme. Bishop and Gasquet, *Bosworth Psalter*, p. 9 note that the Roman version is used to Psalm 100, but that the Gallican is employed thereafter. This has been subsequently followed in D. Panofsky, 'The textual basis of the Utrecht Psalter illustrations', *The Art Bulletin*, 25, 1943, pp. 50–8, at pp. 50–1, n.5, in Harris, 'Marginal drawings', pp. 67–8, and in R. Rensch Erbes, 'The development of the medieval harp: a re-examination of the Utrecht Psalter and its progeny', *Gesta*, 11.2, 1972, pp. 27–36, at p. 35, n.24. Since Gallican readings occur in the 19th and 23rd verses of Psalm 105, the Gallican usage extends beyond Psalm 105, v.20, claimed in C. and K. Sisam, *The Salisbury Psalter*, p. 48, n.1. J.H.A. Engelbregt, *Het Utrechts Psalterium. Een eeuw wetenschappelijke bestudering (1860–1960)*, Utrecht, 1965, p. 83, n.10, states that the first clear Roman reading is at verse 25 – *murmuraverunt*, and verse 25 is subsequently claimed in Alexander and Kauffmann, *English Illuminated Mss.* p. 38, Temple, *Anglo-Saxon Mss.*, p. 81, and Pfaff, 'Eadui Basan', p. 272. The first variant reading between the Gallican and the Roman text on fol. 54r is right at the beginning of line 24 of column a – the Roman *Et* is used, which is absent from the Gallican text for Psalm 105, v.24; the next variant reading between the Gallican and the Roman text on fol. 54r is on line 25 of this column – the Roman *verbis* is used, and not the Gallican *verbo*, also in verse 24 of Psalm 105.

83 J.E. Duffey, 'Inventive group', p. 236, n.3.

Psalter for such a complete transformation in the version of the Psalter text used.[84]

It will be argued below that the Utrecht Psalter itself was the exemplar for the Gallican text, and was followed line by line by D2. The Roman texts of scribe 1 and Eadui show that another manuscript was used for the bulk of Harley's text. Indeed, there is some evidence to suggest that scribe 1 and Eadui were using different textual exemplars. There is no doubt that the Roman texts of both scribe 1 and Eadui are closely related to the second family of Roman texts identified by Weber.[85] Weber used BL Add. Ms. 37517, Cambridge, UL Ms. Ff.1.23, and Cambridge, Trinity College, Ms. R.17.1 to represent this family of texts. As O'Neill has pointed out, this family shares certain variant readings, the frequent addition of *domine*, and a number of Gallican intrusions.[86] However, in Eadui's text I have identified two Gallican readings that cannot be accounted for in any edited Roman text: in Psalm 55, verse 10, Eadui has *cognoui*, not the Roman *agnoui*, in Psalm 72, verse 18 he has *posuisti*, for the Roman *disposuisti*. Also, and unlike the text of scribe 1, there are a number of Gallican readings that lie outside the immediate textual family of Weber's group 2 Roman texts, although they can be paralleled in other ones: Psalm 48 verse 7 *gloriantur*; Psalm 54 verse 18 *et* (added); Psalm 58 verse 7 *uesperam*; Psalm 77 verse 45 *eos*; Psalm 77 verse 49 *eos*. This evidence that two textual exemplars were used for the Roman text of Harley might indicate that a period of time lapsed between the two scribes' work.[87]

Tituli. The *tituli* of the Psalms of Utrecht are written in Uncials. Those to the Harley Psalter are Rustic capitals, written in red, except those by the scribe D2, which are written in Uncials very like those of the Utrecht Psalter (fig. 4). There is a marked difference between Eadui's *tituli* and those that accompany the work of scribe 1, by artist-scribe E (figs. 3 and 5): Eadui's capitals all have pronounced feet, while those to the text of scribe 1 do not; Eadui's tituli have a bow, and not an angle to 'U'; and the 'A' is almost completely closed, not almost completely open.

Verse capitals. The verse capitals of scribe D2's text are elaborately treated (fig. 4). The first stroke of 'A', and the last stroke of 'M', are frequently extended. This also occurs less frequently to the tail of 'Q'. Note also the elaborate treatment of lower case 'b' on fol. 51v/b/3. 'E' is alternately round and square. By comparison the verse capitals to scribe 1's text are very plain, with little that is distinctive (fig. 3). The verse capitals to the text of both these scribes are 'Dunstanesque' in character, rather than 'Aethelwoldan',

[84] There are signs in subsidiary and vernacular texts of changing textual exemplars. See for example C. and K. Sisam in Colgrave (ed.), *The Paris Psalter*, at pp. 15–17, where they note that up to Psalm 50, Paris, BN Ms. Lat. 8824 employs a West Saxon prose paraphrase to parallel the Latin text, and after this an Anglo-Saxon metrical version. [85] Weber, *Le Psautier Roman*, p. ix.

[86] P. P. O'Neill, 'The English version', pp. 123–38, in Gibson, Heslop and Pfaff (eds.), *The Eadwine Psalter*, at p. 138.

[87] From the evidence that he presents, there appear to me to be problems with the tentative conclusion drawn by Pfaff, 'Eadui Basan', p. 272, that there are tiny indications that Eadui was 'thinking Gallicanum': of the three examples he cites, two are found in BL Cotton Ms. Vespasian A.i (the exception is the 'quia' reading of Psalm 51.11), and all three are found in the Bosworth Psalter. Both these are excellent Roman texts, and Eadui may have studied them; he certainly added text to the end of the former (see below, chapter 3, p. 137–8). Eadui wrote a Roman text, and knew that he was writing one. If he thought of editing his Roman text at all, it was only in the hope of improving it.

according to Heslop's characterisation.[88] Verse capitals were never added to Eadui's text (fig. 5).

Psalm initials. With the exception of the interlace *Beatus* initial to Psalm 1, the first letter of each Psalm in Utrecht is a stately capital. Those to the text of scribe D2 in Harley are, for the most part, very similar to those in Utrecht, but larger and in colour (fig. 4). The initial to Psalm 101 was originally of this type, but it was erased and replaced by artist I, and artist I was also responsible for the *Beatus* initial. Both these initials are made up of composite elements, joined and encircled by a clumsy outline. The initial to Psalm 119 on fol. 64r is similar in form, but was probably the work of artist J, who was responsible for all the rest of the initials in quires 1–4 and 9–11. Artist J's initials normally consist of bands of vellum bordered by painted members of varying width, and are frequently elaborated with foliate elements and beast heads (fig. 3). The initials to Eadui's text were left outlined in lead point (fig. 5), but that to the text of Psalm 48 was executed by artist G, and those to Psalm 51 on fol. 29r, Psalm 53 on fol. 29v, and Psalm 57 on fol. 31v were later completed by artist H.

Although there is no coherent hierarchy to the size or colour of the initials, some do receive special attention: the initials to Psalms 1 and 51 are historiated, and those to Psalms 101 and 119 are more elaborate in their decoration, and this reflects the traditional threefold division of the Psalter, and the importance of Psalm 119 in the Office.

Psalm divisions. The Utrecht Psalter has no Psalm divisions. In Harley there are Psalm divisions at all the correct places in the surviving text. However, they were not all executed in one campaign. The Psalm division in Psalm 17 is in the hand of the scribe of the tituli to scribe 1's text: note, for example, the V-shaped 'U', the trailing fourth stroke of 'M', and the upward slant of the foot of 'L'. The Psalm divisions to Eadui's Psalms are identical in their letter forms to the *tituli* that head them. The rest of the Psalm divisions are in a hand very similar to those of Eadui's text, but there are differences: the 'A' is not closed; the third stroke of 'M' comes down below the base line; the second stroke of 'U' curls under the bow of the letter. These features may simply be signs of carelessness on the part of the scribe, and it is not impossible that they too were executed by the same hand. Lines of text were left free for the insertion of divisions on fols. 5v and 9v, but otherwise they were squeezed into the text, and often there was little space for them. The verse capitals following the Psalm divisions to scribe 1's text have been elaborated. At fols. 5v and 9v, they are by the artist of the Psalm initials to scribe 1's text, from fol. 54r onwards by the scribe of the Psalm divisions that precede them, often over erasures of the original undifferentiated verse capitals.

Corrections to the main text. The text of scribe 1 has been corrected. Some examples are as follows:

fol. 2r, Psalm 2 verse 3 *disrumpamus*
fol. 2v, Psalm 2 verse 10 *intellegite*

[88] See Heslop, 'Cnut and Emma', p. 163–4.

fol. 4r,	Psalm 6	verse 10	*asdsumpsit*
fol. 5v,	Psalm 9	verse 26	*pulluuntur*
fol. 7v,	Psalm 13	verse 3	*effundendum*
fol. 8v,	Psalm 15	verse 5	*hereditas*
fol. 8v,	Psalm 15	verse 9	*exultabit*
fol. 9r,	Psalm 16	verse 5	*tuis*
fol. 12r,	Psalm 20	verse 2	*exaltabit*
fol. 12v,	Psalm 21	verse 9	*eripiat / faciat*
fol. 15v,	Psalm 26	verse 6	*exaltauit caput*
	Psalm 26	verse 11	*semitam rectam*
	Psalm 27	verse 2	*et*
fol. 16v,	Psalm 28	verse 9	*reuelabit*
fol. 21v,	Psalm 36	verse 14	*trucidant*
	Psalm 36	verse 21	*soluet*
	Psalm 36	verse 23	*cupiet*
fol. 22v,	Psalm 37	verse 19	*pronuntiabo*
fol. 24r,	Psalm 40	verse 14	*et*
fol. 25v,	Psalm 43	verse 13	*commutationibus*
fol. 26r,	Psalm 44	verse 3	*diffusa*
fol. 26v,	Psalm 44	verse 9	*cassia a*
fol. 54r,	Psalm 105	verse 46	*eos in*
fol. 56r,	Psalm 108	verse 6	*constitue*
fol. 56v,	Psalm 108	verse 18	*eius*
	Psalm 108	verse 25	*obprobrium*
	Psalm 108	verse 28	*benedices*
fol. 57r,	Psalm 109	verse 7	*bibet*
fol. 57v,	Psalm 111	verse 7	*ab auditione*
	Psalm 111	verse 10	*tabescet*
fol. 58v,	Psalm 113	verse 21	*omnes timentes*
fol. 59v,	Psalm 115	verse 16	*disrupisti*
fol. 62r,	Psalm 118	verse 74	*uerbum tuum*
fol. 64r,	Psalm 118	verse 175	*uiuet*
fol. 65r,	Psalm 122	verse 4	*despectio*
fol. 67r,	Psalm 127	verse 5	*ut*
fol. 67v,	Psalm 129	verse 3	*quis sustinebit*
	Psalm 130	verse 2	*ablactatus est super matrem*
fol. 68r,	Psalm 131	verse 9	*sacerdotes*
	Psalm 131	verse 17	*illuc*
fol. 70r,	Psalm 136	verse 8	*tibi*
fol. 71r,	Psalm 138	verse 16	*in eis*
fol. 71v,	Psalm 139	verse 3	*proelia*
fol. 72v,	Psalm 141	verse 7	*in*
fol. 73v,	Psalm 143	verse 1	*proelium*

Most of these corrections were done in a script very similar to that of Eadui Basan, and they may well have been done by him. The letter forms have a comparatively upright aspect, rounded bows, and refined ductus. Occasionally a version of the straight backed 'e' that can be seen in the work of Eadui is employed. The work of scribe D2 and of Eadui himself stands uncorrected.

The illustrations. The great attraction of the Utrecht Psalter as an exemplar for Harley was its illustrations. The division of artistic hands in the Utrecht Psalter has been analysed by Gaehde.[89] Like those in Utrecht, the illustrations in Harley illustrate selected verses of the Psalms that follow them in a literal manner. However, in Harley, many factors other than the Utrecht exemplar also determined the character of the illustrations: the text of the Psalms, contemporary artefacts and ritual, and images in other manuscripts, all played an important role.

Wormald did not give reasons for his 1952 division of the hands in Harley. Later scholars have used various ways of articulating the differences between hands. Carver admirably demonstrated the extent to which each artist responded to his own visual world, as distinct from that which he was seeing in the Utrecht manuscript.[90] Gameson analysed the style of each hand, the extent to which colour was used, the extent to which the sense of space in Utrecht was preserved, and the extent to which each artist deviated from the exemplar.[91] This book will concentrate on the techniques by which the artists worked. These are very different, and they also provide a satisfactory way of articulating the differences between the artists.

In the past the artists' hands have been treated independently of the characteristics of the ruling pattern, and independently of scribal practice. The following analysis, concerned as it is with the interaction of scribe and artist, will be based on the unit of the quire – the unit that dictated scribal and artistic interaction. After Wormald's publication of the division of hands the Psalter was rebound, and this made possible codicological study which largely confirms his brilliant analysis: artistic and scribal divisions frequently correspond to the gatherings in the manuscript. Appendix 1, a tabulated description of the manuscript, demonstrates the extent to which they coincide.[92] Yet why the artists should work by the quire has never been satisfactorily explained. Clearly it is not a case of coincidence, and the question of artistic personality is intimately tied up with scribal practice and the division of labour in the manuscript. This study concentrates on the techniques employed in each of the quires, starting with their ruling patterns, and only then moving on to a consideration of the making of the illustrations and the writing of the text.

The order of the production of the manuscript is not at all self evident, and will be made clear to the reader over the course of the next three chapters. In the meantime, it is wiser not to presume a relationship between quires, and to tackle first that quire which is the easiest to decipher. This turns out to be quire 4, with which I begin my enquiry.

[89] J.E. Gaehde, 'The draughtsmen of the Utrecht Psalter', in K. Bierbrauer, P. K. Klein, and W. Sauerländer (eds.), *Studien zur mittelalterlichen Kunst 800–1250, Festschrift für Florentine Mütherich zum 70. Geburtstag*, Munich, 1985, pp. 49–52.

[90] Carver, 'Contemporary artefacts', *passim*.

[91] Gameson, 'Anglo-Saxon artists', *passim*; Gameson, 'The Romanesque artist', *passim*.

[92] This table is found in Appendix 1 on p. 207.

I

Quires ruled by the artists

Quires 1, 2, 3, 4, and 9 of the Harley Psalter certainly look more like Utrecht than the other six quires. By analysing three of these quires in much the same way, it will be demonstrated that they are themselves very different – so different in fact, that it is only in retrospect that we can see what it is that they really do have in common. It will be seen that the artists of these quires were in command of production procedure to the extent that they not only illustrated before the scribes wrote their text, but also ruled for the lines of the text that the scribe was going to write.

QUIRE 4: ARTIST B and SCRIBE 1

Working procedure

Quire 4, consisting of fols. 20–27, is a regular quire of 8 leaves, with hair side facing flesh and with the hair side on the outside of the quire. The ruling pattern allows for 32 text lines per unillustrated page, arranged in three columns, like the Utrecht Psalter. Overall measurements are also very similar. The ruling in Harley is on both sides of the folio, for the most part in hard point, and usually very faint. At no point does the ruling intrude upon the illustrated space.

It is natural to think that the illustration spaces were left unruled because it was more difficult to draw on areas of vellum that were scored than on areas that were not. However, the Utrecht Psalter itself is ruled throughout, leaving no gaps for the illustration spaces, and the care taken to avoid the areas to be illustrated in Harley is to be contrasted with ruling patterns in most late tenth and early eleventh-century manuscripts. According to Ker, the ruling of each sheet separately became regular practice in the early eleventh century, and before this two or more sheets were commonly ruled at one time.[1] Even in the eleventh century more than one sheet was sometimes ruled at one time: Oxford, Bodleian Library, Ms. Junius 11, which like Harley has illustrations interspersed with the text, was ruled gatherings at a time: quires

[1] Ker, *Catalogue*, p. xxiv.

1–7 were ruled with the sheets flat, while quires 9–16 were ruled after folding, with later folios in the quire reruled as necessary.[2] Certainly ruling can often be seen scoring the illustrated pages of Gospel manuscripts. It is as though the ruling of the illustrated page did not visually offend the eleventh-century viewer, even in *de luxe* manuscripts, and artists were certainly prepared to illustrate on ruled parchment.

This leaves us with the curious situation that in Harley, in which text and illustration combine in such a complicated fashion, the ruling goes out of its way not to intrude upon the illustration area. There are parallels for this procedure. The same phenomenon of ruling on both sides of the folio, with care taken to avoid the illustration space is seen in the eleventh-century Anglo-Saxon Prudentius manuscripts, such as BL Cotton Ms. Cleopatra C.viii, BL Add. Ms. 24199, and Cambridge, Corpus Christi College, Ms. 23 for example.[3] Another remarkable parallel is found in the Old English illustrated Hexateuch, BL Cotton Ms. Claudius B.iv:[4] Clemoes noted that the ruling in this manuscript avoids the illustration spaces, and that ruling was executed on both sides of the folio.[5] Since it was not an aesthetic requirement that illustrated folios should be left unruled, since ruled folios did not present problems for the artists, and since this phenomenon occurs in a group of manuscripts with very complex relationships between text and image, it would seem to be the case that the ruling of these illustrated manuscripts was an integral part of their planning, and their complex formats were, in large part, marked out before anything was written or drawn. Moreover, it is no coincidence that, in BL Cotton Ms. Claudius B.iv and in BL Add. Ms. 24199, the artist at least marked out his illustrations in considerable detail before the scribe wrote his text.[6] It may have been the artists, and not the scribes, who were in charge of the layouts of these two manuscripts. By looking at artistic and scribal practice in Harley, we can discern the purpose of the ruling more clearly, and determine who was responsible for it.

In terms of layout on the page, the artist, who throughout this quire is Wormald's artist B, adhered to Utrecht with precision. Thus on fol. 23r the left-hand angel's wing just intrudes into column b below line 17, as it does in the Utrecht Psalter itself. Similarly, on fol. 22v Christ's right hand is next to the space between lines twelve and thirteen in both manuscripts (compare figs. 6 and 7). Although some of the lines on fols. 22v are not written on in Harley, they were ruled, as can be seen from the diagram of the visible ruling on fol. 22v (fig. 8). Since the horizontal lines were not ruled over the

[2] Temple, *Anglo-Saxon Mss.*, cat. 58. Reproduced in facsimile as I. Gollancz (ed.), *The Caedmon manuscript of Anglo-Saxon biblical poetry, Junius XI in the Bodleian Library*, Oxford, 1927, and the illustrated pages only in Ohlgren, *Textual Illustration*, pp. 534–76. See also Ker, *Catalogue*, cat. 334, pp. 406–8, and B.C. Raw, 'The construction of Oxford, Bodleian Library, Junius 11', *Anglo-Saxon England*, 13, 1984, pp. 187–207, esp. at pp. 199–202.

[3] Temple, *Anglo-Saxon Mss.*, Cats. 49, 48, and 51. In the case of Corpus 23, the ruling is particularly difficult to decipher. A good example of ruling on both sides of the folio is fol. 29.

[4] Temple, *Anglo-Saxon Mss.*, cat. 86. Edited in facsimile by Clemoes and Dodwell, *Hexateuch*.

[5] Clemoes and Dodwell, *Hexateuch*, p. 55–8.

[6] That the illustrations in BL Add. Ms. 24199 were at least sketched in before the text was executed in clear from the illustrations on fol. 22v and 31v, where the text is written around the illustration. The illustrations towards the end of the text in this manuscript are unfinished, but clearly there were underdrawings, in part still visible, because inscriptions work around them. For the Claudius manuscript see Clemoes in Clemoes and Dodwell, *Hexateuch*, p. 56.

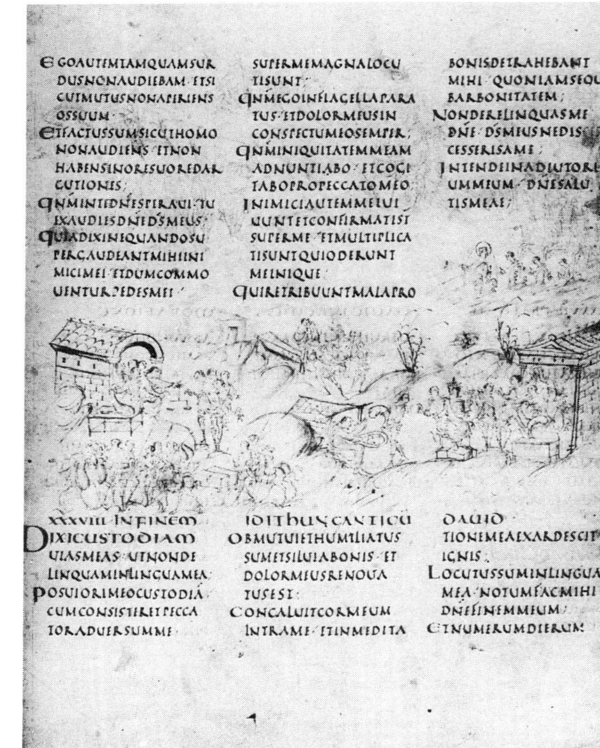

EGOAUTEMTAMQUAMSUR
DUSNONAUDIEBAM ETSI
CUTMUTUSNONAPERIENS
OSSUUM
ETFACTUSSUMSICUTHOMO
NONAUDIENS ETNON
HABENSINORESUOREDAR
GUTIONES
QNMINTEDNESPERAUI TU
EXAUDIESDNEDSMEUS
QUIADIXINEQUANDOSU
PERGAUDEANTMIHIINI
MICIMEI ETDUMCOMMO
UENTURPEDESMEI
SUPERMEMAGNALOCU
TISUNT
QNMEGOINFLAGELLAPARA
TUS ETDOLORMEUSIN
CONSPECTUMEOSEMPER
QNMINIQUITATEMMEAM
ADNUNTIABO ETCOGI
TABOPROPECCATOMEO
INIMICIAUTEMMEIUI
UUNTETCONFIRMATISI
SUPERME ETMULTIPLICA
TISUNTQUIODERUNT
MEINIQUE
QUIRETRIBUUNTMALAPRO
BONISDETRAHEBANT
MIHI QUONIAMSEQUE
BARBONITATEM
NONDERELINQUASME
DNE DSMEUSNEDIS
CESSERISAME
INTENDEINADIUTORE
UMMEUM DNESALU
TISMEAE

XXXVIII INFINEM
DIXICUSTODIAM
UIASMEAS UTNONDE
LINQUAMINLINGUAMEA
POSUIORIMEOCUSTODIA
CUMCONSISTERETPECCA
TORADUERSUMME
IDITHUNCANTICU
OBMUTUIETHUMILIATUS
SUMETSILUIABONIS ET
DOLORMEUSRENOUA
TUSEST
CONCALUITCORMEUM
INTRAME ETINMEDITA
DAUID
TIONEMEAEXARDESCIT
IGNIS
LOCUTUSSUMINLINGUA
MEA NOTUMFACMIHI
DNEFINEMMEUM
ETNUMERUMDIERUM

6

non audiens & non habens
in ore suo increpationes
Quo in te dne speraui, dixi
tu exaudies dne ds meus
Quia dixi ne aliquando in
sultent in me inimici mei
& dum commouentur
pedes mei in me magna
locuti sunt
Quo ego ad flagella paratus
sum . & dolor meus ante
me est semper
Quo iniquitatem meam
ego pronuntiabo & cogita
bo pro peccato meo
Inimici autem mei uiuent
& confortati sunt super
me . & multiplicati sunt
qui oderunt me inique
Qui retribuebant mihi mala
pro bonis detrahebant
mihi : quo subsecutus su
iustitiam
Ne derelinquas me dne ds
meus ne discesseris a me
intende in adiutorium
meum dne ds salutis
meae

IN FINEM IDITHUN
DIXI CUSTODIAM
uias meas ut non de
linquam in lingua mea
Posui ori meo custodiam
dum consisteret peccator
CANTICUM DAVID
aduersum me
Obmutui & humiliatus su
& silui a bonis & dolor
meus renouatus est
Concaluit cor meum in
XXXVIII
tra me & in meditatione
mea exardescit ignis
Locutus sum in lingua mea
notum mihi fac dne
finem meum & numeru

7

6 The Utrecht Psalter, fol. 22v, showing the illustration to Psalm 38.

7 The Harley Psalter, fol. 22v. The illustration to Psalm 38 is by B; the script is by scribe 1; the rubrication is by E; the initial is by J; there is a correction to the text in column b, line 4 from top, pronuntiabo; *additions were made to the illustration by G.*

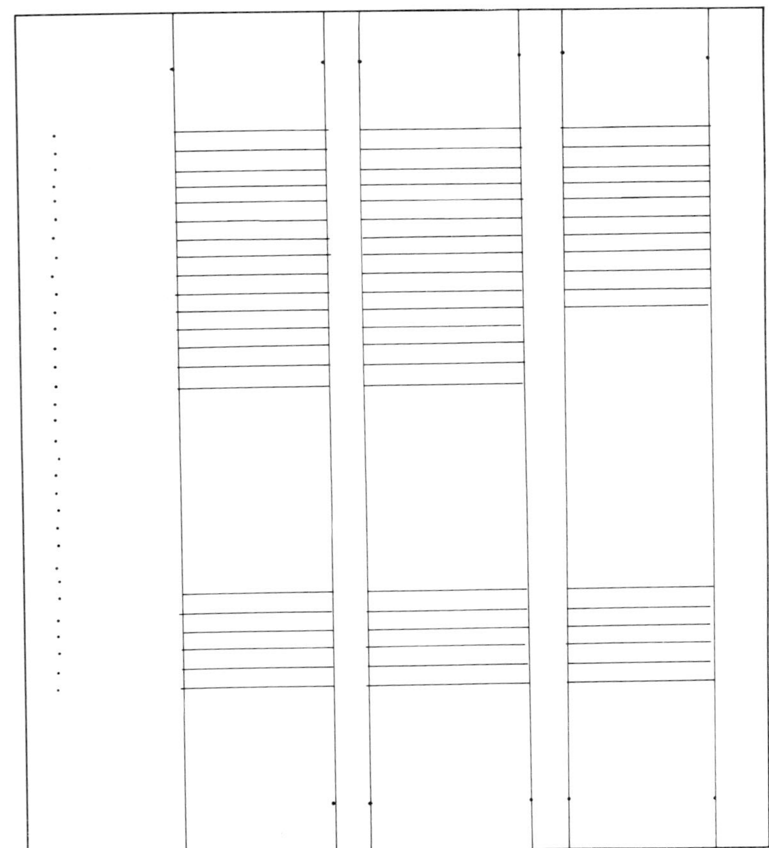

8 The Harley Psalter, fol. 22v, diagram of visible ruling.

illustration space, we can assume that the artist used the ruling pattern to locate his illustration on the page, and to do so in precisely the same location as it is found in the Utrecht Psalter. But, in marked contrast to the ruling pattern and the illustrations, the text shows no such adherence to the Utrecht exemplar. Because the text is in Caroline minuscule, and not Rustic capitals, and the ruling in this quire made no allowances for the smaller area that this text would take up, the scribe had difficulties in using up the area ruled. This led to an unsightly gap on some folios, such as fols. 22v and 23r, where the text does not interact with the illustrations as the form of the illustrations suggests that it should. When he could employ it, the scribe had his own way of countering this problem; he ended his Psalm text on fols. 20r, 21r, 24v, 25v, and 27r, and wrote nothing above the illustrations on the following folios, even though text is found there in Utrecht. This at least avoided an uncomfortable gap between text and picture on the following folio. Sometimes this proved to be a simple operation; for example on fols. 20r and 25v it was a natural consequence of his normal procedure – he wrote out his text which naturally took up less space than the text of Utrecht. However two of these folios show that the scribe had a design of his own that was wilfully at odds with that of the ruler and the illustrator. On fols. 24v and 27v this scribe's practice led to a considerable, and uncomfortable, compression of text in column c: the most visible signs of this are where, on fol. 24v, the eighth line of column c had to be finished on the fifth, and where, on fol. 27v, the last line of column c had to be finished on the third from bottom.[7] It is for this reason that a later artist, G, illustrated to the top of fol. 28r, which, in Utrecht, has lines of text.[8]

It is one of the most enigmatic features of this book that, because of the different lengths of the texts in Harley and Utrecht, there was no scribal reason for following the layout of the Utrecht Psalter, and yet followed it was. This was determined by the ruling of the pages, which does not follow the ruling of Utrecht, nor even the lines of text in Utrecht; rather, it left free of ruling that area of the page which in Utrecht was covered by an illustration. It is unlikely that the scribe was responsible for the ruling of this quire, since he so blatantly ignored the assumption inherent in it that the Utrecht layout would be followed precisely, an assumption with which the artist was quite happy. Rather, the ruling pattern echoes, and complements, the artist's own efforts at duplication. The artist was able to illustrate before the scribe wrote because the ruling pattern determined the parameters of his illustration spaces on the page, which exactly reflected those of the Utrecht Psalter, and this is all that he needed to know. The artist seems to have responded to the ruling pattern in Harley on the unwritten understanding that the scribe would follow the Utrecht layout as well. The scribe did not respond to Utrecht as the artist assumed he would; on the other hand he did respond aesthetically to the problem of integration: far from stretching his text he compressed it to end on the previous folio. I suggest, therefore, that the artist ruled and illustrated his folios, before passing them on to the scribe who wrote the text.

In fact we can relate the two processes of ruling and drawing even more closely, since

[7] *ini|micus* and *reget|nos in saecula* respectively.

[8] See below, chapter 2, p. 94 and forward.

the ruler seems to have paid special attention not to the lines for the script, but to the illustrations. In the last four folios of the quire, the illustrations are circumscribed by a deep ruling wherever there are margins which do not actually interlock with the text. Sometimes these are in lead point, as can be seen on fol. 26v. Indeed the vertical intercolumnar margin rulings here also are in lead point where they pass through the illustration, as if the illustration area was being subdivided into its constituent parts. This is even more evident on fol. 26r, where, as well as a line circumscribing the whole illustration, lead point lines indicate the first and second levels of the composition (fig. 9). These run across the illustration space from the left. As on fol. 26v, this space is further marked out by the ruling lines: through the illustration space the intercolumnar margins are inscribed more heavily than for the text itself. As a result the composition is more regular than in the Utrecht Psalter, drawn on three clear levels, and the position of the forward king, to the lower right, corresponds more closely to the intercolumnar margins of the text below (compare figs. 10 and 11).

The use of lead point in the early eleventh century is exceptional. Ker stated that the use of the pencil was first introduced as an instrument for ruling at the very end of the eleventh century, and had only generally superceded hard point by the third quarter of the twelfth.[9] More will be said on this matter in the discussion of Eadui Basan's quires, when it will be seen that lead point actually fully replaces hard point in the manuscript.[10] It can be said here that, in quire 4, it is directly linked to the fact that the artist of this quire was responsible for its ruling, and artists were used to handling lead point, even if scribes were not.[11] Artist B used it because he needed the parameters of his illustration to be carefully marked out,[12] but as we shall see he continued to use it in constructing the illustrations themselves.

The fact that the ruling pattern seems to pay special attention to the problems of the artist rather than the scribe suggests that the artist ruled the quire. I suggest that the ruling pattern reflected artistic concerns, precisely because the artist was in charge of it. From the artist's point of view the procedure was practical. From the scribe's it was not, and it is remarkable that the artist was given control of production procedure under such circumstances.

The artist's technique

Bearing in mind the artist's adherence to the layout of the exemplar, it would be surprising if this were not also true of his iconography and his style. Artist B did follow the illustrations in Utrecht very closely. This is best seen by his technical approach to the task of recreating the Utrecht images.

After having marked out his illustration spaces, artist B seems to have used the same lead point to execute preliminary drawings of his figures. He is the only one of the

[9] Ker, *Catalogue*, pp. xxiv–xxv. [10] See below, chapter 2, p. 95 and forward.

[11] See M.P. Brown, *Anglo-Saxon Manuscripts*, London, 1991, p. 51.

[12] Vezin, 'La réalisation matérielle', p. 33, notes a similar situation in an evangeliary from the Middle Rhine of *c.* 1000 AD, Paris, BN. Ms. Lat. 9395: lead point was used to guide the artists of the Canon tables.

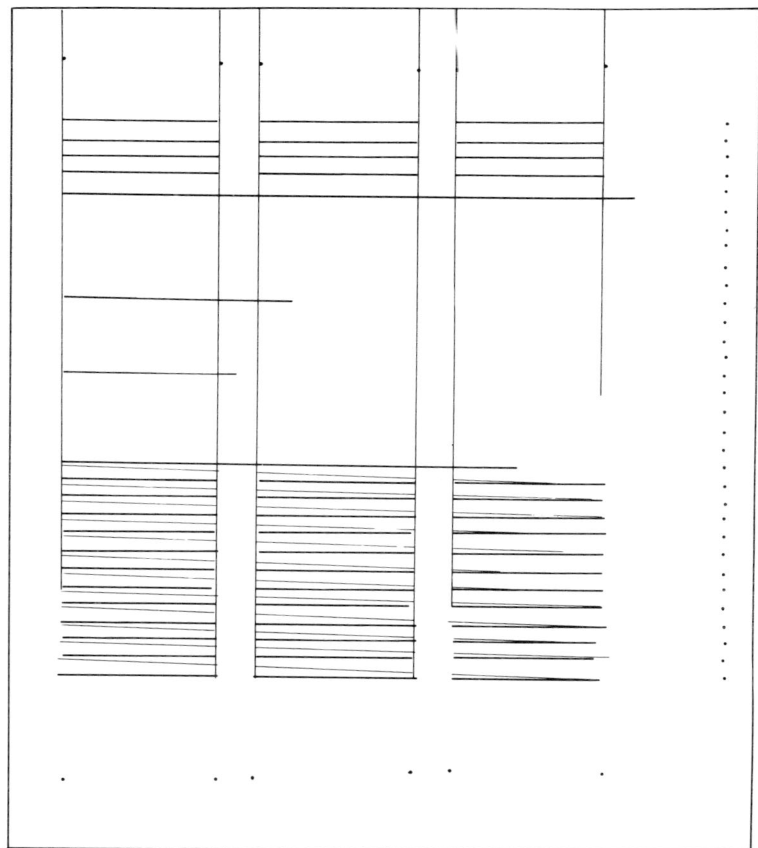

9 *The Harley Psalter, fol. 26r, diagram of visible ruling.*

10 *The Utrecht Psalter, fol. 26r, showing the illustration to Psalm 44.*

11 *The Harley Psalter, fol. 26r. The illustration to Psalm 44 is by B; the script is by scribe 1; the rubrication is by E; the initial is by J; there is a correction to the text in column a, line 4 from bottom,* diffusa.

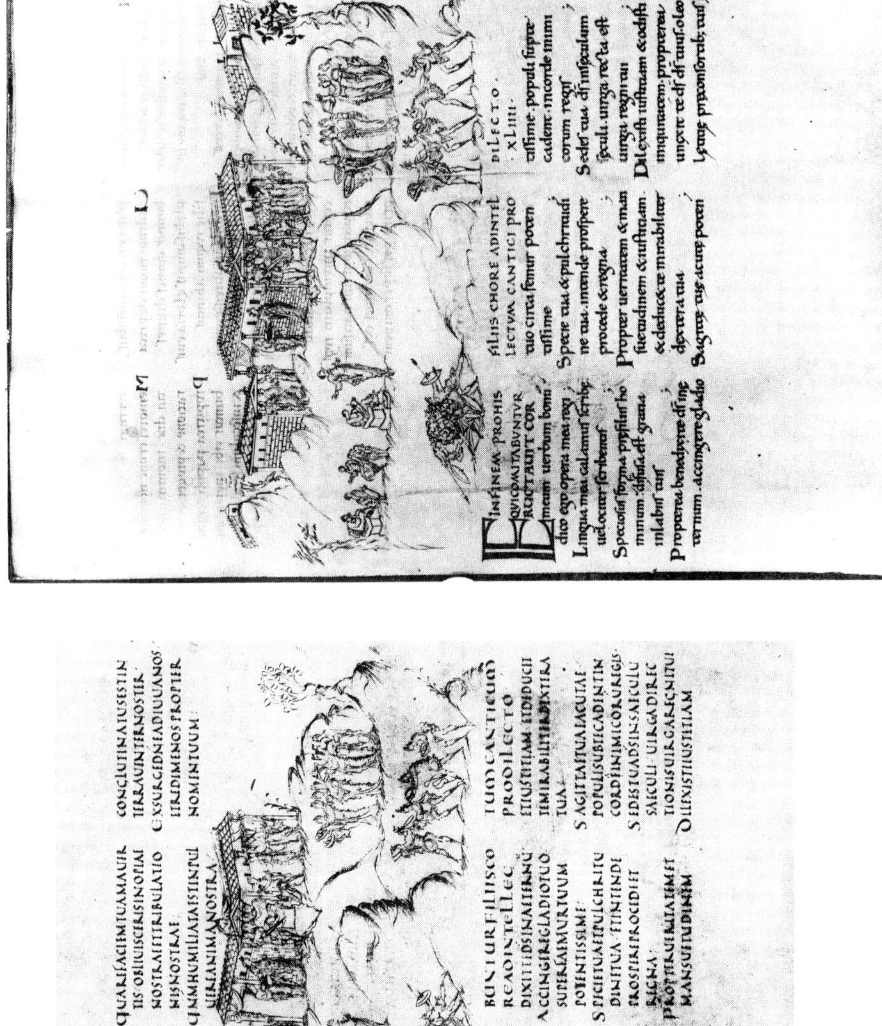

10

11

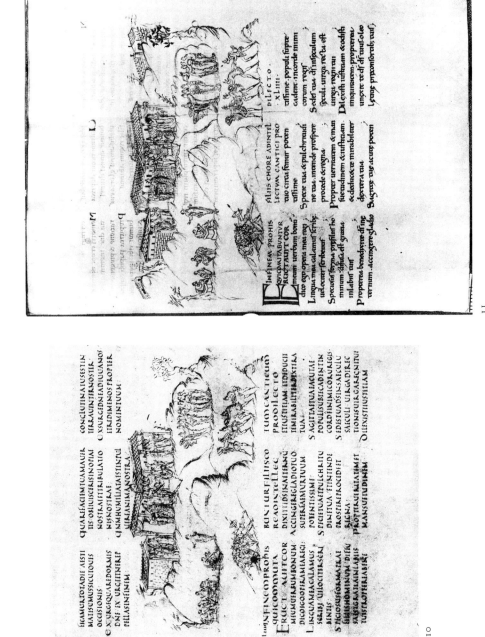

eleventh-century artists for whom there is clear evidence that this was done consistently. It can be seen where he sometimes ignores his under-drawings when colouring his illustrations: it is found around the pediment and cross of the building, and the cock, at the top left of fol. 24r; the head of the upper dog to the bottom right of the illustration on fol. 24v has been rearranged, and the lead under-drawing still shows; the central turrets of the architecture on fol. 26v also show it clearly. There are plenty of other examples. It seems to have been used as the basis for adhering to the Utrecht Psalter compositions remarkably faithfully.

Though the Utrecht Psalter shows many additions by later artists, which are usually difficult to pin down to particular Anglo-Saxon hands, the additions to this manuscript at the bottom right of the illustration on fol. 17r, and that on fol. 24r, may well have been by artist B himself who drew over the Utrecht composition, elaborating and clarifying. As Deshman noted, this certainly explains how Anglo-Saxon artists were able to imitate the Utrecht Psalter so successfully.[13] These illustrations in Utrecht, inked over by the Harley artist, suggest the extent to which this artist distanced himself from the ninth-century artist of Utrecht, commenting and clarifying, and the extent to which he related to and depended on him, using his illustration as a source for his style and composition.

It is no wonder that artist B struggled to come to terms with the style of Utrecht, for his work coincides closely with Gaehde's artist C of that manuscript. This artist executed the illustrations to Psalms 1, 30–50, and the Canticles and Creeds of Utrecht, and, as Gaehde points out, he was the most rapid and prolific of all, who did not stop to delineate coherent contour, and whose figures do not have the weight and density of those of the other artists.[14] Artist B could not but develop a style of his own under such circumstances. This style developed through the course of his work, and will be studied in more detail when we come to consider the relationship between the quires constructed in the creation of the manuscript.[15]

Artist B's colour scale is much more muted than that of artists A and D2, whose work we will analyse later in this chapter. This artist could execute his illustrations quite logically, moving across the entire composition, landscape included, using only two main colours, a ruddy-brown and a black. On four illustrations in this quire an ochre was also used as a background wash – fols. 20v, 21r, 24r, and the illustration to Psalm 42 on fol. 25r. A green was also used to add body to certain trees and illustrations, but without it no iconographic detail would have been missed.[16] In this quire there seems to be only one exception to this: in the illustration to Psalm 43 on fol. 25r, the bed and

[13] Deshman, 'Leofric Missal', p. 157, and n.3.

[14] Gaehde, 'Utrecht Psalter draughtsmen', p. 49.

[15] See below, chapter 3, pp. 125–126.

[16] The limited colour range of this artist has never been adequately stated in the literature, which has always stressed the use of many colours by the artists of the Harley Psalter. The artists of Harley can by no means all be grouped as 'multicoloured' line draughtsmen, especially after additions by artist G are taken into account – see chapter 2. pp. 100–112

clothes of the Lord, and the landscape around the temple to the left, are executed solely in blue. However it is quite possible that the green, the ochre and the blue in quire 4 were actually added by artist G, and a case will be made for this later.[17]

Artist B's use of the two base colours that he employed is deft, and passages such as the alternate light and dark horses at the bottom of the illustration to Psalm 35 on fol. 20v, are particularly impressive. But it will be shown that this handling of two colours simply does not compare in complexity to that of artists A and D2, and technically his work was far easier to execute than theirs: in effect it meant that he could simply transpose his image onto the vellum without having continually to go over it adding details colour by colour. As a result, he left fewer lacunae than either A or D2.

We will see that, iconographically, B was under the spell of his exemplar to a far greater extent than artist A. Carver, in his analysis of contemporary artefacts, notes only six changes in all, and only one of these occurs in quire 4; the rest occur in quires 2 and 3.[18] It was actually more natural for artist B to follow the form of a late antique artefact, than to adopt the images he saw and used in everyday life.

However, B's adherence to Utrecht was far from blind, and if his approach to the task of recreating the Utrecht illustrations was simply workmanlike, it can at least be said that his standard of craftsmanship was extremely high. The degree of his involvement with the illustrations is best gauged by analysing details of compositions. At the bottom right of the illustration to Psalm 36, on fol. 21r,[19] the artist missed out one of the hands of the man holding the bag open, the staff of the character carrying a sack over his shoulder, and the staff of one of the figures in the group to the right. However, in the same detail more riches are being poured into the bag, and the bag feels its greater weight. The crop is sown by a figure who strikes a more energetic pose. The instrument for sharpening the scythe has changed its form, and the crop is more clearly in the process of being cut. These and other changes demonstrate that B was active in his interpretation, thinking about what he was drawing, and how his figures performed. He was drawing from his own physical experience of picking things up, or carrying them, and not just reproducing Utrecht's lines on the page.

This reliance both on the form of his exemplar and on his own experience had some curious repercussions. In the illustration to Psalm 36, the artist misinterpreted the partially erased and redrawn beam of the Utrecht plough as a braced beam,[20] and he was at a loss in placing his ploughman safely to avoid the plough. But he did try to re-interpret the image: the leg of the ploughman is not safe, but at least it is not in between what were, to the artist, the two bars of the braced beam, and the tail of the foremost ox now rests its weight on the beam, as it did not in Utrecht. Similar are small changes wrought by artist B to the harps seen in Utrecht. Rensch Erbes has noted that

[17] See below, chapter 2, pp. 110–111. [18] Carver, 'Contemporary artefacts', pp. 127 and 136.

[19] Illustrated in Wormald, *English Drawings*, plates 12 (a) and (b). Despite the captions, they illustrate the same Psalm.

[20] D. Tselos, 'Defensive addenda to the problem of the Utrecht Psalter', *The Art Bulletin*, 49, 1967, pp. 334–49, at p. 340.

very slight changes were made to the harps on fols. 18v and 24v, while that on fol. 27r has significantly changed its form. However, the alterations were made upon harps that are still essentially of the 'Eastern angle' variety found in the exemplar. The Eastern angle harp is very different to the Anglo-Saxon harp, as it appears on fol. 68r, drawn by artist F, for example.[21] Artist B invested the images of Utrecht with his own experience, but this was only convincing if he was familiar with the image in the first place. When he was not, the result, in the plough as in the harps, was a sort of hybrid that did not really exist at all, and never had done.

The artist's response to the text

Artist B rarely strayed from the iconography of his model, but when he did he revealed an exactitude in his understanding of the text that seems to have eluded his most recent commentator.[22] To the right of Utrecht's illustration to Psalm 38 there is a smudge above the crowned man (fig. 12). If there was any doubt as to the textual reference of this smudge, artist B clarified the issue (fig. 13). On fol. 22v, he has drawn a small animal inside a web, and this refers to part of verse 12 of Psalm 38

tabescere fecisti sicut araneam animam eius.[23]

Utrecht's smudge is a spider's web, and this explains the presence of the web in Harley, which is itself wasting away and curling up as required by the text. As Gameson rightly noted, the animal inside the web looks like a beetle.[24] An arachnid has eight legs, an insect six. This creature has six and a bit legs. But, bearing in mind the text, we are more likely to be correct if we interpret him as a mutilated spider, than if we interpret him as a mutated beetle. Artist B's classification of the natural world may have been a little awry, but his knowledge of the text was not.

Another example is in B's illustration to Psalm 37, verses 4 and 5:

Nec est sanitas in carne mea a uultu irae tuae, et non est pax ossibus meis a facie peccatorum meorum. Quoniam iniquitates meae superposuerunt caput meum; sicut onus graue grauatae sunt super me.[25]

In Utrecht only one of the demons placing the heavy burden on the Psalmist is coloured, while in Harley, on fol. 22r, they are all coloured. Furthermore, unlike Utrecht, the Harley Psalmist himself is coloured in the same brown wash, with details of

[21] Rensch Erbes, 'Harp', p. 29. She goes on (p.33) to trace a development in the harp seen through the artists of Harley in the eleventh century, a development which we will see has no chronological justification. Rather, the changes made to harps depicted in Utrecht by the artists of Harley are an extremely good way of assessing the extent to which late antique images triumphed over contemporary artefacts in each artist, and only demonstrate the very great differences between them. [22] Gameson, 'Anglo-Saxon artists', p. 36.

[23] Thou hast made his soul to waste away like a spider's web.

[24] Gameson, 'Anglo-Saxon artists', p. 36. Characteristically the artist of the Eadwine Psalter, Cambridge, Trinity College, Ms. R.17.1 also missed the textual significance of the spider's web. Uncharacteristically, so did the artist of Paris 8846.

[25] ...Nor is there health in my flesh, because of thy wrath, and there is no peace in my bones because of my sins. For my iniquities are placed over my head; as a heavy burden they are become heavy upon me.

his veins showing, while every other figure that artist B drew is in outline only. It seems here that the illustrator was quite deliberately making a visual connection between the skin of the Psalmist and the demons engaged in stacking the sack carried on his back. The Psalmist is unhealthy because of God's wrath, and his skin is likened to that of the personifications of his sins, which inspired that wrath. The image is thus literal and more appropriate in its reflexive reference than that of Utrecht itself, which merely shows the Psalmist with sores.[26]

Another important change is to the illustration to Psalm 21, on fol. 12r. The smooth cross of Utrecht was not a satisfactory image to artist B, and he has turned it into a rough hewn one (compare figs. 58 and 59, on pp. 127). O'Reilly has given some important clues as to why this should be so: Psalm 21 was sung on Good Friday, and the texts of the liturgy naturally emphasise the Cross, and particularly the fact that it was made of wood. Given Anglo-Saxon predisposition for literal and concrete realisation of textual themes, this is reason enough for the change. The enlargement of the spear and the addition of the title board can be seen in the same light: they are attempts to develop imagery remarkably understated in the plain cross, which, in Utrecht, is neither a jewelled object, nor symbolically the Tree of Life.[27] The understated nature of this image in Utrecht is certainly in sharp contrast to the complex iconography of the crucifixion illustrating another Anglo-Saxon Psalter, Vatican Library, Ms. Reg. lat. 12, a manuscript with which the artists of Harley will be seen to be intimately connected. This illustration was executed in quire 2, and artist B's work in this quire will be further studied in chapter 3.

Another sign of artist B's engagement with his task is in his illustration to Psalm 40 on fol. 24r. Here Christ appears to the two women, having risen from the tomb. This is in response to verse 9 of the Psalm where the iniquitous say:

Numquid qui dormit non adiciet ut resurgat[28]

As Dewald observed, despite the hopes of Pilate and the Jews, the image shows that Christ did rise up again.[29] In Utrecht, Christ is shown twice: once in the tomb, and once before the two women. By contrast, artist B, has omitted the corpse of Christ within the tomb. This is not simply an omission, but rather a difference in emphasis, for, in

[26] Gameson, 'Anglo-Saxon artists', p. 36 notes that the artist ignores the sores of the Psalmist referred to in verses 6, 7, and 8, but it seems clear that they merely take a different form, and that the artist had a rather more subtle intention. The artist of Paris 8846 also imaginatively handled this difficult representation: the sack is not included, and the artist made the demons place a garb over the Psalmist, but they pull on it, so that it becomes a heavy burden for him. The garb actually covers his head, so the Psalmist no longer has to point to his head to demonstrate where the burden has been placed, but can hold out a speech scroll to the Lord. The Eadwine artist is less inventive.

[27] This image is discussed in J. O'Reilly, 'The rough-hewn Cross in Anglo-Saxon art', in M. Ryan (ed.), *Ireland and Insular Art, A.D. 500–1200*, Dublin, 1987, pp. 153–8, *passim*. It should be emphasised that, as she points out (p.153), the cross in the Eadwine Psalter (Trinity College, Cambridge Ms. R.17.1.) is of a very different sort, with irregular projections pointing outwards on both arms, thus imitating a tree, and not two planks constructed of rough wood as in Harley 603, where the projections on both arms point to the left. Neither does the Eadwine Psalter illustration have a title board. It is interesting that both the Eadwine artist and the Harley artist felt the need, at this point, to elaborate upon the Utrecht image, but they did so in very different ways. Compare Gameson, 'Anglo-Saxon artists', p. 46, n.60 and n.61.

[28] Shall he that sleepeth rise again no more?

[29] DeWald, *Utrecht Psalter*, pp. 20–1.

12 *The Utrecht Psalter, fol. 22v. A detail of the illustration to Psalm 38.*

contrast to Utrecht, there is quite clearly a tomb slab over the top of the sarcophagus.[30] The artist here seems to be drawing a parallel, not directly made in the Utrecht Psalter, between the covered tomb in the Holy Sepulchre, which Christ was about to negotiate, and the striking motif of the open sarcophagus from which the iniquitous cannot escape the death that is allotted to them, desired by the Psalmist in verse 6:

[30] Thus T.D. Kendrick, *Late Saxon and Viking Art*, London, 1949, p. 12, can speak of the 'scene at the empty Sepulchre' in Harley, while DeWald, *Utrecht Psalter*, p. 20, with reference to Utrecht, speaks of the Sepulchre as having a corpse in it – a body far more clearly seen in the original than in reproductions. The artist of Eadwine at this point changed the open sarcophagus in the tomb into an altar. Given the choice between the Utrecht and the Eadwine interpretations, the Paris 8846 artist here chose Eadwine's version in his underdrawing, which was later completed by a Catalan artist. The interpretation of Eadwine and Paris may be exegetical. Certainly it is moving further from the literal sense of the text, and the narrative logic of Utrecht's construction, where Christ negotiates the tomb on the left, to appear before the women on the right.

13 *The Harley Psalter, fol. 22v. A detail of the illustration to Psalm 38, by B, with additions by G.*

quando morietur et periet nomen eius.[31]

As well as those deviations from Utrecht that alter the meaning of the illustration, artist B's art involved a measure of 'completion' in those instances where Utrecht appeared unfinished. This involved a degree of invention in pictorial composition, for example in completing the form of the king bringing up the rear in the illustration to Psalm 47 on fol. 27v, and in adding an animated tail to the leeward vessel. The artist never strayed far from the example of Utrecht however, and his innovations are deliberate but small scale. Faults in his workmanship are remarkably few and, for the most part, were faults in pictorial understanding, rather than a failure to appreciate the text.

Artist B's alterations to Utrecht are remarkable precisely because they are so few in number. For the most part he was entirely happy to convey the imagery of his exemplar, but just occasionally he found fault with it. These changes are not simply reversions to more familiar images, simply because, for artist B, Utrecht was the norm in forming his pictorial vocabulary. The change to a rough-hewn cross, for example, is not a neutral pictorial device, but a positive statement. There are, apparently, no alterations to the iconography in the work of artist B to take account of the fact that he was illustrating the Roman, and not the Gallican, version of the Psalter text. The reason for this might

[31] When shall he die and his name perish?

lie, in part, in the mechanics of the book's production, and the degree of his pictorial energy can be gauged by the fact that he consulted the Psalm text, even though, in his own manuscript, it had not yet been written. This is a true testimony to the literate nature of his task. The ruling pattern assumes duplication of Utrecht; in their positioning so do the drawings. This artist studied the page layout of Utrecht and its illustrations; it seems likely that he also referred to its text.

Conclusion

If this analysis is convincing, then it is also extraordinary. In quire 4 of Harley 603 there seems to have been no interaction between the two exemplars used. The Utrecht Psalter thoroughly dominated the iconography of artist B, and the planning of his pages, and the scribe of the Roman text was at a loss. Making Harley was not a simple process, and it could lead to severe organisational problems when it came to the layout of the page.

Quire 1: Artist A and Scribe 1

Working procedure

Quire 1, like quire 4, is a regular quire of 8 leaves, with the hair side facing the flesh, and with the hair side on the outside of the quire. The overall measurements are again very similar to those of Utrecht. As in quire 4, there is a desire not to rule over the illustration space, and ruling was executed, again very faintly, on both sides of the folio. The details of the ruling pattern are difficult to decipher, but it is clear that in quire 1 it was experimental, and that it was difficult to interpret even when it was executed; for example, the last line of text on fol. 2r is half a line too low, and on the recto and verso of the same page lines of text frequently follow different courses, as at the top of fols. 3r and 3v for example. The difficulties of interpreting the ruling pattern do not however prevent us from drawing one important conclusion: in marked contrast to quire 4 the Utrecht layout was not followed. For instance, at the top of fol. 3v there are 11 ruled lines in Harley, and 11 lines of text were written in each of its three columns, while in Utrecht 15 lines of text were written (compare figs. 14, 15, and 16). In his attitude to the Utrecht exemplar, at least on this folio, the ruler of quire 1 stands in marked contrast to artist B: from the determined pictorial equivalence to Utrecht found in quire 4, we have moved to a quire where the format involved careful and calculated adaptation of the exemplar.

A more detailed analysis of the ruling pattern will be helped by an understanding of the order of work in this quire, which was illustrated by artist A, and written by scribe 1. Even though the Utrecht format was not followed exactly, the illustrations were again executed before the text was written. We can see this on fol. 2v where the last line of column b begins 'Non timebo'. Here the scribe indented the text so that the capital 'N' could be fitted in. The scribe must have known that there would be no room in the margin for the capital, and he knew this because the depiction of the Lord was already executed by the artist. If it was not the artist who ruled the manuscript, it was at least the artist who first used the ruling to guide him.

We must now come to terms not with generalities, but with a wealth of detail. The ruling technique varies considerably. On fol. 8v at the top of the illustration there is a hard point line, at an angle on the page, and extending to the pricking, rather than to the outer column margin. This line is independent of the ruling for the text, and seems to have acted as a sort of permeable frame for the artist. Similar lines can be discerned at the lower edge of the illustration on the top of fol. 8r (compare figs. 17 and 19), at the top of the illustration to fol. 4v, and fol. 3v. Clemoes noticed similar ruling lines in BL Cotton Ms. Claudius B.iv, which he thought were lines ruled by the artist, to delineate his illustration space.[32] Given that the artist illustrated before the scribe wrote in this quire, it seems safe to assume that these lines in Harley 603 had the same purpose, and were therefore ruled by the artist. Of course, in quire 4 there was no need for such lines since the artist worked by the lines ruled for the text itself.

While these angled margin lines are used for some illustrations, they are not for others. On fol. 8r, for instance, the text of Psalm 14 has precisely the same number of lines ruled for it as there are lines of text in the Utrecht Psalter (compare figs. 17 and 18). However, the text in columns a and b of Harley leaves the lowest ruled line devoid of script (fig. 19). That part of the illustration to Psalm 15 illustrated by artist A demonstrates an adherence to the ruling pattern, and not to the text: while the tree and the house on the hill were added by artist G, as we shall see,[33] the head of the Psalmist does not protrude into the lines ruled, but cranes into the margin between them. However, in column c, depicting the Lord and angels, the artist has drawn over the ruling pattern, and the result is an interaction with the text, outside the boundaries dictated by the ruling pattern. It seems possible that for this illustration, where even in Utrecht the physical interaction between text and illustration is uneven, the artist ruled all the lines of text, basing his ruling upon that seen in the Utrecht Psalter, but then in column c drew over his own ruling pattern because he knew that the text in his manuscript would be shorter. The scribe for his part wrote the text, but he did not follow the ruling pattern laid out for him.

From this I surmise that the artist ruled horizontal lines independent of the pricking marks to mark out his illustration spaces, and then ruled in the text lines. In those cases where the illustration space was more complicated, the artist did not mark out his illustration space first, but carefully ruled for the lines of text seen in the Utrecht Psalter, which he then adapted in his actual illustrations.

The care taken by the artist to consider the spacing of the text is the clue to why on fols. 3v, 4r, and 4v, he ensured, in his ruling as in his drawing, that the text area that the

[32] Clemoes, in Clemoes and Dodwell, *Hexateuch*, p. 55. [33] See below, chapter 2, p. 107.

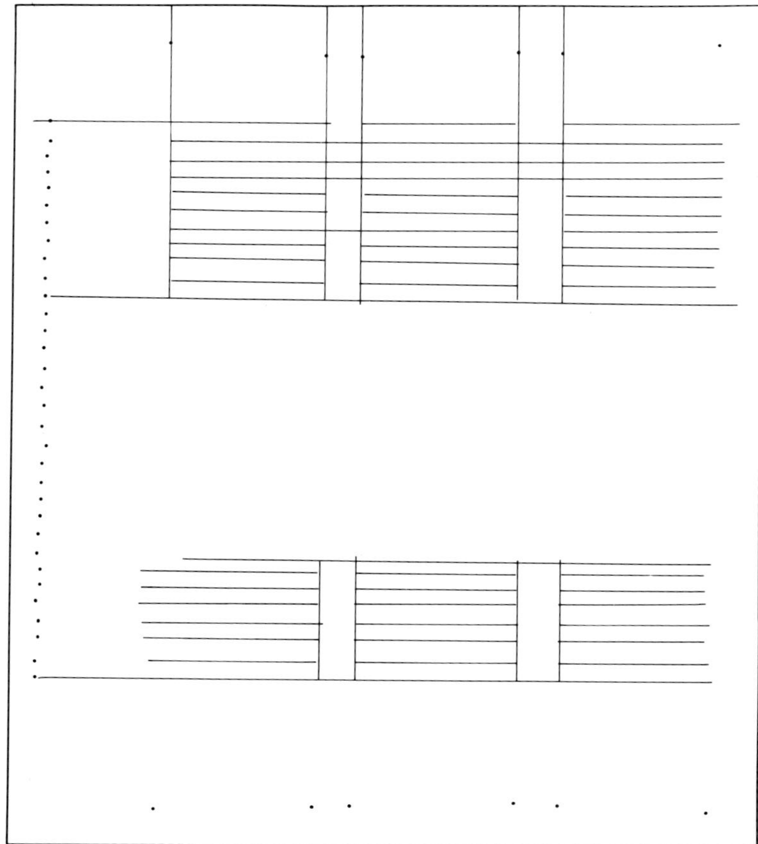

14 *The Harley Psalter, fol. 3v, diagram of visible ruling.*

15 *The Utrecht Psalter, fol. 3v, showing the illustration to Psalm 6.*

16 *The Harley Psalter, fol. 3v. The illustration to Psalm 6 is by A; the script is by scribe 1; the rubrication is by E; the initial is by J.*

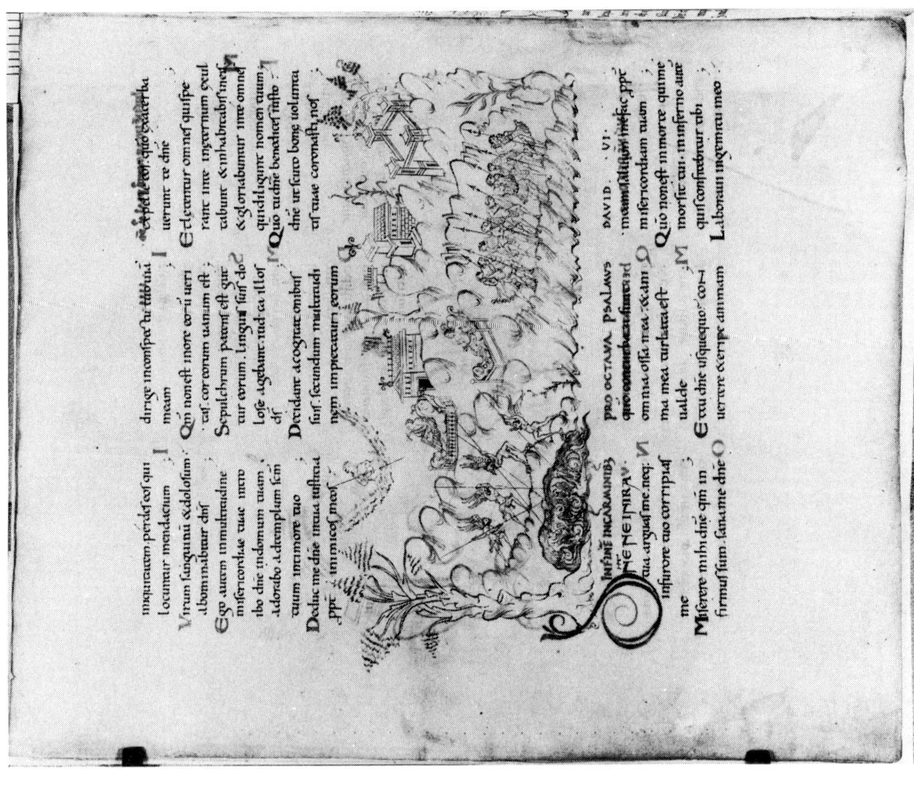

16

15

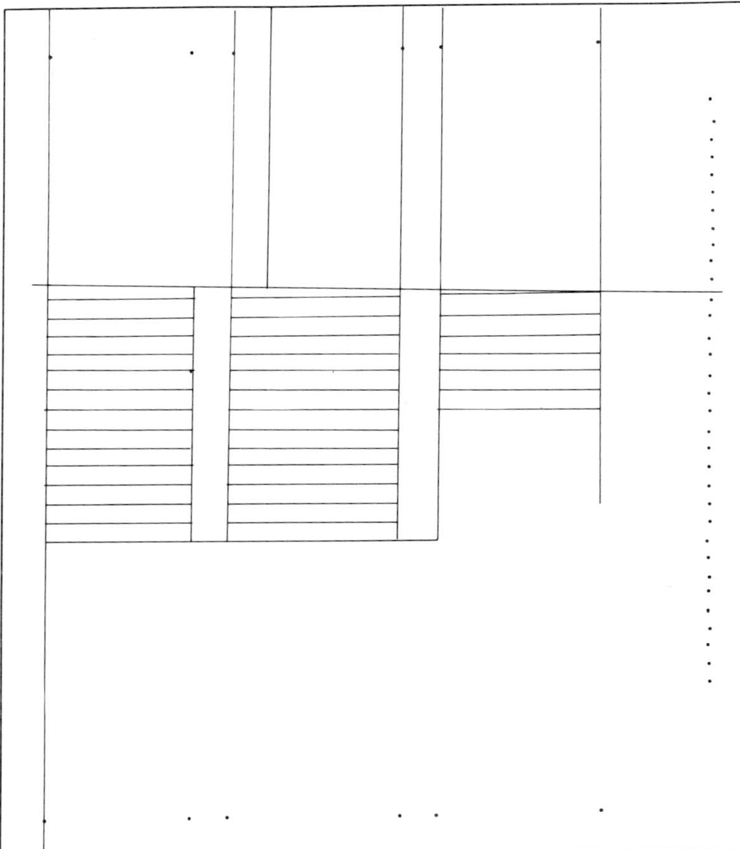

17 *The Harley Psalter, fol. 8r, diagram of visible ruling.*

18 *The Utrecht Psalter, fol. 8r, showing the illustrations to Psalms 14 and 15.*

19 *The Harley Psalter, fol. 8r. The illustrations to Psalms 14 and 15 are by A; the script is by scribe 1, the rubrication is by E; the initial is by J; additions were made to the illustrations by G.*

18

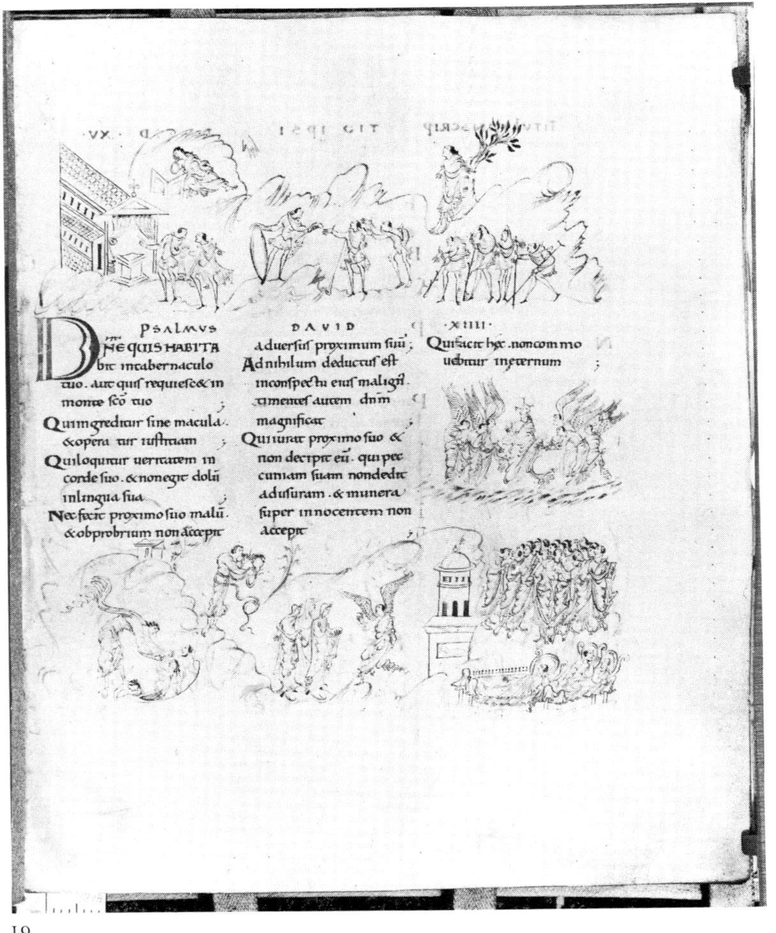

19

scribe would have to cover is less than that covered by the Rustic capitals of the Utrecht Psalter. The integrity of the Utrecht layout was maintained by making the text of each Psalm begin on the same line as it does in Utrecht. It is noticeable that, towards the end of the quire, the artist ceased to adapt the layout of his ruling pattern from that prescribed by the Utrecht Psalter, and that, even though he occasionally still used deeply incised horizontal lines to mark out his illustration space, he normally expected the scribe simply to cover the same area as in the Utrecht Psalter itself. The result is most clearly seen on fol. 6r, where the long text of Psalm 9 ended long before the illustration to Psalm 10.

This would seem to account for the character of the ruling pattern on all folios except fols. 1v and 2r. Why there are signs of ruling at the top left of a verso that was always intended to contain an illustration is difficult to explain. I think it can be put down to the same experimental quality that is seen on fol. 2r, containing the first lines of text in the manuscript (fig. 1, above, p. 4). These lines seem to have been ruled, if not in lead or another type of metal point, then certainly by an instrument which made a 'coloured' guideline, and to have been ruled deep into the Psalm illustration, beyond those lines called for by the exemplar.[34] A not entirely successful attempt was then made to rub this out where it conflicted with the illustration. Not surprisingly, this was discontinued after the text of the first Psalm.

There are no pricking marks on the inner margins of the quire which might imply that the artist ruled by the bifolium. However I suggest that this is unlikely: the ruling pattern seems to develop logically through the quire, moving from experimentation, to adaptation, and finally to an adherence to the exemplar, and this suggests that the page was ruled folio by folio, and not by the bifolium. We should understand, then, that the artist had the open sheet before him, but only ruled one side of this sheet at a time. Such a technique is not entirely unparalleled, and it will be seen to occur later in this manuscript, when we consider the quires of Eadui Basan. Clemoes presumed that ruling a single folio, taking lines from prickings across the width of bifolium, stood contrary to reason, and thus supposed that, in the case of BL Cotton Ms. Claudius B.iv, there was an exemplar which meant that the artist could mark out the first and last folio of his quire in one operation, and know where blank spaces should be left for the illustrations.[35] However, as he also points out, from the thirteenth quire onwards, there are prickings on the inner margins of this manuscript.[36] There are two reasons for having prickings on the inner margin: they are helpful if ruling is done on folded sheets, as was the case with Oxford, Bodleian Library, Ms. Junius 11,[37] and they are helpful if ruling is done page by page. In BL Cotton Ms. Claudius B.iv we know that ruling was done on both sides of the folio, and that therefore there was no point in having pricking in the inner margin for ruling across the folded sheet. I suggest that pricking in the inner margin was adopted from quire 13 of the Claudius manuscript precisely because the

[34] The use of a pigmented ruling pattern before the introduction of the widespread use of lead point is paralleled in Paris, BN Ms. Lat. 259, a late ninth-century Franco-Saxon manuscript, where blood was used on some folios; see Vezin, 'La réalisation matérielle', p. 33. [35] Clemoes, in Clemoes and Dodwell, *Hexateuch*, pp. 57–8.
[36] Ibid., p. 57. [37] See above, pp. 28–9, and n.2.

ruling of each recto and verso was executed singly. This was probably done from the beginning of work on the book, and the fact that pricking in the inner margin only occurs from quire 13 onwards is an indication that techniques of book manufacture were rapidly evolving in the century before the Norman Conquest. Although pricking on both sides of the folio is undoubtedly helpful, it is not absolutely necessary whether ruling is carried out on folded sheets or across the individual folio. In the Prudentius manuscript in Cambridge, Corpus Christi College, Ms. 23, the first quire was certainly not ruled right across the open sheet: the first four folios are ruled without care taken to avoid the illustration spaces, but on the conjoints of these folios, the last four folios of the quire, an attempt has been made to leave some of the illustration spaces devoid of ruling – the ruler of the manuscript changed his mind half way through the quire. The question arises as to how this could be done. It was possible to place one's rule across the entire open sheet, and rule only one half of it. Another possible explanation is that offered by Wright. He supposed that in BL Cotton Ms. Vespasian A.i, where there are no prickings on the inner margin, and where the ruling was executed on folded sheets, some kind of 'T-square' was used.[38]

As a result of this analysis we can say that the ruling of Harley was the artist's concern, and that he was aware of problems of spacing of script, which meant that ideally the Utrecht layout should be adapted. On later folios the adaptation of the ruling pattern proved too complex a problem, but even here, in his illustration to Psalm 15 on fol. 8r, we see him playing with the space suggested by the ruling pattern. When this spatial organisation worked, it worked extremely well: despite the fact that there are four less lines of text at the top of fol. 3v in Harley than there are in Utrecht, the illustration still ties in perfectly with the text; and on fol. 6v the illustration goes to the top of the page in Harley, where in Utrecht there were three lines of text, and the scribe of Harley finishes his text on 6r. How much happier this is than the situation that we saw in quire 4.

The artist's technique

The artist, for his part, seems to have revelled in the artistic possibilities inherent in the larger space he had to use, and in restructuring his composition. One of the most remarkable characteristics of this artist's work is that although the relative placing of his figures changes very considerably compared to Utrecht, the figures normally continue to relate to each other very well. In the illustration to Psalm 6 on fol. 3v, because of the new space to be illustrated the Lord is significantly higher in relation to the two figures confined to their beds, yet they still look to him, and the demons, set further off from the Hell pit than they are in Utrecht, now have significantly more thrust in their spears (compare figs. 15 and 16, above, p. 45); similarly in the illustration to Psalm 9, on fol. 5r, the archer now aims his arrow straight up at the Psalmist, rather than at an angle as in

[38] Wright, *Vespasian Psalter*, p. 18.

Utrecht, and the figure on the turret of the building has to strain his neck further than his counterpart in Utrecht to gaze upon the Lord. These changes are symptomatic of the way artist A rethought the composition in Utrecht, and, having rethought it, carried its implications through to their conclusion in his own Psalm illustration. Furthermore, and unlike artist B, he seems to have done this without the help of any under-drawing: there are one or two touches only, and, bearing in mind A's frequent omissions, we would expect many more. The demonic woman on the right of the illustration to Psalm 7 on fol. 4r has another leg added in pencil, and the bricks fallen from the building in the illustration to Psalm 10 on fol. 6r are also lightly drawn in. Both these examples however, may well be the work of other artists, and not of artist A.

This artist's interpretation of Utrecht went beyond the alteration of spatial relationships between figures. Artist A attempted to imbue every single figure with an internal dynamic which was thoroughly convincing, and very different from its model. This has been briefly but effectively analysed in relation to the horsemen of the illustration to Psalm 13 (compare figs 22 and 23, below, p. 55), on fol. 7v, by Kendrick, who writes,

> There is a greater thrust forward, the forelegs of the horses are raised higher; their hind legs are stretched further back; and the long lances are more impressively and aggressively held.[39]

The technique of drawing from experience found in artist B is seen so much more clearly in the work of artist A, and this is partly because the relationships between figures have been altered so much more.

Artist A was, then, far more daring in his reinterpretation of Utrecht than artist B. But the result of this reinterpretation, particularly the reorganisation of his space, was a much more radical difference in terms of technique. It seems likely that, once his space had been determined, artist A would have drawn his figures first, and presumably the figure that was to be the focus of the Psalm illustration first of all, in order that the other figures could be constructed with reference to it. Buildings generally seem to have been drawn after the figures. This can be seen where figures do not match very well with the structures upon which they rest, as for example in the illustration to Psalm 9, on fol. 5r, where the feet of the character on the turret are not matched correctly with his platform. Evidence is also to be seen in the fact that it is most often the buildings that were left unfinished, and this even when they are next to completed figures: thus the angel in the illustration to Psalm 15 on fol. 8r is finished, but the tombstone on which it sits was not even begun. Finally, and departing from Utrecht most radically, the background landscape was drawn in, making sense of the new relationship between the figures, and between the figures and the buildings. His landscapes bear so little relationship to those in Utrecht, because it is here that we see fully the ramifications of his recomposition of the Utrecht illustrations. The fabulous whirling patterns of this artist are, in part, a consequence of his working procedure, and it is through this new landscape that he ties the new composition together.

This construction technique materially affected the appearance of the illustration.

[39] Kendrick, *Late Saxon*, p. 13.

The late addition of the landscape is why, rather than being set within a landscape, the people in this quire float upon it.[40] And if there was a mistake in an early part of the construction of an illustration, this was reflected later on; thus in the illustration to Psalm 14, on fol. 8r (fig. 19, above, p. 47), the artist did not execute the man lying at the feet of the central character, and therefore later gave this central character a landscaped footing.[41]

Artist A's concern was not to set his figures in a convincing landscape setting, as they are in Utrecht, but rather to give the page a satisfactory overall surface design. The landscape was drawn around figures within it, and it was drawn with a vibrancy and elaboration that Tselos has compared to the landscapes of Van Gogh.[42] Because the surface design was so important, it was essential that illustration and text tied in physically with each other, as so clearly did not happen in quire 4. More than this, the concern for surface design meant that it was perfectly possible for the illustration actually to invade the text space, without any violation of a spatial construction. Integration between text and illustration is found to a far greater extent in quire 1 of Harley than it is in the Utrecht Psalter itself, where the surface pattern of the text is punctuated by the depth of the illustration. Artist A's work normally fills the entire available space: in the illustration to Psalm 6 on fol. 3v the tree to the left of the Utrecht illustration has in Harley grown to enormous heights, its roots designed to sprout from the text below, and the tips of its leaves to penetrate the clouds of text above (compare figs. 15 and 16, above, p. 45). Indeed, in the one illustration in which artist A could not use the text as a permeable barrier for the pattern of his illustration, he had to make one, and in the illustration to Psalm 1 on fol. 1v, not bordered by text, artist A makes a border, which, of course, he then proceeds to break. It was this aesthetic requirement which led him to emphasise the lower edges of his illustrations, and it is precisely when Utrecht's illustrations are less expansive, and involve the assumption that blank vellum is landscaped space to a greater degree, that it is most obvious.[43]

Another theme in this whole process of construction is artist A's use of colour, which was so much bolder than that of artist B, using as he did separate colours to illustrate different parts of the anatomy, and different articles of clothing. If we imagine how the illustration would have looked when half finished, it becomes apparent that this use of colour was only made possible by the fact that there was an exemplar from which to work, and to which reference could be made, when the artist was lost in the complexity of his recreation. Even as it is, there are a number of lacunae in artist A's work – for example the feet and ground underneath the wicked in the illustration to Psalm 1 on fol. 1v, and the hand of the figure being sawn in half at the bottom left of the illustration to

[40] As noted by Gameson, 'Anglo-Saxon artists', p. 38. He notes in particular that the figures on fol. 6r 'lean'; the reason is clear – it is that their ground had not yet been drawn.

[41] The figure was partly executed later by artist G, see below, chapter 2, p. 108.

[42] D. Tselos, 'English manuscript illumination and the Utrecht Psalter', *The Art Bulletin*, 41, 1959, pp. 137–49, at pp. 138–9.

[43] Gameson, 'Anglo-Saxon artists', p. 37, suggests that this was done because artist A worked before the text was written, but artist B, working under similar circumstances felt no such need.

Psalm 13 on fol. 7v (fig. 23, below, p. 55).[44] Unlike artist B, who as I have tried to show, did not have to reconstruct his illustrations, and whose use of colour was far less elaborate, artist A could not follow the Utrecht Psalter's illustrations section by section. Rather he had to work colour by colour, first through figures, then through buildings, and finally through landscape. This is the extent to which these two artists were involved in different technical processes.

The inventiveness claimed for artist A lies partly in his use of images outside those seen in the Utrecht Psalter. In marked contrast to artist B, who shows few signs of assimilating contemporary artefacts in his interpretation of Utrecht's images, Carver has observed that artist A usually did just this. Alterations to the form of contemporary artefacts were not the exception, but the rule, and he has been able to observe that artist A was 'an accurate observer of his surroundings to whom archaeologists are greatly indebted'.[45] In contrast to artist B, it was more natural for artist A to include a contemporary image than it was to emulate an antique one. Artists A and B were making different worlds.

The artist's response to the text

Throughout the work of artist A there is evidence that he intentionally changed certain motifs in order to elaborate upon, or change the emphasis of, the Utrecht illustrations. One of the problems in evaluating these changes is that our interpretation of them is determined by our initial expectations. He has been seen as a not very careful, if extremely talented and inventive, 'facsimilist', who paid little attention to the text of the Psalms.[46] But if the images were read with knowledge of the Psalms, some of his images would be more satisfactory than Utrecht's.

The advantage of having studied the ruling pattern is that we now know that artist A was concerned to adapt the composition of Utrecht, and we can examine the iconographic consequences of this adaptation. In general the consistency with which he maintained the relationships between figures is impressive, but the most remarkable example of his recomposition of an illustration is that to Psalm 4, verse 7,

signatum est super nos lumen uultus tui domine.[47]

On fol. 2v of the Harley Psalter, the Lord is seen above the illustration space proper, and in the margin between columns a and b. The light of the Lord's face is now much more physically '*super nos*' than it is in the rather cramped conditions under column b of text in Utrecht. This change in the composition is catered for throughout the rest of the illustration, and the godly still establish eye contact with the Lord.[48] Indeed more

[44] Gameson, 'Anglo-Saxon artists', p. 37, p. 39, and p. 47, n.71 and 72 also mentions omissions by artist A. The lacunae in A's work will be further explored when we come to consider the additions of artist G in chapter 2.

[45] Carver, 'Contemporary artefacts', p. 121.

[46] Gameson, 'Anglo-Saxon artists', pp. 36–40.

[47] The light of thy countenance is signed upon us O Lord.

[48] The Eadwine artist here placed the Lord's face amongst the other signs above men – the Sun and the Moon. This the Paris 8846 artist also did, but Paris also has the Lord emanating light upon the figure rising from the

people gaze upon the Lord in Harley than in Utrecht, as the priest too is now directing his gaze to Him, and he refers well to verse 2

Cum inuocarem te exaudisti me deus iustitiae meae[49]

The employment of artefacts outside those seen in the Utrecht Psalter may have been, in part, an unthinking reliance on familiar themes. However, sometimes it was not. In his illustration to Psalm 8, on fol. 4v, he greatly elaborated the portrayal of the birds of the air and the fish of the sea in Utrecht, referring to verse 9:

Uolucres caeli et pisces maris, qui perambulant semitas maris.[50]

Instead of a generalised depiction, we have seagulls and, amongst other additions, three sea birds, either herons or cranes,[51] and a number of eels (compare figs. 20 and 21). This is a quite deliberate essay in natural observation, where Utrecht was seen to be somewhat cursory, and, in the light of the text, the artist recognised the pond as the sea and drew a coastal scene. Indeed since the long-legged sea birds of this scene walk beside and on the sea, and one of them actually treads on one of the fish, the artist seems to have taken this a stage further, and made the birds of the air, as well as the fish of the sea, pass through the ways of the sea.

His introduction of motifs drawn from his own experience is also used inventively in the illustration to Psalm 13, which begins

Dixit insipiens in corde suo, non est deus[52]

Here, at the bottom left, the two figures that in Utrecht were fighting over a woman with a bar, are, on fol. 7v of Harley sawing her in half (compare figs. 22 and 23). It certainly conjures up well the atmosphere of a phrase in verse 3,

Contritio et infelicitas in uiis eorum, et uiam pacis non cognouerunt.[53]

There is another change of emphasis in this Psalm illustration: the Harley artist has turned the two snakes wrapped around the columns of the tempietto in Utrecht into far more effective creatures, with twisted animation pulsating through their well articulated bodies. In Utrecht they refer to verse 3:

uenenum aspidum sub labiis eorum.[54]

They are attributes of *insipiens*, and gain their meaning from him.[55] The situation in Harley is very different. While in Utrecht the asp on the right is ineffective, in Harley he

sarcophagus to reinforce the point of the Utrecht illustration, that it is not the light of the Sun or the Moon that is important, but that of the Lord. This point was rather lost on the Eadwine artist, who did not make the figure in the sarcophagus look up to the Lord. [49] When I called upon you you heard me God of my justice.

[50] The birds of the air and the fishes of sea, that pass through the paths of the sea.

[51] Carver, 'Contemporary artefacts', p. 132 identifies them as herons. W.B. Yapp, 'The birds of English manuscripts', *Journal of Medieval History*, 5, 1979, pp. 315–48, at p. 316 identifies them as cranes.

[52] The fool hath said in his heart, there is no God.

[53] Grief and misfortune in their ways, and the way of peace they have not known.

[54] The venom of asps is under their lips.

[55] Compare this mode of reference with that of artist F in his illustration on fol. 71v to Psalm 139, verse 4; see below, chapter 2, p. 85.

20 *The Utrecht Psalter, fol. 4v. A detail of the illustration to Psalm 8.*

21 *The Harley Psalter, fol. 4v. A detail of the illustration to Psalm 8, by A.*

22 *The Utrecht Psalter, fol. 7v. The illustration to Psalm 13.*

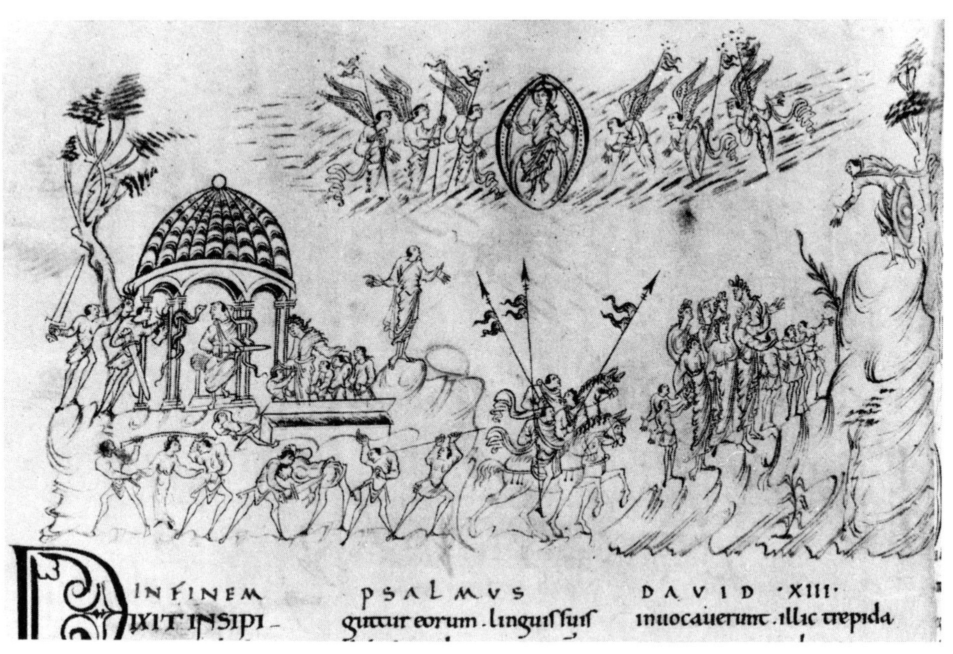

23 *The Harley Psalter, fol. 7v. The illustration to Psalm 13, by A.*

is whispering into the ear of *insipiens*.[56] The one on the left is no longer looking into the mouth of *insipiens*, but staring at him, eyeball to eyeball. The 'venom of asps' is no longer under the lips of *insipiens*, as required by verse 3, and the asps are no longer neatly classified as his attributes. A far more insidious and complex relationship is struck up between the snakes and *insipiens* in Harley. One is polluting his mind by whispering into his ear, and the other is polluting his sight by staring into his eyes.[57]

While the snakes in Utrecht are wriggly little things, that may indeed be asps, the ones in Harley are full-blooded snakes. *Insipiens* is mesmerised by the snake on the left, and elsewhere in Harley close eyeball contact denotes the scheming of evil doers, as in the illustration to Psalm 9 on fol. 5r. A snake-charming a man would have suggested the devil in the early eleventh century: for example, in Aldhelm's riddle of the serpent (*De aspide uel basilico*) on fol. 99r of BL Royal Ms. 12.c.xxiii, the cunning and evil one is interpreted as the devil in the gloss. On page 20 of Oxford, Bodleian Library, Ms. Junius 11, the 'Caedmon Genesis', a winged demon is sent by Satan to bring about the Fall of Man, and he turns into a serpent, very like that in Harley, to speak to the beguiled Eve. The snake on the left is not an attribute of *insipiens*, but his master and his muse, and his presence can be interpreted as alluding to another phrase in verse 3 with a completely different meaning,

Non est timor dei ante oculos eorum[58]

An effective contrast is thereby drawn between *insipiens* and the Psalmist, who so clearly does have God before his eyes.

The occasions when artist A lost interest and creative energy are very few, and when he did, he demonstrates how easy it was to stray from the meaning of the Psalms. Certainly this is true of fol. 6r. After the long Psalm 9, all the merits that we have until now seen in the work of artist A are lost. He did not compensate enough for the text. Given the care with which, as a rule, the artist tried to integrate text and illustration, the '*PAX*', written at the top of the page, can have been of little solace. Carver has noted that the Temple of the Lord in this illustration was probably not executed by artist A.[59] There is iconographic evidence to similar effect. Part of verse 4, Psalm 10, reads:

Quoniam quae perfecisti destruxerunt[60]

and in Utrecht a building is being demolished. In Harley, the same building, as originally designed, had no hole in its wall! Only later was this covered up, and one brick from this hole finally drawn. This shows an insensitivity to the text, and a

[56] The artist of Paris 8846 made the same alteration. This is not necessarily a direct debt to Harley, but in assessing the vigour with which the Utrecht scenes are interpreted, the Harley and Paris Psalters can be usefully contrasted with the stringy lack-lustre versions of Eadwine.

[57] Compare the analysis of Psalm 13 in Gameson, 'Anglo-Saxon artists', pp. 38–9.

[58] There is no fear of God before their eyes.

[59] Carver, 'Contemporary artefacts', pp. 121–5.

[60] For they have destroyed the things which thou hast made.

harshness of drawing quite unlike artist A.[61] Moreover this is one Psalm illustration where the re-composition of the Utrecht image resulted in a loss of interaction between the participants: the figure with the bow is supposed to be firing at the 'upright in heart' (of verse 3) seated on the mountain, but on the Harleian trajectory he would certainly miss. It seems likely that the thin blue bow of this figure was executed by G, and not by the precise delineation of A's pen.[62] Certainly A omitted the bow and hand of the rear archer in the same illustration. But the failure of this illustration is the exception, not the rule, and the exception only highlights the normally close relationship between what the text states and what the artist depicts.

At this point in the analysis of quire 4 it was shown that it is unlikely that artist B considered the Roman text that was to be written in Harley. In quire 1 the situation is more complicated. When it came to the illustration to the first Psalm, on fol. 1v, the text *Beatus uir qui non abiit* was written on the book of the 'Blessed Man': the artist drew the illustration, did not illustrate the squiggles found on this book in Utrecht, but wrote the text in the same ink as that with which he drew the book (compare figs. 24 and 25). Artist A was also a scribe, and he took note of the text that scribe 1 was going to write, and the problems that he would face when he came to write it.[63] Henderson has pointed out that the *uas figuli*, referred to in verse 9 of Psalm 2, on fol. 2r of the Harley Psalter is as yet unbroken (compare figs. 1 and 2, above, pp. 4–5);[64] he has suggested that this is because the text referring to this vessel is found over the page from the illustration, as it is not in the Utrecht Psalter, and the vessel should be seen as 'about to be broken' as one turns the page. The care with which the artist planned his pages in advance to cater for the special requirements of the text, and the success with which he does it in these first few folios, would suggest that this is indeed a possibility: he would have had to know precisely where the verses of the Psalms would be placed on these folios.[65]

We here seem to be at the cutting edge of a creative re-invention of the Utrecht Psalter, where, when all went according to plan, any physical or iconographic interrelation of text and image was possible. Whether these illustrations would be read in this way was of course, not for the artist to decide. This is up to the reader, and whether he would presume a casual relationship between the image and the text, or search for a meaningful one. For example, we cannot know for certain that artist A placed the demon in the illustration to Psalm 5, on fol. 3r, directly above the sarcophagus, as he is not in Utrecht, because he wanted to make clear the reference in verse 11

[61] By contrast with both Harley and Eadwine, the artist of Paris 8846 responded imaginatively to the challenge of this illustration. His illustrations are in full colour, which leaves him with the problem of how to portray this crumbling building without becoming involved in the complexities of its insides. He chose to show the two figures attacking the front of the building as chipping away at its plaster covering (and there are only chips of plaster, not bricks, on the ground), and the figure to the side as chipping away at the mortar between the bricks – an imaginative rationalisation of what are iconographically difficult figures to interpret in the original. The Lord finished his building, before these figures destroyed it. [62] See below, chapter 2, p. 108 and n.54.

[63] In Paris 8846 the cross-nimbed Lord is the *Beatus uir*, and he is holding a quill to an uninscribed open book.

[64] G.D.S. Henderson, 'The idiosyncrasy of Late Anglo-Saxon religious imagery', in C. Hicks (ed.), *Harlaxton Medieval Studies II: England in the Eleventh Century*, Stamford, 1992, pp. 239–49, at pp. 240–1.

[65] In Eadwine the vessel itself is not broken, but the inscription around it labels it as the *vas figuli*; in Paris 8846 the vessel is split horizontally.

24 *The Utrecht Psalter, fol. 1v. A detail of the illustration to Psalm 1.*

25 *The Harley Psalter, fol. 1v. A detail of the illustration to Psalm 1, by A.*

Sepulchrum patens est guttur eorum[66]

but someone who read the text of the Psalms would have made the connection.[67] We do not have to wait until the twentieth century for an interpretation of artist A. This artist had a commentator in the twelfth century, a commentator who demonstrates that, at least a hundred years after they were created, differences between artist A's illustrations and those in the Utrecht Psalter were observed and critically commented upon. He at least, recognised the subtlety with which artist A worked, and saw in him a supreme master of literal illustration. This will be discussed in the section on artist H.[68]

Conclusion

This analysis of artist A articulates more precisely than has previously been possible the nature of his art and the nature of his attitude to the exemplar. The distinction between his work and that of artist B is not simply one of detail, although that is how it manifests itself: while artist B was set on equivalence of the layout, and only very occasional elaboration of the iconography of Utrecht, artist A altered its layout, and reacted to the iconography of Utrecht, setting it into its new formal environment. It was in the nature of A's technique to take, adapt and manipulate his compositions, and consider the problems of the scribe, and in the nature of artist B's simply to clarify, and to ignore future problems. Unlike quire four, there was no conflict between artist and scribe.

Artist A's omissions were the product of his technique, not of illiteracy, and his recomposition of the illustrations demonstrates a dynamic involvement with the text. This positive interpretation of these illustrations accords well with what we know of literal illustration in Anglo-Saxon manuscripts.[69] The occasional disappointments only highlight the supreme mastery found in most of his work.

Quire 9: the artist-scribe D2

The ruling

Quire 9, like quires 1 and 4, is a regular quire of 8 leaves, hair side facing flesh, with hair side on the outside of the quire. The text measurements are the same as those of quire 4, therefore also corresponding closely with those of the Utrecht Psalter. The ruling pattern in this quire has characteristics in common with those already studied: it is faint, on both sides of the folio, and avoids the illustration spaces. Until fol. 52v, those rulings are present that were also found in quire 1, across the width of the page, not adhering to

[66] Their throat is an open sepulchre.
[67] The artist of Paris 8846 also placed the demon further above the open sepulchre; the Eadwine artist placed him beside it. [68] See below, chapter 2, pp. 113–119. [69] For examples, see below, chapter 4, pp. 150–170.

the pricking marks and on a slight angle to the page.[70] On fol. 51v one such line runs across the top of the illustration, and two run along the bottom. The lower two indicate the levels of the composition: one runs through the boats in the sea amidships, the other runs by the bottom of the sea, and the *titulus* to the Psalm is also written on it. As in quire 1, these lines help the illustrator to know where to place his drawings, and they are used only as a permeable barrier and not as a frame: as in the first quire, peaks of the illustration, such as the Lord's halo and the angel's wings, extend beyond them. When the illustrations are guided by these rulings artist D2's compositions are occasionally somewhat larger than the equivalent illustrations in Utrecht: hence on fol. 51v there are 6 lines of text above the illustration in Harley, while there are 8 in Utrecht. However after fol. 51v, we find the exact pictorial equivalence to the Utrecht Psalter in the ruling pattern, as it is found in quire 4, and here the illustrations are also the same size as those found in Utrecht. On fol. 57r for example, 12 lines were ruled for, and, although there are 12 lines of text in Utrecht's columns a and b, column c has one less line (compare figs. 26, 27, and 28). As in quire 4, the ruling was determined by the illustrations of Utrecht, not its lines of text. As will be demonstrated, the artist who illustrated this quire was also the scribe who began it. It is safe to assume that the same person ruled it.

The illustrations

Artist D2 was by far the most accurate interpreter of Utrecht's images. It is not enough to compare what the images in the two manuscripts look like, because our eye will be seduced into assuming an identity between them. We have to try to understand how artist D2 worked, and once his technique is understood, we can truly begin to appreciate the extent of the illusion. His method was as fundamentally different from that of A and B, as those of A and B were from each other.

We have seen that artist B used lead point, upon which he added his colours, while artist A seems to have used nothing. Artist D2 frequently used hard point, at least to outline his buildings. This is now only visible in a very few areas, where he did not fill in the spaces that he had marked out: for example, in place of the capital on the arch of the building at the top right of fol. 54v there are two marked lines, like those coloured in to form the capitals of the building on fol. 53v; similarly, on fol. 50r, the pediment of the building on the left betrays its hard point precursor; another case is that of the stocks on fol. 54v which do not follow the originally intended proportions. This shows a level of planning in the drawing of the buildings, combined with an interest in Utrecht, very different to that of artist A. Indeed there are signs, on fol. 50r, that D2 also drew out his landscape in hard point before going over it, and on fol. 51v it is just possible to discern a hard-point circle for a nimbus to the Lord that was never painted. There is, however, no indication that he used lead point or hard point to articulate his figures.

Similar hard point lines have been observed demarking parts of all four Evangelist

[70] See above, p. 43.

portraits in the Copenhagen, Royal Library, Ms. G.K.S. 10, 2°.[71] Their purpose is not entirely clear, but it might not be coincidence that both manuscripts seem to have had close iconographic precursors. In this respect the remarks of Clemoes on the derivative nature of BL Cotton Ms. Claudius B.iv, are particularly pertinent. He writes

> It might or might not have been possible to recreate the freshness that the pictures undoubtedly have [if the manuscript were copied]. And in the nature of things we cannot say whether or not there was any tracing, which would prove that the pictures were copied into B: owing to elasticity in the fibres of the parchment, any shallow grooves left by tracing would have lasted only long enough to act as temporary guides.[72]

In fact there are many such shallow grooves in Claudius B.iv, and artist D2 can allay Clemoes's fears that the freshness of the original might not be recreated.[73] Could the hard-point lines that can be seen in Harley, in the Hexateuch, and in the Evangelist portraits of the Copenhagen Gospels be signs of a tracing technique? The survival of the Utrecht Psalter gives us the perfect opportunity to find out. The vellum of Harley 603 is not itself transparent enough for straight transposition. We would have to suppose that tracings were taken in lead or hard point through linen paper or transparent vellum from Utrecht, and that then hard-point lines were scored through the tracing onto the vellum of Harley.[74] We can see the first stage of the process in the 'Very Last Manuscript Copy of the Utrecht Psalter', BL Add. Ms. 26104: in *c.* 1830 the illustrations of Utrecht were traced on tracing paper with great skill, and then struck onto a paper backing.[75]

The simplest way to compare the dimensions of illustrations in the two manuscripts is to use scale reproductions of them, and superimpose one image upon the other.[76] The results are curious. For example, in the illustration to Psalm 106 on fol. 54v, the Lord and his angels, the Psalmist, and the oxen, are very similarly placed in relation to each other as they are in Utrecht (compare figs. 29 and 30). In the same illustration, the building on the left, the chair on the left, and the ploughman also relate to each other as they do in Utrecht. However, these two sets of relationships do not work well together in Harley: the ploughman has to plough downhill, not on the level, the chair is positioned above the Psalmist, not beside him, and the left-hand angel is uncomfortably close to the chair. The left-hand side of the illustration is a whole centimetre higher in relation to the right than it is in Utrecht. The consistency in error would imply a slip of method. It is as if the artist is starting the process of recreating the illustration from

[71] Heslop, 'Cnut and Emma', p. 193. [72] Clemoes, in Clemoes and Dodwell, *Hexateuch*, p. 57.

[73] These occur throughout the manuscript. One good example is on fol. 113v, in the illustration of the invocation for blessing the Israelites (Numbers, ch.6, vv. 22–7). The pointed central dome of the building replaces a clearly defined articulated cone. Another is on fol. 118r: the inhabitants of Eschol, strong men of great stature (Numbers ch.13, vv. 28, 32), were, in hard point, even larger.

[74] Theophilus advises the use of Greek parchment, made of linen cloth, for the making of gold leaf (C.R. Dodwell (ed.), *Theophilus. De Diversis Artibus*, Oxford, 1986, Book 1, ch.23; see the introduction, p. ix). I am grateful to Sandy Heslop for bringing this to my attention. [75] See Engelbregt, *Het Utrechts Psalterium*, plate 62.

[76] Those interested can perform this operation for themselves, reasonably accurately and cheaply. The Warburg Institute possesses a set of full-page 95 per cent to scale photographs of the Harley Psalter, which were ordered by Adelheid Heimann, and have notes by her on the back. These can be xeroxed and enlarged onto transparent overhead projector paper, and placed over the illustrations in the Graz facsimile of Utrecht, which is to scale.

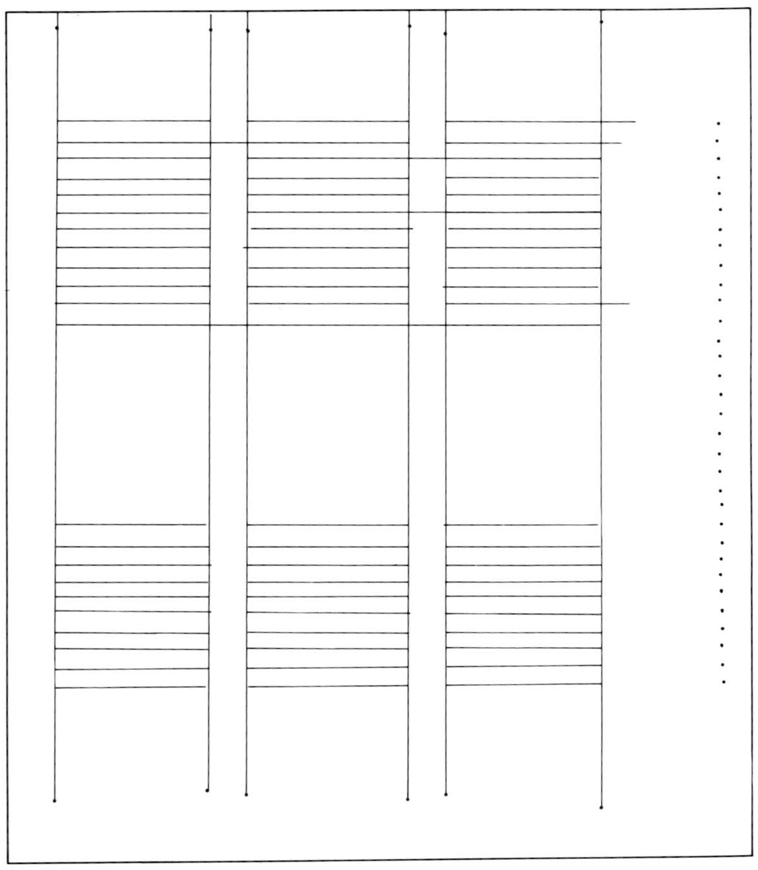

26 *The Harley Psalter, fol. 57r, diagram of visible ruling.*

27 *The Utrecht Psalter, fol. 65r, showing the illustration to Psalm 110.*

28 *The Harley Psalter, fol. 57r. The illustration to Psalm 110 is by D2; the script is by scribe 1; the rubrication is by E; the initials are by J; there is a correction to the text in column 3 line 5,* bibet*; additions were made to the illustration by G.*

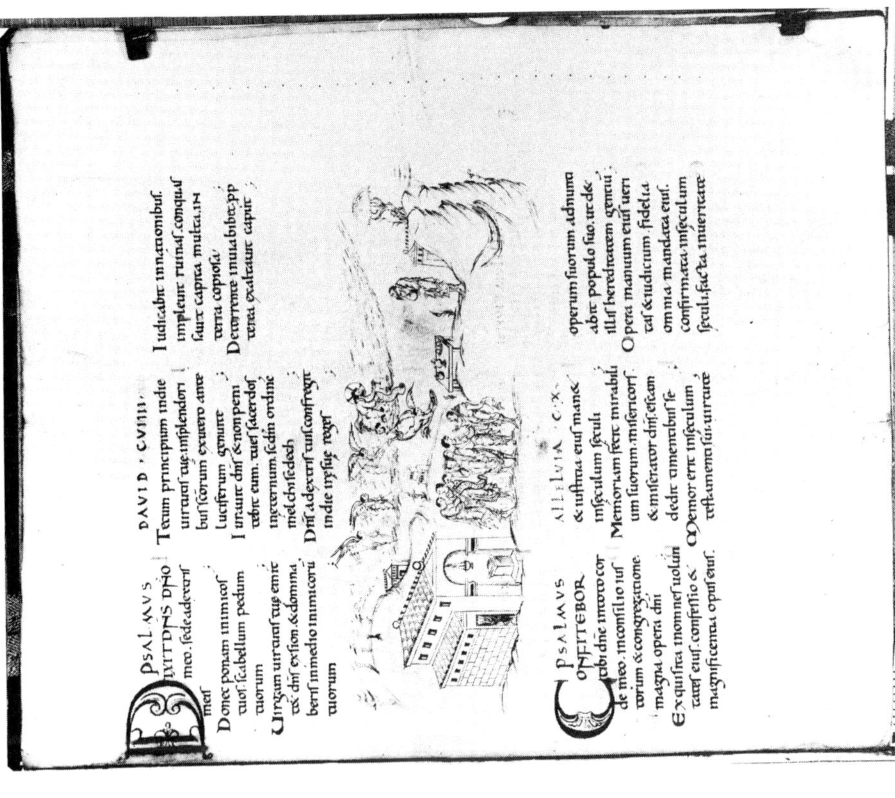

28

27

29 *The Utrecht Psalter, fol. 62v. The illustration to Psalm 106.*

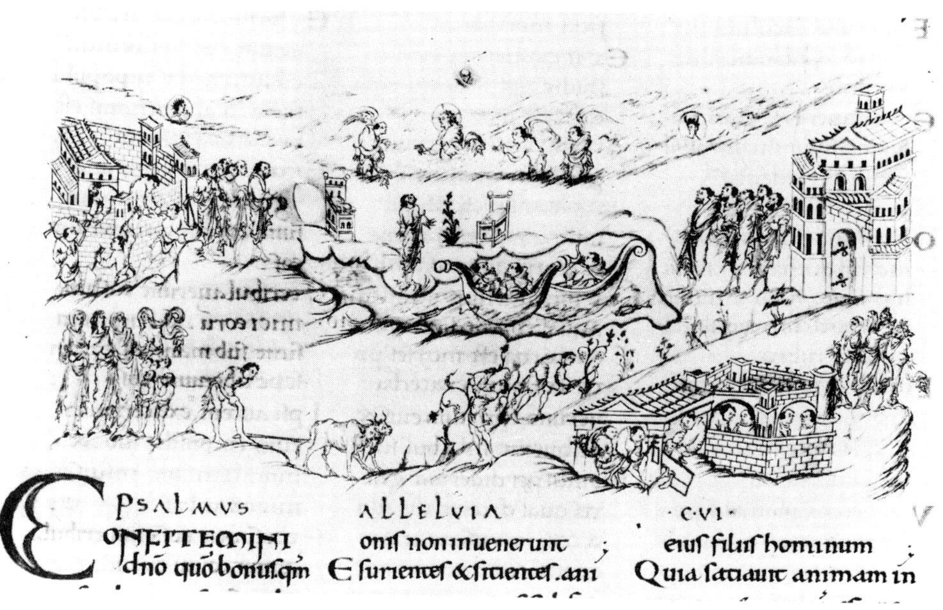

30 *The Harley Psalter, fol. 54v. The illustration to Psalm 106, by D2, with additions by G.*

two different points, not correctly related to each other. As a result some elements have to be squeezed in where possible. The right-hand chair does not relate to anything in the same way as it does in Utrecht, and the artist has made the sea more horizontal than it is in the original. A similar phenomenon can be observed in the illustration to Psalm 107, on fol. 55v.

This could mean that the artist traced the illustration in two goes, as it were, or that the Utrecht Psalter slipped while he was tracing, but I do not think that the relative proportions are consistent enough to demonstrate this. While individual lines have astonishingly similar dimensions, so similar that they rule out the possibility that artist D2 was drawing by eye alone, there are probably too many discrepancies in the overall proportions of the illustrations, and a number of occasions on which the dimensions are not so close. Rather, I think we can reconstruct the artist's procedure as follows: first, he took two features on either side of an illustration in Utrecht and marked their positions in Harley; secondly he took independent sets of measurements from these two points to features nearby them and plotted them in Harley; he then made up much of his illustration in hard point, using a straight edge for architectural elements; any inconsistencies resulting from the fact that he started his relative measurements from two different fixed points, he dealt with by eye.

Artist D2 did sometimes make mistakes, probably more than artist B, and it is interesting to note where he took liberties. For example, he missed out a window in the building on the right of the illustration to Psalm 101 on fol. 50r, and he did not finish the wall of the building on the right; on fol. 53v he omitted a doorway, and the decoration to the pediment of the building on the right; he did not draw the capital to the arch of the building on the right of fol. 54v, and from the same building he omitted the finial decorating the pediment (compare figs. 29 and 30); on fol. 55v he omitted three windows in the turret of the building on the right; on fol 57v he also omitted bases to the columns of the right of the building, and the hanging bowel above the head of the *Beatus uir*. He also only wrote the bottom line of text to the book held by the *Beatus uir* (as he sees it), just enough to make the pictorial reference to the text.[77]

Most of these omissions were made in architecture, and the portrayal of Utrecht's architectural elements had less fascination for him than the elucidation of figures and landscape. Like those of the other artists, all D2's architectural elements were made with a straight edge, while Utrecht's were drawn free hand. It is perhaps for this reason that it is in the buildings that most of his elaborations can be discerned: for example, he added an extra decoration to the left throne in the illustration on fol. 54v, giving an extra square black notch to the top of its back (compare figs 29 and 30); he added crenelations to the buildings in the centre and on the right of fol. 55v; on fol. 56r, he added another window to the building on the left; and on fol. 57v, two of his roofs are different from those in Utrecht. It is as if the buildings did not hold the challenge of technical virtuosity in penmanship that the landscape and figures so clearly did.

The departures from Utrecht's architecture may have been casual. Otherwise he

77 Gameson, 'Anglo-Saxon artists', p. 46, n.45 mentions four further omissions: fol. 51r Christ has a nimbus but no halo; fol. 51v omits right table strut; fol. 53v unfinished back wall on left of town; fol. 54v unfinished figure on left.

stuck to Utrecht's images extremely closely. Artist D2's technical approach to individual figures was also fundamentally different to that of artists A and B. He was the only artist who set out to reproduce the precise form of the lines of Utrecht's illustrations: he flexed his pen in the same way that it had been flexed two hundred years earlier. Artist D2 was also lucky enough to have illustrated Psalms that were illustrated in Utrecht by Gaehde's artist G, whose articulation of landscape, architecture, and people, was comparatively solid, with carefully tapered penstrokes that described well shaded objects.[78] Artist D2's task was very different to that of artist B, and he was able to approach it in a very different way. To state that he rarely changed the composition or the iconography of his model is to tarnish his achievement with an irrelevant consideration, and since this study is not concerned with iconographic innovation *per se*, this artist is just as interesting for us as the others in the book, being symptomatic of an attitude to the exemplar not otherwise displayed in the manuscript. If Anglo-Saxon artists were close observers of natural phenomena, this one can be noted for the same accuracy with regard to observing what he saw in the Utrecht illustrations.[79] We can go further, for with the quality of his penmanship, and with his use of colour, in apparently imitating the Utrecht illustrations, he enlivened them beyond anything achieved by the exemplar. His figure style never became dry, his technique never slackened – he was imaginatively engaged in the task of following Utrecht with extreme precision.

It was an operation brilliantly realised, and the result is that while we have evidence that artists A and B imbued their adherence to Utrecht with an understanding of the text that they were illustrating, and with comprehension of the qualities of the objects that they were depicting, it is difficult to say the same of artist D2. His technique of emulation was so good that it appears that he could match anything that the Utrecht artist intended to portray, without reference to any such understanding. There are just a few occasions when we can see it however. One elaboration by artist D2 is the fish in the sea on fol. 54v, in the illustration to Psalm 106 (compare figs. 29 and 30, above, p. 64). This fish is not to be found in Utrecht, but in Harley, they that go down to the sea in ships to do their works (verse 23) have something to catch. Artist D2 imagined the scenes of Utrecht as real while he was copying them. The most daring elaborations upon the iconography of Utrecht by artist D2 are the door hinges added to the building on the right of the same illustration. What was in Utrecht an arched opening, set in oblique perspective, with the inside of the arch shaded and the rest left blank, has become in Harley an arched opening set flat to the picture plane with a gate opening inwards. Gameson interprets this as the miscomprehension by artist D2 of a recessional device used in Utrecht.[80] However, D2 had come across the same recessional device, and included it perfectly, in the immediately preceding Psalm illustration, and was to employ it again. Furthermore, the fact that the hinges are themselves set at an angle would imply that this artist understood recessional devices perfectly well. On the

[78] Gaehde, 'Utrecht Psalter draughtsmen', p. 51. He notes that Psalms 105–6 were executed by E, who also used broad strokes to articulate his figures.

[79] See M. Schapiro, 'The image of the disappearing Christ: the Ascension in English art around the year 1000', *Gazette des Beaux-Arts*, 6th ser. 23, 1943, pp. 135–52, esp. at p. 148 for his comments on BL Cotton Ms. Julius A.vi.

[80] Gameson, 'Anglo-Saxon artists', p. 35.

contrary, the hinges are a virtuoso display of opportunism that demonstrates that artist D2 had a thorough understanding of the construction of pictorial space, which he could use when it suited him to employ it. He betrays his knowledge of the Psalms in his illustration to Psalm 108, on fol. 56r. In verse 23 of the Psalm the Psalmist is likened to a shaken locust. This locust is difficult to spot, and difficult to identify in Utrecht's illustration, but it is quite clear and painted green in artist D2's; it is hard to imagine the Harley artist correctly identifying the creature on the basis of Utrecht's illustration alone.[81]

Only very occasionally, then, did he see fit to depart from the model intentionally, and when he did he only managed to convey the fact that he was revelling in the artistic possibilities that imitating the Utrecht Psalter had presented to him. He remained so aware of what it was to adhere to Utrecht, line by line, that changes in minute detail are not signs of his being lax, but indications of his involvement in what he was doing. He slightly altered the form of the crown of the foremost king in the illustration to Psalm 101 on fol. 50r,[82] and he repeated this alteration on the crowned figure to Psalm 107 on fol. 55v. The king with his head transfixed by a spear in the illustration to Psalm 109 (the head is crushed; see verses 5 and 6), on fol. 56v, has a crown different from these two, and different from the exemplar. Also in the illustration to Psalm 101, he altered the form of the ewer on the table,[83] as he did the ewer below the tree in the illustration to Psalm 108 on fol. 56r. While the beast-headed prow of the ship in Utrecht's illustration to Psalm 103 is rather insipid, artist D2's on fol. 51v actually barks at one of the birds swimming on the sea (compare figs. 52 and 53, below, pp. 104–5). In the illustration to Psalm 105, on fol. 53v, the rod with which Moses strikes the Red Sea has been given nodes; it has become a lopped staff. In the illustration to Psalm 107 on fol. 55v, the Eastern angle harp has taken on some of the characteristics of the western harp; the artist has rounded the junction of the string arm and the sound chest, and allowed the sound chest to expand just below the junction.[84] In the same illustration the Lord in the mandorla is given an orb to stand on. Artist D2 also added a cross to the Lord's book in the illustration to Psalm 108 on fol. 56r,[85] and a buckle to the garment hanging from the tree. Even in the landscape and figures he corrected Utrecht, adding legs to the figures in the arched opening to the left of the composition on fol. 57v and ground on which to stand them. In the illustration to Psalm 106, on fol. 54v, he finished the female figure fourth from the left at the bottom of the composition, which is left without a midriff by Utrecht (compare figs. 29 and 30, above, p. 64). But these alterations are very much exceptions in his operation.[86]

There is no doubt that from his own point of view artist D2, like artist A, thought that he was improving upon the illustrations in Utrecht. Artist D2 was certainly not

[81] The Eadwine artist did not manage to do so; the locust is absent.
[82] Carver, 'Contemporary artefacts', p. 136 and p. 128. [83] Ibid., p. 136 and p. 128.
[84] Rensch Erbes, 'Harp', p. 30, not noted in Carver 'Contemporary artefacts'.
[85] Gameson, 'Anglo-Saxon artists', p. 46, n.46 observes this alteration.
[86] There are certainly more than those enumerated here, but some of these are probably the work of another artist altogether, artist G. His contribution will be analysed in more detail in the next chapter. Carver, 'Contemporary artefacts', p. 128 and p. 136 also considers the two inventions on fol. 53r as by artist D, the winged spear and the three thong flail with rings; however this composition is clearly the work of hand E, as will be investigated in chapter 2, pp. 91–3.

above criticising the overall appearance of the Utrecht page; he thought that the illustration to Psalm 111 was too far to the left in Utrecht, so he moved it over to the right in Harley, on fol. 57v. That artist D2 was concerned with the appearance of the page at this stage is important, because at this stage the page was unwritten. In this quire too, the illustrations were executed before the text. Thus, following the layout of Utrecht, the artist drew his illustration to Psalm 108 at the top of fol. 56r, but the scribe could not finish his text to Psalm 107 on fol. 55v, and so had to go onto the illustration on fol. 56r, avoiding the heavenly sky, and the tree in the left-hand margin, which were already drawn.[87]

The script

The scribe of fols. 50r–54r/a/23 is primarily puzzling because, as was first pointed out by Bishop and Gasquet,[88] he employed the Gallican version of the Psalter. Based on a misreading of the text in Psalm 101 verse 4, they supposed that the scribe was following the Utrecht Psalter text. But, as Backhouse has noted, this misreading is not uncommon, and their reasoning is far from conclusive.[89] It has been maintained by Brooks that the use of the Roman text by scribe 1 was in accord with liturgical norms at Christ Church, Canterbury.[90] The question arises, therefore, as to why scribe D2 should return to the Gallican text employed in the exemplar, a version which scribe 1 had deliberately avoided. Since, of all those who worked on the manuscript, this scribe is most closely associated with Christ Church, his text cannot be seen as reflecting the liturgical usage of another community.[91]

Historians have tackled this problem in a variety of ways. Bishop and Gasquet, for example, considered that the reliance on the Utrecht text was due to the scribe's lack of familiarity with the Gallican version of the Psalter text.[92] Yet scribes frequently had to contend with texts with which they were not familiar. Brooks has argued that the Gallican text of scribe D2 was added after the Roman of scribe 1.[93] But the fact that the Roman text returns at fol. 54r/a/24, again written by scribe 1, renders such an explanation dubious. The Gallican cannot be seen, in any chronological sense, as a sign of a gradual change to a Gallican usage at Christ Church in the eleventh century. Its presence remains a puzzle; another approach is required.

As we have seen, in quire 4 scribe 1 showed no signs of adhering to the Utrecht Psalter layout, and in quire 1 he did not have to. This is in marked contrast to the practice of scribe D2, who began this quire. The disposition of text in the Utrecht Psalter was his guide in negotiating the vellum between one illustration and another. He frequently followed it line by line. This occurs, for example, in the first six lines of fol. 50r (compare figs. 31 and 32). The clearest example however is found on fol. 50v,

[87] As noted by Duffey, 'Inventive group', p. 18.
[88] E. Bishop and F. Gasquet, *The Bosworth Psalter*, London, 1908, p. 9.
[89] Backhouse, 'Making', p. 112, n.12. [90] Brooks, *The Church of Canterbury*, pp. 261–5.
[91] See below, chapter 3, p. 136, and p. 144, and n.87. [92] Bishop and Gasquet, *Bosworth Psalter*, p. 9.
[93] Brooks, *The Church of Canterbury*, pp. 380–1, n.28.

where the composition of text in Harley was guided not by the width of the ruled column, but by the placing of text as it is found in Utrecht: the parallel is almost exact.

Further evidence for the fact that the Utrecht Psalter itself was used by the scribe as the textual exemplar is to be found in the *tituli*. We see in those to Psalms 100–105 an adherence to the Utrecht Psalter conspicuously lacking in other quires. In the rest of the manuscript, the *tituli* are written in rustic capitals with the Psalm number written after the title. In Psalms 100–105 the *tituli* are in Uncial script,[94] with the Psalm number before the title, and in this they are exactly the same as those in the Utrecht Psalter itself. Even the placing of these *tituli* on the page is nearly identical to that found in Utrecht, and when it is not there are specific reasons for it. For example the *titulus* to Psalm 101 in Utrecht is a line and a half above the start of the main text, whereas in Harley, on fol. 50r, it is simply written one line above. This is understandable because, as we have seen, throughout the Utrecht manuscript the ruling was on a grid system of 64 lines per page: this allowed for 'half-lines' to be written on, while in Harley only full lines were ruled for.[95] It therefore makes sense that the last words of the *titulus*, which could not be fitted onto the same line, are above it in Harley, and half a line below it in Utrecht. What is extraordinary here is not that these last words are squeezed in in different places, but that scribe D2, who clearly had the Utrecht Psalter in front of him, did not compensate for the spatial error in Utrecht, and that in both cases the last letters of the title are written in the right-hand margin. It shows a rigid adherence to the Utrecht exemplar that is so conspicuously lacking in the text of scribe 1.

Bishop and Gasquet were right, albeit for the wrong reason. Scribe D2 did have the Utrecht Psalter in front of him; passages of precise line-by-line duplication of Utrecht by the scribe leave no room for doubt.[96] This provides us with a key to one of the most important problems associated with the Psalter – why it is that scribe D2's work is in the Gallican. The question should be phrased rather differently: why should it be that here scribe D2 followed the layout of the Gallican Utrecht Psalter, while scribe 1 and Eadui did not, but used a Roman text instead?

One great advantage of following the Utrecht text was that it allowed the scribe to spread out his text to the full extent between the illustrations to each Psalm, which were placed approximately in the same position as they were placed in the Utrecht Psalter. Since this scribe was writing the text of particularly long Psalms, this was of great importance. Unless the text was carefully spread, large areas of vellum would remain blank, as we have seen occurred on fol. 6r, with scribe 1. In using the Utrecht Psalter as a way of spacing out his script, scribe D2 inevitably had to occupy just one or two lines of text less than the exemplar, simply because of the different types of script used. The result of the spacing of script according to the Utrecht Psalter can be clearly seen in these folios. By comparison with the work of scribe 1, the columns of text appear insubstantial and ragged. Column a on fol. 52r suffers particularly badly in this respect,

[94] Duffey, 'Inventive group', p. 236, n.2, noted that this scribe used uncials for his *tituli*, but did not draw the connection with those in the Utrecht Psalter. [95] See above, Introduction, p. 21.

[96] Duffey, 'Inventive group', p. 17, notes the coincidence in the spacing of script, but does not acknowledge the implications of her own analysis.

C PSALMUS DAUID
MISERICORDIAM
ETIUDICIUM· CANTABO
TIBIDNE;
PSALLAMETINTELLEGAM
INUIAINMACULATA·
QUANDOUENIESADME
PERAMBULABAMININNO
CENTIACORDISMEI· IN
MEDIODOMUSMEAE
NONPROPONEBAMANTEO
CULOSMEOSREMINIUSTAM
FACIENTESPRAEUARICATI
ONESODIUI
NONADHAESITMIHICOR
PRAUUM·DECLINANTEM
AMEMALIGNUMNON
COGNOSCEBAM.
DETRAHENTEMSECRETO
PROXIMOSUO·HUNCPER
SEQUEBAR
SUPERBOOCULOETINSACI
ABILICORDE·CUMHOC
NONEDEBAM;
OCULIMEIADFIDELESTRAE·
UTSEDEANTMECU·AMBU
LANSINUIAINMACULATA
HICMIHIMINISTRABAT·
NONHABITABITINMEDIO
DOMUSMEAE·QUIFACIT
SUPERBIAM·QUILOQUI
TURINIQUA·NONDIREX
ITINCONSPECTUOCULO
RUMMEORUM;
INMATUTINOINTERFICI
EBAMOMNESPECCATORES
TERRAE·UTDISPERDEREM
DECIUITATEDNIOMNES
OPERANTESINIQUITATE;

CI ORT PAUPERIS
DNEEXAUDIORA
TIONEMMEAM
ETCLAMORMEUSADTE
UENIAT;
NONAUERTASFACIEMTUA
AME· INQUACUMQUEDIE
DUMANXIUSFUE
TRIBULORINCLINAAD
MEAUREMTUAM;
INQUACUMQUEDIEINUO
CAUEROTEUELOCITEREX
AUDIME
QUIADEFECERUNTSICUTFU
RITETCORAMDNOEFU
DERITPRAECESSUA
MUSDIESMEI· ETOSSAMEA
SICUTCREMIUARUERUNT
PERCUSSUSSUMUTFAENUM
ETARUITCORMEUM· QUI
AOBLITUSSUMCOMEDERE
PANEMMEUM

31 *The Utrecht Psalter, fol. 58r, showing the illustration to Psalm 101.*

M·C·PSALMUS DAUID
MISERICORDIAM
& iudicium cantabo
tibi dne ;
P sallam & intellegam
inuia inmaculata
quando uenies ad me ;
P erambulabā in innocentia
cordis mei: in medio domus meæ;
N on proponebam ante
oculos meos rem iniustā:
facientes preuaricatio
nes odiui ;

Non adhesit mihi cor prauū:
declinantē a me malignum
non cognoscebam ;
D etrahentē secreto proximo
suo: hunc persequebar ;
S uperbo oculo & insatiabili
corde cū hoc non edebam ;
O culi mei ad fideles terræ
ut sedeant mecū ambulans
in uia inmaculata hic
mihi ministrabat

N on habitabit in medio dom
meæ: qui facit superbiam:
qui loquitur iniqua: non
direxit in conspectu
oculorum meorum ;
I n matutino interficiebā
omnes peccatores
terræ: ut disperderem
de ciuitate dni omnes
operantes iniquitatem ;

ORATIO PAUPERIS CUM ANXIUS FUERIT ET CORAM DNO EFFU DERIT PCES SUAS·

D NE EXAUDI ORA
tionem meam · et
clamor meus ad te
ueniat ;
N on auertas faciem tuā
a me: in quacumq· die

tribulor inclina
ad me aurem tuam ;
I n quacumq· die inuoca
uero te uelociter
exaudi me ;
Quia defecerunt sicut

fumus dies mei. & ossa mea
sicut cremiū aruerunt ;
P ercussus sum sicut faenū
& aruit cor meum: quia
oblitus sum comedere
panem meum ;

32 *The Harley Psalter, fol. 50r. Everything on this page, which contains the illustration to Psalm 101, is by D2, with the exception of the 'D' initial to Psalm 101. The original 'D' was by D2, but it was erased, and replaced by I.*

but the contrast to scribe 1's technique can be most clearly seen where the latter resumes his text on fol. 54r, column a, line 24: the ragged right-hand margin of scribe D2's script has been replaced by the justified and condensed script of scribe 1.

Even with this procedure, scribe D2 still occasionally lost a line compared to Utrecht: on fol. 53r he occupied two lines less than on the equivalent folio of the exemplar. One wonders, therefore, if the fact that Harley's illustrations early in this quire are slightly larger than those of Utrecht was an attempt to compensate for this: it is certainly because the scribe lowered his text a line compared to Utrecht after the illustration on 51v that he ended up on the same line on fol. 52r. If so, there were problems involved, as a closer analysis of the spacing of text and illustration shows. At the top of fol. 50r, the Harley Psalter artist left space for 12, 12, and 11 lines of main text in columns a, b, and c respectively, while Utrecht has 13, 13, and 12 lines respectively. The scribe dealt with this situation by following the Utrecht text word for word for the first six lines, and then squeezing verse 3 into two lines, where in Utrecht it took up three; he then carried on, ending this column with the same word as in Utrecht, maintaining almost exactly the same physical relationship between the text and the illustration. In the next two columns the Harley scribe lost not one line compared to Utrecht, necessary because the illustration took up one extra line, but two. In the case of column b, this may have been because the scribe did not want such a close interaction between text and the top of the illustration as is found in the Utrecht Psalter, where the text actually 'treads' on the mandorla. In the case of column c it is harder to see the reason, and looking at the disposition of lines one wonders whether it was not forced on him by the change in script. Certainly the scribe regretted his decision. At the top of the weather vane of Jerusalem on the right of the illustration, is a cock. This is simply free invention upwards of an already complete, and an already completely copied, weather vane found in the Utrecht Psalter. The addition of a cock is out of character with this artist's efforts at duplication and in the ink of the scribe. It seems to have been added to fill the gap of one line between the text and the illustration at the end of this column, which would only have become apparent after the text had been written.

The initials to Psalms 100, 102, 103, 104, and 105 are plain and monumental, and follow the form of those in the Utrecht Psalter itself. There are two differences: the initials are somewhat larger, and they are executed in colour. Their painterly quality makes them very different to those in the rest of Harley, and, sharing as they do the concern of the *tituli* and the Psalm text itself to follow the Utrecht Psalter so closely, we can assume that they were executed by the same hand. The one initial of which this is not true is that initial to Psalm 101 on fol. 50r: however a plain monumental 'D' initial, like that in Utrecht has been erased, and replaced by the floriate 'D' of artist I, who clearly thought that the traditional division of the Psalter needed some signalling.

Finally we come to the verse capitals. These also seem to have been executed by scribe D2 contemporaneously with his script. They are of considerably higher quality than those in the rest of the book, and are characterised by certain peculiarities which the capitals in other sections of the Psalter do not share. For example square and rounded 'E's are used alternately, while the only square E in the verse capitals of fols. 2r–27v and fols. 54r/a/24–73v is on fol. 54v, and this I take to be a response to scribe D2's practice. Scribe D2 did leave out two capitals: the 'T' of *Terminum* at the bottom of column c on fol. 51v, and the 'E' of *Et uocauit* in the middle of column c on fol. 52v. This may indicate that the capitals were executed together, in one operation, after the text was written.

Conclusion

I am now in a position to make the case for what I have hitherto assumed; that artist D and scribe 2 are one and the same. The similarity in approach to the exemplar between scribe 2 and artist D, who is by far the closest imitator of the style and iconography of Utrecht, is striking. The fact that the scribe used Utrecht to space his text more successfully than scribe 1 did, does not explain why he used Utrecht's Uncial script for his *tituli*, nor why he followed the mistake in spacing that Utrecht made in his *titulus* to Psalm 101. It seems that, within the boundaries dictated by the use of colour and the type of script used, both artist and scribe were aiming for a pictorial equivalence to the exemplar quite beyond that seen in other quires. Furthermore, the need to follow Utrecht in order to space text is hardly in itself enough to account for the change in the version of Psalter text used. Both the scribe and the artist were following Utrecht line by line – literally. The scribe's skill as an artist is witnessed in his initials and the weather cock on fol. 50r. His concern to integrate his text with the illustrations is seen in the rubric to Psalm 101, again on fol. 50r: to the left of the raised line of *titulus*, there is a squiggly line that runs down from the illustration, and contraction marks above the 'P' seem almost decorative. Moreover, there may be some independent corroboration that this scribe was also an artist, for if, as Bishop maintained, he wrote the text of BL Harley Ms. 1117(ii) (Bede, Lives of St Cuthbert), he also executed the two accomplished Type II(b) initials on fol. 45r.[97] For these reasons I propose that artist D and scribe 2 are indeed the same person. This person, an exceptional scribe, and an exceptional artist, appears in neither of these guises anywhere else in the book. He executed his illustrations first, and only reached fol. 54r in writing his text. For these few folios of the Harley Psalter, as in the first few, the text and the illustrations overcame the problems posed by the exemplar's layout. Yet they do this in entirely different ways: in the first folios of quire 1 the spaces of the illustrations differ from those of Utrecht, and are adapted to the projected space of the script; in those of quire 9 the text is spaced as it is in the exemplar, to take into account the spacing of the illustrations, which was determined by Utrecht.

D2 stopped writing at fol. 54r/a/23, and scribe 1 took over. He would have

[97] Bishop, 'Notes VII', p. 420, but see below, chapter 3, p. 136, n.27. The initials are illustrated in Temple, *Anglo-Saxon Mss.*, ills. 108–9.

considered fols. 50r-54r/a/23 to be complete when he stopped working. Scribe 1's response to scribe D2's practice is examined in chapter 3.

Conclusion to chapter 1

The ruling technique is different from quire to quire, and the differences reflect artistic responses to the exemplar. That the ruling changes between quires, with artist, and in ways which are not conducive to scribal practice, are compelling reasons for supposing that these quires were ruled by artists and not by scribes. The governing characteristic of all three quires studied is, then, that the artists were in command of the working procedure. In these quires, they were given four unmarked sheets each to make up the quires that they then ruled and illustrated, before the scribes wrote on them. Even when, in quire 9, the scribe and the artist were the same person, this person ruled his folios in order to mark out his illustration space, which he filled first, before writing his script. The script had to fit into the mould set by the illustrations, and not vice versa. The mould set by the illustrations was that of the Utrecht Psalter. Even in quire 1, where the illustration spaces sometimes differed considerably from those of the exemplar, the base of the illustration space was on the same line as it was in Utrecht.

The importance of scriptorium procedure in the appearance of manuscripts, and in deciphering their idiosyncrasies, has been noted by Heslop.[98] He demonstrates that in some cases, such as Cambridge, Trinity College, Ms. B.10.4,[99] lavishly illustrated pages were placed in the hands of the artist, while folios intended to contain only script were written as part of a separate exercise. This meant that the text of the verso of the illustrated page, which was written after the decoration was executed, was written after the text on the following recto. As Heslop notes, such a *modus operandi* is asking for trouble. So it seems was that employed in these quires of Harley. However, the scribes and artists clearly had their reasons for using these procedures. These reasons might have to do with the division of labour in the scriptorium, but equally, they might have to do with more fundamental assumptions that lay behind the procedures that they employed. This chapter has demonstrated that the quires studied were ruled by artists, but it has left untouched the reasons for this practice. This question will be tackled in chapter 4.

Despite certain similarities of production, it is clear that the three quires studied, which form part of what has been termed the 'first phase' of production in the Harley Psalter, have within them the manifestations of very different attitudes to the exemplar.[100] Of course, in assessing eleventh-century approaches to the task of creating the Psalter, it is very important to know in the first place if, and in the second how, these quires related to each other. For example – was the original intention to produce a

[98] Heslop, 'Cnut and Emma', pp. 167–9, and pp. 188–95.

[99] Temple, *Anglo-Saxon Mss.*, cat. 65, Keynes, *Anglo-Saxon Mss. in Trinity*, cat. 20.

[100] The phrase 'first phase', current in recent literature on the Harley Psalter (Backhouse *et al.*, *Golden Age*, pp. 74–5, Backhouse, 'Making', pp. 98–9, Gameson, 'Anglo-Saxon artists', p. 30), derives from Wormald, *English Drawings*, p. 30ff, and pp. 69–70. Its meaning is not entirely clear.

coloured version of the Gallican Utrecht Psalter, written in Caroline minuscule, as in quire 9, or was it to take account of the different script used, and to make an illustrated Roman Psalter, with the Gallican intrusion of D2 an indication that not only the form, but also the content of the text was dictated by artistic concerns? These are some of the questions that will be addressed in chapters 3 and 4.

2

Quires ruled by the scribes

When we move from fol. 57v to fol. 58r in the Harley Psalter, we move into a different world: in the last two quires of Harley the illustrations are very different from those in Utrecht. In the past this increased distance from Utrecht has been explained in a number of ways, all of which involve circumstances that are external to the mechanics of the book's creation. But it is essential to determine the mechanics of the book's manufacture before we can understand why the change occurred. The very different character of quires 10 and 11 first has to be set within the context of the technical procedure by which they were made. This is altogether different from that which was employed in quires 4, 1, and 9.

QUIRES 10–11: SCRIBE 1 AND ARTISTS F AND E

Working procedure

In complete contrast to the quires examined in the last chapter, there are signs on nearly every folio of quires 10 and 11 that scribe 1 wrote his text before the artist executed his illustrations, and the artist frequently drew over the text. We might presume from this fact alone that the scribe was responsible for the ruling pattern. Certainly it shows few of the concerns for the artists that were such a conspicuous feature of the ruling patterns discussed in the last chapter. In contrast to them, in quires 10 and 11 hair side faces hair, and the page is completely ruled, with no care taken to avoid the illustration spaces, and there is no sign that the spaces for them were planned in advance (see fig. 33). The only concession to the artist is that in these quires too, the ruling was executed very faintly on both sides of the folios. The ruling on both sides is not consistent, but it occurs too frequently to be dismissed as occasional reruling. Often difficult to see, it is obvious where lines of text on the recto follow a different course to (equally straight) lines of text on the verso of a folio. This procedure was followed presumably in order that the membrane was not scored too heavily on one side. We must understand, then, that the scribe approached his unwritten page with no indication as to where he should place his text. In contrast to the quires studied already, it was up to him to decide. He placed his text as he saw fit, and, in writing it, he determined where the illustrations would be inserted.

Scribe 1 did not follow the example of the Utrecht Psalter in the placing of his text. On the first folio of quire 10, fol. 58r, the text is similar to that in Utrecht in its spacing, but this spacing is simply practical and logical. On the verso of this folio it looks as if the scribe initially intended to leave an illustration space at the bottom of the page rather than at the top of the next one, as it is in Utrecht, but miscalculated the length of his text. In fact, from fol. 59v onwards, the spacing of text on the pages of Utrecht and Harley is normally very different. The independence of the scribe from Utrecht is well illustrated in his treatment of Psalm 118 on fols. 61r–64r. This long Psalm is divided into sections, and in Harley these sections were grouped together in twos: thus on fol. 61r, Aleph's section starts off the Psalm in column a; this goes down to line 18 and then the text returns to the top of column b, where Beth's text starts on line 8; after line 18 in column b the Psalm text returns to the top of column c, where it finishes on line 12. Below this, Gimel's section starts on line 20, column a, and the same format is repeated. This is in marked contrast to Utrecht where the whole Psalm is written out column by column down the page as usual. Independence from the Utrecht layout was not a guarantee of a satisfactory page however: one of the great achievements of the exemplar was that it left very few untidy gaps at the bottom of folios, and scribe 1 could not match this achievement. On fols. 64r and 65r, for example, the spaces at the bottom of the page are not large enough for full illustrations. Artist F normally left these spaces blank and, whether he knew it or not, they would later be filled in by artist E. He did illustrate one particularly large space however, and as a result there are two illustrations for Psalm 115, at the bottom of fol. 59r and at the top of fol. 59v. Despite the new working procedure, there were still some uncomfortable areas of blank vellum left on the folios.

This procedure is the complete inverse of the process by which the quires studied in the last chapter were made, and it is obviously of the greatest importance in understanding the different character of the last two quires of the manuscript. It is necessary to see the work of artist F in the context of the consequences of the scribe's procedure: the mould of the illustrations was determined by the script, and it differed so radically from Utrecht that recreation of its compositions was frequently impossible. For example, F could not emulate the vertical composition at the right of the illustration to Psalm 116 in Utrecht, where column c is five lines shorter than the first two, because the text on fol. 59v of Harley left no room for it. It was upon this basis that artist F worked, and therefore his deviations from the Utrecht Psalter are not proof of the absence of the Carolingian manuscript.

Artist F

In fact, despite the differences between the illustrations of this artist and those in the Utrecht Psalter, it is quite clear that it was F's study of the Utrecht images that initially formed the backbone of his pictorial repertoire, and it was to their compositions that he

33 *The Harley Psalter, fol. 59r, diagram of visible ruling.*

34 *The Utrecht Psalter, fol. 67r, showing the illustrations to Psalms 114 and 115.*

35 *The Harley Psalter, fol. 59r. The illustrations to Psalms 114 and 115(i) are by F; the script is by scribe 1; the rubrication by E; the initial is by J; additions were made to the illustrations by G.*

34

35

frequently responded and reacted.[1] There are a number of close pictorial parallels in illustrations to the same verses of the same Psalms in the two manuscripts, that are not directly warranted by the text. For example, in the Harley illustration to Psalm 113 on fol. 58r, the composition bears a marked similarity to that in the bottom left-hand corner of the illustration to the same Psalm in Utrecht, only it is reversed: two figures are prominent at the bottom of a slope, with the sea rising up before them; at the back of the group in both cases are a number of women; the one male figure in Utrecht has been multiplied to form the whole crowd of Israel, depicted in another part of the illustration in Utrecht. In the illustration to Psalm 114, on fol. 59r of Harley, the Lord has three angels in attendance in both illustrations, an element not textually required (compare figs. 34 and 35). Similarly, in the first illustration to Psalm 115, on the same folio, the text does not account for the mechanics of the death of the Lord's saints, which are pictorially similar in both Utrecht and Harley.

Artist F's use of Utrecht was not static; it developed. It is in the first Psalm illustrations that he executed that we see his debt to Utrecht most clearly. He takes specific motifs, and although he changes them in details, they have the same textual meaning. This is true of the princes seated at the right of the illustration to Psalm 112, on fol. 58r, for example referring to verse 8. This example is curious because, in using the image in Utrecht, artist F has not made his own references clear. We have to rely on a comparison with the Utrecht illustration to read artist F's correctly. Artist F wished to show the poor man of verse 7 literally *cum principibus populi sui* rather than soon to be between them, as he is in Utrecht. It is only because of the absence of the empty chair, placed between two sets of princes and which is so clear in the centre of the composition in Utrecht, that we are driven to find the poor man resuscitated with the princes on their bench, second from the left. He is only just distinguished by the glances of the other three princes, and by his lack of a sword and blue attire.[2] Later on artist F became more experimental. It is, in fact, impressive testimony to the influence of the Utrecht Psalter on Harley that it provided images for artist F which he proceeded to employ in very different textual settings. The most extreme example of this is in the illustration to Psalm 117, on fol. 60r of Harley. The long staff aimed at the Psalmist in Utrecht was the visual cue for the angel in Harley to cause the *portas iustitiae* to be opened (verse 19), and the upright spears of the Psalmist's persecutors in Utrecht, are, in Harley, used by the angels as a solid wall of protection for the Psalmist, emphasising that the Lord is the Psalmist's strength (verse 14). Artist F seems to have worked Psalm by Psalm, and with each Psalm illustration he distanced himself more from the pictorial vocabulary of Utrecht. But even towards the end of

[1] Wormald, *English Drawings*, p. 44 and p. 79, Dufrenne, 'Les copies anglaises', p. 187, Duffey, 'Inventive Group', esp. pp. 97–105, Backhouse *et al.*, *Golden Age*, p. 75, Carver, 'Contemporary artefacts', p. 132, and Gameson, 'Anglo-Saxon artists', pp. 31–2, all agree that the Utrecht Psalter was available to artist F. James, *Canterbury Psalter*, p. 2, n. 4, Dodwell, *Canterbury School*, p. 3, and Hasler, 'Zu zwei Darstellungen', p. 322, n. 29, did not think that it was.

[2] Duffey, 'Inventive group', pp. 34–37, notices these differences, and states that 'For some reason, the artist wanted to make one of these figures more important than the others.' Clearly, as I have suggested the reason is to be sought in the text. Her subsequent discussion (pp. 108–10) of the impact of the ritual of carrying swords on the illustration, if tenable, might have made the image more clear to an eleventh-century reader.

the manuscript he did not entirely free himself from his exemplar. Psalm 136 recounts that the Israelites sat down and wept by the rivers of Babylon. Verse 2 of the Gallican version reads

In salicibus in medio eius, suspendimus organa nostra.[3]

In its wider sense '*organum*' means 'instrument'; in its narrower, it means 'organ'. However, to illustrate his text the Utrecht artist has shown harps, and this corresponds more precisely to the '*citharas*' of Jerome's Hebrew text of the Psalter (fig. 36).[4] Harley's Roman text also reads '*organa*', and artist F has been careful to include an organ in the trees of his illustration on fol. 70r, referring to his own text (fig. 37). But he has also included a harp. He did not do this without thinking about it: the harp is very different in form to the ones in Utrecht, probably drawn from artist F's experience of harps; and he demonstrates his knowledge of his own text in depicting the organ.[5] Artist F was either drawing attention to the wider meaning of the word '*organa*', or he was including harps to draw attention to the Hebrew variant. Nonetheless, the harps are a visual idea implanted by the exemplar, and not strictly necessary to articulate his text.[6] Looked at from the point of view of the text, artist F was not so emancipated from his exemplar as the contemporary image would imply.

In his increasing emancipation from the exemplar, artist F necessarily referred to images, like the harp, that lay outside the realms of Utrecht's iconography. The extent to which he drew from his own experience has been well researched by Duffey,[7] and Carver traced a greater degree of first-hand natural observation in his later work.[8] Even when he was free from his exemplar however, the relationship between contemporary images and the Psalter text was not free of problems. Harley's Roman Psalm 128, verses 6 and 7, read

Fiant sicut foenum aedificiorum, quod priusquam euellatur arescit.
De quo non impleuit manum suam qui metit, nec sinum suum qui manipulos collegit.[9]

Harley's text differs from that of Utrecht: it suggests that the grass is of the buildings (*aedificiorum*), while the Gallican text reads that the grass is of the rooftops (*tectorum*). Consequently, rather than depict wilted grass on the roof of a barn without walls, as Utrecht does, on fol. 67r artist F depicts the 'grass' of a wattle hut, without a roof (compare figs. 38 and 39).[10] Artist F calls attention to the grass itself by showing it handled by three figures. He may have wanted to clarify verse 6, but in doing so he obscured its sentiment, and a possible reference to verse 7. There is no textual

[3] On the willows in the midst thereof we hung up our organs. [4] Panofsky, 'Textual basis', p. 57.

[5] Rensch Erbes, 'Harp', pp. 31–2.

[6] Ibid., p. 32 and p. 35, n. 44, states that artist F is here 'literal minded', and she quotes from the King James Bible to demonstrate this. However the King James Bible adheres to the Hebrew version of the Psalter, while artist F is illustrating not a Hebrew text, nor, as Rensch Erbes suggests, a Gallican text, but a Roman text. The Roman agrees with the Gallican, and therefore refers to *organa*, not *citharas*. The illustration of artist F cannot be explained here simply by reference to his text, but his literal mentality is undoubted.

[7] Duffey, 'Inventive group', esp. pp. 160–73. [8] Carver, 'Contemporary artefacts', p. 132.

[9] Let them be as grass of the buildings, which withereth before it be plucked up. Wherewith the reaper filled not his hand, nor he that collected sheaves his bosom. [10] As noted by Duffey, 'Inventive group', pp. 135–6.

36 *The Utrecht Psalter, fol. 77r. A detail of the illustration to Psalm 136.*

justification for the process of construction that seems to be going on: the whole point is that the grass of verse 6 is useless and withered, like the wicked, and it is the fact that the figures cannot gather the bundles to their breasts, as required by verse 7, that should be visually stressed. It is possible to interpret the figures in Harley not as constructing the hut, but as deconstructing it, and finding the grass, which is flying madly in the wind, difficult to handle. This would fit the text much better, and the figures would be reaping and gathering. However, if this is the case, it is far from clear, and the contemporary image that F chose for verse 6 has within itself implications that run counter to the meaning of verses 6 and 7. By contrast, the Utrecht artist's interpretation of verse 7 is clear, and he sensibly separates it from verse 6: the stooping gatherers are clearly having trouble collecting the grass. It was precisely this success in the difficult task of illustrating such verses that was the attraction of the Utrecht Psalter.

Of course, these are just a few images by an artist who had a vivid pictorial imagination, and frequently he found pictorial equivalents to Utrecht's images that surpassed those of the Carolingian manuscript. Knowing that he had Utrecht in front of him, we can see how he developed Utrecht's visual ideas in the light of his own concerns. In the illustration to Psalm 125 in the Utrecht Psalter the only sign of the Lord is the *Manus Dei*, while in Harley, on fol. 66r, the fact that it was God himself who overturned the captivity of Sion (verse 1) is made clear by the fact that he stretches out his arm from a flaming mandorla, personally sending forth his axe-bearing angels, who tumble out to work their havoc.

Similarly, on fol. 69r to illustrate his text to Psalm 134, verse 7

37 *The Harley Psalter, fol. 70r. A detail of the illustration to Psalm 136, by F.*

Qui producit uentos de thesauris suis[11]

artist F makes the Lord himself conjure up the winds from his left hand, like a magician. This is in stark contrast to Utrecht, where the winds are merely coming from the base of the mandorla. In the illustration to verse 2 of Psalm 140,

Dirigatur oratio mea, sicut incensum in conspectu tuo.[12]

Utrecht has the Psalmist at prayer, in a temple with its doors held open and curtains fastened back, holding up a censer. In the detail of Utrecht, it is just possible to see lines between the censer and the outstretched hand of God (fig. 40). Evidently these are the fumes of the incense, but it is odd that they seem to be directed from God's outstretched hand, rather than directed to his sight. On fol. 72r, artist F, who was evidently dissatisfied with Utrecht's composition to this Psalm, made the censer appear in the guise of a torch, similar to the one that the Lord holds to illuminate the eyes of the Psalmist in Harley's illustration to Psalm 12 on fol. 7r (fig. 41). However, the rays of the torch are collected up in the right hand of the Lord, as if they were being swung by him

[11] [The Lord] who bringeth forth winds out of his stores.

[12] Let my prayer be directed, as incense in thy sight.

38 *The Utrecht Psalter, fol. 74r. A detail of the illustration to Psalm 128.*

39 *The Harley Psalter, fol. 67r. A detail of the illustration to Psalm 128, by F.*

like the chains of a censer. The Lord has taken up the Psalmist's prayer, indeed, it is now he who is directing it.

Artist F's illustration on fol. 71v, to Psalm 139, verse 4 is also impressive. The verse reads,

Acuerunt linguas suas sicut serpentes, uenenum aspidem sub labiis eorum.[13]

In Utrecht's illustration, those that have sharpened their tongues like serpents, and who have the venom of asps under their lips, are merely holding snakes. Artist F has portrayed the figures with serpents for tongues, and they are spitting venom. These examples show firstly that artist F was concerned to make God more active in his participation in terrestrial activity, and secondly that elucidation of the text was his prime concern, and one of the main sources of his conception.[14]

The influence of the text on artist F's interpretation of Utrecht's motifs can be demonstrated in another way; written before the illustrations were drawn, it had an impact on their form. In Harley's illustration to Psalm 112 on fol. 58r, as in Utrecht's, the composition is divided both into three horizontal tiers, and into three vertical bands formally related to the three columned format of the text below. The compositions also share pictorial motifs: two outstretched hands were used to establish an element of dynamism above the space between columns a and b of the text; four figures were placed on a bench in the middle right of the composition. However, despite these similarities, in Harley the placements of the motifs corresponds to the physical positioning of the text beneath. Thus in column a of the text, and directly above in the illustration, we find the children of the Lord praising the name of the Lord (verse 1); in the centre of the illustration we find the Lord above all the people who are praising him, and below them the pauper raised from the dust, corresponding to verses 4 and 7 in column b of the text; similarly, the princes of the Lord's people are at the top right of the illustration, just as they are mentioned at the top of column c of the text (verse 8), and below them is the joyful mother of children mentioned in the last verse of the Psalm. The spacing of the text in Utrecht is similar to that in Harley – clearly the principles which guided the placing of motifs were very different. As he progressed artist F became bolder in his placing of his illustrations to relate to the physical placement of his own text. The relationship between text and illustration is never so close as in the illustration to Psalm 138 on fol. 71r, where the hell mouth is actually drawn around the reference to the *infernum* (verse 8). It was the text, as much as it was the Utrecht illustrations, that moulded the compositions of artist F.

While artists A–D2 followed the Utrecht Psalter extremely closely, artist F did not. What does this mean in terms of how the images were made? Artists A–D2 were primarily engaged in the task of adhering to Utrecht's imagery, and referring to the text for clarification of a difficult image or because a different emphasis was wanted. This is why they occasionally omitted textually significant details. Artist F was concerned

[13] They have sharpened their tongues like serpents, the venom of asps is under their lips.

[14] The concern for concrete and literal realisation of the divine is a characteristic of Anglo-Saxon art, for which see especially, M. Schapiro, 'Disappearing Christ', *passim*; see also R. Mellinkoff, *The Horned Moses in Medieval Art and Thought*, London, 1970, pp. 27ff; also Henderson, 'Idiosyncrasy', *passim*.

40 *The Utrecht Psalter, fol. 79r. A detail of the illustration to Psalm 140.*

41 *The Harley Psalter, fol. 72r. A detail of the illustration to Psalm 140, by F.*

primarily to elucidate the text with images that he then invented, often using Utrecht for his pictorial repertoire, and this is why there are fewer lacunae in artist F's illustrations. Artist F's illustrations are much simpler than those of Utrecht, but they appear to have been fully worked out before they were placed on the page. Unlike the other artists in the book, artist F may well have had to experiment and draft his designs before placing them in Harley. There are very few signs of under-drawing, and it is hard to envisage how he could have composed his multicoloured schemes if he had not first experimented on scraps of parchment or wax tablets.[15] In his execution of the illustration he drew his figures and his buildings, and then drew in the great swathes of land and sky that connect the disparate elements of the compositions. The Utrecht images were the basis from which artists A, B, and C worked; the Harley text was the basis from which artist F worked, and he had much more liberty to experiment. Technically, the processes of creation are very different.

Despite the difference between the construction techniques of artist F and the other artists of the manuscript, there are points of contact. Artist A did not follow the Utrecht layout precisely for example, and it is no coincidence that both artists executed their figures first and worked their landscapes around them. Like artist F, artist A reorganised his compositions, he included many elements from the contemporary world, and he was not concerned to preserve the sense of space created in Utrecht. Above all, in the work of artists A, B, and F, there is evidence of textual reference over and above that made by the Utrecht Psalter. Artist F's illustrations are entirely compatible with those of artist D2. His illustrations are still placed ahead of the Psalms, and they illustrate them by visualising selected verses of each Psalm and combining them to make coherent compositions. He frequently illustrated fewer verses than the artists of the same illustrations in Utrecht. Thus, in the illustration to Psalm 113, Utrecht alludes to the dead that praise not the Lord (v. 25) by corpses in coffins, and those that go down into hell (v. 25) by a ladder down which people fall into a personified hell, together with their displaced idol (v. 16). Artist F, on fol. 58r, ignored all this and merely illustrated Israel going out of Egypt through the Red Sea (v. 3), while making it clear that the mountains skip like rams (v. 4).[16] But there is nothing in this that makes these illustrations incompatible with other illustrations in the Psalter. It is not as if Utrecht images were comprehensive in their coverage of the Psalmist's imagery. For example Psalm 104 recounts Jewish history from the time of Abraham through to nearly the end of the Exodus, yet both in Utrecht and in Harley, on fol. 52v, little more is illustrated than the tribe of Israel praising the Lord (vv. 1–3), the Word of the Lord (v. 8), and possibly three of his prophets upon whom the story is hung. Similarly artist F's stress on the immediacy and active participation of the Lord in terrestrial affairs is frequently at odds with the somewhat reticent iconography for the Deity in illustrations to the same Psalms in Utrecht: for example in the illustration to Psalm 118, on fol. 60v,

[15] A glimpse into the (almost) lost world of drafting on vellum and on wax is provided by Eadmer: See R.W. Southern, *The Life of St Anselm by Eadmer*, Oxford, 1963, p. 150–1. On wax tablets more generally, see M.P. Brown, 'The role of the wax tablet in medieval literacy: a reconsideration in the light of a recent find from York', *British Library Journal*, 20.1, 1994, pp. 1–16.

[16] Dufrenne, 'Les copies anglaises', p. 187, also analyses this Psalm.

the Lord himself is present before the people who praise him, not merely his temple with his Word inscribed upon a lectern. But while this insistent presence of God in Harley is not paralleled in illustrations to the same Psalms in Utrecht, it is found earlier in the Psalter, and it is no surprise that in his first illustration to Psalm 115 on fol. 59r, artist F is happy to borrow his motif from the illustration to Psalm 12. Artist F's illustrations may not look like the Utrecht Psalter's, but his concerns were actually very similar to those exhibited by artists A and B, and similar to those exhibited in the Utrecht Psalter itself, which was so assiduously followed by artist D2.

The only reason that the voices of those scholars who have claimed that the Utrecht Psalter was available to artist F have not held universal sway is that they have not been able to explain the departure from the Utrecht programme. In the light of this analysis, we can begin to redefine the problem. Technically, artist F was engaged upon a different operation from that of the artists examined in the last chapter. The use of these techniques was the inevitable consequence of the scribe's departure from the example of the layout of the Utrecht Psalter. To explain the appearance of these two quires, then, we have to start by asking why the procedure employed in making them was in such marked contrast to that employed in the quires ruled by artists, and why the scribe spaced the text as he did.

Artist E

So far in my analysis I have been careful not to assume that any of the artists worked before or after any others. From now on, the situation is easier to decipher. Artist E added to work already started in other quires, except those written by Eadui Basan. Artist G added to the work of all the other artists, except to that of artist H, and artist H himself followed on from artist G's work on fols. 28r and 28v. Many of the iconographic inventions of these artists cannot be understood without bearing in mind this sequence, and this is in itself important. I will demonstrate that the artists become increasingly concerned not just with the Utrecht Psalter, but with the earlier work in Harley.

Scholars have been understandably reticent in interpreting the illustrations of artist E.[17] Their iconography is puzzling in the first place because there is no self-evident textual context for them: they fill gaps left by scribe 1, mainly in quires 10 and 11, and, with the exception of his work on fols. 15r and 15v they are not placed at the head of Psalm texts. Moreover, they lack virtuosity and clarity: artist E's pictorial ambition was far greater than his manual dexterity. He did not, for example, shirk from portraying horsemen with their backs to us so that only the bonnets on their heads are showing, as we see them in the illustration to Psalm 26 on fol. 15r. He even managed to elaborate the tent pegs and their tug on the canvas. But he had little felicity of line and almost no ability to compose a grand scene, even when basing it on Utrecht.

17 Wormald, *English Drawings*, p. 70, states that his drawings bear no relation to the text. Gameson, 'Anglo-Saxon artists', p. 33 refers to his additions as 'apparently meaningless doodles'.

Artist E worked after the artists discussed so far, and he borrowed motifs from them. For example, in his illustration on fol. 61r, in the text of Psalm 118, he borrowed from the composition of artist F that heads the Psalm. We have seen that Psalm 118 has a complicated layout, and it seems clear that in this, and in the other sketches that he adds to this Psalm, he tried to clarify it.

The involvement with the text and the illustration already depicted in Harley's Psalm 118 is, in other illustrations, complemented by an interest in Utrecht's iconography. It has been noted above that in the Harley illustration of the Psalmist's prayer as incense (Psalm 140, verse 2), artist F was elaborating on the illustration in Utrecht, relating the prayer more closely to the incense, and attaching it more tightly to the Lord.[18] In artist E's illustration at the bottom of column c of the text on fol. 70v we see a further development (fig. 42); now the censer is held by the Lord, not by the Psalmist at all. It is the third stage in the process of the guiding of the prayer: having left the Psalmist in Utrecht's illustration, its journey to the Lord is seen in F's illustration, and here we see it in the *Manus Dei* itself. The Lord has received the prayer in the guise of the censer, and is stretching forth his right hand to the Psalmist who prays to him. Artist E's temple, with its curtains and open doors looks rather like the temple in the Utrecht image, but its position means, of course, that it cannot relate to Psalm 140. Rather, it relates to Psalm 137, which it follows, and which is almost entirely concerned with the Psalmist's prayers being answered. There is no reference to a censer in the text, but if we understand it as a visual metaphor for a prayer in the light of artist F's illustration to verse 2 of Psalm 140, then three verses of Psalm 137 are particularly pertinent. In verse 1 is found,

Confitebor tibi Domine in toto corde meo, quoniam exaudisti omnia uerba oris mei[19]

in verse 2

Adorabo ad templum sanctum tuum, et confitebor nomini tuo.[20]

and in verse 7

saluum me fecit dextera tua[21]

There may be an element of criticism of artist F's illustration to Psalm 137, for the contact so clearly established between the Psalmist and God in the illustration in Utrecht is rather lost.[22] Certainly the image on the left of artist E's composition is illustrating verse 7 of Psalm 137 to which artist F fails to refer

Si ambulauero in medio tribulationis uiuicabis me[23]

[18] See above, pp. 83–4.

[19] I will give glory to you O Lord with my whole heart, because thou hast heard all the words of my mouth.

[20] I will worship towards the holy temple, and I will give glory to thy name.

[21] Thy right hand hath saved me.

[22] That there is an element of criticism here is contemplated by Duffey, 'Inventive group', p. 214.

[23] If I shall walk in the midst of tribulation thou wilt quicken me.

IPSI DAVID. CONFITEBOR
tibi dne in toto
corde meo. qm exaudis
ti omnia uerba oris mei.
& in conspectu angelorum
psallam tibi ;
Adorabo ad templum scm
tuum. & confitebor no
mini tuo ;
Sup misericordia tua
& ueritate tua. quo mag
nificasti sup nos nomen
scm tuum ;

.C.XXXVII.
In quacumq: die inuoca
uero te exaudi me. multi
plicabis in anima mea
uirtutem tuam ;
Confiteantur tibi dne
omnes reges terre. quia
audierunt omnia uer
ba oris tui. & cantent in
canticis dni ;
Quo magna est gloria
dni. quo excelsus dns
& humilia respicit. &
alta a longe agnoscit ;

Si ambulauero in medio
tribulationis uiuificabis
me. & super iram ini
corum meorum extendisti
manum tuam. & saluum
me fecit dextera tua ;
Dne retribue pro me dne
misericordia tua in seculum.
& opera manuum tuarum
ne despicias ;

42 *The Harley Psalter, fol. 70v. The script is by scribe 1, the illustration heading Psalm 137 by F, the rubrication and the illustration at the bottom of the page are by E; the initial is by J.*

However, to illustrate this verse artist E used a motif drawn from Utrecht's illustration to Psalm 142, verse 11, with similar wording

propter nomen tuum domine uiuicabis me in aequitate tua
educes de tribulatione animam meam[24]

The same desire to comment on F's illustrations lies behind artist E's composition below the text of Psalm 128 on fol. 67r. This alludes to verse 7 of this Psalm, in which, as we have seen, the sinners are likened to grass that cannot be collected.[25] In Utrecht's illustration the stooping gatherers are shown having great difficulty in collecting their sheaves. By contrast in artist E's illustration the sheaves have certainly been bound by six people, three either side of the Lord, who are holding them aloft, as if they are prized possessions, and quite clearly they have been successfully reaped and collected.[26] Here, as in the illustration to Psalm 137, artist E is reacting to the illustration in Utrecht. But here he is more free in his comment on the Psalm, emphasising that those who do not hate Sion, but love the Lord, are like healthy sheaves. Artist E was trying to clarify the textual reference that was ambiguously presented by artist F.

In his illustration on fol. 53r artist E also shows a desire to comment on artist D2's illustration to Psalm 104, on fol. 52v, just as in his illustration to Psalm 137 he did to artist F's (fig. 43). As Duffey has observed, the lower group of the angel striking at two demons is derived from part of artist F's illustration to Psalm 124 on fol. 65v,[27] which illustrates verse 3 (fig. 44),

Quia non derelinquet dominus uirgam peccatorum, super sortem iustorum.
Ut non extendant iusti ad iniquitatem manus suas[28]

While Psalm 124 is a Psalm celebrating the relationship between the Lord and Israel, Psalm 104 describes the wanderings of the tribe of Israel, and particularly their bondage in Egypt. However, as noted above, the illustration by artist D2 to this Psalm, imitating the Utrecht Psalter, depicts none of the wanderings of Israel, but rather depicts the tribe celebrating the Lord. If artist E wished to extend the visual allusions to this Psalm's text, a particularly relevant verse may have been verse 15. What in verse 3 of Psalm 124 is noted as observed action by the Lord, is here turned into his direct command:

Nolite tangere christos meos et in prophetis meis nolite malignari.[29]

If we look at artist E's illustration, the two figures in the upper section are looking towards the Lord from across the page, while underneath an angel is ensuring that the

[24] For thy name's sake, O Lord, thou wilt quicken me in thy justice. Thou wilt bring my soul out of tribulation. Artist F used the same motif in his illustration to Psalm 129, *De profundis*, on fol. 67v. He also used the Utrecht image for Psalm 142. But artist E used the Utrecht image, appropriate to the very words of his text.

[25] See above, pp. 81–2.

[26] Duffey, 'Inventive group', p. 257, n. 263, attributes a suggestion that they are bags of wheat to Wormald, *English Drawings*, 1952, but does not give a page reference. I can find no reference to this in Wormald, *English Drawings*. At p. 212, she suggests that they are flaming suns.

[27] Duffey, 'Inventive group', p. 210.

[28] For the Lord will not leave the rod of the wicked, upon the lot of the just. That the just stretch not their hands to iniquity.

[29] Touch ye not my anointed and do no evil to my prophets.

43 *The Harley Psalter, fols. 52v–53r, showing the illustration to Psalm 104. The script, the illustration heading the Psalm, and all the rubrication except the Psalm division is by D2; the illustration at the bottom right is by E; the Psalm division is an addition, perhaps by Eadui Basan.*

44 *The Harley Psalter, fol. 65v. A detail of the illustration to Psalm 124, by F.*

demons do not touch them, in this case with a flail, and not a rod. Artist E looked at Harley's illustration to Psalm 124, which like the illustration to Psalm 104 has Israel praising the Lord, chose the one element from it lacking in the illustration to Psalm 104, and added it at the end of that Psalm, replacing the rod with a flail. This implies a knowledge of artist F's illustration, of the text of Psalm 124, the text of Psalm 104, and criticism of artist D2's illustration to Psalm 104, which so accurately reflects the Utrecht Psalter itself.[30]

Not all of artist E's work can be deciphered with precision, but it is clear that it is not always mere decoration, and elements can be discerned which shed light on artist E's attitude both to Utrecht and to Harley. Unlike the other artists, artist E invented his compositions on the page. This might account for their 'doodle-like' quality, but they are not meaningless doodles. The gaps left an excellent opportunity to comment on the text, on the illustrations in Harley, as well as those in Utrecht, and even on the relationship between them, as a sort of pictorial commentary.

[30] Duffey, 'Inventive group', p. 210 states that this illustration is 'possibly related to Psalm 118'. I cannot see why; a connection with Psalm 104 would seem more appropriate.

Quires 5–8: Eadui Basan and artists G and H

Working procedure

Quires 5–8 were written by Eadui Basan. The folios are arranged so that hair side faces hair; some of it was poorly prepared.[31] The overall text space is the same as before, with three columns of 32 lines. However, there are a number of features that require explanation. Most importantly, unlike quires 1–4 and 9, but like 10–11, the Utrecht layout was not followed closely, while, like quires 1–4 and 9, but unlike quires 10–11, the illustration spaces are unruled. Since those illustrations that were completed were executed after the text, it is clear that the scribe was responsible for the ruling.

We must decide whether Eadui had the Utrecht layout to hand as a possible model. There is evidence that he did, and that at first he intended to stick to it. At the top of fol. 28r Eadui did not rule lines for the three lines of text that are to be found on the equivalent folio in the Utrecht Psalter; as we have seen, the text was finished by scribe 1 at the bottom of fol. 27v (compare figs 47 and 48, below, pp. 98–9). He did however start his rulings 18 lines from the bottom of the page, which is very close to Utrecht's 17, and on fol. 28v he started his ruling 8 lines from the bottom of the text block, like Utrecht, even though there are 6 less lines of text at the top of this folio than there are in the exemplar. Even after he was forced to give up the Utrecht layout, the Utrecht Psalter still exerted an influence: the illustration space on fol. 41v to Psalm 77, *Adtendite populus meus*, is very large, as it is in Utrecht, and indeed in both manuscripts sufficient space is left at the bottom of the preceding recto for a normal size illustration. It is curious that this remnant of the Greek Psalter emphasis on Psalm 77 should find itself manifested not only in the Utrecht Psalter, but also in its first Anglo-Saxon derivative.

There is other evidence to suggest that Eadui had the Utrecht Psalter to hand. His text is much more justified and regular than that of scribes 1 and D2. As a result his columns are closer than those of scribes 1 and D2 to those of Utrecht in their appearance, where the rustic capitals are similarly tightly packed and justified. If scribe D2 followed the Utrecht Psalter line by line, Eadui Basan was far more faithful than any other scribe in the book to the overall appearance of Utrecht's columns.

Perhaps in order to adhere to the Utrecht layout Eadui also slightly reduced the width of his text columns, from *c.* 64 mm to *c.* 62 mm: there was marginally less room for the minuscule which therefore took up more lines.[32] However, if this was the case it did not work. His text still took up less space than it did in the Utrecht Psalter, which is why there are fewer lines of text at the top of fol. 28v than there are on the equivalent folio in Utrecht. Artist G, who clearly illustrated after Eadui had written his text,

[31] Fol. 46 is particularly transparent, greasy, stiff, and thick: see T.J. Brown, 'The distribution and significance of membrane prepared in the insular manner', in J. Bately, M.P. Brown, and J. Roberts (eds.), *A Palaeographer's View: The Selected Writings of Julian Brown*, London, 1993, pp. 125–39, at p. 126. The paper was given at *La Paléographie Hébraïque Médiévale*, Colloques internationaux du Centre National de la Recherche Scientifique, a symposium of 11–13 September, 1972.

[32] A difference of 2 mm may not sound much. However, multiplied by 32 it is 64 mm – slightly more than one of his column widths: it had the same effect as ruling each page for 31 lines, not 32.

therefore had to make his illustrations substantially larger than the equivalent compositions in Utrecht.

Eadui soon realised that he could not maintain the Utrecht format without making the illustration space too tall for the artist to follow its illustrations, especially after a long Psalm. The folio after fol. 28 is now wanting, but the present fol. 29r demonstrates that by this stage Eadui had radically reconsidered his approach to his task, and he no longer followed the Utrecht Psalter's layout. In departing from Utrecht Eadui was doing no more than conceding to the inevitable. He showed nothing of the cavalier attitude to the interests of the artist that we saw in quires 10 and 11. The Utrecht layout was only sacrificed so that the artists could adhere to its compositions, and Eadui was careful not to leave spaces at the bottom of the page that were too small for an illustration, and yet large enough to create an eye-sore.

Eadui had instigated another important change in his preparation of the text block by the time he started fol. 29r: instead of hard point, he had begun to use lead point in his ruling.[33] In the first half of the eleventh century this is most unusual;[34] as we have seen artists used lead point for preparatory drawings, and, as an extension of this, artist B was seen to use it in his ruling,[35] but for scribes it was a different matter. Rand pointed out that the ninth-century Tours, Bibliothèque Municipale, Ms. 22 was executed in lead point,[36] and it was also used in a sacramentary of *c.* 1000, Paris, BN Ms. Lat. 817, on fols. 76r and 79v, in order not to score fully illustrated pages.[37] Eadui's use of lead point ruling can similarly be linked to the desire to take the artist into consideration, and perhaps also to the fact that he was an artist.[38] Its advantage over hard point was that when text lines had to be ruled on one side of a folio, they did not score what were potentially illustration spaces on the other side; unlike all the other ruling in the book, Eadui's did not have to be faint. The one advantage of hard point ruling – that the recto and verso of more than one folio could be ruled at one time – was not material, since all the folios in the manuscript were ruled on both sides and separately.

This procedure left Eadui with a problem. Without an exemplar to follow it was difficult to work out in advance where the illustration spaces would go. Despite the absence of pricking marks on the inner margins of his quires, Eadui is most unlikely to have ruled individual text lines by the bifolium: he would have had to have calculated in advance the page layout on the last page of a quire before he had written the first. This would have been an astonishing achievement. He sometimes may have ruled the bounding lines of his text block across bifolia, but individual text lines can, I think, only have been ruled a few folios in advance.[39] Evidently, while Eadui's ruling technique was innovative, he had either pricked his quires before he had thought through the

[33] None is present on fol. 28r, perhaps a little on fol. 28v. It is only in the next quire that he finally adopts it unreservedly.

[34] Ker, *Catalogue*, p. xxiv–xxv: it started to appear at the very end of the eleventh century, but only became a regular feature in the twelfth.

[35] See above, chapter 1, pp. 32–36.

[36] E.K. Rand, *A Survey of the Manuscripts of Tours*, 2 vols., Studies in the Script of Tours 1, Cambridge, Massachusetts, 1929, p. 102, with illustrations in Vol. 2 (Plates), plates XXXIV and XXXV.

[37] Vezin, 'La réalisation matérielle', p. 33, and n. 12.

[38] The case has most recently been made in Heslop, 'Cnut and Emma', p. 176.

[39] I have already suggested that artist A probably ruled individual rectos and versos independently of each other; see above, chapter 1, pp. 48–49.

implications of his procedure, or he never considered pricking in the inner margins as a possibility. It is important to remember that, in the eleventh century and before, pricking in both margins in insular manuscripts is associated with a different type of ruling altogether – ruling on sheets already folded. The practice of ruling across single folios, one at a time, from prick to prick and in lead point, was a twelfth-century development; Eadui would have found this procedure useful, but he probably had no precedent for it.[40] The only example I know of pricking in the inner margin for ruling across individual page in the first half of the eleventh century in England is that of BL Cotton Ms. Claudius B.iv, and then it only occurs after quire 12.[41] Like artists A and D2, Eadui defined the limits of the illustration spaces with lines that do not conform to the column bounding lines, and frequently extend to the pricks in the outer margin. He then added the text lines. Sometimes he miscalculated, but this did not matter; he simply ruled extra lines as he needed. This can be seen on fol. 49v: the last line of Psalm 96 has an extra line in column c, and an extra line was needed in all three columns for Psalm 97 (compare figs. 45 and 46). When one realises how labour intensive this process was compared to that used in quires 10 and 11, for example, it is possible to see how concerned Eadui was to ensure that his section of text should combat the problems that adapting the Utrecht Psalter involved.

Eadui's quires witness a closer appreciation of Utrecht than quires 10 and 11. It is therefore clear that he intended the Utrecht compositions to be followed closely by the artist who illustrated after he wrote.

Artist G

Just as Eadui was more faithful to Utrecht than scribe 1, so artist G was more faithful than artist F, and on fols. 28r and 28v he shows an impressive interpretation of the Utrecht compositions. Like artist A, artist G was less concerned to create a sense of depth than to create a satisfactory surface, and he too altered the spatial relationships of Utrecht's figures. In his illustration to Psalm 48 on fol. 28r the sheep are placed more firmly in the bottom left, and the tree above them has been enlarged to establish the corners of the composition (compare figs. 47 and 48). Although these changes do not affect the interpretation of the Psalm others are more curious, and, unlike artist A, artist G filled in background landscape with new iconographic elements. For example, a personification of the Sun has been placed at the top of the illustration, defining its upper limit, and below the Sun is a temple. These elements draw a useful contrast between the house of God and the house of the rich man, which will be a sepulchre (verse 12), and the personification of the Sun above the house of God draws attention to the fact that the rich man will never see the light (Verse 20). The fact that one of the two speakers addressing the inhabitants of the

[40] See Ker, *Catalogue*, p. xxiv, and, for more details of twelfth-century practice see also N. R. Ker, *English Manuscripts in the Century after the Norman Conquest*, Oxford, 1960, pp. 41–4.

[41] See above, chapter 1, p. 48.

45 *The Harley Psalter, fol. 49v, diagram of visible ruling.*

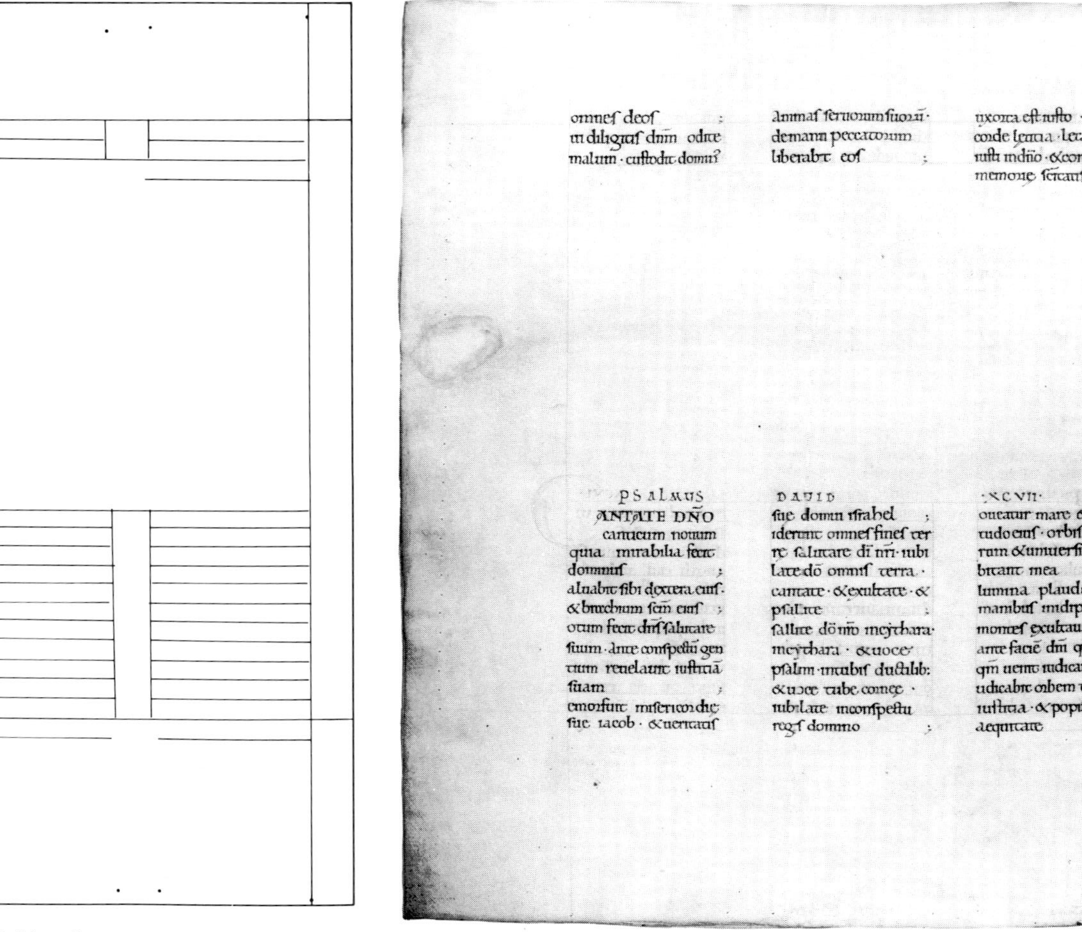

46 *The Harley Psalter, fol. 49v. Everything on this page, which ends with the text to Psalm 97, is by Eadui Basan.*

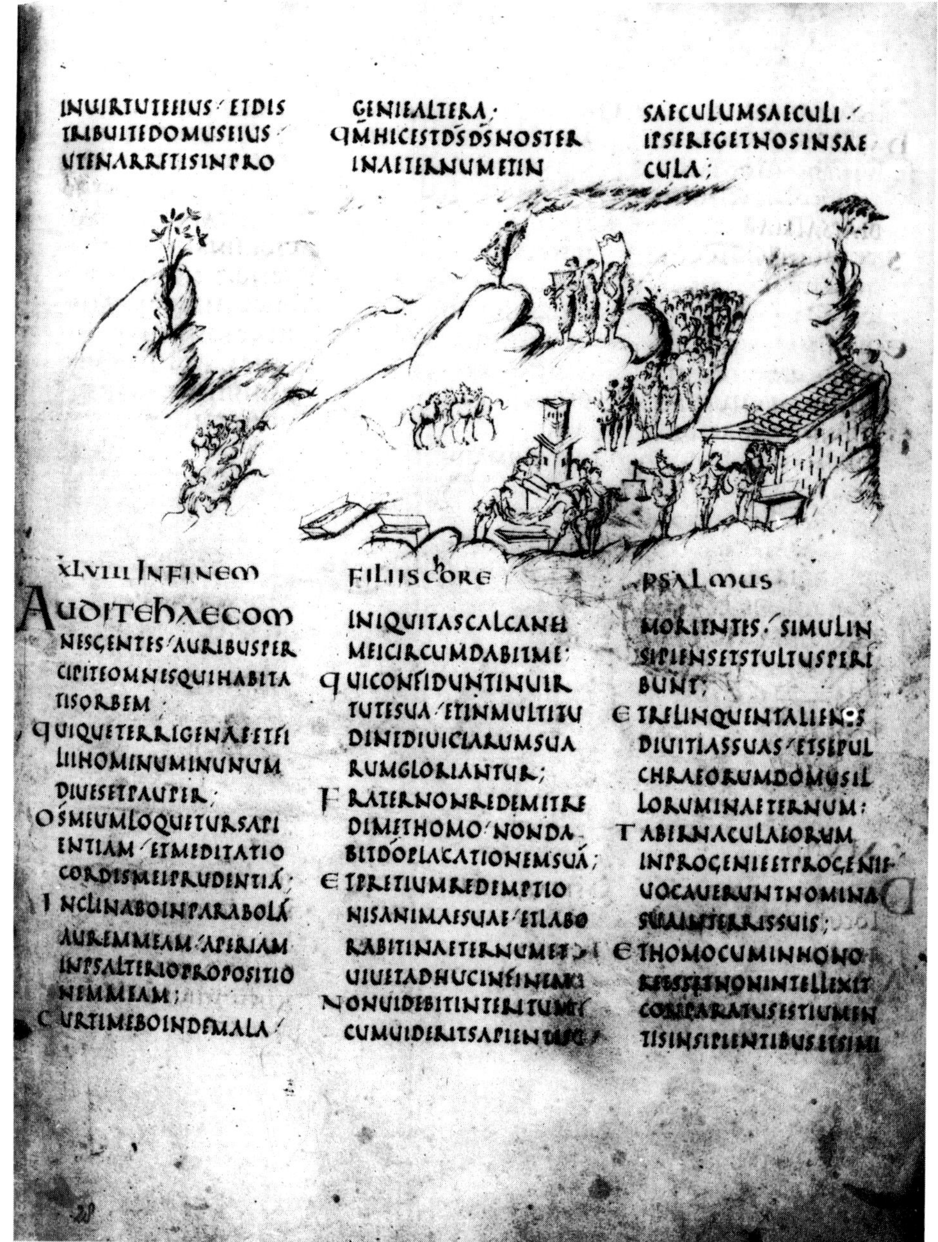

47 *The Utrecht Psalter, fol. 28r, showing the illustration to Psalm 48.*

48 *The Harley Psalter, fol. 28r. The script and the* titulus *are by Eadui Basan; the illustration to Psalm 48 is by G, who also executed the initial.*

49 *The Harley Psalter, fol. 17r. The illustration to Psalm 30, by B, with additions by G.*

earth carries a standard rather than a whip may have been an idle matter of preference rather than a reflection of artist G's interpretation of the Psalm. However, the fact that the money of the rich man is no longer being entered into a money chest, and that the rich man is now entering a building with an altar, would suggest a deeper intent. There is no apparent textual justification for this change, and this is all the odder because, in his additions to the work of other artists, artist G will demonstrate an acute awareness of the text.

One of Gameson's important contributions to the study of Harley was his observation that artist G added details to the illustrations of the other artists.[42] The following analysis attributes further additions to G. They are in fact so substantial that they materially affect our understanding of the work of earlier artists in the book.

As Wormald first noted, artist G added the small composition on fol. 17v of Harley (fig. 50).[43] In doing so he drew from elements in the composition on fol. 17r, at the head of Psalm 30 (fig. 49), which alluded to verses 5 and 13 of that Psalm. However his invention did not stop here, but rather went on to fol. 18r. Artist B adhered closely to the iconography of the Utrecht Psalter, and his palette was muted. The figure at the lower left of the illustration to Psalm 31 is not to be found in Utrecht, and he is depicted in red (compare figs. 50 and 51). He is quite out of character with the rest of artist B's work. We do not have to rely on stylistic parallels to know that this figure is by artist G,

[42] Gameson 'Anglo-Saxon artists', pp. 43–4, lists the additions that he attributes to artist G.

[43] Wormald, *English Drawings*, p. 70. Ohlgren, *Textual Illustration*, p. 24, attributes it to Hand E, but he is clearly mistaken.

and not artist B as Gameson suggests.[44] The eyes of this character look to the composition on fol. 17v; he also points with his right arm to the Lord depicted at the top of the illustration to Psalm 31. In this way, as a précis of the illustration to Psalm 30, artist G's illustration is more comprehensive, linking as it does the Psalmist to the Lord, who is also present in the illustration to the earlier Psalm. This extension of the composition on fol. 17v onto fol. 18r is paralleled by the text. At the bottom of the second column of the text of Psalm 30 on fol. 17v, stretching to the top of the third column, verse 23 reads,

Ego autem dixi in pauore meo, proiectus sum a uultu oculorum tuorum.
Ideo exaudisti uocem deprecationis meae, dum clamarem ad te.[45]

The added figure on fol. 18r is pointing out the presence of the Lord to the Psalmist, a castaway at the bottom of the preceding page, and the fact that he has heard his cry. In pictorial terms artist G responded to the cry of the Psalmist to the Lord in verse 17,

Inlumina faciem tuam super seruum tuum[46]

The very specific gestures of this cheerful character make no sense without the illustration by artist G on fol. 17v, and, since this illustration was not even there when artist B illustrated Psalm 31, it must be by artist G, and must be best understood as an integral, if disguised, part of the composition on fol. 17v. Given this identification, we can note other elements not to be found in Utrecht, executed in the same pigment, and ascribe them to the same artist: another figure just to the right of the centre behind a hillock, and an extra fish in the sea, again to the right. The halo of the Lord is rather more curious. Originally this was a simple cross nimbus. The nimbus was then coloured green, and finally another cross was added to the nimbus, outside the green, and at a different angle to the rest of the cross. I think we can safely ascribe the second cross, executed in red, to G, and read it as an attempt to highlight his composition – one that he was not unnaturally proud of. In several instances a red cross has been added to the nimbus of an earlier artist. All of these should be ascribed to G because they are consistent in form throughout quires 1–4, are normally in his distinctive hues, and are similar to the nimbus seen in BL Cotton Ms. Caligula A.xv, which Gameson rightly attributes to this artist.[47] The green of the nimbus on fol. 18r is a more difficult matter and one to which I shall return.

At the table in the illustration to Psalm 103, on fol. 51v, Harley has one more figure than Utrecht (compare figs. 52 and 53). This figure is attributed to artist D2 by Gameson.[48] But, as we have seen, it is most unusual for artist D2 to extend his imagery beyond that of the Utrecht Psalter. The figure is executed in the characteristic red hue that we saw in the addition on fol. 18r, and it also has a profile resembling those in BL Cotton Ms. Caligula A.xv. For these reasons I ascribe this figure to artist G.

44 Gameson, 'Anglo-Saxon artists', p. 46, n. 57.
45 But I said in my fear, I am cast away from the countenance of thy eyes. Therefore thou hast heard the voice of my prayer, when I cried to thee.
46 Make thy face to shine upon thy servant.
47 Temple, *Anglo-Saxon Mss.*, cat. 106, ills. 317–18; Gameson, 'Anglo-Saxon artists', p. 40; see also below, Chapter 3, p. 139, and p. 142.
48 Gameson, 'Anglo-Saxon artists', p. 46, n. 46.

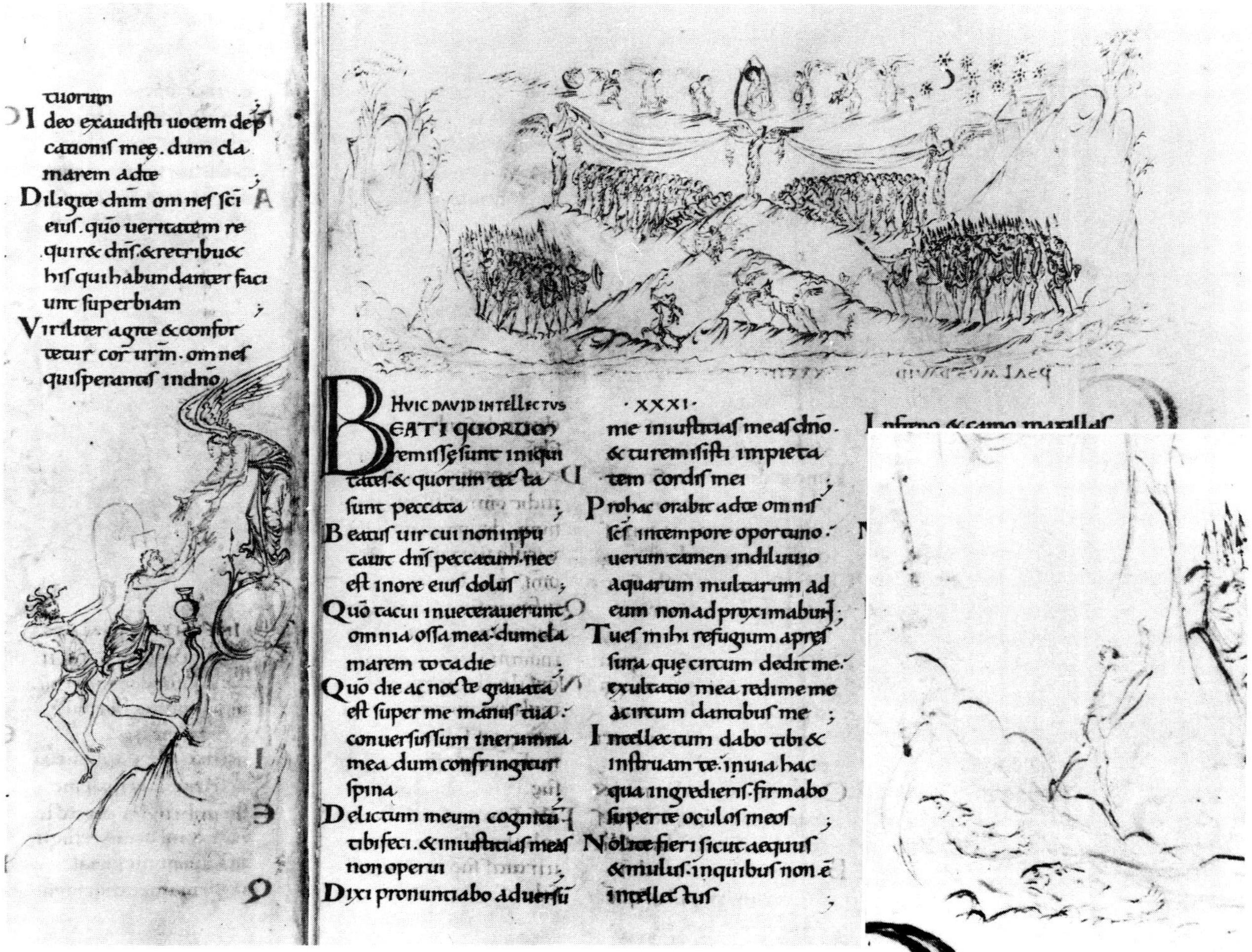

50 *The Harley Psalter, fol. 17v–18r. The illustration heading Psalm 31 is by B, the script is by scribe 1; the rubrication by E; the initial by J; the addition on fol. 17v is by G, who also added details, including the inset, to the illustration to Psalm 31.*

XXXI HUICDAUID INTELLECTUS

BEATIQUORUM
REMISSESUNTINIQUI
TATES· ETQUORUMTEC
TASUNTPECCATA:
B EATUSUIRCUINONIN
PUTABITDNSPECCATU·
NECESTINSPUEIUSDOLUS:
Q NMTACUIINUETERAUE
RUNTOSSAMEA· DUM
CLAMAREMTOTADIE:
Q NMDIEACNOCTEGRA
UATAESTSUPERMEMA
NUSTUA· CONUERSUS
SUMINAERUMNAMEA
DUCONFIGITURSPINA:
DIAPSALMA
D ELICTUMMEUMCOGNI
TUMTIBIFECI ETINIUSTI
TIAMEANONABSCONDI·

D IXICONFITEBORADUER
SUMMEINIUSTITIAMMEA
DNO· ETTUREMISISTIIMPI
ETATEMPECCATIMEI:
DIAPSALMA
P ROHACORAUITADTEOM
NISSCSINTEMPOREO
PORTUNO:
U ERUMTAMENINDILU
UIOAQUARUMULTA
RUADEUMNONADPROXI
MABUNT:
T UESREFUGIUMMEUM
ATRIBULATIONEQUAE
CIRCUMDEDITME EXUL
TATIOMEAERUEMEACIR
CUMDANTIBUSME·
DIAPSALMA
I NTELLECTUMTIBIDABO

ETINSTRUAMTE· INUIA
HACQUAGRADIERIS·
FIRMABOSUPERTEOCU
LOSMEOS·
N OLITEFIERISICUTEQUUS
ETMULUS· QUIBUSNON
ESTINTELLECTUS:
I NCHAMOETFRENOMA
XILLASEORUMCONS
TRINGE· QUINONAD
PROXIMANTADTE:
M ULTAFLAGELLAPECCATO
RIS· SPERANTEMAUTEM
INDNOMISERICORDIA
CIRCUMDABIT:
L AETAMINIINDNOETEX
SULTATEIUSTI· ETGLO
RIAMINIOMNESRECTI
CORDE:

4

51 *The Utrecht Psalter, fol. 18r, showing the illustration to Psalm 31.*

52 *The Utrecht Psalter, fol. 59v. The illustration to Psalm 103.*

Psalm 103 is perhaps the most beautiful Psalm in the Harley Psalter. It is held to be a prime example of the work of artist D2.[49] There are, however, more additions by artist G in this illustration than just the figure at the table. The following examples are all executed in a turquoise of a distinctive character, used by G, and which has some depth to it. None of these is found in the Utrecht exemplar:

The aura around the head of the Lord, within the nimbus.
The right and left-hand emanations between Heaven and Earth.
An extra tree of substantial proportions in the mountains to the left.
Two extra trees, immediately above the oxen.
Touches to the robes of the minister of the Lord pouring oil on the central figure behind the table.
Five separate additions of foliage to the tree on the extreme left of the illustration, and a single, outlined leaf to the little plant at the extreme lower left.

How can we tell that these details are the work of artist G? First, this colour is found in artist G's established work: it occurs, for example, on fol. 28v in the tiles of the building on the left. More importantly, the same turquoise appears on other folios, used for what are clearly additions to illustrations already drawn; the most striking example of this is the addition to the Lord's hair on fol. 11v.

[49] E. Kitzinger, *Early Medieval Art in the British Museum*, London, 1940, plate 29a; Talbot Rice, *English Art*, p. 203, discusses and illustrates this Psalm (Plate. 66 a); Wormald *English Drawings*, pp. 31–2 and ills. 11(a) and (b). Backhouse *et al.*, *Golden Age*, colour plate XIX. D.J. Bernstein, *The Mystery of the Bayeux Tapestry*, Chicago, 1986, pp. 61–5, plates 23–4, goes into some detail in his analysis. But note M.P. Brown, *Anglo-Saxon Manuscripts*, London, 1991, p. 75, and plate 73.

53 *The Harley Psalter, fol. 51v. The illustration to Psalm 103, by D2, with additions by G.*

Another colour used by G was magenta. This can be seen in the tree that artist G added to the illustration on fol. 11r, as noted by Gameson.[50] G also used magenta in elaborating upon B's illustration to Psalm 21 on fol. 12r: the mandorla is not found in Utrecht, and was executed in magenta; in the same colour, G added the flagstaffs to the angels, and highlights to the sides of the hills and the landscape at the bottom; moreover, while B did not include the nimbus seen in Utrecht in his illustration to this Psalm, it is possible that it was G who added the cross to the head of the Lord (compare figs. 58 and 59, below, p. 127). Magenta additions can also be seen in the illustration to Psalm 106 on fol. 54v. In the group of people to the right of Harley, there is a completed robe for a figure which, in Utrecht, is left unfinished. This robe is in the characteristic colour used by artist G, and the somewhat broader folds, which do not imitate those of Utrecht, are also a signature of the later artist. Another notable addition is the decoration of the chair on the right of the Psalmist, also executed in magenta.

Gameson notes no additions by G to the last two quires, and this raises the possibility that artist F may have been responsible for these additions; certainly much turquoise is found on his folios. However in the illustration to Psalm 119, on fol. 64r, the tree was executed in magenta, and seems certainly to have been by artist G, and not by artist F who, at this stage in his campaign, was still not interested in earthly details and did not use this pigment (fig. 66, below, p. 153).[51] The tree should be paralleled with that on 11r. In this same Psalm, there are also later additions in turquoise: it has been added to the shield held by the Psalmist, thus making it distinct from those carried by the angels, and to the Lord's robes, around his left thigh, in a similar way to that in which it was added

[50] Gameson, 'Anglo-Saxon artists', p. 43.

[51] See Carver, 'Contemporary artefacts', p. 132. Carver considers this illustration to be the first folio on which artist F shows his naturalistic tendencies. However the tree was added at a later date by artist G.

to the robes of the figure pouring oil in the illustration to Psalm 103 on fol. 51v. The extra line of landscape which nonsensically stops in front of the foremost angel was also executed in this colour.

Artist G also employed green in his illustrations. It was frequently employed as a tint to articulate buildings and landscapes. This is how it was used in the building to the right on fol. 28r. One wonders, therefore, whether touches of green added to artist B's illustrations in quire 4, are not in fact by artist G. It has been noted that green was added to the nimbus of the Lord on fol. 18r: since we know that G was interested in this illustration, and since it has been demonstrated that he tinted the nimbus of the Lord in the illustration to Psalm 103, we can suggest that the artist also added the green here. The same tint has been added to the nimbus on fol. 19v. It was also used for architectural details in quire 4, such as the finials of the building on fol. 26v. It is clear that someone has gone over B's illustrations, adding very little to the iconography of the illustrations, in a second wave of colour, after they were originally completed. This wave stopped at fol. 24v, and there is very little green from fols. 25r–27v. Artist B was quite happy to execute his illustrations in two colours alone, and therefore it seems likely that this green tinting is by G.

This hypothesis is given some substantiation by the fact that it was G's style to tint outlines already drawn in other colours.[52] This is true, for example, of the garments of the Psalmist and the angel on fol. 17v. These blue tints are very like the green tints found in quire 4. We have seen that G was interested in the figure of the Lord within a mandorla on fol. 18r, and the blue tinting of the inside of the mandorla may be attributed to him. This blue tinting is also found on the group of women at the bottom of the illustration on fol. 18v, culminating in one figure whose entire robe is blue. There seems no reason to give this figure special emphasis, and it seems possible that it was actually added by G, making up a lacuna in the iconography of B. Certainly the same blue, attributed by Gameson to G, is found in the illustration on fol. 22v. Similarly, on fol. 18v, the water being poured out of the vessel seems to be by G. We have seen that in quire 4 artist B's colour is muted; for example the sea in the illustration to Psalm 47 on fol. 27v is executed in buff brown, its fluid nature being characterised by the complexity and ever varying density of buff brown strokes; that on fol. 18v is depicted in a blanket blue, and this concentration of local colour is at once untypical of his usually muted palette, and unsuccessful in that it unbalances the composition. There is also blue tinting on the body of the serpent rising out of the sea which I attribute to G. The obvious question, then, is whether G was also responsible for the use of blue in the illustration to Psalm 43 on fol. 25r. Once again there is no clear reason why the ground to the left should be executed in blue, and, although there is more to be said for depicting the Lord's bedclothes in this colour, the fact that they were begun in B's usual ink may suggest that the change in colour coincided with a change in hand. If so, this illustration might be said to have been genuinely unfinished until the arrival of G.

52 Talbot Rice, *English Art*, p. 202, notes that in some cases in Harley 603 the tints were never added to the drawings. Perhaps he was thinking of the work of artist B here. However, it is certainly not the case that the figures in the manuscript were all outlined first, and then tinted, as he maintains.

Since it has been established that artists B and D2 adhered closely to the Utrecht Psalter, we can search for further examples of G's work by comparing their illustrations with the exemplar. If we take the example of the illustration to Psalm 110, on fol. 57r of Harley, we see slight differences from Utrecht that are of a character that we can now ascribe to G (compare figs. 27 and 28, above p. 63): the capitals of the building on the left are decorated in blue, while they are not shaded in Utrecht; there is an extra plant just to the right of the table, and another one to the bottom right of the illustration; the bowl of meat brought down from Heaven by the angel has blue additions; the Almighty himself has been given a cross nimbus. These additions seem unlikely to have been added by someone so concerned with his model as was D2, even though they are executed in a similar hue to the landscape on the left of the illustration, and the foliage on the tree at the top right. But the plants are not similar to others by D2, they are not found in the Utrecht Psalter, and a similar instance is to be found in the little plant just to the right of the angels staff in the illustration to Psalm 102 on fol. 51r. Similar additions in blue can be seen in the illustration to Psalm 111 on fol. 57v, at the base of the throne of the *Beatus uir*, and on the object that he gives to the poor man on the left.

In assessing the contribution of artist G to quires 2, 3, 4, and 9, we are significantly helped by the fact that the artists adhered so closely to the Utrecht exemplar. The problem of deciphering separate hands is obviously more complicated in quires 1, 10 and 11. I attribute the prostrate man below the central figure in the illustration to Psalm 14 on fol. 8r to artist G, not just on grounds of colour, but because artist A takes no account of him in his drawing of the landscape (compare figs. 18 and 19, above, p. 47). Similarly, in the illustration to Psalm 15 on the same folio, artist A had carefully ensured that the head of the Psalmist would appear in the margin flanked by both columns of text, but the scribe did not use the last line, and it must therefore have been artist G who drew the house and the tree on the hill, below the first column of text, and the plant below the second. These were executed in the same red pigment as the dome to the Sepulchre, and the figure lying inside. Sometimes artist G's additions make no sense: the turquoise tree-top beside the Lord in the illustration to Psalm 7 on fol. 4r, for example, has no trunk, and branches of the tree on the right of the illustration to Psalm 5 on fol. 3r, also in turquoise, are not integrated with the tree. Turquoise is also used to articulate the undergarment of the personification of the Sun on the left of the same Psalm illustration.

The following is a list of the details that I think, in varying degrees of probability, are ones that artist G made to the work of other artists. Most of those that are not simply tints are not found in Utrecht's illustrations.

fol. 2r The illustration to Psalm 2 (fig. 1, above, p. 4)

The tree in the foreground with characteristic touches of turquoise. Originally placed there by artist A, the tree is not found in the Utrecht Psalter, and was here used as a space filler.

Another turquoise tree at the back right.

fol. 3r The illustration to Psalm 5

Two turquoise branches of the tree at the right of the illustration, and touches to the tree next to it. Not present in Utrecht.

The turquoise the body underneath the cloak of the personification at the top left. Not present in Utrecht.

fol. 4r The illustration to Psalm 7

The turquoise tree-top without a trunk just to the left of the Lord carrying his weapons. Not present in Utrecht.

fol. 4v The illustration to Psalm 8

Tops of the staffs of the angels. Not found in Utrecht. These were evidently drawn in reaction to the gap between the illustration space and the text, and therefore must have been executed after the illustration itself. The angels at the top right of G's illustration to Psalm 49 have similar tops to their staffs.[53]

A plant to the right of the animals. He also seems to have added other foliage.

fol. 6r The illustration to Psalm 10

The bow of the foremost archer, executed in blue, with none of the precision seen in the implements of A's other characters.[54]

The quiver of the second archer.

The arrows in the quiver were executed by the same artist who drew the single brick below the building under attack. This was not the hand of artist A; it may have been G.

Much, if not all, of the blue landscape.

fol. 6v The illustration to Psalm 11

The cross of the nimbus.

fol. 7r The illustration to Psalm 12

The turquoise plant at the top left.

The cross of the nimbus.

fol. 7v The illustration to Psalm 13

The cross of the nimbus.

fol. 8r The illustration to Psalm 14 (fig. 19, above, p. 47)

Red highlighting of the *Manus Dei*.

The three red hands of the two figures approaching the temple.

The red unfinished figure, lying prostrate at the feet of the figure in the centre of the composition.

fol. 8r The illustration to Psalm 15 (fig. 19, above, p. 47)

The red house and the tree on the hill at the top left.

The red dome of the sepulchre and the red body inside it.

The cross of the nimbus.

fol. 8v The illustration to Psalm 16

The cross of the nimbus.

fol. 9r The illustration to Psalm 17

The cross of the nimbus.

[53] Carver, 'Contemporary artefacts', p. 135, attributes these to hand A.

[54] Ibid., p. 135, interprets this as a double-outline bow, while Gameson, 'Anglo-Saxon artists', p. 37, suggests that here artist A has misunderstood the depiction of a bow.

fol 10v The illustration to Psalm 18
The magenta cross of the nimbus.
The magenta lines in the sky.
fol. 11r The illustration to Psalm 19
Two magenta trees on the hill.
The turquoise top of another tree.
The magenta orb on which the Lord sits within the mandorla.
The magenta shading of the bricks.
fol. 11v The illustration to Psalm 20
The cross of the nimbus.
The turquoise added to the crown being placed on the Psalmist's head.
The turquoise additions to the hair of the Lord.
The turquoise tree on the left of the composition.
Three trees on the right.
fol. 12r The illustration to Psalm 21 (fig. 59, below, p. 127)
The magenta flags of the staffs of the angels.
The magenta mandorla of the Lord.
The cross behind the head of the Lord.
The magenta highlighting of the hillside.
The magenta landscape at the bottom of the illustration.
fol. 13v The illustration to Psalm 23
The three red trees.
The red tinting of the right gate tower.
The cross of the nimbus.
A touch of red tinting underneath the powerful king.
fol. 14r The illustration to Psalm 24
The torch of the Sun personification.
The cross of the nimbus.
The red bands on the urn.[55]
A red tree.
Small red traces in the sky.
fol. 14v The illustration to Psalm 25
The cross of the nimbus (here the outlines of the original nimbus, by artist C, are still visible).
fol. 16r The illustration to Psalm 28
The cross of the nimbus.
fol. 16v The illustration to Psalm 29 (fig. 56, below, p. 125)
The torch of the Sun personification.
The cross and shading of the nimbus.
The red dashes in the sky above the Manus Dei.
The three red trees.

[55] Carver, 'Contemporary artefacts', p. 136, attributes the bands on the urn to C.

The red and orange flashes in the hell pit.
The orange hook to the staff of the demon, that, in Utrecht, is holding a trident.
The touches on one of the angel's wings.
The blue touches on the top of the Lord's staff, adding a flag, and greatly enlarging the cross.
The blue landscape to the left and right.
The orange landscape below the Psalmist.
The two blue trees, and a blue sprout to a third.

fol. 17r The illustration to Psalm 30 (fig. 49, above, p. 100)
The blue tree.
The blue bottom of the pit.
The blue line around the sarcophagus.
Four windows in the city.
The blue touches to the right foreground.

fol. 17v (fig. 50, above, p. 102)
The entire composition.

fol. 18r The illustration to Psalm 31 (fig. 50, above, p. 102)
The red figure at the bottom left.
The red figure at the lower right behind the hillock.
One red fish, and highlights on two others.
The blue touches on the Lord's mandorla.
The blue touches on the hill to the left.
The green shading and the red cross of the nimbus.
The green highlighting of some figures on the right, and of the central landscape.

fol. 18v The illustration to Psalm 32
The cross of the nimbus.
The blue touches and the robe to one whole figure in the group of women at the bottom left.
The green tinting of the pediment and the green of the drape, which (now barely visible) was once drawn by artist B.
The green building on the left, not seen in Utrecht.
The water being poured out of the vessel.
The blue tinting on the body of the serpent rising out of the sea.

fol. 19r The illustration to Psalm 33
The green plant on the hill on the left.
The green plant on the hill on the right, not seen in Utrecht.

fol. 19v The illustration to Psalm 34
The red cross and green shading of the nimbus.
All the green shading in this illustration.

fol. 20v The illustration to Psalm 35
The cross of the nimbus.
The ochre landscape and architecture.

fol. 21r The illustration to Psalm 36

The cross of the nimbus.

fol. 22r The illustration to Psalm 37

All the touches of green.

fol. 22v The illustration to Psalm 38 (fig. 7, above, p. 30)

The cross of the nimbus.

The blue of the background landscape.

The blue of the arch on the left.

The blue shading in the house.

The blue base of the throne.

The blue around the pediment of the building on the right.

All the touches of green.

fol. 23r The illustration to Psalm 39

The magenta tree on the left.

The blue tree on the left.

All the touches of green.

fol. 24r The illustration to Psalm 40

All the green touches.

All the ochre touches.

fol. 24v The illustration to Psalm 41

The green touches to the tent.

fol. 25r The illustration to Psalm 43

All the blue elements.

fol. 27r The illustration to Psalm 46

The cross of the nimbus.

fol. 27v The illustration to Psalm 47

The weathercock on the turret.

The red sky line with a tree on it at the back right.

fol. 28r The illustration to Psalm 48 (fig. 48, above, p. 99)

The entire illustration, and the initial.

fol. 28v The illustration to Psalm 49

The entire illustration.

fol. 51v The illustration to Psalm 103 (fig. 53, above, p. 105)

The turquoise shading of the nimbus.

The turquoise emanations between Heaven and Earth.

The turquoise tree in the mountains to the left.

The two turquoise trees above the oxen.

The touches on the robes of the minister of the Lord pouring oil on the central figure behind the table.

The turquoise additions of foliage on the tree on the extreme left of the illustration.

The single, outlined leaf of the little plant at the extreme lower left.

fol. 54v The illustration to Psalm 106 (fig. 30, above, p. 64)

The magenta detailing of the chair on the right of the Psalmist.

A fish in the sea.

The magenta clothing of one of the men in the group at the top right.
The green plant.
Magenta flowers of one of the plants on the hill.

fol. 56r The illustration to Psalm 108
The green of the nimbus.

fol. 56v The illustration to Psalm 109
The blue of the Lord's seat on the left.

fol. 57r The illustration to Psalm 110 (fig. 28, above, p. 63)
The cross of the nimbus.
Two plants.
The capitals of the building.
Blue touches on the bowl born by the angel.

fol. 57v The illustration to Psalm 111
The blue tinting of the crust given to the beggar on the left.
The blue touches to the base of the throne.
The blue tinting to the foremost beggar's hair on the right.
The green tops to two plants above the hell pit, and a green plant to the left of the hell pit.

fol. 59r The illustration to Psalm 114 (fig. 35, above, p. 79)
The green tinting of the three trees on the right.
Psalm 115(i) (fig. 35, above, p. 79)
The green tinting of the figure holding the cup of salvation.

fol. 64r The illustration to Psalm 119 (fig. 66, below, p. 153)
The magenta tree.
The turquoise landscape.
The decoration of the shield of the Psalmist.

Altogether G is a fascinating character, and a much better 'doodler' than artist E. His sheer wizardry in assimilating himself into the compositions of other artists is evidence that Anglo-Saxon artists were able to reproduce styles as successfully in the middle of the eleventh century as they were in its early decades.

Artist G was clearly prepared to take great liberties with the exemplar, but his own full-page compositions in Harley indicate that he was very far removed from the approach seen in the work of artist F. In his additions G has in fact tried to balance out the very different character of the various artists of Harley, adding colour to those bare of it, and deviations from Utrecht in those illustrations that most adhered to it. He also tied the illustrations more closely to the text than was originally possible, and tried to complete those illustrations that were originally left unfinished. It is as if artist G analysed the manuscript in much the same way as this study has done, and tried to compensate for the very problems in the making of the manuscript that this study has examined.

Artist H

The work of artist H is normally considered separately from the other artists of the manuscript.[56] It should not be. The starting point for his style was that of artist G, from whom he took over. Wormald characterised the style of artist G as 'Revived Utrecht'.[57] That of artist H could perhaps be termed 'Revived Revived Utrecht'. The palette was essentially the same as G's, with almost exclusive use of red, blue and green, and the later artist started his illustrations on fol. 29r by attempting to emulate the earlier's technique. Broad strokes of colour were used by artist G to give more body to the figures than was given to those in the earliest illustrations in the Psalter, and wispy strokes were used to suggest movement and impression; in contrast to earlier artists, there is very little outline in any true sense of the term. However artist H could not emulate his predecessor: he did not have the same control of colour to indicate the bulk of his figures, and these figures are stiff by comparison. As he progressed, artist H wrestled to come to terms with a style that would blend with those of the rest of the manuscript, and yet with which he also felt comfortable: for the figure of the bishop in the illustration to Psalm 53 on fol. 29v, he gave up the relatively broad strokes of artist G in an attempt to gain greater clarity, and he used a multitude of thin blue strokes to articulate the bishop's clothing. The green, used almost as a wash on the figure of *insipiens* in the illustration to Psalm 52, also became progressively more tightly controlled. He struggled to capture the impressionism of artist G until fol. 32r, where a thin dark line was used to outline the chair legs, the dogs outside the wall, and to help articulate the Psalmist himself. It was dropped again until the uncoloured and unfinished illustration on fol. 34r, where not a black, but rather a soft brown outline is employed, which shows few traces of impressionism. In his approach to the composition of the illustrations, as in their style, artist H owed much to artist G: the number of figures was reduced, they were made larger, and the illustrations take up the entire available space. In his sketch for the never finished illustration to Psalm 66 for example, on fol. 34v, artist H placed the Lord centrally, bending over his scales, and thus provided a more satisfactory image than the rather lacklustre equivalent in Utrecht, where the centre of the composition is very weak, and the Lord is seen to the right. The result has been called 'infelicitous'.[58] It was certainly a struggle, and eventually the struggle was lost as the artist reverted to a thick outline. Furthermore, not one illustration is completely finished. But it is also punctuated by superb pieces of draughtsmanship, most notably in the 'Q' initial to Psalm 51 on fol. 29r, and the dogs outside the city walls on fol. 32r.

Gameson, in a lengthy study of this artist, was rather more positive in his interpretation of his contribution than Dufrenne, who considered his work maladroit and unoriginal, but who noted that the iconography in the illustration to Psalm 52 on fol. 29r was more elaborate than that of Utrecht (compare figs. 54 and 55).[59] It is clear

[56] Kauffmann, *Romanesque Manuscripts*, cat. 67. [57] Wormald, *English Drawings*, pp. 53–4.

[58] Dodwell, *Canterbury School*, p. 27.

[59] R. Gameson, 'The Romanesque artist', pp. 24–61, and S. Dufrenne, 'Les copies anglaises', pp. 189–90.

54 *The Utrecht Psalter, fol. 30v. The illustration to Psalm 52.*

that many differences between the illustrations to Psalm 52 in the Utrecht and Harley Psalters are the consequence of the Harley artist borrowing motifs from the illustration to Psalm 13, on fol. 7v of both Utrecht and Harley (see figs. 22 and 23, above, p. 55).[60]

The Utrecht Psalter's illustration to Psalm 52 is certainly very different from that of artist H. The figure of *insipiens* is seated cross-legged within a domed tempietto. His head rests upon his right hand, while his left clutches a sword pointing out to the left. Two men carrying swords and severed heads approach him from the left. A further figure lies crumpled at the foot of the platform upon which *insipiens* is seated. God himself is 'looking down from the heavens upon the sons of men', as demanded by verse 3 of the Psalm. The only attribute he has to signify his status is his cross-staff. To the lower left are the 'sons of men', not one of them doing good, as demanded by verse 4. The group to the lower right represents Israel, and the figure on the hill probably Jacob, from verse 7. The Psalmist is in the centre gesturing towards *insipiens* and looking up to God.

God himself is not nearly as clearly identified in the illustration to Psalm 52 of Utrecht as he is in that to Psalm 13, and this may have been felt all the more acutely because *insipiens* himself said *non est Deus.* Tselos has argued that the scratchy arc in the Utrecht Psalter below the figures of heaven in the illustration to Psalm 52 was derived from a clearly defined arc of heaven, which would have made God's status clearer; this was especially necessary in this Psalm illustration, as it is one of the few that does not depict God symmetrically flanked by the Company of Heaven.[61] The Harley artist reached his own solution and borrowed the idea of the mandorla from the very similar Psalm 13.

[60] As noted in Ohlgren, *Textual Illustration*, p. 29, and Gameson, 'The Romanesque artist', p. 45. Ohlgren says that the iconography is reproduced from fol. 7v (that is Psalm 13 of Harley), and Gameson that the iconography of Psalm 13 simply grafted.

[61] G.R. Benson & D.T. Tselos, 'New light on the origin of the Utrecht Psalter', *The Art Bulletin*, 13, 1931, pp. 13–79, at p. 76. Certainly the artist of Paris 8846 felt he had to introduce a more clearly defined 'Arc of Heaven' into this Psalm.

55 *The Harley Psalter, fol. 29r. The illustration to Psalm 52, by H.*

However, he has been careful to retain features of the composition to Psalm 52: the cross of the cross-staff of the Lord in the Utrecht illustration to Psalm 52 has been given to the Lord in Harley, and the angel that does the 'looking down', just as the Lord looked down in Utrecht, has been given the staff. As the figure of the Lord in the illustrations to Psalm 13 of both Psalters holds nothing, we can be sure that this change is a direct consequence of the Harley artist's thinking through of the implications of his iconographical borrowings upon the meaning of Psalm 52.

The reasons for this reliance on the iconography of Psalm 13 are not difficult to find. The Harley artist was illustrating a Roman text, which is even more like Psalm 13 than the Gallican.[62] In the Utrecht Psalter the iconography of Psalm 13 is more weighty than the liturgically more important Psalm 52. There was clearly a perceived need on the part of the Harley artist to add to the particularly reticent iconography of Psalm 52 in the Utrecht Psalter: the imagery of Psalm 13 was the most obvious starting point for iconographic accretion. Similar though these illustrations are, as Tselos has observed, where they are alike the text suggests that they should be different, and where they are dissimilar there is no textual justification for their dissimilarity.[63] This is partly the result of the fact that very often the images are not simply literal, but formulaic, and artist H played upon the formulae.

The artist of the Harley Psalter felt the need to embellish the iconography of the Fool in this Psalm as well. In the Harley version also, *insipiens* is seated. Unlike the Utrecht image, Harley's is crowned: his status as '*le mauvais prince*', as Dufrenne calls him, is

[62] It includes an extra *non est usque ad unum* in verse 2, like Psalm 13 in verse 1.

[63] D. Tselos, *The Sources of the Utrecht Psalter Miniatures*, Minneapolis, 1955, pp. 31–2.

articulated by an attribute.[64] His left hand now points with an extended finger out to his right to a winged figure with demonic features, peering out from behind the building and pointing with an extended finger back at him. In his right hand he holds the sword which points out to the left. His legs have been double-crossed, and the figure below the seat of *insipiens* in the Utrecht illustration has been activated, and now clutches his feet.

In a general sense the winged demon conversing with *insipiens* can be interpreted as the opposite of the Holy Spirit in the form of a dove who in the full page *Beatus* initial in the St Albans Psalter in Hildesheim, for example, inspires David as Psalmist.[65] Indeed, in the Utrecht Psalter's illustration to the Apocryphal Psalm, we find precisely this role being played; as David is anointed by an angel, the Spirit of the Lord having come down upon him, so Saul sits to the left of the composition, not with a bird-headed sceptre, but with a sceptre that seems to have some pagan deity *all'antica* at its head. This seems to correspond to the text of 1 Samuel ch. 16 v. 14., for when the Spirit of the Lord entered David, so

> The Spirit of the Lord departed from Saul, and an evil spirit from the Lord troubled him.

But what provoked the inclusion of such an evil muse, in this particular form, in the illustration to Psalm 52 in the Harley Psalter?

One phrase not found in Psalm 52, but which is in Psalm 13, verse 3 is:

> *uenenum aspidum sub labiis eorum.*[66]

This is illustrated in the image to Psalm 13 by two snakes which wind up the columns of the tempietto to the foolish man. There is every reason to connect our winged demon with these two snakes.[67] The snakes are not textually warranted in Psalm 52, and were not transposed from the illustration to Psalm 13, but we know that the Harley artist looked to the illustration to Psalm 13 and they do provide a visual cue for the demonic figure. This visual cue is clearly owed not to the illustration of Psalm 13 in the Utrecht Psalter, but to the corresponding illustration on fol. 7v of Harley. While the snakes of the illustration to Psalm 13 in Utrecht are literal interpretations to a phrase of the Psalm and therefore attributes of *insipiens*, in Harley, as we have seen, a more dynamic

[64] Dufrenne, 'Les copies anglaises', p. 190. *Insipiens* is crowned as a ruler: for pictorial parallels for crowns see M. Archibald, 'Coins', in G. Zarnecki *et al.*, *English Romanesque Art 1066–1200*, (Exhib. Cat.), London, 1984, pp. 320–41, p. 332, cat.417 (King Henry I), and p. 355, cat. 439, (King Stephen), and ills. on p. 331. Gameson, 'The Romanesque Artist', pp. 45–6, sees the depiction of the fool of Psalm 52 as a specifically anti-Jewish image, because of his headgear. There are two questions here. The first is whether a Jewish hat would make an image of *insipiens* specifically anti-Jewish. Images of Jewish fools are difficult to identify as anti–Jewish, because they are in part Jewish already: as Gameson rightly notes, the fool had had a Jewish streak in his complex character since the time of the Church fathers. The second is whether the hat is a Jewish hat. It seems no more specifically Jewish than that worn by the prince on the right of the bench in Harley's illustration to Psalm 112 on fol. 58r, and that of the king leading all the kings of the Earth in the illustration to Psalm 137 on fol 70v. Even hats that did look Jewish could carry other meanings as well; the Sun in Psalm 120 of Harley, on fol. 64v, sports a 'Jewish hat', but it is unlikely that the hat was employed to indicate that he sprang from the seed of Abraham. The fool of Harley's Psalm 52 is a prince wearing an exotic crown, and he is no more Jewish than the fool of Psalm 13.

[65] Illustrations of all the images in the St Albans Psalter in Hildesheim are found in O. Pächt, C.R. Dodwell, and F. Wormald, *The St Albans Psalter (Albani Psalter)*, London, 1960.

[66] The venom of asps is under their lips.

[67] This is also noted by Gameson, 'The Romanesque artist', p. 45. He does not give his reasons for his speculation in n. 108. The basis of the following analysis is to be found in W.G. Noel, 'The Making of BL Harley Mss. 2506 and 603', unpublished Ph.D. dissertation, Cambridge 1993, pp. 241–51.

relationship is set up. The snake on the left was eyeballing *insipiens*, which actually implied that it had demonic powers independent of him.[68] In the illustration to Psalm 52 in Harley the devil is leering at *insipiens* in just the same way as the snake in the illustration to Psalm 13. The puzzle is that there is no textual justification for this image. Not only is the phrase *uenenum aspidum sub labiis eorum*, not found in Psalm 13; also absent is the phrase

Non est timor dei ante oculos eorum[69]

Artist H also owes a debt to the other snake of artist A's illustration to Psalm 13. In the Harley Psalter, but not in Utrecht, the serpent on the right is whispering into the ear of *insipiens*, but in the illustration to Psalm 52 the statement is more overt and out in the open. Precisely those motifs of speaking and staring that were articulated by artist A and not found in Utrecht are here realised by artist H. Of course, artist H has embodied the malevolence of the two snakes into one demon, but the curtain hanging down to the right of *insipiens* and looping around the column, emulates the animated second serpent in the Harley illustration – something that the stringy creature of Utrecht could not suggest. The subtle changes wrought by artist A on the iconography of his Psalm 13 are here being acknowledged by an artist who, as we shall see, was working a hundred years later.

The relationship between the devil and *insipiens* is more elaborate than the relationship between the snakes and Insipiens in the illustration to Psalm 13 of Harley. The devil has provoked *insipiens* into speech, and his index finger is raised. Together, the figures are actually having a conversation.[70] This refers well to another phrase found in verse 3 of Psalm 13:

Quorum os maledictione et amaritudine plenum est[71]

And again, it is not found in Psalm 52. The fool's senses are being attacked, he does not have the fear of God before his eyes, he is speaking curses and hearing bitterness. In his speech, hearing and sight, he is reflecting what he is saying only in his heart: *non est Deus*.

If artist H was making textual parallels as he worked, he actually had to look no further than to the illustration to Psalm 5 of Harley for the qualities of his demon, on fol. 3r.[72] Here a similarly winged demon with flaming hair and a hirsute appearance is prancing above an open sepulchre to illustrate verse 11:

Sepulchrum patens est guttur eorum, linguis suis dolose agebant[73]

which is repeated in Psalm 13, but not in Psalm 52.[74]

[68] See above, chapter 1, p. 56. [69] There is no fear of God before their eyes.

[70] In this transformation, the image falls in well with the outline of the development of the fool in D. J. Gifford, 'Iconographical notes towards a definition of the medieval fool', *Journal of the Warburg and Courtauld Institutes*, 37, 1974, pp. 336–42, esp. p. 338. The fool as an evil prince superintending rapine and carnage is becoming the fool as disputant. [71] Their mouth is full of cursing and bitterness. [72] See above, chapter 1, pp. 57–9.

[73] Their throat is an open sepulchre, with their tongues they dealt deceitfully.

[74] Gameson, 'Romanesque artist', p. 45 gives other parallels for the figure of the demon. None are as close in their physical characteristics, or in their proximity to Psalm 13. We need look no further than the snakes of Psalm 13 in Harley for malevolent beings inspiring a human.

The imagery is developed yet further. The purpose of the crumpled man at the feet of *insipiens* in the illustration to Psalm 13 of Utrecht and Harley is not entirely clear. It may be to illustrate verse 3:

ueloces pedes eorum ad effundendum sanguinem.[75]

This figure turns up again in the illustration to Psalm 52 of the Utrecht Psalter, but he seems to be an iconographic hangover from the earlier Psalm: there is no textual justification for him. As this figure is employed in the illustration to Psalm 52 of Harley, however, he has been given a role and a decapitated companion. There can be no doubt about the text that is being referred to. The feet of *insipiens* are speedy indeed, having been double crossed, they tread on the hands of the man whose blood he is spilling. One of his evil minions is also treading on the newly introduced decapitated corpse. Yet again, this phrase is not found in Psalm 52, but it is in verse 3 of Psalm 13.

In the Utrecht illustration to Psalm 52, the two figures to the bottom left of the illustration are fighting each other over a woman, with a long pole. This is very similar to the Utrecht illustration to Psalm 13. We have seen that artist A, in his illustration to Psalm 13, no longer has the two figures tugging over the woman, whose arms are comparatively relaxed, but rather they are sawing her in half.[76] Since artist A looked to illustration to Psalm 13 in Harley, as well as to that of Psalm 52 in Utrecht, it seems very likely that artist H took inspiration from the work of artist A in making the figure in the middle, not the subject of a possessive battle, but the joint object of persecution, and this time not by sawing, but by stoning. Moreover, while artist H has changed the sex of this figure, since the scene is no longer one of rape but rather one of martyrdom, its head is closer to the head of the woman in the illustration to Psalm 13 of Harley than to the illustrations of either Psalm in Utrecht.[77] Just as artist A did, artist H has used a different device from Utrecht. Like all the other characteristics of foolishness that artist H has devised, this one helps illustrate another phrase not found in Psalm 52

Contritio et infelicitas in uiis eorum, et uiam pacis non cognouerunt.[78]

I suggest that in his illustration to Psalm 52, artist H's intention was to elaborate upon the qualities of *insipiens*. These are largely left unstated in Psalm 52 where we find his actions, but not his characteristics. They are found in all that part of verse 3 that is not found in Psalm 52. There is something deliberately allusive about the iconography, which is perhaps the best way to deal with a figure as elusive as *insipiens*. But nonetheless, this image, like others of the time, is heavy in the weight of its mysteries.[79]

The relationship that the fool of Psalm 52 has with a demon in Harley was to be a popular subject in Psalter illustration of the later Middle Ages.[80] An early example, one

[75] Their feet are swift to shed blood. [76] See above, chapter 1, p. 53.

[77] The Paris 8846 artist also rationalises this illustration as two people fighting over one: this time, it is not a saw that is being used, nor stones, but rather the two figures to the sides are seemingly pulling the central character apart.

[78] Grief and misfortune in their ways, and the way of peace they have not known.

[79] See T.A. Heslop, "Brief in words, but heavy in the weight of its mysteries", *Art History*, 9, 1986, pp. 1–11, *passim*.

[80] The role of the fool in Medieval art and drama is to be discussed in a forthcoming publication by Professor V.A. Kolve.

wonders whether the Harley artist is following a broader development, or instigating it. The illustration to Psalm 38, *Dixi custodiam*, on fol. 55r of the 'Little Canterbury Psalter' (Paris, BN Ms. Lat. 770), is particularly similar to it in iconography.[81] The illustration to Psalm 38 is in two parts: on the right is a king, seated, before a demon; on the left is a scene of execution. The former has the king not taking care of his ways, and sinning with his tongue, in contrast to the first words of the Psalm:

Dixi custodiam uias meas
ut non delinquam in lingua mea
posui ori meo custodiam
dum consisteret peccator aduersum me[82]

Caviness identifies this scene as Saul plotting the death of David, which would certainly fit into her narrative framework. But her explanation for the scene on the left is unconvincing. The title of the Psalm, she says, promises that Christ will lay hold of us because of our sins and correct us, and the pictorial commentary interprets this as a threat to evil kings.[83] However, elsewhere in this Psalter the commentary has no part to play in the iconography, the figure being executed is not a king, and the picture has few trappings of the divine. The scene would seem far more likely to be the physical consequence of the king's speech – the brutal murder of an innocent – rather than a scene of speculated, and divinely instigated, regicide. In the illustration to Psalm 52 in Harley we find similar motifs expressing a similar idea: a devil is provoking a ruler into speech, and to the left are scenes of execution. The two thugs are similar to the representations of Psalm 13 and 52 in the Utrecht Psalter tradition, yet only in the Harley Psalter is the snake, an attribute of *insipiens*, turned into a demon, debating with *insipiens*, in Psalm 52.[84]

In the illustration to Psalm 52 it is no longer clear which is the exemplar – the Utrecht Psalter, or the earlier illustrations in Harley. In later illustrations, where there is no such immediate parallel with illustrations executed earlier in the book, artist H adhered more closely to the Utrecht Psalter itself, although he still had reference to other sources for his illustrations.[85] However, artist H is a good artist with which to finish this survey.

81 See M.H. Caviness, 'Conflicts between *Regnum* and *Sacerdotium* as reflected in a Canterbury Psalter of ca. 1215', *The Art Bulletin*, 61, 1979, pp. 38–58, and fig. 8 at p. 43. Caviness argued that this Psalter, made *c.* 1210–20 at Christ Church, has a pictorial cycle which programmatically sets out to illustrate the conflict between *Regnum* and *Sacerdotium*, a subject of great relevance to the community at Christ Church from the time of Becket until after the death of King John. For this manuscript see also Avril and Stirnemann, *Manuscrits enluminés*, pp. 52–3; see also Morgan, *Early Gothic Mss. (1)*, Cat 34, pp. 83–4.

82 I said I will take heed to my ways, that I sin not with my tongue. I have set a guard to my mouth, when the sinner stood against me.

83 Caviness, 'Conflicts', p. 42.

84 Quite what the scene represents, if it is more than an example of bad kingship in a generic sense, is difficult to determine; there is no suitable subject that will fit into Caviness's narrative sequence. The subject of Psalm 26 is Saul throwing a spear at David; the next Old Testament subject, at Psalm 52 is David receiving the bread and sword at Nob. A possible interpretation of the scene under discussion is David ordering the death of Urias the Hethite, and Urias' death (2 Kings, chapter 11).

85 Kauffmann, *Romanesque Mss.*, Cat 67, p. 96, observed that the priest of Psalm 53 in Utrecht has been turned by artist H into a bishop. See also Gameson, 'The Romanesque artist', p. 41. On pp. 38–9 Gameson also draws a parallel between artist H's sketch of the Lord riding on his chariot in Psalm 67, and the depiction of Luxuria's overturned chariot in illustrations to Prudentius, *Psychomachia*. See also below, chapter 4, p. 164 for a relationship with the Bury Psalter.

Although in the past he has been considered a 'copyist' of the Utrecht Psalter, in fact he demonstrates that the programme of Harley has nearly turned full circle: it is finally the earlier work of the Harley Psalter, as much as the Utrecht Psalter, which informs his style and iconographic subtleties, and it could be to the artists of the Harley Psalter, as well as to those of the Utrecht Psalter, that later Medieval artists looked for inspiration.

Conclusion to chapter 2

Duffey is the only scholar to have analysed the planning of the illustrated pages of Harley in any detail, and her opinions can be significantly modified.[86] She supposed that the scribes were responsible for the planning of all the illustrated pages, because on some folios the text is finished, whereas the illustrations are incomplete.[87] As we have seen, in quires 1, 4, and 9, the artists were responsible for the ruling pattern, although in quire 9 there is a case to be made for supposing that the artist and the scribe of fols. 50r–54r/a/23 are the same. In her analysis Duffey goes so far as to state the following:

> That some of the illustrations as well as the spaces for them may have been completed prior to the text raises the question of how far the artist and scribe worked together in planning.[88]

But because she never allows for the fact that the artists were in charge of the ruling pattern in some of the quires of the Psalter, she does not appreciate the importance of scribal ascendancy in determining the characteristics of quires 10–11 and 5–8. In marked contrast to the quires examined in the last chapter, the illustrations had to fit into a mould set by the text, and not vice versa, and the mould set by the text was not that of the Utrecht Psalter.

Scribe 1 seems not to have paid any attention to the Utrecht Psalter layout. Even in the first few folios of quire 10, where the Harley layout is similar to Utrecht, this seems to have been simply coincidental. Artist F, for his part, may have had little choice in the decision not to follow the Utrecht compositions closely, and he began by basing his illustrations closely on the ideas of Utrecht's imagery; it was only later that he had the confidence to depart more radically from the Utrecht compositions. However, in marked contrast to scribe 1 in quires 10 and 11, in quires 5–8 Eadui believed that Utrecht was an excellent vehicle upon which the artists could base their illustrations. The artists, for their part, agreed with him.

Before we work out why so many different techniques were employed to make the Harley Psalter, we should discuss how the various quires relate to each other, and examine when and where they were made.

[86] Duffey, 'Inventive group', pp. 13 and forward. [87] Ibid., pp. 14–15. [88] Ibid., pp. 18–19.

3

The origin and dates of the Harley Psalter

In the preceding two chapters I examined the making of the Harley Psalter by analysing the techniques by which its various quires were made. We are now in a position to sort out the sequence of production of the quires, to date them, and to discuss where they were made.

The sequence of production

Quires 5–8

Quires 5–8 were written by Eadui Basan. Quire 5 starts on fol. 28r, and quire 8 ends on fol. 49v (see fig. 48, above, p. 99, and fig. 46, above, p. 97). The juxtaposition between fol. 49v and fol. 50r (fig. 32) is particularly dramatic, and immediately arouses the suspicion that this whole section was written after the section that follows it.[1] Not only were many of the illustrations to these quires never even started, but also Eadui's text was never finished. Although he executed his own *tituli*, and added Psalm divisions at Psalm 68, verse 16, and Psalm 77, verse 36, verse capitals and Psalm initials were never added to his text. He also left the first few lines of text to Psalm 51 on fol. 29r to be written in display script, like those of Psalm 1 on fol. 2r, and they were never written. It is conceivable that Eadui intended to complete the rubrication himself. Certainly that is how scribe D2 operated. But the rubrication of scribe 1's text is unlikely to have been done by scribe 1, since it was not part of the same operation. The rubrication of scribe 1's text followed after artist F's illustrations, and these were, in their turn, executed after the text. Thus, in Psalm 128, on fol. 67r (fig. 39, above, p. 84), the 'C' of *canticum* was written over the legs of one of the builders; and in Psalm 129, on fol. 67v, the 'G' of *graduum* was written over the toes of a figure; in Psalm 131, on fol. 68r, the last numeral of the *titulus* was written over the ground; in Psalm 139, on fol. 71v, the *titulus* was written over the hell mouth, while the main text was written underneath it; and in Psalm 140, on fol. 72r,

[1] Fol. 27v is shown next to fol. 28r, and fol. 49v is shown next to fol. 50r in W.G. Noel, 'The division of work in the Harley Psalter', in Linda L. Brownrigg (ed.) *Making the Medieval Book: Techniques of Production*, Los Altos Hills, 1995, pp. 1–15, figs. 3, 5, 7 and 9.

the second D of *David* was written over the toes of the flogged man (fig. 41, above, p. 86).

It seems far more likely that the rubricator to scribe 1's text was artist E. He also worked after artist F, but whether he worked before or consecutively with the rubricator is not so clear: on fol. 15r, which has an illustration partly by E, the *tituli* do not follow the lines ruled by the scribe, but rather a 'marginal ruling' left there by an artist ruler for his illustration. Here the rubrics act as a support for E's illustration, and it is just possible that the illustration was executed after the rubric. Artist E's compositions are executed in two tones, a dark scribal ink, and a rather lighter one.[2] The lighter tone sometimes seems identical to that of the rubrics.[3] The character of artist E's work adds further weight to this hypothesis. He appears only very infrequently until Psalm 118. Having avoided 'space filling' in general, it was the spaces in this Psalm that he chose to articulate, and to make clear a page layout that is, at best, difficult to read. As Gameson points out, what is most remarkable about artist E is that he gained access to the book at all.[4] There was certainly no great want of talented artists in Canterbury, and yet artist E was far from being a great draughtsman. We are looking for someone with artistically unwarranted access to the book. I think it safe to conclude that artist E did not get his hands on the book through artistic excellence, but first and foremost in his capacity as rubricator, and that the illustrations are his increasingly bold experiments as he works through the book. Backhouse supposed that the absence of artist E in Eadui's quires indicated in itself that they were later than those of the rest of the manuscript.[5] While it could be claimed that E's illustrations are too unsystematic to be certain, the fact the rubricator of the manuscript did not work on Eadui's unfinished text, suggests strongly that Eadui's quires were indeed written later.

The same can be said of the initial letters to the Psalms. The initials that accompany scribe 1's script are also very different in character to those on fols. 50r–53v. They are the work of two hands, and they do not correspond to the other artistic divisions in the manuscript. This is not surprising as they were, in terms of the order of production, physically distant from it. The earlier of the two hands executed the initial to Psalm 101, on fol. 50r, which was written over an erasure of an initial D that was originally executed by D2 (fig. 32, above, p. 71). This complex initial is not well executed, and it is made up of composite elements bounded by a solid line. One characteristic is a garish green. These same elements, and this same hue, are to be seen in the *Beatus* initial to Psalm 1, on fol. 2r (fig. 1, above, p. 4). The artist of the initial also seems to have been responsible for the first few inept lines of display script. Despite the lacklustre beasts heads and the pedestrian foliage in the initial, the figures of the Lord and of the archbishop are rather accomplished. Rather than divide the Beatus initial into the work of two artists, I ascribe the Trinity illustration, sublime in its conception, but surprisingly crude in execution of its architectural elements, to the same hand, artist I. The rest of the initials to scribe 1's text were executed by another

[2] There is but one exception to this: on fol. 15r one of the horsemen is depicted in green.

[3] For this reason alone Duffey ascribes the drawings by E to the rubricator – see Duffey, 'Inventive group', pp. 209–10.

[4] Gameson, 'Anglo-Saxon artists', p. 33. He speculates that artist E was either a scribe or the archbishop depicted on fol. 2r in the *Beatus* initial.

[5] Backhouse, 'Making', p. 105.

hand, artist J, who seems to have borrowed the decorative vocabulary of artist I for the initial to Psalm 119 on fol. 64r.[6] These initials were executed after the *tituli* to these quires: the 'I' initial of Psalm 30, on fol. 17r, was worked around the verse capitals in column a; and the 'B' of *Bonitatem* which begins Teth's section of Psalm 118, on fol. 62r, was worked around the Q, executed by E, which begins the verse directly above. This initials artist was a talented draughtsman, of a character quite unlike artist E, or artist I. Impressive examples of his flair are the dragon-tailed Q to Psalm 124 on fol. 66r; the dragon-headed initial to Psalm 35, *Dixit iniustus*, on fol. 20v, which rises to speak to the iniquitous in the illustration; and the dragon-headed L to Psalm 116, *Laudate dominum*, on fol. 60r, which is looking to praise the Lord in the illustration to Psalm 115 on fol. 59v.

Therefore two hands, E and J, that articulated the text in all the other quires of the book, and another, I, that worked in quires 1 and 9, are not found in Eadui's section. These hands worked after quires 1–5 and 9–11 had otherwise been finished, and, we can be sure, before Eadui's text was written.

It can, then, be argued that Eadui's text was written later because hands found elsewhere in the manuscript are not found in Eadui's section. The same point can be made by the reverse procedure: hands present in Eadui's section are found adding to quires that had already been completed. It was probably Eadui who corrected scribe 1's text throughout the manuscript, and artist G, who began illustrating Eadui's section, is found adding details to the work of all the other artists.

The most conclusive evidence that Eadui's text was started after quire 9 had been started comes from the quire arrangement of the volume, which indicates that Eadui's section bridged a gap between quires 4 and 9. However one reconstructs Eadui's section, his last quire, quire 8, ending on fol. 49v, cannot have been a regular one of eight leaves.[7] It was an irregular quire because it had to come to an end with the illustration space to Psalm 100, the text of this Psalm already having been written by scribe D2 on fol. 50r. The internal evidence that Eadui's quires were written after all the other quires in the book is unequivocal, and this is despite the fact that they are found in the centre of the book.

Humphrey Wanley was the first to note that Eadui's script was written later than that of the rest of the manuscript.[8] He, like Janet Backhouse, supposed that the manuscript was damaged, and then repaired.[9] However, it is extremely difficult to see how a once completed manuscript could have had its central folios so damaged that they were beyond repair without leaving a single sign of such damage on the immediately preceding and subsequent folios, fols. 27v and 50r. Furthermore, it is remarkable that the supposed damage coincides precisely with perfectly regular quire divisions: it would have to be supposed that this were simply coincidence, or that quires only partly damaged were excised from the manuscript. Both are unlikely. Another solution is needed, and to uncover it we have to return to the beginning of the book.

[6] Ibid., p. 108, noted that the foliage in the *Beatus* initial is similar to that of the initial to Psalm 119, on fol. 64r.

[7] See above, introduction, p. 17, and Appendix 2, p. 214

[8] See Noel, 'The division of work', p. 9.

[9] Backhouse, 'Making', pp. 105–6.

The early artists

Towards the end of quire 1 artist A began to omit iconographically significant details from his illustrations. Though minor slips occur throughout the quire, the first psalm illustration that can be characterised as unfinished is that to Psalm 10, on fol. 6r.[10] But apart from this folio, which we have seen is unsatisfactory in its layout, it is not until fol. 8r that we see significant errors, and we should understand artist G as trying to finish the illustration to Psalm 15 (fig. 19, above, p. 47).[11] These omissions continue in artist A's illustrations in the next quire. For example, in the illustration to Psalm 17 on fol. 9r, the artist omitted to depict the stones on the altar of the Lord, the wings of the wind upon which the Lord flies, and the flail which in Utrecht is carried by the right-hand angel descending to the Psalmist in the centre of the composition.

From the brilliant heights of the first few folios this gradual decline in the work of artist A can be traced in other ways. From the illustration to Psalm 15 on fol. 8r onwards his treatment of landscape became more cursory: from the energised torrent of strokes that articulated the landscape on fol. 3v, he moved to outline only, and on fol. 10v even this outline was barely sketched in. This is symptomatic of a much more illuminating trend in artist A's work: he ceased to adapt the spatial relationships of his figures from those prearranged in the Utrecht Psalter, and therefore no longer needed to depict the figures first, the buildings second, and finally the landscape around them. Indeed his illustrations on fols. 11r, 11v, 16r, and 16v reflect the Utrecht landscape reasonably closely (compare figs. 56 and 57). The whole attitude of this artist to his work was slowly changing.

Artist A's use of colour also became far less ambitious as his work progressed. The angel destroying the enemies in the illustration to Psalm 8 on fol. 4v has a blue undergarment and a green cloak; the details of his limbs are delineated in a thin dark brown, and substance is given to his wings with a buff-coloured brown. On fol. 8v the green is dropped from the range of colours, and while blue is still used for the background on the right-hand side of the illustration on fol. 9r, the bodies are simply brown. His illustrations on the bifolium 11/16 are even simpler, and that on fol. 16v was originally monochrome; there is some blue and some red in the background, but these are later additions by artist G.[12] In all these characteristics artist A seems to be approximating more closely to the technique of artist B in quire 4.

Furthermore, there is less detail in artist A's work in quire 2: compare, for example, the relatively cursory treatment of the demonic figures in the illustration to Psalm 29 on fol. 16v with those in that to Psalm 6 on fol. 3v (fig. 57, above, p. 125, and fig. 16, above, p. 45). Artist A degenerated so much that artist E felt it necessary to add to his work – a figure and some landscape to the left of the central table in the illustration to Psalm 16 on fol. 8v, and the chariot – if not associated figures – in the illustration to Psalm 19, on fol. 11r.

In his illustrations artist A seems to have executed quire 1 before quire 2, and to have

[10] See above, chapter 1, pp. 56–7. [11] See above, chapter 2, p. 107. [12] See above, chapter 2, pp. 109–110.

56 *The Utrecht Psalter, fol. 16v. The illustration to Psalm 29.*

57 *The Harley Psalter, fol. 16v. The illustration to Psalm 29, by A, with additions by G.*

started quire 2 working by the Psalm. Thus from fol. 9r he did not illustrate fol. 17r, but moved on to fol. 10v. However, he also illustrated a bifolium, fols. 11 and 16, executing 11 before 16.

If artist A finished his stint of work in quire 2, artist B started his work in Harley on the same quire. The illustration on fol. 17r is artist B's weakest (fig. 49, above, p. 100). The question is whether this reveals him as a raw novice yet to come to terms with his task, which he so clearly did in quire 4, or whether this is one of his last illustrations, executed quickly. Looking at his work in quires 3 and 4, this illustration would seem to be rather the tentative beginnings of his work on the Psalter, and to imply that he had yet to settle down in quire 3, and only to achieve a stylistic integrity of his own in the fourth. On fol. 17r, for example, artist B tried to emulate the impressionism of the model, suggesting multiplicity by a lack of clarity in definition. Thus the spears of the group just below and to the right of the building are, as in Utrecht, sketchy in detail – a mass of lines on the page that do no more than imply their form. But by fol. 24v in Harley, the point of each spear is filled in with an inky black. They have become clearly elucidated spear heads and are much more tangible as a result, making a staccato pattern across the face of the page which relates his work in terms of style to the work of artist A. Indeed we can see the development in his treatment of spears on fol. 18r (fig. 50, above p. 102); those on the left reflect his treatment of them on fol. 17r, while those on the right are more like those on fol. 24v. This change is consistent with his use in quire 4 of a much darker pigment than he ever employs in fol. 17r, and which he only occasionally uses on fol. 18r. In terms of figure articulation also, on fol. 19r, B was still experimenting as he attempted to come to terms with the style of Utrecht, and here he employed a rather darker ink than on fol. 17r, but the figures are still articulated by a multitude of short, cropped strokes. It was only in quire 4 that he settled down to a consistent style. Moreover, as he developed his style, his colour range became wider. The monochrome illustration on fol. 17r is the exception; on later folios he used a darker base colour than that which he employed on fol. 17r, and complemented it with a ruddy brown. In short, quire 3 seems to be an exploratory precursor to quire 4, and the illustration on fol. 17r is a prelude to both. It is not surprising, therefore, that the clarity with which he conveyed the Utrecht images in quire 4, is missing on fol. 17r. Fol. 17r was not the work of a master craftsman losing interest in his task, but that of a novice struggling to come to terms with his exemplar.[13]

In general terms then, it seems that quire 2 was begun after quire 1, but before quires 3 and 4. But artist B also started the bifolium 12–15, and to place his work here is a rather more difficult matter (compare figs. 58 and 59). We cannot use the spears as a guide to his development because, although they are solid, they are likewise in the exemplar, which was at this point illustrated by a different hand.[14] They were executed after the illustration on fol. 17r, because they are executed in two colours, but they exhibit none of the mastery of definition shown in later folios. This being the case, it is strange that he did not complete the bifolium 12/15, while he did complete quires 3 and 4. Artist E completed the illustration on fol. 15r, and was entirely responsible for that on fol. 15v,[15] and artist G added extensively to the illustration on fol. 12r.[16]

[13] Duffey, 'Inventive group', p. 225, supposes that B is an older, well-tried artist, and states that 'perhaps his peculiar fuzziness of line is in part shakiness of age, part quirky reluctance to give up a favourite pen'. There is little to substantiate this suggestion.

[14] See Gaehde, 'Utrecht Psalter draughtsmen', p. 50 – his artist B.

[15] J. Kiff, 'Images of war: illustrations of warfare in early eleventh-century England', *Anglo-Norman Studies*, 7, 1985, pp. 177–94, at p. 184, confuses Wormald's attributions for fol. 15r, and attributes the lower half of the drawing to artist B. Artist B did the upper half, artist E the lower half.

[16] See above, chapter 2, p. 109.

58 *The Utrecht Psalter, fol. 12r. The illustration to Psalm 21.*

59 *The Harley Psalter, fol. 12r. The illustration to Psalm 21, by B, with additions by G*

Another problem concerns the appearance of the bifolium 13–14. This is normally attributed to artist C, but this artist's very identity has been brought into question by Janet Backhouse, who thought that his work was actually by artist A.[17] Although it is certainly very different to artist A's work in quire 1, it is much more similar to his work in quire 2. A's last illustrations are executed largely in one colour like those on the bifolium 13–14, and, as a logical consequence of his following its landscape and

[17] Backhouse, 'Making', p. 99.

60 *The Utrecht Psalter, fol. 14v. A detail of the illustration to Psalm 25.*

composition much more accurately, he preserved the illusion of depth seen in Utrecht's illustrations. I nonetheless consider artists A and C to be two separate hands. The important difference between the illustrations on fols. 13r, 13v, 14r, and 14v, and the work of artist A, is really in the type of pen used, and in the colour of the pigment. Even in his later work, artist A preserved the sharp delineative crispness of his pen and his stark base colour. The artist of the bifolium 13/14 had an altogether softer touch, and this is symptomatic of a totally different attitude to the Utrecht images. Of all the Harley artists, including artist D2, artist C was the only one to be interested in the fall of light. The others treated shade either as blackness, or as an excuse for another colour, or they ignored it altogether. Artist C set out to recapture it. The shading around the turrets of the walled town on fol. 13v, the modelled falling of light on the head of naked tethered figure in the centre of the illustration on fol. 14v (compare figs. 60 and 61), and the underbellies of the sheep and goats on fol. 13r, all bear witness to this interest. Artist A was never interested in the fall of light to articulate bulk. In the Utrecht Psalter, the goats next to the altar on fol. 11r, the lion on fol. 8v, and the sepulchre in the lower illustration on fol. 8r are all heavily shaded, but artist A did not recapture the same effect. Although the mannerisms of these two artists are very similar, the sensitivity to Utrecht's tones on the bifolium 13/14 indicates that we should probably envisage three artists, and not two, working by the bifolium in this quire.

The relationship of artists D2 and F to the other hands is problematic. Artist F's work is entirely confined to quires 10 and 11, and artist D2's work was entirely confined to

61 *The Harley Psalter, fol. 14v. A detail of the illustration to Psalm 25, by C.*

quire 9. Artists A, B, and C did not contribute to these quires. No account of artistic practice alone can elucidate where, in the sequence of production, they are to be placed. However the observation that artist D was scribe 2 suggests that more might be learnt of the relationship between these quires by an analysis of scribal practice.

The early scribes

The one hand common to quires 1–4 and 9–11 is scribe 1, and in retrospect we can see how his practice developed as he wrote out the Psalter text. We have seen that, in the first quire, the artist-ruler made concessions to the problems of spacing that the scribe would inevitably face. However, when confronted with an obvious scribal problem on fol. 6r, the scribe did not try to end his text on fol. 5v, as we have seen he tried to do in quire 4, for example on fol. 24v. Taken with the fact that the illustrations were drawn before the text was written, and that those in quire 1 were executed before those in quire 4, this may be used as corroborative evidence that he wrote quire 1 before he wrote quire 4. It is as if only when the artists failed to take account of the scribe did scribe 1 slowly develop his own way of tackling the increasingly evident problem of spacing his text.

The artist-scribe D2 started on fol. 50r, and with a fundamentally different premise from scribe 1 – that the Gallican Utrecht Psalter text should be followed as closely as possible. One possible reason for following Utrecht line by line is precisely that in doing so scribe D2 knew that he would thereby avoid the difficulties faced by scribe 1 in the first quire, and this might imply that scribe D2 started work after scribe 1.[18] We would certainly not expect the project to have started at Psalm 101 rather than Psalm 1.

When scribe 1 took over from scribe D2, on fol. 54r, the text was once again written out without thought to the space that it was supposed to occupy. The result is that on fol. 54v the text is 4, 4, and 2 lines short of the following illustration in columns a, b, and c. Scribe 1 was a slow learner! But he did eventually learn: for the text of the rest of the Psalms in this quire, he did try to space out his text to achieve a felicitous physical relationship between text and illustration. There is, however, no evidence that he used the Utrecht Psalter to do so. Rather he seems to have worked by the verse, justifying all but the last line of any given verse, which frequently contains only one word. The amount of text space that the script occupied was similar. Thus, at the top of fol. 55v, he was only one line short of the illustration. However he never fully came to grips with this difficulty – hence the problem at the top of fol. 56r, already referred to.[19] Similarly on fol. 56v he decided to leave out the bottom line ruled in columns a and b, only to find that he had to compress his text densely in column c. At no point in the first four quires did scribe 1 try to 'stretch' his text as he did here, and this indicates that he wrote his section of quire 9 after he had written the first four quires. It would seem, therefore, that the artist/scribe D2's work was executed either very shortly after scribe 1 had started on the manuscript, or at the very same time.

Although it is clear that the last two quires of the manuscript were completed before Eadui's section was started, they still have to be placed in relation to quires 1–4 and 9. They surely must be placed after them. Certainly quire 10 could not have been started until after quire 9 hade been planned, because scribe 1 would not otherwise have known to start it by leaving an illustration space for Psalm 112 at the top of fol. 58r. There is no reason to think that scribe 1's work in quire 10 is anything other than consecutive to his work in quire 9. Artist F therefore worked after artists A–D2.

Codicological considerations

In the first four quires, the artists illustrated before the scribes wrote, and, this might account for the appearance of quire 2. I suggest that the scribe was in fact so much faster at writing than the artists were at illustrating, that the characteristics of quire 2 might be seen as the result of an attempt to speed up artistic procedure. Work was divided amongst the three artists, each artist being responsible for a bifolium. I also suggest that artist B did not finish his bifolium of quire 2 because the scribe needed to write on it. This hypothesis is substantiated by a consideration of the ruling pattern in this quire.

18 The scribe of the Salisbury Psalter, Salisbury Cathedral Ms. 150, also copied his exemplar line by line; see C. and K. Sisam, *The Salisbury Psalter*, p. 2.
19 See above, chapter 1, p. 68.

The ruling pattern in quire 2 adheres much more closely to that of Utrecht than does quire 1. Indeed, while still occasionally employing those ruling lines that extend into the outer lateral margins of the folios, seen in the first quire and quire 9, it approaches the precision of quire 4. Artistic responses to the ruling pattern varied considerably however: on fol. 9r, artist A overruled the ruling pattern by two lines; artist C, having followed the margin ruling which delimits his illustration space on fol. 13r exactly, on fol. 14v made his composition adhere to the upper limit, but drop way below the lower ruling; and artist B, on fol. 17r, adhered to the ruling absolutely. Different responses by different artists should not disguise the fact that the ruling pattern, as originally conceived, followed the Utrecht Psalter. It is unlikely that this pattern was constructed primarily with the scribe in mind. Certainly it did not help the scribe, who had a greater problem in integrating text and illustration than he did in quire 1. As with the ruling in quires 1, 4, and 9, it seems more likely that the ruling was executed with a view to the illustrations being executed first and the text second, and therefore by the artists illustrating their respective bifolia.

Nevertheless, there is one very revealing oddity in the ruling of this quire: although in general care was taken that the illustration spaces were left free of ruled lines, on fol. 15v the ruling runs right through the illustration space to Psalm 27.[20] It is this Psalm illustration that was entirely undertaken at a later date by artist E, who illustrated around a prewritten text, and it seems likely that the fact that the ruling pattern ignores the illustration space is in some way related to this (compare figs. 62 and 63). I suggest that since the artist had not illustrated this folio, he had not ruled it either, and that in fact the scribe ruled it, ignoring the illustration space. As we have seen, this is precisely what he did when he ruled quires 10 and 11.[21] It is no coincidence therefore that on this folio, in columns a and b, above what is now the illustration, uniquely in this quire, the text extends one line below its position in the Utrecht Psalter, and is consequently much shorter in column c: the scribe was not guided by a pre-existing ruling pattern, nor by an illustration. This evidence of the scribe as ruler on this folio may be explained if, as I have suggested, he was catching up in his writing with the artists in their drawing.

Yet if the hypothesis that work in the quire was divided up amongst artists working on their respective bifolios in order to expedite its production is plausible, then some physical realities must be borne in mind. For example, artist A could not work at the same time as artist C, because they would be in each other's way all the time, unless, of course, the Utrecht Psalter was at this point unbound, the bifolia of its second quire separated, and given to the different artists. If this were the case, then the unbound folios of Utrecht would have to match the folios to be illustrated by the separate artists in Harley. It is remarkable that they do. The Utrecht Psalter is constructed in quires of 8, except for the first folio, which is a singleton. Thus the first quire of Harley, which is a regular 8 including the first folio, does not coincide with that of Utrecht. However, because fol. 10 is a singleton, the bifolium 13/14 which artist C illustrated is also a

[20] The ruling pattern on this folio is confused, as it is on many other folios, presumably because lines were not drawn right across the page between the two sets of pricks.

[21] See above, chapter 2, pp. 76–77.

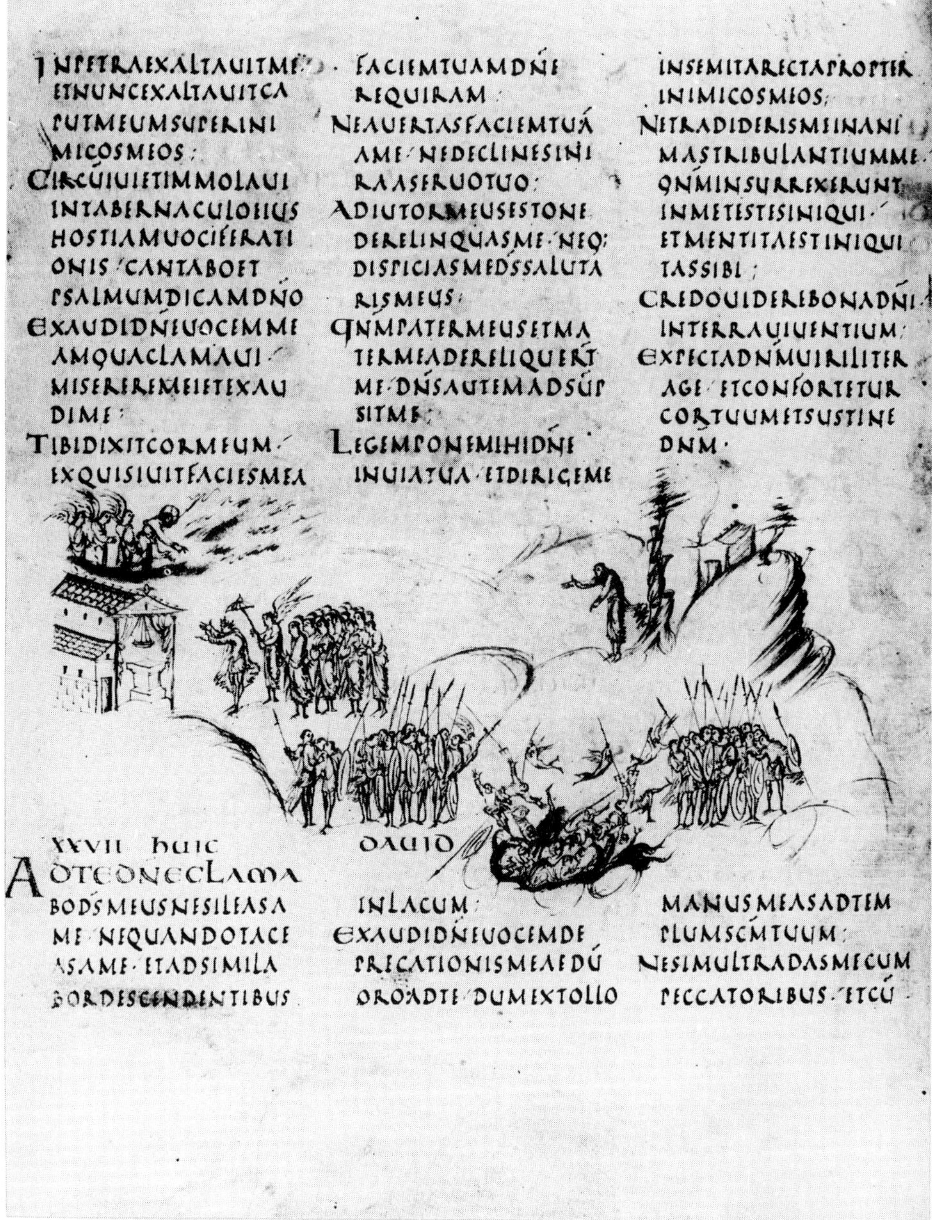

INPETRAEXALTAUITME
ETNUNCEXALTAUITCA
PUTMEUMSUPERINI
MICOSMEOS;
CIRCUIUIETIMMOLAUI
INTABERNACULOEIUS
HOSTIAMUOCIFERATI
ONIS CANTABOET
PSALMUMDICAMDNO
EXAUDIDNEUOCEMME
AMQUACLAMAUI
MISEREREMEIETEXAU
DIME
TIBIDIXITCORMEUM
EXQUISIUITFACIESMEA
FACIEMTUAMDNE
REQUIRAM
NEAUERTASFACIEMTUA
AME NEDECLINESINI
RAASERUOTUO
ADIUTORMEUSESTONE
DERELINQUASME NEQ;
DISPICIASMEDSSALUTA
RISMEUS
QNMPATERMEUSETMA
TERMEADERELIQUERT
ME DNSAUTEMADSUP
SITME
LEGEMPONEMIHIDNE
INUIATUA ETDIRIGEME
INSEMITARECTAPROPTER
INIMICOSMEOS;
NETRADIDERISMEINANI
MASTRIBULANTIUMME
QNMINSURREXERUNT
INMETESTESINIQUI
ETMENTITAESTINIQUI
TASSIBI;
CREDOUIDEREBONADNI
INTERRAUIUENTIUM;
EXPECTADNMUIRILITER
AGE ETCONFORTETUR
CORTUUMETSUSTINE
DNM

XXVII huic dauid
ADTEDNECLAMA
BODSMEUSNESILEASA
ME NEQUANDOTACE
ASAME ETADSIMILA
BORDESCENDENTIBUS
INLACUM
EXAUDIDNEUOCEMDE
PRECATIONISMEAEDU
OROADTE DUMEXTOLLO
MANUSMEASADTEM
PLUMSCMTUUM;
NESIMULTRADASMECUM
PECCATORIBUS ETCU

62 *The Utrecht Psalter, fol. 15v, showing the illustration to Psalm 27.*

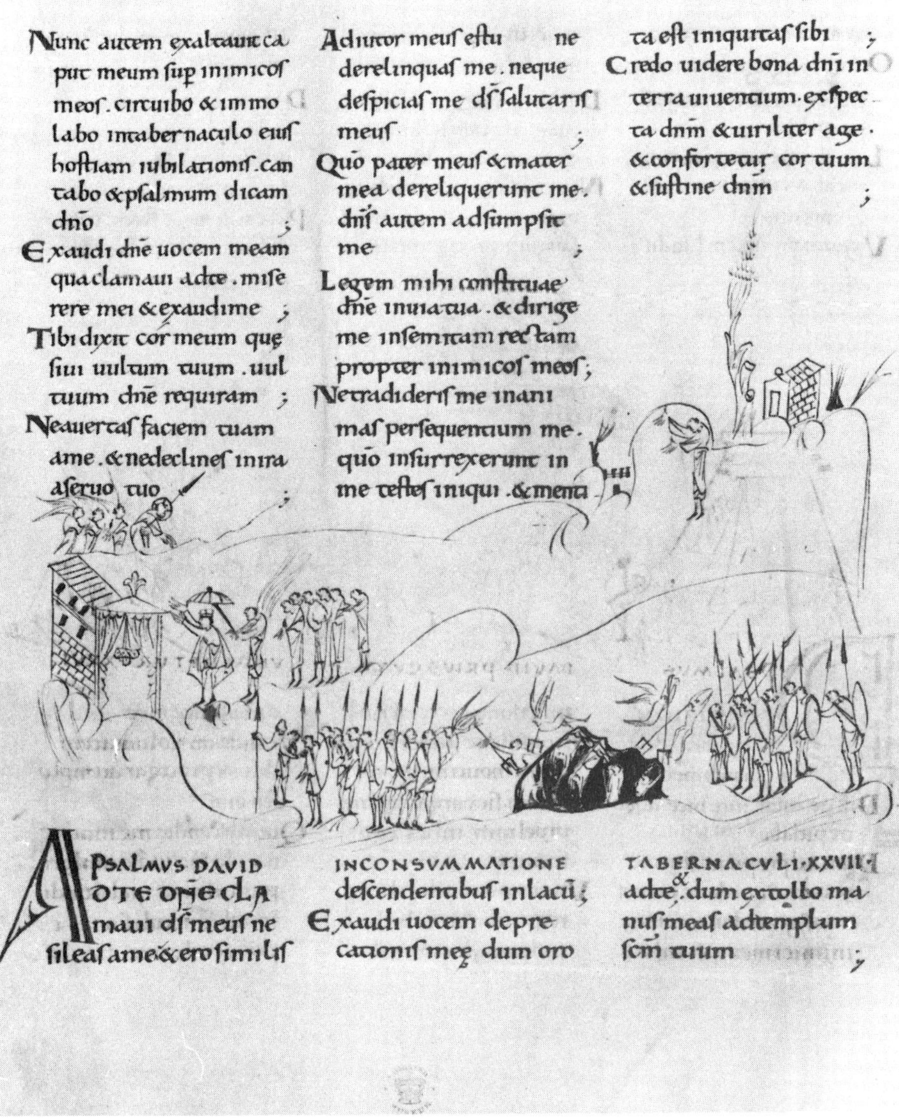
Nunc autem exaltauit ca
put meum sup inimicos
meos. circuibo & immo
labo intabernaculo eius
hostiam iubilationis. can
tabo & psalmum dicam
dno ;
Exaudi dne uocem meam
quaclamaui adte. mise
rere mei & exaudi me ;
Tibi dixit cor meum que
siui uultum tuum. uul
tuum dne requiram ;
Neauertas faciem tuam
ame. & nedeclines inira
aseruo tuo ;
Adiutor meus estu ne
derelinquas me. neque
despicias me ds salutaris
meus ;
Quo pater meus & mater
mea dereliquerunt me.
dns autem adsumpsit
me ;
Legem mihi constitue
dne inuia tua. & dirige
me insemitam rectam
propter inimicos meos ;
Netradideris me inani
mas persequentium me.
quo insurrexerunt in
me testes iniqui. & menti
ta est iniquitas sibi ;
Credo uidere bona dni in
terra uiuentium. exspec
ta dnm & uiriliter age.
& confortetur cor tuum
& sustine dnm ;
PSALMUS DAVID
ADTE DNE CLA
MAUI ds meus ne
sileas ame & ero similis
INCONSUMMATIONE
descendentibus inlacu ;
Exaudi uocem depre
cationis meę dum oro
TABERNACULI XXVII
adte & dum extollo ma
nus meas adtemplum
scm tuum ;

63 *The Harley Psalter, fol. 15v. The script is by scribe 1, the rubrication and the illustration to Psalm 27 is by E; the initial is by J; there are corrections to the text in column a, line 1,* exaltauit caput, *in column b, line 11,* semitam rectam, *and in column c, third line from bottom,* et.

bifolium in Utrecht, as is the bifolium 11/16 which artist A illustrated, and the bifolium 12/15 which artists B and E illustrated, as is demonstrated below.[22]

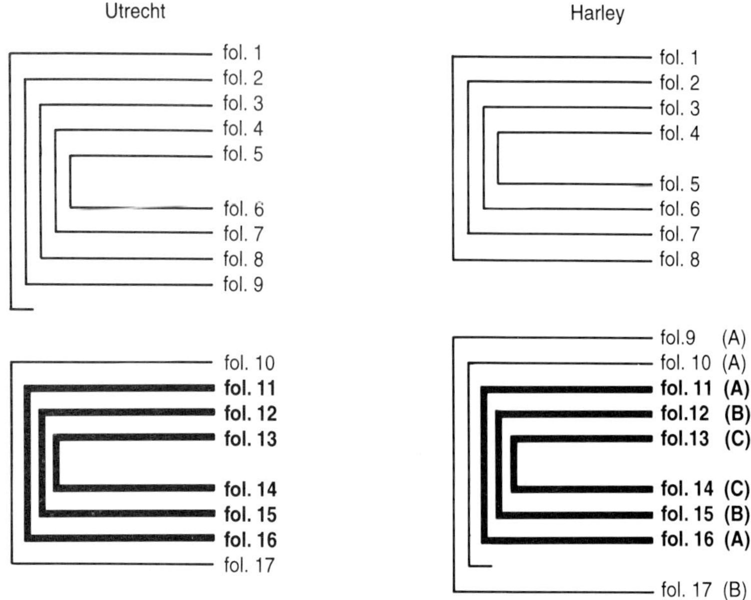

The central bifolia of quire 2 are the only bifolia which correspond to those in Utrecht, except those in quire 9. Quire 9 of Harley corresponds exactly with quire 8 of Utrecht.[23] It was illustrated by a different artist. Once again, if the Utrecht Psalter was disassembled, it would have made simultaneous working a real possibility, and this is precisely what is indicated by the evidence of the work of scribe 1 and D2, recounted above.

I would suggest that the Utrecht Psalter was unbound when artist A finished illustrating his quire 1, when it was realised precisely how complex and prolonged the task of illustrating Harley would be. It was at that stage that it was decided to make fols. 9 and 17 (rather than 16) conjoint leaves. Since the bifolium 9–17 is not matched by one in Utrecht, after having finished fol. 9, artist A left it and illustrated the singleton, fol. 10. After having finished with fol. 10, he gave artist B the bifolium 10–17 of Utrecht, and artist B executed fol. 17r of the bifolium 9–17 of Harley that artist A had started. Work on the central bifolia of quire 2 was then divided between artists A, B and C. At the same time, a second front to the Psalter was started by artist-scribe D2 at quire 9, on fol. 50r. This second front was begun at an extremely logical place, the text for Psalm 100 and the illustration to Psalm 101: since the original intention was probably to execute the set of Canticles, the Lord's Prayer, the Creed, the *Quicunque Uult* and the additional Psalm *Pusillus eram*, as they are set out in the Utrecht Psalter, this would have been about half way through the project – there were sixty-six illustrations to execute after Psalm 100, and if, as I suppose, quire 1 had already been illustrated, there were eighty-four to illustrate up to and including Psalm

[22] I have emboldened the corresponding bifolia for the sake of clarity. [23] See Appendix 2, p. 214.

100. The fact that Utrecht was unbound explains the single appearance of artist C on his bifolium, and the use of a second scribe for four pages and 23 lines: scribe 1 and artists A and B were working at the same time on other parts of the book.

The decision to unbind Utrecht was an *ad hoc* one, and not planned from the start of the campaign. In its actual execution, there were some problems. Despite the division of work, scribe 1 caught up with the artists in quire 2, and started to write on the bifolium 12/15, that artist B had just begun. Artist B did not complete the bifolium, and went on to illustrate quire 3, which is also a bifolium, and quire 4, which is a regular one of 8 leaves. Scribe 1 went on to write the rest of quire 2, which had already been illustrated, before following in the wake of artist B in quires 3 and 4.

If the artists of Harley were working by the quire, and were using an unbound exemplar, then Eadui's quires can come quite logically in the sequence of production, and damage hypothesised by Wanley and Backhouse is not needed as an explanation. The curious order of production would thus be resolved. Eadui's quires are a continuation of the making of the first half of the book, started after the making of the second half had begun.

The strength of the hypothesis that the Utrecht Psalter was unbound is that it can explain many of the apparent anomalies in the sequence of production in the Harley Psalter remarkably economically, and provide a single motive for them. The hypothesis cannot be 'proved', but the history of the binding of Utrecht does not contradict it: the Carolingian manuscript was rebound, at least twice, before it was acquired by Sir Robert Cotton in *c.* 1600.[24] Moreover scribes had worked from an unbound exemplar at Christ Church Canterbury, and in the last quarter of the tenth century, not long before Harley was made. Bishop noted that the six scribes of Cambridge, UL Ms. Ff.4.43 (Smaragdus, *Diadema monachorum*) divided their work by quires, and that three scribes wrote severally sheets i and iv, ii, and iii of quire 4.[25] He saw evidence in the spacing of the script at the end of quires for supposing that scribes were copying from an unbound exemplar, and also for some evidence of line by line copying. He could see no evidence of problems with spacing to suggest that quire 4 was independently copied from the unbound bifolia of an exemplar, but it is difficult to see any other explanation, especially in view of evidence that the exemplar was indeed unbound. In fact, the second sheet, containing the large script of Bishop's scribe 4, extends well over the margins of the text block, and the scribe of the third sheet has very eccentric line endings, which might suggest line by line copying. In Harley of course, the fact that fol. 10 is a singleton seems to point to the fact that the bifolia of Harley were matched with those of Utrecht precisely so that the bifolia of Utrecht could be duplicated by the several artists of Harley.[26]

[24] See above, Introduction, p. 16, n.57. [25] Bishop, *Caroline Minuscule*, p. 6.

[26] I am grateful to the many scholars with whom, since 1989, I have discussed the sequence of manuscript production in the Harley Psalter. A special debt is owed to George Henderson and to Michelle Brown, who know the argument as well as I do by now, and who can clearly see its faults. I am also indebted to Peter Kidd, for his part in a discussion that lead to the realisation that the bifolia in quire 2 of both manuscripts corresponded, Linda Brownrigg, who provided me with auxiliary evidence good enough to persuade me that I might be right, and Koert van der Horst, who supplied me with the evidence I needed for it to be possible. For a cursory presentation of related material see Gameson 'After Dunstan', p. 204, and p. 205, n.75.

The dates of production

Bishop identified scribe D2 with the scribe of BL Stowe Charter 35.[27] He had good reason. Generic similarities include the slight clubbing of ascenders, the tapering of descenders to the left, the use of the 'figure 2' 'r', and the occasional use of the 'oc' form of 'a'. Note in particular the following forms: 'h', with its elegant crescent; 'x', with a high waist; the occasional use of insular half uncial 'n' at the beginning of words; 'g', which comprises a round bow, with a separate tail stroke, and a small wedge where they join, and tall 's', which has a disappointingly clumsy shoulder. The script in the diploma does have slightly more breadth and rotundity, but this does not outweigh the use of similar letter forms, and can be put down to the different nature of the two documents. One difference is the last stroke of the ampersand, which in Harley is often extended to the top right, but this seems to be a deliberate contrivance; when it is not used, the ampersand in Harley is similar to that in B.L. Stowe Charter. 35.

BL Stowe Charter 35 was written in 1002 or 1003.[28] Dating Harley in relation to it is problematic. Bishop considered them closely contemporary.[29] It is remarkably neat that Harley appears very near the end of Bishop's list of manuscripts that have hair side universally facing flesh, that Bishop saw the change from insular to continental practice in the arrangement of parchment as occurring at about the time that Stowe Charter 35 was written, and that the last two quires of Harley have hair side facing hair, something that Bishop did not note.[30] However, the reasons for the change in practice within Harley are not chronological, but rather due to the fact that scribe 1 took over from the artists in arranging his vellum. It would be unwise to place too much faith in a set of circumstances that may well be coincidental. That Harley has any quires with hair side facing hair might make it difficult to date it to the end of the tenth century, but the terminus ante quem is uncertain. Scribes could live a long time. Good evidence that Style II Caroline minuscule persisted at Christ Church into the third decade of the eleventh century is provided by detailed notices of the translation of Alphege added to the fragmentary calendar of Paris, BN Ms. Lat. 10062 fols. 162r–163v, as Bishop noted.[31] It is quite possible that scribes 1 and D2 were working in the second decade of the eleventh century.

27 Bishop, 'Notes vii', p. 420, where it is also maintained that this scribe wrote BL Harley Ms. 1117(ii), and BL Royal Ms. 7.c.iv, . Dumville, *Caroline Script*, pp. 109–10, has questioned all these identifications. BL Stowe Charter 35 is P. H. Sawyer, *Anglo-Saxon Charters, An Annotated List and Bibliography*, Royal Historical Society Guides and Handbooks 8, London, 1968, n.905; and reproduced in W.B. Sanders (ed.), *Facsimiles of Anglo-Saxon Manuscripts*, 3 vols., Southampton, 1878–84, vol. 3, n.36.

28 Bishop, 'Notes vii', p. 420 accepted that it was written in 1003, the date that it bears. S. Keynes, *The Diplomas of King Aethelred 'The Unready' 976–1016: A Study in their use as Historical Evidence*, Cambridge, 1980, p. 259, and p. 108, n. 70, observed that its witness list suggests a date of 1002. Dumville, *Caroline Script*, pp. 100–1, noted that the third minim in the date was a later addition; but see P. Chaplais' review of Dumville, *Caroline Script*, in *The Journal of the Society of Archivists*, 16, 1995, pp. 105–7 esp. pp. 106–7.

29 Bishop, 'Notes vii', p. 420.

30 Ibid., p. 420–1. Paris, BN Ms. lat. 6401a in fact has hair side uniformly facing flesh with the hair side on the outside of the quire, although it is the first manuscript in Bishop's list of manuscripts that have hair side facing hair.

31 Bishop, 'Notes vii', p. 420. Bishop noted that the main text of the calendar is similar to scribe D2's own work. To borrow his terminology, it is rather more 'denatured'. Bishop's important observation undoubtedly extends the life of Style II Anglo-Caroline beyond 1011, its normal *terminus ante quem*.

Since the Utrecht Psalter was unbound so that the artists and scribes of Harley could work on it simultaneously, it is safe to conclude that the work of scribe 1, artists A, B, C, and the artist-scribe D2 in quires 1,2,3,4, and 9 of the manuscript was executed within a few months. Moreover, there is no need to think that scribe 1's work in quire 10 was anything other than immediately after that in quire 9. We cannot explain their different appearance by assuming a time gap between the two quires, indeed, as we will see in the next chapter, the opposite is true.

Since Bishop's 1971 analysis of the oeuvre of Eadui Basan,[32] this scribe has attained a reputation and importance in the eyes of twentieth-century students of Anglo-Saxon manuscripts only matched by the admiration that he himself looked for from those who studied them in the eleventh: financially independent,[33] yet *sacerdos et monachus*;[34] not only *scriptorum princeps*,[35] but also poet,[36] artist,[37] and forger;[38] scarred,[39] and portly,[40] this larger than life figure has been credited with influencing the script of England for over one hundred years.[41] It is where his work in Harley 603 fits into his oeuvre that is a matter of importance to the present study.

The dating of Eadui's section of Harley 603 is controversial. One good reason for this is that it is surrounded by examples of a type of script that is usually dated to the first decade of the eleventh century, while dated examples of script that have been attributed to Eadui with certainty fall into the second and third decades. BL Stowe Charter 38 is dated 1018, and BL Arundel Ms. 155 is dateable to between 1012 and 1023.[42] Pfaff, and Alexander and Kauffmann, worked from the assumption that Eadui's script was co-eval with that of scribes 1 and 2. Alexander and Kauffmann accounted for this by giving a late date to the work of scribes 1 and 2, and dating the manuscript to *c.* 1020.[43] Pfaff, noting the poor quality of Eadui's work in Harley, chose to interpret it as that of a junior member of the scriptorium, and therefore dated his section early, and the manuscript as a whole to the first decade of the eleventh century.[44] My analysis of the construction of the codex would indicate that this was not the case. Eadui certainly worked later than scribes 1 and 2, the rubricator and the initials master. The question is, simply, how much later?

Attempting to place a work in a scribe's career on the basis of style alone is a particularly subjective endeavour, but it is necessitated by the peculiar appearance of Eadui's script in Harley. Bishop allied it to this scribe's work in BL Cotton Ms. Vespasian A.i, fols. 155–60, which he called 'late and degenerate'.[45] Eadui's work in Harley 603 is

[32] Bishop, *English Caroline*, p. 22, and figs. 24 and 25; Eadui signed himself in a colophon on fol. 183v of Hannover, Kestner-Museum, Ms. W.M. XXIa, 36. [33] See Heslop, 'Cnut and Emma', p. 175.

[34] This is the implication of the citation in Bishop, *Caroline Minuscule* p. 22, of A. Boutemy, 'Two obituaries of Christ Church, Canterbury', *The English Historical Review*, 50, 1935, pp. 292–9, where *Eadwius, sacerdos et monachus* is listed on p. 297. He is found on the second flyleaf of Lambeth Palace Library, Ms. 430, which was once inserted between fols. 19 and 20 of the Christ Church obituary in BL Cotton Ms. Nero C.ix.

[35] Pfaff, 'Eadui Basan', esp. pp. 282–3. [36] Ibid. [37] See Heslop, 'Cnut and Emma', p. 176.

[38] Brooks, *Early History*, pp. 257–9. [39] Pfaff, 'Eadui Basan', p. 280.

[40] Dumville, *Caroline Script*, pp. 123–4. [41] Ibid., pp. 111–38.

[42] For BL Arundel Ms. 155, see above, Introduction, p. 10, n. 40. Stowe Charter 38 is Sawyer, *Anglo Saxon Charters*, n. 950, reproduced in Sanders, *Facsimiles*, vol. 3, n. 39.

[43] Alexander and Kauffmann, *English Illuminated Mss.*, p. 39. They date the manuscript to 1015–25.

[44] Pfaff, 'Eadui Basan', pp. 272–3.

not nearly as accomplished as that in Vespasian A.i. In the latter manuscript the effect of uniformity relies on the firm base line of the script, on the consistency of its height, on its upright ascenders and descenders, and on the close spacing of the letter forms. In Harley 603 this consistency is lost. Spacing between words and letters, although still compressed, is very variable; the letters are of very different heights within the same words; the ascenders and descenders veer both to the left and to the right, sometimes within the same word. Having said this, all the peculiarities of Eadui's script are present. It also occasionally lapses into the idiosyncracy of the hooked 'e' that is consistently applied in the Vespasian manuscript, and in that manuscript alone. In Harley 603 Eadui seems not to be developing his skills, but losing the ones he already had. There is no need to consider Eadui's career as bounded by the dates that we can glean from surviving manuscripts.[46] I would explain the difference between Eadui's script in Harley and that seen in his other works by supposing that it is later than dated examples.[47]

One good reason for supposing that Eadui was a well-established master scribe by the time he came to write his section of Harley 603 is the nature of the task that he was set: it is unlikely that a beginner, working in an altogether different style, would be asked to complete work on the text of such an ambitious project. This judgement is corroborated by both the importance of the task, and the extreme difficulties that it presented. Eadui is likely to have been asked to contribute on the basis of a reputation that he had already established. I would suggest that he was working in the third or fourth decades of the eleventh century. He is extremely unlikely to have been working contemporaneously with scribes 1 and 2.

Artist F executed his illustrations at some time between the work of scribe 1 and Eadui. Wormald dated his work to the second quarter of the eleventh century.[48] More recent scholarship has tended to place it rather earlier, around *c.* 1020. Artist F has been compared with work in other manuscripts.[49] Such parallels should be used cautiously in

[45] Bishop, *Caroline Minuscule*, p. 22.

[46] Dumville, *Caroline Script*, p. 125, states that 'There is little in his surviving output to suggest that his career, distinguished as its results were, need be reckoned as extending over a lengthy period. It is striking that those specimens of his writing which permit of dating cluster around and perhaps just before 1020, 1012 x 1023 being the outer limits indicated.' 1012–23 might be the outer dates indicated by dated examples, but the dates of Eadui's career should not be defined by dated examples of his work. The length of his career remains undefined.

[47] Pfaff, 'Eadui Basan', p. 273, considered that there was not a shred of evidence to place any of Eadui's work after *c.* 1023, but on. pp. 278–9 he ascribes the script of the document in BL Cotton Ms. Claudius A.iii, fols. 2r–6r, to Eadui (Sawyer, *Anglo-Saxon Charters*), n. 914. Some agree with this attribution: see O. Homburger, *Die Anfänge der Malschule von Winchester im X. Jahrhundert*, Leipzig, 1912, p. 56 and n.1; P. Chaplais, 'The Anglo-Saxon chancery : from the diploma to the writ', *Journal of the Society of Archivists*, 3,1966, pp. 160–76, at p. 174, and n. 118; B. Barr 'The history of the volume', in N. Barker (ed.), *The York Gospels*, pp. 101–117, at p. 103, and n. 4. Others have been less certain: see Ker, *Catalogue*, cat. 185 art. a, Dumville, *Caroline Script*, p. 126, n. 75. Bishop, *Caroline Minuscule*, p. 22 does not mention it, perhaps speaking volumes. It is the type of prestige work that Eadui would undertake. N. Ker 'Membra disiecta', *British Museum Quarterly*, 12, 1938, pp. 130–5, at pp. 130–1, noted that it was once inserted into BL Cotton Ms. Tiberius A.ii, Gospels that King Athelstan gave to Christ Church (see S. Keynes, 'King Athelstan's books', in M. Lapidge and H. Gneuss (eds.), *Learning and Literature in Anglo-Saxon England*, Cambridge 1985, pp. 143–201, at pp. 147–53). Brooks, *Early History*, pp. 257–8, demonstrated that it is a forged charter, supposedly of AD 1006, that cannot have been written before 1032.

[48] Wormald, *English Drawings*, pp. 69–70.

[49] Temple, *Anglo-Saxon Mss.*, p. 101, like other commentators, compares him to the artist of BL Arundel Ms. 155, dated 1012–23, and also to the artist of Vatican Library, Ms. Reg. lat. 12 which cannot have been made before 1032; see below, chapter 4, p. 150, and n. 2.

considering the date of his work. In considering line drawing, Wormald's entire 'Progressive Style' consisted of only four manuscripts;[50] BL Arundel Ms. 155 (1012–23) is the only one that can be dated.[51] Fully painted works in a comparable style are dated to after *c.* 1015.[52] It is difficult to envisage artist F working before *c.* 1010. The *terminus ante quem* for artist F is best defined by the date we ascribe to Eadui's work in Harley.

There seems to be no good reason to consider the work of artist F as very much later than that of artists A–D2 and scribes 1 and D2. In a scriptorium as prolific and quickly developing as Canterbury apparently was we should expect to find examples of stylistic overlap.[53] The differences between artist F and artists A–D2 could be accounted for by the adherence of the first four artists to their exemplar. Artist D2 owed so much to his exemplar that it would be difficult to find his work anywhere else; it would be unwise to use artist B for stylistic comparisons, as he seems to have started off his campaign of work in this manuscript as a novice, and to have altered his style in order to tackle his demanding task. I think that the exaggerated expressiveness of the figures of artist A as compared with Utrecht, especially in the illustration to Psalm 12 on fol. 7r, has much in common with the style of artist F.[54] It is certainly possible that F's work was executed contemporaneously with the work of scribe 1.

There is no indication from an analysis of style that Eadui worked later than artist F. However, they lie a good distance apart in the production of the manuscript, while artist F worked consecutively to scribe 1. The contributions of the artist E, I, and J separate the work of artist F from that of Eadui, and it therefore seems more likely that artist F is co-eval with scribes 1 and D2, than that he was co-eval with Eadui. I would therefore date the work of scribes 1 and D2 and artists A–F to the second decade of the eleventh century, Eadui's section to the third or fourth decade, and the work of artists E, I, and J to sometime between the two.

Artist G was also responsible for the drawings on fols. 122v and 123r of BL Cotton Ms. Caligula A.xv.[55] The illustrations in the Caligula manuscript have been dated variously to 1053,[56] 1073,[57] and 1076,[58] on the basis of a perceived change of hand in the annals. I see little reason to suppose a change in hand after 1053, and, after that date, the script and ink are consistent to 1073. This would imply that the entries to 1073 were executed in one campaign rather than separately for each year. A date of *c.* 1073–6 can stand for this campaign. There are no other examples of the Revived Utrecht Style

[50] Wormald, *English Drawings*, pp. 42–9. These are B.L. Arundel Ms. 155, Harley 603, Paris, BN Ms. Lat. 8824, and the single drawing on fol. 84r of B.L. Royal Ms. 15 A.xvi; the drawings in BL Cotton Ms. Tiberius A.iii, Durham, Cathedral Library, Ms. B.III.32, and the Vatican Library, Ms. Reg. Lat. 12, he considered to be rather later.

[51] See above, Introduction, p. 10, n. 40.

[52] Such as BL Harley Ms. 76 (Temple, *Anglo-Saxon Mss.*, cat. 75, where the manuscript is dated to *c.* 1020–30).

[53] See the remarks in Heslop, 'Cnut and Emma', p. 169.

[54] Gameson, 'Anglo-Saxon artists', p. 40, compares the work of artist A to the Arenberg Gospels (New York, Pierpont Morgan Library, M. 869 (Temple, *Anglo-Saxon Mss.*, cat. 56)); but, even if one accepts this connection, there are no secure dates for the Arenberg Gospels either – see Heslop, 'Cnut and Emma', pp. 169–70, and, for a different view, Dumville, *Caroline Script*, pp. 106–7.

[55] Gameson, 'Anglo-Saxon artists', p. 40 (Temple, *Anglo-Saxon Mss.*, ills, 317 and 318).

[56] That would seem to be the implication of Backhouse, in Backhouse *et al.*, *Golden Age*, p. 78.

[57] Wormald, *English Drawings*, p. 54.

[58] Ker, *Catalogue*, p. 175, he notes a change of ink, but attributes the entry of 1076 to the same hand.

which we can date with greater accuracy. Eadui and artist G are very unlikely to have been contemporaries.

It is certain that there was a considerable gap between the work of artist G and that of artist H, whose work Wormald dated to the twelfth century.[59] A useful way to date artist H is by the mitre of the bishop on fol. 29v. Heslop has demonstrated that the bishop's hat was replaced by a mitre in the early eleventh century, that by *c.* 1140 its lateral lobes were being replaced by points, and that by 1150 the mitre was appearing in the shape that we know it today.[60] The bishop in Harley has a lobed mitre, though it is difficult to tell whether they are lateral or not. Artist H's work is from the first half of the twelfth century, but finding parallels for it is difficult, and none are securely dated.[61]

The place of production

The question of the origin of Harley is linked to the question of its dates for the reason that it is necessary to try to establish where the manuscript was at all the different times that it was worked on. If it is possible to determine where it was at any period of its construction, this can be used as excellent supporting evidence that it was at the same place at another period: although the evidence of later provenance is normally not very satisfactory in determining where a manuscript started its life, especially for decorated Anglo-Saxon manuscripts of the first half of the eleventh century which were often not made for the house that produced them,[62] this is a special case. Here we are dealing with the provenance of two manuscripts, not one: as I have demonstrated, Harley was dependent on Utrecht throughout its manufacture and, if they moved at all while Harley was being made, the two manuscripts moved together. It is a difficult circumstance to envisage, and cogent reasons have to be put forward for it, especially since Harley was never really in a position to travel from the scriptorium. For this reason, provenance provides the backbone of this inquiry. Since the best evidence for the origin of both manuscripts comes from the twelfth century, I start with the latest work on the book and work backwards.

That the twelfth-century artist of Harley worked at Canterbury is indicated by independent evidence of the presence of the Utrecht Psalter at Christ Church. This is provided by the Eadwine Psalter, Trinity College Cambridge Ms. R.17.1. Made in the mid-twelfth century, this book was written by known Christ Church scribes, it includes a Christ Church Calendar and a representation of the waterworks constructed there by

59 Wormald, *English Drawings*, p. 70.

60 T.A. Heslop, 'The Romanesque Seal of Worcester Cathedral', *British Archaeological Association Conference Transactions*, 1, Worcester Cathedral, 1978, pp. 71–9, esp. pp. 73–4.

61 One is the artist of a Prudentius *Psychomachia* manuscript, BL Cotton Ms. Titus D.xvii, fols. 1v–34r, for which see R.M. Thomson, *Manuscripts from St Albans Abbey, 1066–1235*, 2 vols., Bury St Edmunds, 1982, vol. 1, p. 10, pp. 17–19, pp. 91–2, and vol. 2 plates 26–30. The manuscript shows a similar concern to recapture an Anglo-Saxon style with formidable vigour. The impact of the Alexis Master's style is more evident than it is in the work of artist H.

62 See Heslop, 'Cnut and Emma', esp. pp. 178ff.

Prior Wibert.[63] Equally certainly, the illustrations are taken directly from the Utrecht Psalter. It is therefore perfectly reasonable to assume that Utrecht, Harley, and Eadwine, were all at Christ Church in the twelfth century.[64]

The Utrecht Psalter and its progeny are also anchored at Christ Church by their influence on the stained glass of the Cathedral, the provenance of which is secure, and which, we can presume, was executed *in situ*. One example of this influence is the depiction of the Exodus from the Second Typological Window in the north choir aisle at Christ Church, Canterbury, probably made in the last quarter of the twelfth century.[65] The group of the women of Israel, in classical garb, with their children accompanying them, is very similar in the glass and the illustration to Psalm 76 of Utrecht, as Caviness noted.[66] However, it is also matched by a similar group in the illustration to Psalm 13. Pictorially, the scene in the glass is made to match that of Christ Leading away the gentiles, its partner as a type for the scene of the Magi before Herod. However, if it is turned round, the whole scene bears a striking formal resemblance to the entire composition to Psalm 13 in Utrecht, which shows *insipiens* in the top left of the illustration, and the people of Israel being beckoned out of captivity by Jacob on the hill. Pharaoh takes the place of *insipiens* at the left, the people of Israel walk stage right, the Red Sea finds an echo in the slope of the hill, and the Pillar of Fire is matched by the figure of Jacob. The Utrecht Psalter not only provided details for the designer of the glass, but may also have provided the inspiration for this entire composition.

The value of the stained glass in the context of this argument is that it provides further evidence that Harley in particular was also at Canterbury in the twelfth century. In one case, at least, it seems that elements from an illustration in Harley were deliberately chosen by the designers of the glass, in preference to an illustration to the same Psalm in Utrecht. Caviness supposed that the scene of the siege of Canterbury by the danes, one of the panels in the north choir aisle gallery recounting the life of St Alphege,[67] was derived from an ancient pictorial tradition and better suited to line drawing than to stained glass.[68] It has four people defending the city against its attackers. The defenders are symmetrically placed, two of them hurl boulders, and two thrust spears against the assailants. In Utrecht's illustration to Psalm 59, the defenders of the city are not symmetrically placed, and it has only one stone thrower. The buildings are set in oblique perspective, and not crenelated. It is not very similar to the glass design. However, although the Harley illustration to this Psalm by artist H, on fol. 32v, is clearly derived from the Utrecht Psalter, it is much more similar to the design in the glass. Like the glass, it has a building within a wall, both of which are crenelated and

[63] See the recent comprehensive study of Gibson, Heslop, and Pfaff (eds.), *The Eadwine Psalter*, *passim*, esp. pp. 209–10.

[64] M.T. Gibson, in Gibson, Heslop, and Pfaff (eds.), *The Eadwine Psalter*, p. 209 uses the supposed Christ Church origin of Harley to help establish the origin of Eadwine, but Eadwine provides such conclusive evidence of its own that there is no danger of the argument becoming circular.

[65] Window n. xv. in accordance with the usage of M.H. Caviness, *Corpus Vitrearum Medii Aevii. Great Britain Volume II: Christ Church Cathedral Canterbury*, London 1981, pp. 78–9 and pp. 85–99, fig.156. See also M.H. Caviness, *The Early Stained Glass of Canterbury Cathedral c. 1175–1220*, Princeton, 1977, p. 26.

[66] Caviness, *Early Glass*, pp. 124–5

[67] Caviness, *Corpus Vitrearum GB II*, window Nt.ix, pp. 70–1, fig. 131.

[68] Caviness, *Early Glass*, pp. 144–6.

set in frontal perspective; it has its defenders symmetrically spaced, and there are two stone throwers, and two with spears. The buildings and the figures would have been less difficult than those in Utrecht to use in a glass design.[69] The designers of the glass referred to the pictorial treasure house of the Christ Church Library, and referred to both Utrecht and Harley, and masterfully adapted their line drawings into a different medium.[70] We can conclude that Harley was at Christ Church in the twelfth century.[71]

Artist G might have worked elsewhere,[72] but he did work at Christ Church. The Christ Church origin of BL Cotton Ms. Caligula A.xv, on which he worked, is established by annals attached to the table of years which relate to events at Christ Church (fols. 133–7).[73] Moreover, his compositions in the annals demonstrate an intimate knowledge of the pictorial tradition of Utrecht and Harley: the temple on fol. 122v owes its pictorial vocabulary to the buildings on fols. 15r and 16r of both manuscripts; the crouching monks in the same illustration are to be paralleled by the entourage of the Lord, those on fol. 51v of Harley possibly being the best example; the cherubim either side of the mandorla on fol. 123r of the annals are derived from those in the illustration to Psalm 17 on fol. 9r, and textual justification for them is provided in verse 11; and the angels holding staffs either side of the Lord might be paralleled with those in the illustration to Psalm 21 on fol. 12r of Harley, to which artist G himself added the banners. Artist G supplies corroborative evidence for what we would expect; that Harley and Utrecht were together in the same scriptorium in the second half of the eleventh century as they were in the first half of the twelfth.[74]

As far as we can place Eadui anywhere, we can place him at Christ Church. This is witnessed by his production of BL Arundel Ms. 155, and by charters written for the community.[75] However, Eadui's work was not all for the Christ Church community,

[69] Ibid., p. 66. Caviness considers that the scene of the storming of Jericho on New York, Pierpont Morgan Library, M. 724, one of the four leaves originally attached to the Eadwine Psalter (see M.R. James, 'Four leaves of an English Psalter', *Walpole Society*, 25, 1936–7, pp. 1–23), had a common model with the glass. Certainly both stem from the Utrecht Psalter tradition, because these leaves were originally attached to the Eadwine Psalter: see T.A. Heslop, in Gibson, Heslop, and Pfaff (eds.), *The Eadwine Psalter*, pp. 25–9, who substantiates, beyond reasonable doubt, the suggestion first made in H. Swarzenski, 'Unknown Bible pictures by W. de Brailes', *Journal of the Walters Art Gallery*, 1, 1938, pp. 65–9.

[70] The Eadwine artist follows Utrecht closely in this Psalm; it was not illustrated by the artist of Paris 8846.

[71] Dodwell compares Harley's artist H with the artist of a known St Augustine's book, BL Royal Ms. 1.B.xi (Dodwell, *Canterbury School*, p. 28, n.1., and plate 21b). However, the comparison is not close.

[72] Artist G was probably responsible for the illustrations on fols. 26v–33v of BL Add. Ms. 24199, Prudentius, *Psychomachia* (Wormald, *English Drawings*, p. 66; his Hand II); the manuscript is of a different textual tradition to the Christ Church manuscript, BL Cotton Ms. Cleopatra C.viii, and, unlike library books at Christ Church it is written in Style I Anglo-Caroline: See G.R. Wieland, 'The Anglo-Saxon manuscripts of Prudentius *Psychomachia*', *Anglo-Saxon England*, 16, 1987, pp. 213–321, esp. at pp. 218–20, and Bishop, *Caroline Minuscule*, p. xxii.

[73] See Temple, *Anglo-Saxon Mss.*, p. 122.

[74] Dodwell, *Canterbury School*, p. 3, n. 2. considered that artist G was working from earlier underdrawings. The underdrawings are his own, and his debt to Utrecht can clearly be seen in his additions to other artists' work, for example in Psalm 15, see above, chapter 2, p. 108.

[75] The calendar of BL Arundel Ms. 155 indicates a Christ Church origin (Korhammer, 'Origin of the Bosworth Psalter', at pp. 175–6 and 179–80); see also Wormald, *English Kalendars Before 1100*, pp. 169–81. As well as writing and illustrating this manuscript, Eadui added documents referring to the community in BL Royal Ms. I.D.ix, for which see P. Chaplais, 'The Anglo-Saxon Chancery' at p. 174, and Ker, *Catalogue*, cat. 247, p. 317; and possibly he wrote the forged document in BL Cotton Ms. Claudius A.iii, once in BL Cotton Ms. Tiberius A.ii, for which see above, p. 138, n.47.

and it may not all have been written at it. Heslop supposes that he was working semi-independently from the scriptorium at Christ Church,[76] while Dumville probes further the possibility that his early training may have been outside the Christ Church scriptorium.[77] The question of the origin of Eadui's section of the manuscript has not yet been clarified.

That Eadui's work in Harley 603 was written after his work in BL Arundel Ms. 155 is important in establishing where it was carried out. In Arundel 155, on fol. 133r, we see a figure, prostrate before the feet of St Benedict, wearing a Benedictine habit with a girdle inscribed *zona humilitatis*, and presenting a *lib(er) ps(almorum)* to St Benedict.[78] A representative of the community carries another book, open, and inscribed with the first words of the Rule. The *Manus Dei* holds a banderole on which are inscribed two phrases. The one delivered to Benedict reads *qui uos audit me audit*, and the one to the monks *Obedientes estote prepositi uestro*. That this image is a powerful affirmation of Benedictine values has been pointed out.[79] In particular, it is linked to chapter 5 of the Rule, on obedience; the words *qui uos audit me audit* are given twice in this short chapter. Deshman follows Higgit in supposing that the whole image is adapted from an earlier prototype that served as a preface for the *Regularis Concordia*.[80]

In Arundel 155, the image comes at the end of the Psalms, before the canticles. It is integral to the structure of the volume, appearing on the recto of the fifth leaf of a quire of eight leaves. The Psalm text ends on the preceding verso, and the canticles commence on the following verso. It not a prefatory image, as it was in the prototype, but rather a colophon. The book being presented is no longer the *Regularis Concordia*, but a Psalter.[81] In a manuscript that was almost certainly illustrated, as well as written by Eadui,[82] I would suggest that we see him presenting to St Benedict the Psalms that he was asked to make as an integral part of his manual labour.[83]

Whatever the circumstances of Eadui's early career, from the point of Arundel 155 onwards, we should probably understand his role to be that of performing tasks at the command of his superiors, for the benefit of the Christ Church community. Bearing in mind that artists H and G worked on the Harley Psalter with the Utrecht Psalter to hand at Christ Church, it seems likely that Eadui did the same, and that either he was asked to make the extremely short journey to St Augustine's to execute the additions to the BL

[76] See the analysis of T.A. Heslop, 'Cnut and Emma', pp. 173–6.

[77] Dumville, *Caroline Script*, pp. 126–8.

[78] Temple, *Anglo-Saxon Mss.*, cat. 66, ill. 213.

[79] Brownrigg, 'Review', pp. 253–4, and subsequently R. Deshman, '*Benedictus Monarcha et Monachus*. Early Medieval Ruler Theology and the Anglo-Saxon Reform', *Frühmittelalterliche Studien*, 22, 1988, pp. 204–40, esp. pp. 211–19.

[80] Higgit, 'Glastonbury, Dunstan', pp. 283f; Deshman, '*Benedictus Monarcha et Monachus*', pp. 215–16.

[81] Higgit, 'Dunstan, Glastonbury', pp. 283–4, supposed that in the prototype the figure prostrate before St Benedict represented St Dunstan; Deshman, '*Benedictus Monarcha et Monachus*', p. 219, suggested St Aethelwold.

[82] The case for Eadui illustrating this Psalter is made most fully in Heslop, 'Cnut and Emma', p. 176.

[83] Deshman, '*Benedictus Monarcha et Monachus*', p. 215, suggests that this figure is the abbot of the monastery. This is a Christ Church manuscript, and Christ Church did not have an abbot. He also considers the same figure to be the donor of the manuscript. It is unlikely that a monk could be a donor of the manuscript in the sense that he paid for it; the inscriptions in the illustration shows great adherence to the letter of the Rule, which prohibited private wealth.

Cotton Ms. Vespasian A.i, or that this manuscript went to Christ Church for the same purpose.[84]

Further support for a Christ Church origin for Harley is provided by the archbishop in the Beatus initial, on fol. 2r, which was executed before Eadui's work, and after the work of artist E, by artist I. Bearing in mind the other evidence for a Canterbury origin for the manuscript, this archbishop is unlikely to have been from York. His role in the book will be examined later, but the fact that he is there at all presents a strong *prima facie* case for a Christ Church origin for the volume at this stage.[85]

There is no evidence to separate Utrecht from Harley in quires 10 and 11; indeed the opposite is true. Artist F had the Utrecht Psalter to hand. Unless the two manuscripts moved together, they were written in the same scriptorium as that in which Eadui's quires were written and illustrated. These two quires were started immediately after quires 1–4 and 9, and their origin can be linked to the evidence of scribe 1 and his certain contemporaries, as well as to that of artist F. All the independent evidence is palaeographic, and would suggest that Harley was executed at Christ Church. Following Bishop, Dumville is happy to accept that both scribe 1 and D2 of Harley were Christ Church scribes.[86] Moreover fols. 50r–54r/a/23 were written by a the same scribe as BL Stowe Charter 35, *scripta in ciuitate dorobernensis quae est metropolis cantuariorum*.[87] Quite apart from the evidence that this scribe was also artist D2, he himself had the Utrecht Psalter to hand, and followed it line by line.

James and Dodwell explained the appearance of Harley by supposing that the Utrecht Psalter was only intermittently available; they thought that Utrecht was at Christ Church, while Harley was at St Augustine's.[88] There is, in fact, no evidence to

[84] The association of St Augustine's and Harley goes back at least to 1903, and sometimes has had a strange eventful history. M.R. James, *The Ancient Libraries of Canterbury and Dover*, Cambridge, 1903, at p. lxxi and p. 532, attributed the manuscript to St Augustine's on palaeographical grounds. James, *The Canterbury Psalter*, p. 4, n. 2. embellished the argument by explaining the deviation from the exemplar in Harley by supposing Utrecht was no longer available. Dodwell, *Canterbury School*, pp. 1–3 took up James's explanation and, at p. 1, n. 1, further supposed that the script of the scribe of the liturgical additions to the Vespasian Psalter, BL Cotton Ms. Vespasian A.I, was similar to scribe 1 of Harley 603. Dodwell supposed that the Vespasian Psalter was at St Augustine's in the eleventh century, a view substantiated in Wright, *Vespasian Psalter*, pp. 37–41. T.A.M. Bishop, 'Notes on Cambridge Manuscripts Part v: Mss. connected with St Augustine's Canterbury, continued', *Transactions of the Cambridge Bibliographical Society*, 3.1, 1959, pp. 93–5, at p. 94, n. 1, noted that the scribe of additions to the Vespasian manuscript was not similar to the script of scribe 1 in Harley, but was similar to the script of fols. 28–49 in Harley, a view that he expanded upon in 1971 (Bishop, *Caroline Minuscule*, p. 22), when he stated that both were the work of Eadui. Bishop, 'Notes v', p. 94, n. 1, constructs a chain of 'chain of less than certain inferences', that demonstrate that he was unhappy in his support of St Augustine's origin for Harley. In 1963, Bishop, 'Notes VII', pp. 420 and 423, lays emphasis on the Christ Church nature of the script of scribe D2, and in *Caroline Minuscule*, p. 22, he gives the origin of the additions to BL Cotton Ms. Vespasian A.i as Christ Church. Dodwell went to considerable lengths to maintain James' theory – see above; n. 74, and n. 71.

[85] See Backhouse, 'Making', pp. 108–10. [86] Dumville, *Caroline Script*, p. 107, n. 124.

[87] See above, p. 136, and n. 27. Dumville, *Caroline Script*, pp. 109–10, considers that BL Stowe Charter 35, as a royal diploma, would more naturally have been written by a royal official. If, as I maintain, it is written by artist/scribe D2 of Harley, this royal official must have come from Christ Church, or retired to Christ Church, where he worked on the Psalter. But, under these circumstances, it is more natural to think that the diploma was written by a scribe who was never in royal employ: the king might have relied on a scribe from the community to supply the document; on the other hand, even if it is correctly dated, the diploma could be a contemporary copy by a member of the community (see above, p. 136, n.28). Taunton, Somerset County Museum, DD/SAS.PR.502, of AD 995, is another diploma written apparently by a Christ Church scribe (Sawyer, *Anglo-Saxon Charters*, n. 884; and S. Keynes, *Facsimiles of Anglo-Saxon Charters*, London, 1991, n. 11.); see Bishop, *English Caroline*, p. xxvi, and 'Notes VII', p. 421–2 (his scribe xv), and the comments of Keynes, *Diplomas of Aethelred*, p. 120.

separate Utrecht from Harley at any stage, this is useful for three conclusions: first, all the evidence presented above for a Christ Church origin of the manuscript is mutually supportive, even though it spans at least a hundred years; secondly, the independent evidence that the scribes and artists of Harley worked at Christ Church provides the best evidence available for the eleventh century provenance of Utrecht; thirdly, Harley's deviations from the exemplar have to be explained in another way.

Conclusion to chapter 3

Without a calendar, a litany, a cover, a *de claustro* inscription, or any other additional material, we are fortunate to have such a mass of circumstantial evidence of a Christ Church origin for Harley 603, and it would be perverse, for the moment, not to assume that Harley was made there.

The date margins that I have proposed for the various sections of Harley are necessarily wide, and are based on examples of other dated work already available to the scholar. However, if codicological, palaeographical, and artistic considerations are all brought to bear, it is possible to refine our understanding of the developments of the Christ Church scriptorium, and to set up a relative chronology of undated manuscripts at Christ Church. For an example, I look to the illustrated Christ Church Prudentius, BL Cotton Ms. Cleopatra c.viii. This manuscript's scribe comes earlier in Bishop's stemma of Christ Church scribes than scribe D2 of Harley 603,[89] its vellum is arranged so that hair side faces flesh, and its illustrations show no sign of the Progressive Style, and some of Wormald's First Style which can be found in the last quarter of the tenth century.[90] These three features combined indicate that the comparatively ambitious Harley is a slightly later essay in manuscript production than the Cotton *Psychomachia*, by the same scriptorium. Individually however, none of these features is convincing: it would be unwarranted to suppose that the scribe of the Prudentius manuscript and the first two scribes of Harley could not have overlapped in their careers; Harley's quires 1–4 and 9 have hair side facing flesh; and one of the artists of the Prudentius also illustrated the York Gospels, partly written by Eadui Basan.[91] But it remains the case that Harley would have to have been a precocious document to have been earlier than the Cotton manuscript. Another useful comparison is with BL Arundel Ms. 155. Possible dates for this manuscript are 1012–23.[92] Eadui's section of Harley 603 was written after it. But, in the earlier sections of the manuscript, only the illustrations of F and E are of the same generation as the work of Eadui; otherwise Harley is a relatively less advanced document.

The questions raised by the script of Harley run right to the heart of our understanding of book production in this period. Three unresolved and related factors

[88] James, *Canterbury Psalter*, p. 4, n. 2; Dodwell, *Canterbury School*, pp. 1–3; see above n. 84.

[89] See above, Introduction, p. 2, n. 6.

[90] For example the Sherborne Pontifical, Paris, BN Ms. Lat. 943. See Temple, *Anglo-Saxon Mss.*, cat. 35.

[91] See above, Introduction, p. 2 [92] See above, Introduction, p. 10, n. 40.

are involved: differences in script between volumes reflect differences in date,[93] in origin,[94] and possibly in the type of book being written.[95] Differences within volumes might indicate that a number of styles were available co-evally, or alternatively, that a manuscript was executed over a number of years. Though the answers are still far from clear, Heslop and Dumville have, in very different ways, shed raking light on the problems.[96] Harley is of importance to the debate simply because it is an extensively illustrated manuscript with a secure origin, and such are none too plentiful. Since it was started in style II Caroline minuscule, it would indicate that fully formed style I, in which most *de luxe* manuscripts of the period were written, was not current at Christ Church in the early years of the eleventh century. Eadui, to whom Dumville attributes the birth of his 'style IV' English Caroline, may have been writing other books at the same time as scribes 1 and D2 were writing Harley, but he himself tackled Harley after they had finished work.

It is an important point that the origin of Harley establishes the provenance of Utrecht. Utrecht Psalter imagery was not confined to Christ Church. It is found in manuscripts that were at Winchester and St Bertin, at Bury St Edmunds, St Augustine's, Canterbury, and in a number of manuscripts without known early Medieval provenance.[97] Of itself, the presence of Utrecht Psalter imagery in Harley is no indication of origin. It is the fact that the book itself must have been there that is helpful, and although Utrecht's imagery spread, it is no surprise that the three surviving Medieval versions of the entire cycle were all made at Christ Church. This leaves the interesting question of how Utrecht imagery spread elsewhere. It might be that Harley was not the only Anglo-Saxon version of Utrecht: it is unlikely that all the versions of the Utrecht Psalter have survived, and it is possible that another one did move between communities. But debts to Utrecht in other manuscripts are piecemeal, and wax tablets or scraps of vellum are more plausible suggestions. Looking at works like the so-called 'Quinity' on fol 75v of the Winchester manuscript BL Cotton Ms. Titus D.xxvii, fol. 75v,[98] which is a conflation of imagery seen on various folios of

93 For the most recent survey see Dumville, *Caroline Script*, pp. 86–140. Heslop, 'Cnut and Emma', *passim*, has attempted to overturn the conventional dating of many Christ Church manuscripts, but his brilliant series of deductions are in large part based on the still unchallenged fact that, although different styles could be co-eval, Style II is infrequently found after *c.* 1015, and that apparently pioneered by Eadui is rarely found before that time.

94 For example, while Dumville, *Caroline Script*, pp. 86–120 attempts to break down Bishop's conclusion that only style II was practised at Christ Church until *c.* 1010, it remains certainly true that no style II is found at Winchester.

95 See Dumville, *Caroline Script*, pp. 106–7.

96 Ibid., *passim*, and Heslop, 'Cnut and Emma', *passim*. The 'Missal' of Robert of Jumièges (Rouen, Bibliothèque Municipale, Ms. Y.6) is a classic problem case. Heslop, 'Cnut and Emma', p. 155 and n. 12, and pp. 160–1, n. 25, dates it to the 1020's and thinks that it is from Peterborough. Dumville, *Caroline Script*, pp. 115–20, proposes a Christ Church origin in about 1010. See also T.A. Heslop's review of Dumville, *Caroline Script*, in *Journal of Theological Studies*, 45, 1994, pp. 378–81.

97 At Winchester, BL Cotton Ms. Titus D.xxvii and BL Stowe Ms. 944 (Temple, *Anglo-Saxon Mss*, cat. 77 and cat. 78); at St Bertin, Boulogne, Bibliothèque Municipale, Ms. 20; at Bury, Vatican Library, Ms. Reg. Lat. 12 (Temple, *Anglo-Saxon Mss.*, cat. 84); and at St Augustine's, BL Royal Ms. 15.A.xvi (Temple, *Anglo-Saxon Mss.*, cat. 85)

98 Temple, *Anglo-Saxon Mss.*, cat. 77, ill. 245.

Utrecht, separated from the literal meaning of the text, we can imagine separate drawings being made, and then the imagery being thoughtfully rearranged at Winchester.[99] The drawing of a building in BL Royal Ms. 15.A.xvi is also particularly pertinent.[100] Wormald noted that the towers at either end of the building are later additions, that otherwise the building is similar to that in the illustration to Psalm 26 of the Utrecht Psalter, and that it is stylistically related to hand E in Harley.[101] The relationship to the illustration to Psalm 26 in Utrecht and Harley is uncannily accurate. The roof of the rectangular building below the central tower has two types of tiles: at the extreme left are two panels of the type that in Utrecht is always used to represent round buildings: the artist of the drawing did not understand that the building in the Psalm illustration had a rounded apse, but nonetheless included the tiles of the apse at the end of his own rectangular building. However, it seems that he looked to the Harley image on fol. 15r, by artist B, since the tiles that were over the apsidial tiles in the Royal manuscript resemble those in Harley much more closely than they do those in Utrecht: to borrow the terminology of Carver, the Royal and Harley manuscripts share a type 5a roof, while Utrecht has a style 5b.[102] It would certainly account for the similarity in the ground of the Royal illustration and the grounds created by artist E in Harley if the drawing was a conflation of imagery seen in the Anglo-Saxon manuscript. This looks suspiciously like a first-hand interpretation of Harley's image onto a piece of spare vellum.[103] The Royal manuscript has a thirteenth-century St Augustine's pressmark, but this is not evidence of a St Augustine's origin of Harley;[104] there is no more reason to place Harley at St Augustine's because of this drawing than there is to place Utrecht at Winchester because of the Winchester 'Quinity'. We see the same process of gradual assimilation of Utrecht Psalter imagery going on in the Royal manuscript, but at an earlier and less sophisticated stage, in the Christ Church scriptorium itself.

99 For a thorough analysis of this image, and its context see Kantorowicz, 'Quinity', *passim*. A similar process of rearrangement of the forms of the Utrecht Psalter was undertaken, probably at Christ Church, by the artist of the Arenberg Gospels, New York, Pierpont Morgan Library, M. 869, for which see J.E. Rosenthal, 'The historiated canon tables of the Arenberg Gospels', unpublished D.Phil. thesis, University of Columbia 1974, and J. Rosenthal, 'The unique architectural settings of the Arenberg Evangelists', in K. Bierbrauer, P. K. Klein, and W. Sauerländer (eds.), *Studien zur mittelalterlichen Kunst 800–1250, Festschrift fur Florentine Mütherich zum 70. Geburtstag*, Munich, 1985, pp. 145–53, esp. pp. 149–50.

100 Temple, *Anglo-Saxon Mss.*, cat. 85, ill. 211.

101 Wormald, *English Drawings*, pp. 44–5.

102 See the annotated diagrams of types of roof in Carver, 'Contemporary artefacts', p. 122. On p. 144, n. 51 Carver suggests that the artist of the Royal manuscript copied Harley and not Utrecht because they both differ from Utrecht in the type 3 roof that they have over the main rectangular building. But these roofs are quite differently interpreted: Royal's tiles are well articulated and pegged, while Harley's are little better than circles.

103 See the discussion in Brooks, *Early History*, pp. 46–8.

104 Carver, 'Contemporary artefacts', p. 144, n. 51, tries to find support for Dodwell's hypothesis that Harley was at St Augustine's without Utrecht in this drawing. However this flies in the face of all the evidence for a Christ Church provenance for Harley that we do have, it places too much weight on the thirteenth-century pressmark for the origin of the Royal manuscript, and there seems to me no reason to suppose that Harley was in a different house to Utrecht just because the artist of the Royal manuscript chose to use the Anglo-Saxon manuscript as his exemplar, rather than the Carolingian one.

Monks, scribes, and artists took books with them when they travelled, to read and to give, and to collect pictorial motifs.[105] A case in point is the Anglo-Saxon artist of BL Harley Ms. 2506, an astrological compilation probably made at Fleury.[106] This artist also worked at St Bertin, for example on Boulogne, Bibliothèque Municipale, Ms. 11.[107] There he would have seen the Leiden Germanicus, Leiden, UL Vossianus Ms. Q. 79,[108] which was being used as an exemplar in the St Bertin scriptorium at about the same time, to create Boulogne, Bibliothèque Municipale, Ms. 188.[109] The illustration of Cygnus in Harley 2506, on fol. 38r,[110] closely resembles that on fol. 46v of the Leiden Germanicus. The evidence would suggest that the artist made his interpretation of the Leiden Germanicus image at St Bertin, and employed it at Fleury. Such an operation, repeated frequently by the artist when consulting books, would explain the prodigious iconographic range seen in his works.[111] Such an operation, repeated by several artists consulting one or two books, would explain how Utrecht Psalter imagery spread from Christ Church.[112]

Artists clearly had some degree of mobility, and exemplars were important in forming style. If we cannot use Utrecht iconography to locate manuscripts, we cannot use comparisons with the style of other decorated manuscripts to help secure their origin either.[113] These factors should make us question what we mean by a house style when it comes to lavish manuscript production, especially as *de luxe* manuscripts seem often to have travelled from their place of origin so quickly after they were made.[114] It is our lack of understanding of how style was transmitted in the early eleventh century that allowed Higgit to suppose that the illustrations in the Harley Psalter may have been started at Glastonbury, with the Christ Church scribes writing after it had moved to Christ Church,[115] and Gameson to suppose that the artists of Harley might have come from Winchester, and might have returned there.[116] But I have argued that scribe D2 was indeed a Christ Church scribe, that he had the Utrecht Psalter to hand, and that he can be identified with an artist, Wormald's artist D. Moreover, the construction of the

[105] See D. Gaborit-Chopin, 'Les Dessins d'Adémar de Chabannes', *Bulletin Archéologique du Comité des travaux historiques et scientifiques*, Nouv. Ser. 3, 1967, pp. 163–225, for a continental example.

[106] For details of this manuscript see below, chapter 4, pp. 174–83.

[107] Temple, *Anglo-Saxon Mss.*, cat. 44. See also A. Boutemy, 'Un monument capital de l'enluminure anglo-saxonne: le Ms. 11 de Boulogne-sur-mer', *Cahiers de Civilisation Médiévale*, 1, 1958, pp. 179–82.

[108] *Aratea*, Faksimile Verlag, Luzern, 1989, with a commentary volume by B. Bischoff, B. Eastwood, T. Klein, F. Mütherich, and P. Obbema.

[109] See C. Kelleher, 'Illumination at St-Bertin at St-Omer under the abbacy of Odbert', unpublished D.Phil thesis, University of London, 1968, pp. 292–310.

[110] Illustrated in McGurk *et al.*, *Anglo-Saxon Illustrated Miscellany*, Plate XII, fig. 95.

[111] The artist was also responsible for illustrating BL Harley Ms. 2904 (Temple, *Anglo-Saxon Mss.*, cat. 41), New York, Pierpont Morgan Library, M. 827 (Temple, cat. 45), and Orléans, Bibliothèque Municipale, Ms. 175 (Temple, *Anglo-Saxon Mss.*, cat. 43).

[112] There is no need for the Utrecht Psalter to have left Christ Church once it had arrived; whenever we have evidence for its location, we have evidence that it was at Christ Church. The Utrecht Psalter may yet have left Christ Church and returned at frequent intervals, like a yo-yo.

[113] Dumville, *Caroline Script*, pp. 119–20, notes that art historians would be happy with a Christ Church origin for the 'Missal' of Robert of Jumièges (Rouen, Bibliothèque Municipale, Ms. Y.6) on stylistic grounds. It is a point that does not bear repeating: there is hardly a style at Christ Church that cannot be found elsewhere.

[114] For a discussion of 'house style' in Carolingian scriptoria, and problems with the term, see R. McKitterick, 'Carolingian book production: some problems', *The Library*, 6th Series, 12, 1990, pp. 1–33.

[115] Higgit, 'Glastonbury, Dunstan', p. 282. [116] Gameson, 'Art after Dunstan', p. 208.

volume indicates that the artists of Harley 603 were well integrated into the production procedures of the scriptorium, and were given first use of the vellum, which they even ruled for the scribes. It is clear that Harley 603 was a Christ Church book not only in the sense that it was made there, but also in the sense that it was made by members of that community.

4

Four perspectives on the making of the Harley Psalter

In the preceding three chapters I have explained how the Harley Psalter was made, discussed the sequence of production in the manuscript, and attempted to date the various hands. This was an account of the appearance of the Harley Psalter, not an explanation for it; from now on, I will be concerned not with how the Harley Psalter was made, but why it was made in the way that it was, and indeed why it was made at all.

The Harley Psalter is normally considered in relation to the Utrecht Psalter. Its similarities to Utrecht are noted, and its differences from Utrecht interpreted. There are many ways of analysing the Harley Psalter other than by reference to its principal exemplar. In this chapter I look at the making of Harley from four different angles: from the perspective of another illustrated manuscript tradition; in the light of the problems encountered in integrating text and illustration by artists and scribes engaged on related projects; by determining assumptions that lay behind the initial working procedure; and by examining the extent to which working procedures were conducive to the completion of a manuscript in which coloured illustrations were integrated with text.

MAKING THE ILLUSTRATIONS: THE BURY PSALTER AND THE HARLEY PSALTER

There are many possible answers to the question 'When is a copy not a copy?', but one might be when the first artist, the last artist, and several in between had access to another manuscript altogether in making their illustrations.

The date of the Bury St Edmunds Psalter, Vatican Library, Ms. Reg. lat. 12,[1] is much disputed, but the Calendar indicates that it cannot have been made before 1032, or after 1095.[2] The manuscript has been ascribed to Christ Church Canterbury on iconographic

[1] For a technical description of the manuscript see A. Wilmart, *Codices Reginenses Latini*, I, Vatican, 1937, pp. 30–5. Full page plates are to be found in Ohlgren, *Textual Illustration*, pp. 249–97.

[2] The calendar is printed in full in Wormald, *English Kalendars before 1100*, pp. 239–51. It records the day of the dedication of the Church of St Edmund in the original hand, and a note added to the Easter tables of the manuscript makes it clear that it took place in 1032 – see E.M. Thompson *et al.* (eds.), *The New Palaeographical Society Facsimiles of Ancient Manuscripts*, 2nd series, London, 1903–30, Plates 166–8 and text. Since the translations

and stylistic evidence, and to Bury St Edmunds on liturgical and palaeographical evidence.[3] It was certainly made for use at Bury, and we can assume that it was there shortly after it was made. The Bury St Edmunds Psalter itself was therefore almost certainly never available to the artists of Harley: as we have seen artists A–F worked before 1032, and all the artists of Harley worked at Christ Church Canterbury. Nevertheless, using the work of Robert Harris as a starting point, I aim to demonstrate that Bury is such a powerful tool in understanding some of the perplexing imagery in Harley, that Harley must have been dependent on a manuscript that looked very similar to it throughout the course of its construction.[4]

It helps that there is good evidence that the Bury Psalter had an iconographic precursor. The Odbert Psalter, Boulogne, Bibliothèque Municipale, Ms. 20, was written at St Bertin in AD 999.[5] In his dissertation on the marginal illustrations in Bury, Robert Harris demonstrated that all seven marginal illustrations added to Odbert shortly after it was completed closely reflect some of those in the Bury Psalter.[6] For example, in the illustration to Psalm 21, verse 22, on fol. 28v of Odbert, and on fol. 36r of Bury, both manuscripts show the Lord and his mandorla rising from a base of cloud, to come to the aid of the Psalmist with a shield and a spear (compare figs. 64 and 65). Although the Bury drawings are placed exactly beside the relevant verses of the Psalm text, those in the Odbert Psalter were not, but rather were squeezed in where there was space left by the gloss,[7] sometimes at some distance from the verse to which they refer. Based on the fact that the illustrations in Odbert are displaced, Harris made a cogent case for supposing that there was a model of Odbert in which the illustrations were placed beside the relevant verse, as they are in Bury;[8] he judged from their style, untypical of other works from the St Bertin scriptorium, that this model was

of Saints Jurmin and Botulf are also in the calendar in the same hand, and local tradition, in the form of Oxford, Bodleian Library, Ms. Bodley 297, attests that their remains were translated in the abbacy of Leofstan (1044–65), it may well have been made after 1044. The editors, *New Pal. Soc.*, Ser. II, Plates 166–8, discovered ambiguity in the entry in Bodley Ms. 297, but see A. Wilmart, 'The Prayers of the Bury Psalter', *The Downside Review*, 48, 1930, pp. 198–216, at pp. 198–9. The text is printed in T. Arnold (ed.), *Memorials of Bury St Edmunds Abbey*, vol. I, Rolls Series, London, 1890, pp. 340–58, at p. 352. The manuscript was not made after 1095 because the translations of Saints Edmund, Jurmin, and Botulf, which took place in that year are not entered; see Dumville, *Caroline Script*, pp. 42–3.

3 Harris, 'Marginal drawings', pp. 553–9, ascribes the manuscript to Canterbury. It was clearly made for Bury, and this is some *a priori* evidence that it was made there. The evidence of the calendar and prayers and litany is most fully recounted in Wilmart, 'Prayers of the Bury Psalter', *passim*. R.M. Thomson, 'The library of Bury St Edmunds Abbey in the eleventh and twelfth centuries', *Speculum*, 47, 1972, pp. 617–45, at p. 623, n. 25; looking for parallels from Bury, he cites the example of Cambridge, Pembroke College, Ms. 20, a missal which he dates to *c.* 1050–75.

4 Harris, 'Marginal drawings', pp. 101–231, and 553–9. His work is the background against which my discussion takes place. Harris's unpublished dissertation is one of the most important texts for this period, and it is a great pity that it has never been published.

5 The Boulogne manuscript was in part illustrated by Abbot Odbert of St Bertin, and is dateable to AD 999, see Leroquais, *Psautiers*, vol. I, pp. 94–101, and esp. p. 99.

6 Harris, 'Marginal drawings', p. 114, notes that the Odbert scriptorium ceased to flourish after his death in *c.* 1007, and it seems unlikely therefore that they were executed long after the text. On the relationship between Bury and Odbert see Harris, 'Marginal drawings', pp. 110–19. See also below, n. 9.

7 On the planning of Odbert as a glossed text, see G. Lobrichon, 'Le Psautier d'Otbert', in J. Vezin and J-H. Martin (eds.), *Mise en page et mise en text du livre manuscrit*, Paris, 1990, pp. 175–8.

8 Harris, 'Marginal drawings', pp. 115–9.

64 *Boulogne, Bibliothèque Municipale, Ms. 20, fol. 28v. The illustration to Psalm 21, verse 20.*

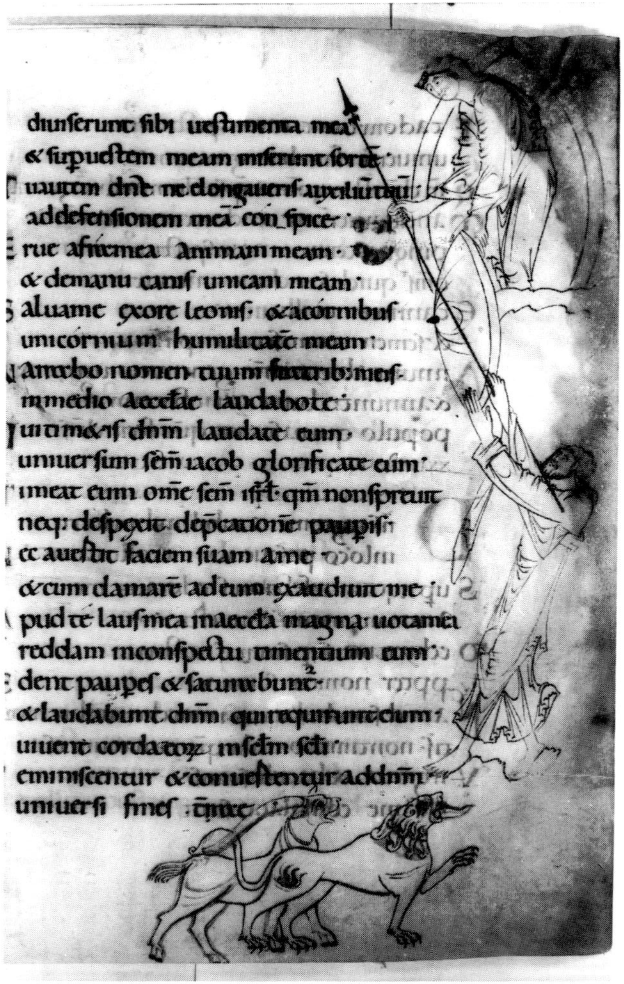

65 *Rome, Vatican, Biblioteca Apostolica, Ms. Reg. lat. 12, fol. 36r. The illustration to Psalm 21, verses 20–2.*

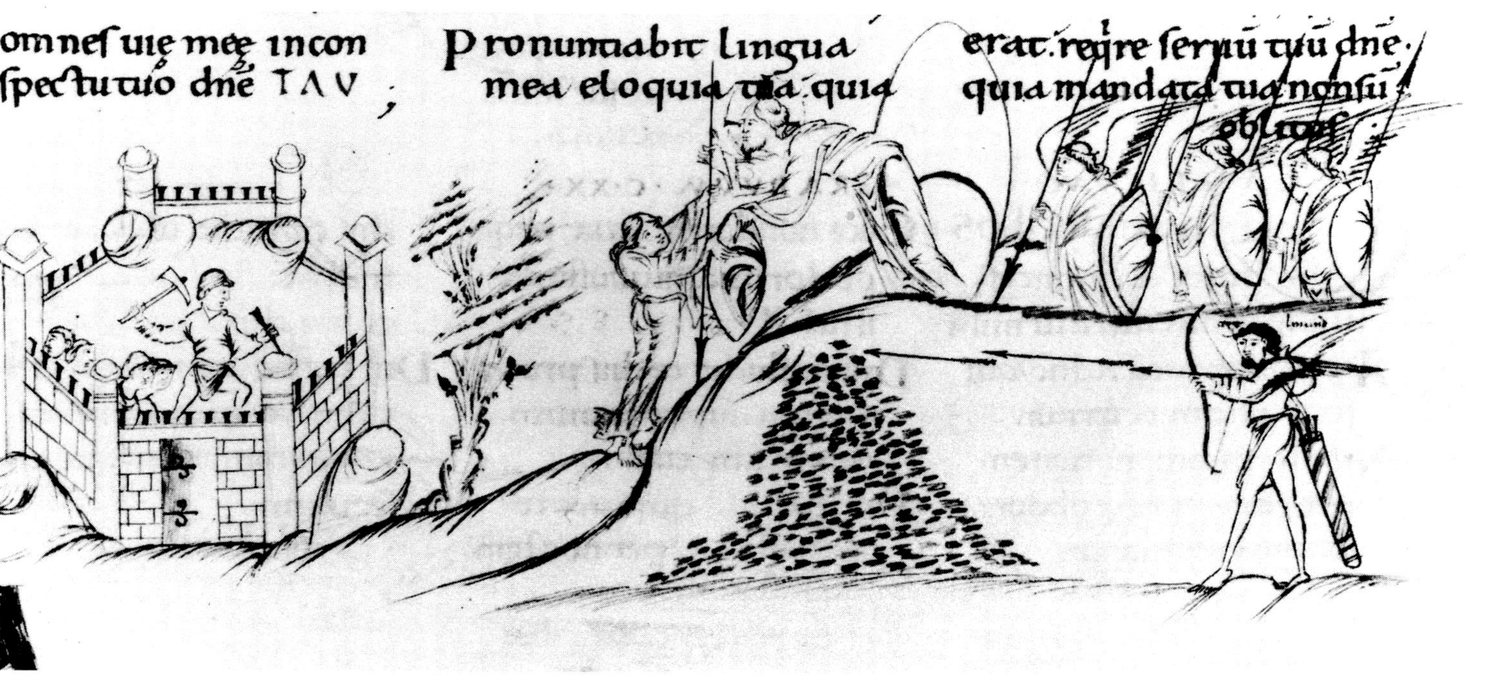

66 *The Harley Psalter, fol. 64r. The illustration to Psalm 119, by F, with additions by G.*

Anglo-Saxon;[9] and he raised the possibility that the model was only partially reflected in the illustrations added to Odbert.[10] There is evidence, independent of Harley, that there was a prototype for at least some of Bury's imagery before Harley was made, and that this prototype was made in England.

That there is a connection between the Odbert/Bury tradition and the Harley Psalter is demonstrated by Psalm 119 in Harley, on fol. 64r (fig. 66). At the top right of Utrecht's illustration to Psalm 119 is a group of angels armed with arrows (fig. 67). The leading angel hands one of these, shaft first, to the Psalmist, as the Lord looks on. This illustrates verses 3–4:

> *Quid detur tibi et quid adponatur tibi ad linguam dolosam*
> *Sagittae potentis acutae cum carbonibus desolatoriis*[11]

The Psalmist is pictorially being invited to help in the chastisement of the iniquitous. Artist F's illustration to this Psalm is different. Certainly he looked to the Utrecht Psalter: in Utrecht, as in Harley, the Lord is accompanied by an angelic retinue not warranted by the text, and in both manuscripts the members of this retinue hold the same weapons as the Psalmist. However, in Harley's illustration, the Psalmist does not receive an arrow from an angel, but a shield and a spear from the Lord. It is less clear what is meant by the Harley image.

In departing from Utrecht artist F shows a striking parallel with the Bury illustration to Psalm 21, verses 21–22.[12] Both make the Lord himself deliver the weapons to the Psalmist, and in both, his legs and the lower half of the mandorla are obscured. In both manuscripts a spear and a shield are used, and they are held by both protagonists in a similar way. The pictorial justification for the spear and shield held by the Psalmist and the Lord in the Bury manuscript came from the exemplar that Odbert also used. There is no such self-evident context for the shield and spear in Harley, and this indicates that the Harley artist looked to a manuscript similar to Bury, derived through the archetype for Odbert.[13] It was this manuscript that provoked the Harley artist to incorporate the Lord as an active participant, rather than as a spectator in his illustration.

The composition was appropriate in the illustration to Psalm 21 of Bury and Odbert, because the weapons were the vehicle by which the Lord plucked the Psalmist from peril in the form of the lion and the unicorn. In the light of these illustrations we can interpret artist F's illustration in a similar way. He refers to verses 1 and 2

> *Ad dominum dum tribularer clamaui, et exaudiuit me.*
> *Domine libera animam meam a labiis iniquis, et a lingua dolosa.*[14]

[9] Ibid., pp. 134–7, notes that they owe a strong stylistic debt to the artist of Boulogne, Bibliothèque Municipale, Ms. 11, a manuscript also produced at St Bertin in the time of Odbert, and illustrated by an Anglo-Saxon artist (see above chapter 3, p. 148, and n. 107).

[10] Harris, 'Marginal drawings', p. 119

[11] What shall be given to thee and what shall be added to thee, to a deceitful tongue? The sharp arrows of the mighty, with coals that lay waste.

[12] Harris, 'Marginal drawings', pp. 138–42.

[13] Ibid., pp. 139–40. Harris suggests that the Utrecht Psalter illustration to Psalm 143 may have influenced the design of either the Harley, or the Vatican illustration. It is worth stressing that although the artists of both these illustrations may have looked at Psalm 143 in Utrecht, it cannot explain the shared debts that the two manuscripts have outside it, for in Psalm 143 the weapons are a shield and a sword, and the Psalmist is holding neither.

[14] In my trouble I cried to the Lord, and he heard me. O Lord deliver my soul from wicked lips, and a deceitful tongue

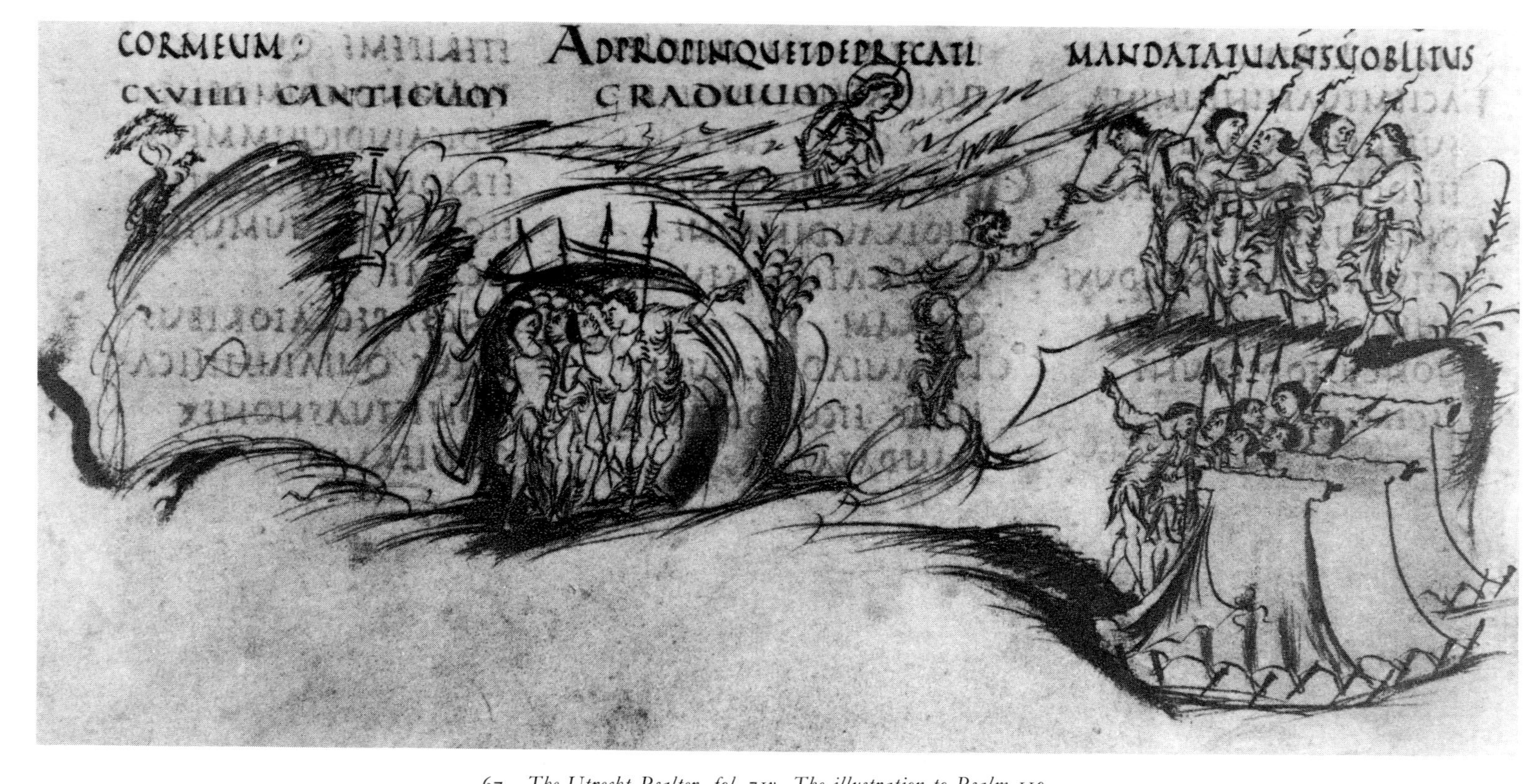

67 *The Utrecht Psalter, fol. 71v. The illustration to Psalm 119.*

This left artist F with the problem of what to do with the arrows that were textually warranted in his Psalm, and so he gave them to the figure at the bottom right of his illustration. Unfortunately, although this character is meant to be delivering the arrows to the iniquitous inhabitants of Cedar, he looks as if he is firing at the Psalmist. The difficulty is not helped by the ambiguity of Harley's own text to verses 3 and 4 of the Psalm:

Quid detur tibi aut quid adponatur tibi; et a lingua dolosa.
Sagittae potentis acutae, cum carbonibus desolatoriis[15]

The status of this figure is curious, and clearly caused some trouble at the time. It was for this reason that a later hand felt it necessary to clarify his position and name him *aegelmund.*[16]

As Harris pointed out, this illustration indicates that a member of the Odbert/Bury tradition was available to the Harley artists. I will now demonstrate the extent of its influence on Harley, going through the Harley artists in sequence. It is with the first artist, artist A that I start.

In the Utrecht Psalter's illustration to Psalm 7 there is a figure lying on the ground, suckling two of her three offspring (fig. 68). She refers to verse 15,

Ecce parturiit iniustitiam, concepit dolorem, et peperit iniquitatem.[17]

In artist A's illustration of the same figure in Harley, on fol. 4r, despite adherence to many details of Utrecht's illustration, including the snake-like locks of hair and the drapery, the breasts of this woman are lost, and she now holds not three, but four offspring (fig. 69). The change in detail betrays a radical alteration in meaning. The figures are no longer being suckled as the text would suggest they should be. There is no justification in the words of the Psalm for the loss of the two breasts and the addition of another misery.[18] If it is not injustice, sorrow or iniquity, what is it?

In illustrating the same verse, on fol. 25r, the Bury artist parallels artist A, for the breasts of the woman are also lost here, and the offspring have further multiplied (fig. 70). What is more, the Bury illustration shares the upright stance of the figure in the Harley Psalter. That the Harley artist should depart from Utrecht at precisely this point, and find a formal parallel in this departure with the Bury image, is surely significant. Heimann thought it so, even though she did not notice that a fourth misery had been included.[19] Certainly we know that this verse also occupied the mind of the artist of Paris, BN Ms. Lat. 8824, who, on fol. 6r, also departed from Utrechtian imagery to illustrate the Anglo-Saxon text, and in doing so, he demonstrates a relationship with the

[15] What shall be given to thee or what shall be added to thee; *and from a deceitful tongue*. The sharp arrows of the mighty, with coals that lay waste.

[16] On the etymology of *Aegelmund* see Hasler, 'Zu zwei Darstellungen', pp. 330–8, but see also below, chapter 5, p. 198, and n. 60.

[17] Behold, she hath been in labour with injustice, she hath conceived sorrow, and brought forth iniquity. (The Douai Bible interprets the progenitor of the evils as male, but the image here would seem to dictate a female of the species; Heimann, 'Three illustrations', p. 57, had the same problem.)

[18] Ohlgren, *Textual Illustration*, p. 20, citing verse 15 of the psalm for textual justification, states that this female nurses triplets. This is precisely not the case: in spite of the text she is holding quadruplets, and this needs an explanation.

[19] Heimann, 'Three illustrations', pp. 56–9.

Bury manuscript.[20] It was singled out by Anglo-Saxon artists for special treatment. Moreover, artist A's interest in elaborating upon Utrechtian demonology has been thoroughly demonstrated: it consists in altering small details of the figures to transform their type utterly, as occurs, for example, in Psalm 6 on fol. 3v (compare figs. 15 and 16, above, p. 45),[21] and in Psalm 2 (compare figs. 1 and 2, above pp. 4–5).[22]

The iconography is much more fulsome in the Bury illustration. As Harris has pointed out, the woman holds the *uas mortis*, referring to the *uasa mortis* of verse 14, and, in medieval exegesis, interpreted as signifying a species of evil spirits.[23] The figures held within the cloak of the woman are thus representatives of the species, and the species itself has a label. In the light of the Bury illustration, the figures in Harley can be interpreted in the same way. However, lacking their label, they cannot be fully understood without the help of the more elaborate and explicit illustration, and this indicates that although they are closely related to those seen in the Bury manuscript, they have been modified to fit into the Utrecht context of the entire Harley Psalter.[24]

Because he was engaged in a technically different process, it is in the work of artist F that we see the influence of the Odbert/Bury tradition most clearly. As we have seen, artist F took advantage of the possibility of portraying Psalm 115 twice.[25] The pose of the figure holding the chalice used by artist F in his first illustration to this Psalm, on fol. 59r, is taken from the figure holding the chalice to Christ Crucified in Utrecht's image for the same Psalm (compare figs. 34 and 35, above, p. 79). This figure no longer holds anything in his extended left arm and with his right he supports the Lord balanced on the top of the cup referred to in verse 13:

Calicem salutaris accipiam[26]

However, the figure holding the chalice in artist F's second illustration to Psalm 115, on fol. 59v, bears a similarly striking formal resemblance to the equivalent figure in the Bury Psalter, on fol. 120v (compare figs. 71 and 72). This is the only Psalm illustrated in the Bury Psalter that coincides with one by artist F in Harley, but it is no coincidence

[20] R.M. Harris, 'An illustration in an Anglo-Saxon Psalter in Paris', *Journal of the Warburg and Courtauld Institutes*, 26, 1963, pp. 255–63, esp. pp. 255–7; also Harris, 'Marginal drawings', pp. 158–60.

[21] The first to note changes to the Utrecht demons wrought by artist A was Tselos, 'English manuscript illumination', p. 139. Contrary to his supposition, artist A cannot be seen as the progenitor of a 'new demonology'. There are clearly antecedents, most obviously on fol. 50r of the Leofric Missal, Oxford, Bodleian Library, Ms. Bodley 579 (Temple, *Anglo-Saxon Mss.*, cat. 17) – see L. Jordan, 'Demonic elements in Anglo-Saxon iconography' in P. Szarmach (ed.), *Sources of Anglo-Saxon Culture*, Kalamazoo, 1986, pp. 283–317, at p. 295, and the correction to this view in Gameson, 'Anglo-Saxon artists', p. 47, n. 84. At p. 47, n. 78 Gameson notes the four children of Harley, but did not draw a connection with Bury. Yet the formal parallel between the Harley and Vatican figures would indicate a tangible relationship between the two illustrations.

[22] DeWald, *Utrecht Psalter*, p. 21 terms the figures above the iniquitous to Psalm 2 angels. They are ambivalent because they are in the sky. Otherwise they are quite unlike Utrecht's angels, which are always robed. Three of these are naked, and two wear clothing reserved for humans. They can, in fact, be interpreted as demons doing the Lord's work, like those that appear in Utrecht's Psalm 5 or Psalm 27. Evidently artist A interpreted them as such, and felt the need to divest them of any qualities that might be considered angelic; four are now naked, the genitals of one of them are more obvious, and none of them has wings. The artists of the illustration to Psalm 2 in Eadwine and Paris 8846 make these figures much more obviously angelic in character.

[23] Harris, 'Marginal drawings', pp. 163–4.

[24] For a wider iconographic context for the image in Bury see Harris, 'Marginal drawings', pp. 158–66.

[25] See above, chapter 2, p. 77. [26] I will take the chalice of salvation.

68

69

68 *The Utrecht Psalter, fol. 4r. A detail of the illustration to Psalm 7.*

69 *The Harley Psalter, fol. 4r. A detail of the illustration to Psalm 7, by A.*

70 *Rome, Vatican, Biblioteca Apostolica, Ms. Reg. lat. 12, fol. 25r. Part of the illustration to Psalm 7, verses 14–15.*

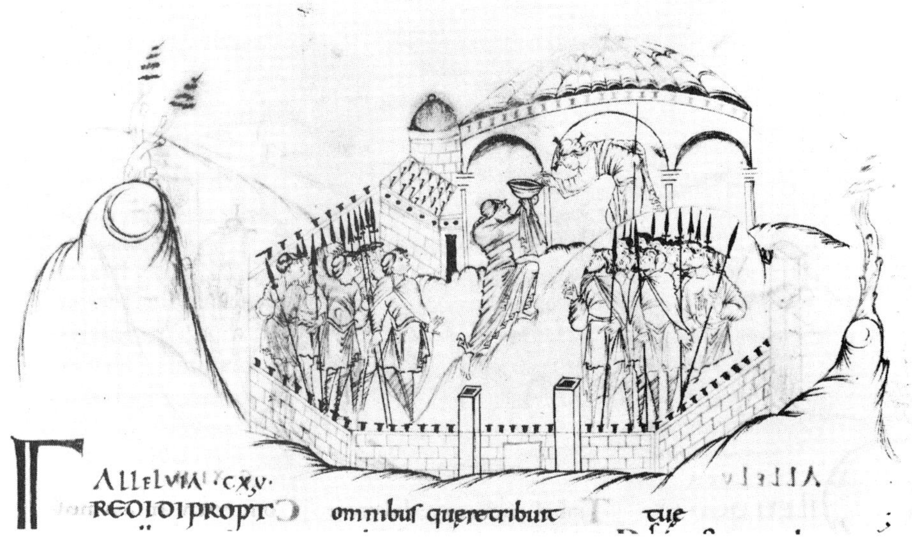

71 *The Harley Psalter, fol. 59v. The illustration of Psalm 115(ii), by F.*

72 *Rome, Vatican, Biblioteca Apostolica, Ms. Reg. lat. 12, fol. 120v. The illustration to Psalm 115, verse 13.*

that there is a close iconographic similarity between them.[27] Although it would make more sense for Harley's image to be the sacrifice of thanksgiving that the Psalmist offers to the Lord in verse 17, pictorially speaking this image looks like a repeat of the cup of salvation in the preceding illustration. This is confirmed by the placing of the illustration in Bury, where the chalice is precisely beside the word *calicem* of verse 13. It is as if the Harley artist has at last been given the opportunity to draw from two different pictorial traditions, and this in the illustrations to a Psalm with a strongly eucharistic tone.[28] The former illustration he adapted from the Utrecht Psalter, and the central image of the latter from that now seen in the Bury manuscript.

One of the majesterial characteristics of the Bury Psalter is that its imagery stretches through text and across page-spreads. This can be seen in its illustration to Psalm 7, verses 13–15: the demon is placed next to verse 13 at the bottom of fol. 24v, but he fires arrows at the demonic figure placed next to verses 14 and 15 at the top of the following recto. Another example is on fols. 87v–88r of the Bury manuscript, illustrating Psalm 78, where the Jews on the outer margin of Bury's verso throw stones across the text block at Stephen Protomartyr on its inner margin. Stephen himself looks to the *Manus Dei* on the inner margin of the following recto, as his soul in the form of a bird ascends to it. The *Manus Dei* itself is obviously the receptive vehicle of the Trinity placed in the upper margin of the recto. It seems that this characteristic has not yet been observed in other eleventh-century Anglo-Saxon manuscripts. To allow imagery to run across the page presupposes a quite different formal attitude to that seen in Utrecht, where the whole point of combining the verses illustrated into pictorial compositions was to create the illusion of coherence through three-dimensional relationship on a two-dimensional surface. It is remarkable then, that the same characteristic is seen in artist E's addition on fol. 53r in Harley. As we have seen, artist E set out to illustrate verse 15 to Psalm 104,

Nolite tangere christos meos et in prophetis meis nolite malignari.[29]

He linked it to artist D2's illustration on fol. 52v, and he too, uses a glance to do it.[30] In doing so, he demonstrated a sophisticated appreciation of the text of the Psalms, and of two illustrations in his own manuscript. It was surely the imagery of the Odbert/Bury tradition that lent this artistic 'Smierfink', as Heimann called him,[31] the pictorial audacity to consider such a bold device. But the formal parallel is complemented by an iconographic one, because it was the Odbert/Bury tradition that provoked artist E to illustrate verse 15. In the margin of Bury's text to this Psalm the sons of Jacob are depicted, clearly referring to the sons of Jacob mentioned in verse 6. However, Reuben and Simeon, the first of these sons, are placed not where there is room for them opposite this verse on fol. 108v, but opposite verse 15, on fol. 109r, already quoted (fig. 73). We have seen that Bury's images were normally carefully placed in relation to their text; the

[27] As noted in Harris, 'Marginal drawings', pp. 555–6, and Duffey, 'Inventive group', p. 116.

[28] The eucharistic element to the illustration of this Psalm in Utrecht is noted in B.C. Raw, *Anglo-Saxon Crucifixion Iconography and the Art of the Monastic Revival*, Cambridge, 1990, p. 77. Clearly in Harley 603 it is even more marked. See Duffey, 'Inventive group', pp. 115–17.

[29] Touch ye not my anointed and do no evil to my prophets.

[30] See above, chapter 2, pp. 91–3, and fig 43.

[31] Adelheid Heimann, unpublished notes in the Warburg Institute.

73 *Rome, Vatican, Biblioteca Apostolica, Ms. Reg. lat. 12, fol. 109r. A detail of the illustration to Psalm 104, verse 15.*

point here is not only that they are Abraham's seed, but also that they are the Lord's anointed, and that they are not to be touched. It was this illustration that encouraged artist E to elaborate upon the very same verse in the Harley Psalter, and therefore the two figures in E's illustration represent the two untouchable prophets that could be squeezed into the small space that was left by scribe D2.

Artist G's contribution to the Harley Psalter can be used to summarise the arguments presented so far, and to substantiate them further. Four of his images can be linked to the Bury Psalter. Like artist E, artist G's illustration to Psalm 30 on fols. 17v–18r was inspired by the Odbert/Bury tradition.[32] As in the Bury illustrations his illustration runs across the page spread, and the visual link is made with nothing more substantial than a glance, as it is with Stephen Protomartyr. Like Bury's illustration to Psalms 23 and 24, on fol. 37v, where the monk illustrating verse 1 of Psalm 24 is lifting his soul to the King of Glory of verse 8 of the previous Psalm on the other side of the page, artist G uses the imagery of one Psalm to bolster the imagery of another.

In his illustration to Psalm 48 on fol. 28r (fig. 48, above, p. 99), artist G shows the woman weeping at the tomb with similar hair and facial type to those of the distraught

[32] See above, chapter 2, pp. 100–1, and fig. 50.

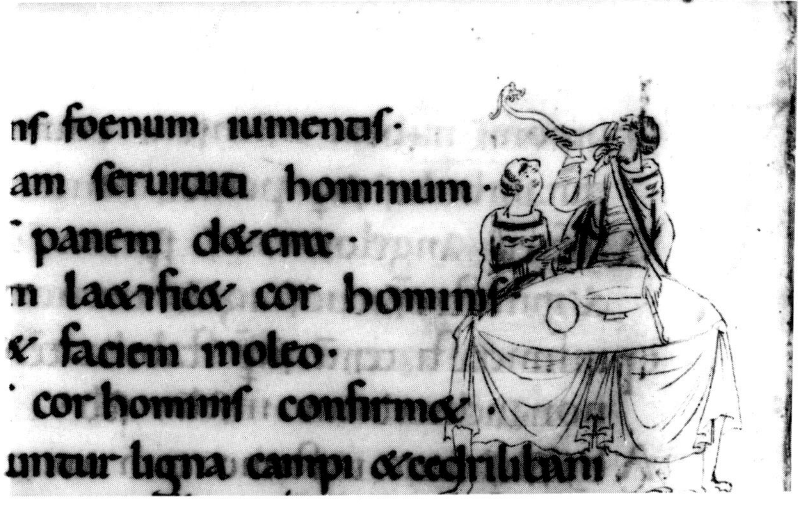

74 *Rome, Vatican, Biblioteca Apostolica, Ms. Reg. lat. 12, fol. 107v. The illustration to Psalm 103, verse 15.*

'Rachel' in Psalm 78, on fol. 87v of the Bury manuscript.[33] It was a member of the Odbert/Bury tradition that provoked the Harley artist to deviate from the Utrecht Psalter.

In the Utrecht Psalter there is no mandorla around the Lord in Psalm 21. In Harley, on fol. 12r, there is, and this is one of a number of artist G's additions to this Psalm.[34] It is paralleled in the illustrations of Odbert and Bury to this Psalm – the Lord's hand protrudes from the mandorla, and the mandorla itself is similarly pointed and cut off below the Lord's knees.

The illustration to Psalm 103 verses 14–15, on fol. 107v of the Bury manuscript (fig. 74), is taken from the same illustration to the same verse in the Utrecht tradition (fig. 52, above, p. 104). There are important changes: the figures are now made to hold the cutlery with which they are to eat, and the horn of oil is held by the figure on the right himself, and it is held so that it more or less covers his face. It seems that this character is now drinking from the horn, and therefore the horn may refer to the wine that cheers the heart, as much as to the oil that brightens the face, of the man referred to in verses 14–15 of the Psalm. The Psalmist has told the Lord that the earth is full of the fruit of his works, bringing forth grass for the cattle, and herb for the service of man:

Ut educas panem de terra et uinum laetificat cor hominis.
Ut exhilaret faciem in oleo et panis cor hominis confirmat.[35]

[33] Harris, 'Marginal drawings', pp. 302–3.

[34] Compare figs. 58 and 59 on p. 127, and for the extent of artist G's contribution to this Psalm, see above, chapter 2, p. 109.

[35] That thou mayst bring bread out of the earth and that wine may cheer the heart of man. That he may make the face cheerful with oil and that bread may strengthen man's heart.

The image is rather more effectively realised in Bury than it is in Utrecht, where, although the messenger of the Lord is pouring oil over the face of the character at the right of table, his face is not cheered, and where the figure on the left is not in the process of drinking from his horn – it is just being offered to him. The image in the Bury manuscript is more literal than the image in the Utrecht Psalter from which it derived. In adding another figure at the table to the illustration of this Psalm on fol. 51v of the Harley Psalter,[36] artist G demonstrates a parallel development to that seen in the Bury manuscript (fig. 75). Like the Bury artist, artist G felt the need to elaborate on the reference to verse 15: the artist concentrated on the face of the figure, and, painted in red, this figure does indeed seem exhilarated. Moreover, this figure is located in a similar place at the table as the figure on the left in the Bury manuscript, and has approximately the same pose, looking upward, at the horn of oil. Artist G has added literalism to the image in the manuscript, trying, within the framework of the Utrecht illustration, to raise it to a par with the imagery now seen in the Bury manuscript.

The illustration to Psalm 60 by artist H can be paralleled with the Bury Psalter as well. Verse 7 of this Psalm reads

[D]ies super dies regis adicies annos eius usque in diem saeculi et saecula[37]

As Heimann masterfully demonstrated, the Bury illustration to this Psalm verse, on fol. 68v, represents Hezekiah, who looks on in supplication as God the Creator alters his sundial (fig. 76).[38] The story comes from the Second Book of Kings, chapter 20. Hezekiah wants a sign from the Lord that he will indeed add fifteen years to his days as he promised, and the Lord makes the shadow go back 10 degrees on the sundial of Ahaz. We do not have the Lord adding days to the King's life here, although that is what is in the Psalm text. Instead, we have the sign that he would do what he said. In the Utrecht Psalter, by contrast, we have a literal interpretation of the Psalm text. The Lord is bestowing a laurel upon the King, by implication adding days to his days (fig. 77). But in the Harley Psalter, on fol. 33r, we move back to the specific sign that was bestowed on Hezekiah (fig. 78). As Heimann observed, the twelfth-century artist of the Harley Psalter has turned the laurel into the Sun, and the Lord has brought it back on its course across the sky.[39] The Lord's mastery of the Sun is further indicated by the fact that he holds a torch, which, in Utrecht as in Harley, is an attribute normally held by personifications of the Sun. The methods of presenting the miracle are obviously very different. In Bury, the Lord moves the sundial, in Harley, and in accordance with the usual portrayal of this scene, he moves the Sun. Heimann did not consider connecting the two illustrations in any direct way. But, in the light of other parallels with the Odbert/Bury tradition, I would suggest that it was an image similar to that which we see in the Bury manuscript that provoked the Harley artist to deviate so subtly from his exemplar.

That parallels can be drawn with the Odbert/Bury tradition at all is indicative of the

[36] See above, chapter 2, p. 101–5.
[37] Thou will add days to the days of the king, his years even for ever.
[38] Heimann, 'Three Illustrations', pp. 46–56. [39] Ibid., pp. 55–6.

75 *The Harley Psalter, fol. 51v. A detail of the illustration to Psalm 103, by D2, with an addition by G.*

76 *Rome, Vatican, Biblioteca Apostolica, Ms. Reg. lat. 12, fol. 68v. The illustration to Psalm 60, verse 6.*

invention with which the artists of Harley adapted the iconography of Utrecht. There are other parallels cited by Harris in artist F's work, which further demonstrate the connection between the two manuscripts.[40] Frequently the parallels he observed merely demonstrate that the artists were working 'in the same visual world'. However there are specific connections between the two manuscripts that would indicate a very much closer relationship than that. In Psalms 7, 21, 60, 103, 104, and 115, the artists of Harley elaborate the very same verses, and in Psalms 7, 21, 103, and 115 they use similar forms

[40] See Harris, 'Marginal drawings', pp. 553–9, for a summary.

77 *The Utrecht Psalter, fol. 34v. The illustration to Psalm 60.*

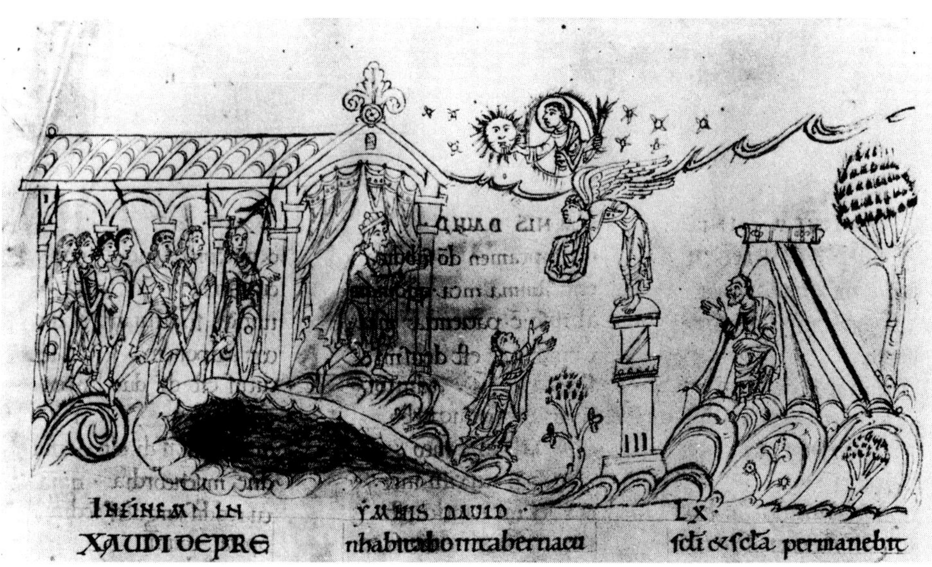

78 *The Harley Psalter, fol. 33r. The illustration to Psalm 60, by H.*

to do so – forms that lie outside those found in the Utrecht Psalter itself. In the illustrations to Psalms 115 and 7, the Bury manuscript presents images more precise and satisfactory than their relatives in the Harley manuscript: the iconography is more coherent, and more closely tied in with the text. It seems more likely, therefore, that there has been a conscious effort on the part of the Harley artists to incorporate the imagery now seen in the Bury Psalter, than that the Bury artist has chosen to elaborate comparatively unsatisfactory images in Harley. Indeed, to recognise the parallels between the two manuscripts, it has been necessary to compare Utrecht and Harley, looking for iconographic divergence. We would have to suppose that the Bury artist had done the same, and then concentrated upon elaborating Harley's divergences, if we considered that the direction of influence flowed from Harley to Bury. Without attempting to place the Bury Psalter therefore, I suggest, as Harris hypothesised, that a manuscript very similar to it was present at Christ Church from the early eleventh century, for which there is some independent evidence in the Odbert Psalter.[41]

The reliance on the Odbert/Bury tradition by artists from all of the 'phases' of the Harley Psalter, shows that the notion that Harley is a 'copy' of Utrecht is unsustainable. The artists of the manuscript, even one of the so-called 'facsimilists', looked to other manuscript sources, including an earlier eleventh-century prototype of the Bury Psalter. Harley has to be reclassified: like the Bury Psalter, the Harley Psalter, from start to finish, is one of a number of 'Problematic relatives of the Utrecht Psalter';[42] like the third 'copy' of the Utrecht Psalter, Paris, BN Ms. Lat. 8846, the Harley Psalter is not a copy of the Utrecht Psalter, but a conflation of imagery from at least two different manuscripts;[43] and like the compilers of the *Regularis Concordia*, the Harley artists behaved like bees; they went to more than one flower to make their honey.[44]

If I were not to point out, at some stage, that many of the illustrations to this book are very tiny details of the Harley illustrations, I should be accused of misleading my readers. The artists that worked on this book were precisely concerned with this level of articulation, and as Wormald noted, the miniature scenes are seen best in enlargements of some details.[45] There are good reasons for this. As he also pointed out, the compositions of Utrecht may look coherent, but they are an artificial concoction. As a whole they have no textual message.[46] Artist F's departures from the overall compositions of Utrecht are therefore deviations from something that earned no textual meaning. His illustrations make textual sense in the same way that Utrecht's do: individual details mean something in relation to the text; the overall compositions do not. None of the illustrations in Utrecht and Harley are illustrations of any given Psalm; all the illustrations in both manuscripts are illustrations that accompany a Psalm, and make reference to selected phrases within it. This is why in this book I have referred to illustrations to Psalms and not illustrations of Psalms, and this is why, in other manuscripts, such as the Bury Psalter itself, and in Paris, BN Ms. Lat. 8824 discussed below, individual incidents could be extracted from the Utrecht Psalter cycle so effectively. In using Utrecht, the Harley artists missed many of its references to the text,

[41] The implications of this analysis for the tradition of marginal Psalter illustration in late Anglo-Saxon England will be further explored in W.G. Noel, 'A prototype for the Bury St Edmunds Psalter' in A. Gransden (ed.), *British Archaeological Association Conference Transactions : Bury St Edmunds*, forthcoming. Compare R. Gameson, 'English manuscript art in the mid-eleventh century: the decorative tradition', *The Antiquaries Journal*, 71, 1990, pp. 64–122, p. 87, and n. 140.

[42] The phrase comes from Tselos, 'English manuscript illumination', pp. 148–9, where other relatives are discussed.

[43] See Stirnemann, *Manuscrits enluminés*, pp. 46–7, and Dodwell, 'Final copy', *passim*.

[44] T. Symons (ed.), *Regularis Concordia*, Edinburgh, 1953, Forward; see also W.H. Stevenson, *Asser's Life of King Alfred*, Oxford, 1904, pp. 302–3: Aldhelm used it in the *De laudibus uirginitatis*, and Stevenson cites two more Canterbury related examples; see also T.A. Heslop, in Gibson, Heslop and Pfaff (eds.), *The Eadwine Psalter*, p. 34.

[45] Wormald, *English Drawings*, p. 31. [46] Wormald, *Utrecht Psalter*, pp. 1–2.

but they incorporated hundreds of them. When we have evidence that the Harley artists read Utrecht's images in the light of the text, they only demonstrate further their concern with extraordinarily detailed visualisation of particular verses, sometimes outside the iconography that Utrecht itself provided. Those that made Harley seem to have tackled references to verses of the Psalm text with a care similar to that seen in Bury and Paris 8824, where individual verses were illustrated with separate compositions. It is simply that, in following Utrecht more closely, they were more comprehensive in the verses that they covered. It is probably no coincidence that when artist F departs from Utrecht, the figures that he uses to articulate his references to the text are comparable in size to those seen in the Bury manuscript, and markedly different to those seen in Utrecht or the early quires of Harley. However, the size of the image is no indication of the intellectual effort that went into making it, and we cannot assume that a reader would find the size of the image a barrier to literate understanding of it. If the reader of Harley understood its images in the same way that the artists of Harley understood Utrecht's images, then the work of all the artists of Harley is compatible, and there is no need to think that the aims of the campaign changed during the course of construction. This brings us to the threshold of the next chapter.

Making the illustrated page: Paris BN Ms. Lat. 8824 and the Harley Psalter

In one important respect, the artists who contributed to the imagery of the Odbert/Bury tradition had a much easier task than the makers of the Harley Psalter. The great advantage of the format of the Odbert/Bury tradition was that images could be left out, or incorporated and invented for the first time, without upsetting the layout of the book. The first experiment to incorporate Utrecht Psalter imagery into a Psalter text in England was not Harley, but drawings taken from the Utrecht Psalter, and placed in the margins of a pre-written Psalter text with ample margins. This is an altogether less ambitious task than to incorporate Utrecht's images into the body of a new text, as a comparison with other manuscripts demonstrates.

Paris, BN Ms. Lat. 8824, is a manuscript made in the second quarter of the eleventh century, possibly at Christ Church.[47] It is a Psalter containing parallel Roman and Anglo-Saxon versions of the Psalm text.[48] Most of its illustration has been excised. It was once worthy of being in the collection of Jean, Duc de Berry:[49] full-page illustrations prefaced the major divisions of the Psalter, and every other verse initial in both the Latin and the Anglo-Saxon versions was executed in gold. However, a number

[47] For notices of this manuscript see B. Colgrave (ed.), *The Paris Psalter*; Avril and Stirnemann, *Manuscrits enluminés*, pp. 18–19; the long study in Harris, 'Marginal drawings', pp. 28–73; Harris, 'Anglo-Saxon Psalter in Paris', pp. 255–63; Temple, *Anglo-Saxon Mss.*, Cat 83, pp. 99–100; Ohlgren, *Textual Illustration*, pp. 3–4 and 298–302; J. Vezin, 'Manuscrits des dixième et onzième siècles copiés en Angleterre en minuscule caroline et conservés à la Bibliothèque nationale de Paris', in *Humanisme actif. Mélanges d'art et de littérature offerts à Julien Cain*, 2 vols., Paris, 1968, vol. 2, pp. 283–96, at pp. 291–2.

[48] For the text see the contribution of K. and C. Sisam in Colgrave (ed.), *The Paris Psalter*, pp. 15–17.

[49] For the history of the manuscript see the contribution of J. Bromwich to Colgrave (ed.), *The Paris Psalter*, pp. 11–12.

of illustrations were inserted within the body of the text, where gaps were left because one version of the Psalter was longer than the other. These exhibit the same concern as the Harley artists to adopt and adapt Utrechtian motifs to illustrate particular verses of the Psalter text in a literal manner.[50] Thus, on fol. 2r, the figure of the Lord smashing the iniquitous like a potter's vessel, as demanded by the text of Psalm 2, verse 9, is clearly derived from the same figure in Utrecht and Harley. It is instructive to see the designers of Paris 8824 tackling the problems of layout that so beset Harley.

At first glance, one might suppose that the illustrations in Paris 8824 were the result of later opportunism by an artist with a passing interest in the manuscript. But this is not the case. On the contrary, they were always meant to be part of the design of the book, and the manuscript was to be punctuated throughout with them. Some one-line spaces, and every space of two lines or more, are occupied by an illustration until fol. 8r. On these folios the justification of the columns is good, except occasionally where there are illustrations, where the correct space was left for them. As the scribe was writing his text he was thinking of the illustration to be inserted, and, as Rickert has observed, the illustrations were actually executed before the scribe wrote his subsequent text.[51] Moreover, very soon after the illustrations stop, the scribe decided to employ another method of filling up the gaps created in his text: from fol. 10v he centred his Latin verses within the ruled space, and the text takes up an increasingly small amount of the width of the column as the verse closes; dissatisfied with this solution, on fol. 13r he ranged his text to the left, and gave up the right-hand margin; finally, from fol. 17r onwards he reverted to the gaps between verses again. This fruitless struggle to construct an alternative solution implies that the illustrations were contemporaneous with the writing of the text, and integral to the conception of the book. Too time consuming they may have been, but without them the scribe had to try to overcome his problem another way.

As has been stressed in the literature, there are precedents in late antique systems of book production for images being inserted into columns of text.[52] However, Paris 8824 probably owed nothing more to late antique systems of book illustration than the fact that it inspired contemporary parallels for columnar illustration, some of which may have ultimately been derived from them.[53] The manuscript itself shows every sign of being an original product of late Anglo-Saxon England, containing an Anglo-Saxon text, and an Anglo-Saxon illustrated variant.[54] Certainly late antique systems of

[50] We cannot be sure whether the artist of Paris 8824 looked to Utrecht or to Harley for his images. That 8824, on fol. 3v, has the whale-like Mouth of Hell also found on fol. 71r of Harley, and not in Utrecht, might lead us to suggest a direct connection between the two works. But this type of Hell Mouth was a common image by the first half of the eleventh century; it is also found in the 'Quinity' of Winchester (on fol. 75v of BL Cotton Ms. Titus D.xxvii), on pages 3 and 16 of the Caedmon Genesis (Oxford, Bodleian Library, Ms. Junius 11), and on fol. 7r of BL Stowe Ms. 944. See also Tselos, 'English manuscript illumination', p. 149. However, the Harleian version is not the decorative first beginnings of this type of Hell Mouth as Tselos proposes, for, as L. Jordan, 'Demonic elements', at p. 298 notes, it is found in a late eighth or early ninth-century Anglo-Saxon ivory in the British Museum; see J. Beckwith, *Ivory Carvings*, cat. 4, pp. 118–19, and ills. 1 and 16.

[51] M. Rickert, *Painting in Britain: The Middle Ages*, London, 1954, p. 56, n. 60.

[52] Harris, 'Marginal drawings', pp. 37–40, and H. Toubert, 'L'illustration dans les colonnes du texte', in J. Vezin and J.H. Martin (eds.), *Mise en page et mise en texte du livre manuscrit*, Paris, 1990, pp. 355–9.

[53] Notably the *Herbarium* in BL Cotton Ms. Vitellius C.iii, and (Temple, *Anglo-Saxon Mss.*, cat. 63) and the Marvels of the East in BL Cotton Ms. Vitellius A.xv (Temple, *Anglo-Saxon Mss.*, cat. 52), and BL Cotton Ms. Tiberius B.v (Temple, *Anglo-Saxon Mss.*, cat. 87).

[54] See above, pp. 156–7.

illustration cannot explain what is truly extraordinary about 8824, its size – the text space is *c.* 425 by *c.* 100 mm, the overall dimensions, slightly trimmed *c.* 530 by 185 mm:[55] even trimmed, the manuscript is nearly three times as high as it is wide. For this we need another explanation. Although undoubtedly it is, and was, a physical oddity, as Sandy Heslop has pointed out to me, it is the same shape as the codices that are carried by figures in prefatory pages of Gospel books. Christ in Majesty holds one such book closed on fol. 16v of Cambridge, Trinity College, Ms. B. 10.4, and St Matthew holds another one open on fol. 17v of the same manuscript.[56] Conceptually it was a familiar size to an Anglo-Saxon, and it may have gained a certain status by being the size that it was.

But what was so special about this manuscript that it should be this size? The Psalter is laid out in two thin columns of equal width, with 45 lines per column. On the left is the Roman text of the Psalms, and on the right, running parallel to it, is the Anglo-Saxon translation. Since the Anglo-Saxon translation is longer than the Latin, it would have made better sense if the columns were wider, or at least that the Anglo-Saxon text column was wider than the Latin. The gaps between each Latin verse would have been much smaller if this had been the case. It is not just that the size of the manuscript is extraordinary in itself, but also that, for parallel texts of different lengths, it was extraordinarily inappropriate. I would like to propose the following hypothesis to explain this curious circumstance. We have in fact been looking at the reasoning of the planner of the manuscript the wrong way round. The gaps between the Roman verses were not mistakes at all. Rather, they were designed to be there, and to be filled with images. In fact the Paris 8824 layout is very clever: the columns were made thin to create gaps, and the artist could insert imagery where it was possible. The page dimensions of the volume were a necessary consequence of the planning of the gaps between verses. The gaps that were created through trial and by error in scribe 1's work in Harley were created quite deliberately by the planner of Paris 8824. Because the parallel columns of text were so thin, few verses could be fitted on any one folio. The solution was to make the manuscript very tall.[57] The placing of the illustrations in Paris 8824 might have been determined by the text in its construction, but the proportions of the text block itself were determined by the desire to leave spaces for the illustrations.[58]

The difficulties generated by the desire to incorporate imagery into the text area

[55] Harris, 'Marginal drawings', p. 39, cites the late antique example of the Ravenna Annals, discussed by B. Bischoff and W. Koehler, 'Un' edizione illustrata degli annali Ravennati del Basso Impero', *Studi Romagnoli*, 3, 1952, pp. 1–17. Bischoff, on p. 1, estimated the original size of the folios of the annals (Merseberg, Biblioteca Capitolare, Ms. n. 202), at 280 by 220–30mm. It was not a tall thin manuscript.

[56] Temple, *Anglo-Saxon Mss.*, cat. 65, and ills. 212 and 214.

[57] As it is, the manuscript is very thick for its height, comprising 186 medieval folios, even in its mutilated state. Another alternative would have been to produce the manuscript in two volumes of normal height, but this would have meant that the reader would have had to turn the pages of the volumes inconveniently frequently.

[58] This explanation for the appearance of the manuscript depends upon its size being the result of planning considerations. It is weakened by the extent to which other books, without the same problems, have the same size. Another tall thin book is BL Harley Ms. 5431 (Temple, *Anglo-Saxon Mss.*, cat. 38) for example, containing the Rule of St Benedict, of *c.* 1000, and from St Augustine's, measures 230 × 85 mm. It is less than half the size of Paris 8824; it is written in one column. Bischoff, *Latin Palaeography*, p. 26, n. 50, notes the extraordinary size of Paris 8824, which he compares to Florence, Biblioteca Laurenziana. Ashburnham Ms. 1814, an eleventh-century manuscript from Poitiers, measuring 455 by 140 mm, which I have not seen. Compare Gameson, 'Decorative tradition', p. 90.

meant that great feats of organisation were admired and imitated. For example, the colossal task of designing the layout of the second version of Utrecht, the Eadwine Psalter, demanded a figure in overall control, and Dodwell is surely right to suppose that Eadwine's portrait in this manuscript was as much a celebration of his achievement in orchestrating the layout of this enormously complicated book, as it was of his skills in writing.[59] When the third version was made, some fifty years later, its designer stuck to the Eadwine layout extremely closely.[60] The planners of this manuscript were not slaves to tradition, and they did not 'copy' Eadwine's illustrations, but they did find the Eadwine Psalter extremely useful in the planning of their pages.

There is a great deal of difference between a layout being followed because it was necessary to follow it, and a layout being followed because the purpose of the book was to imitate the model. If the Utrecht layout was also followed in Harley because it had the authority of tradition behind it, then we are faced with the inescapable conclusion that quires 10–11 and 5–8 are generically different to quire 9. But all the indications are that this was not the case. After all, when the project was first started, artist A did not follow the Utrecht Psalter layout; on the contrary, he deliberately and laboriously took up more space than the illustrations of Utrecht. His solution was strikingly similar to that arrived at by the scribe Eadui, on fol. 28. The Utrecht layout was no more canonical to the makers of Harley than the Rustic capitals of its text. The designers of Harley were not, then, ever faced with the problem of reproducing the layout of the Utrecht Psalter. Rather, just like designers of a number of other Psalters employing Utrecht imagery, they were faced with the problem of how to incorporate it into their text block.

So far I have looked at the question of the layout of the Harley quires from the point of view of the artists, and from the point of view of the scribes. In fact there is good evidence to suggest that this neat distinction between artists and scribes should be blurred. In this period the artists of intricate initials were also frequently the scribes of their texts, and their artistry is such that there is no reason in theory why they could not be responsible for more sumptuous decoration.[61] When one considers that the development of coloured line drawing can be placed in the context of the development of coloured initials, the possibility that scribe and artist were frequently one and the same certainly arises.[62] Adémar of Chabannes from St Martial, Limoges, was both a scribe and an artist,[63] as was Odbert of St Bertin.[64] We can add others to the list from textual sources: notably St Dunstan, able to make pictures and form letters, as Osbern

[59] Dodwell, 'Final copy', p. 26. See also M.T. Gibson, 'Who designed the Eadwine Psalter?', in S. Macready and F.H. Thompson (eds.), *Art and Patronage in the English Romanesque*, London, 1986, pp. 71–6, where the method of construction of this book, as well as its designer, is discussed. See T. Webber, 'The script', in Gibson, Heslop and Pfaff (eds.), *The Eadwine Psalter*, pp. 13–24, for Eadwine's limited contribution to its writing.

[60] See P. Stirnemann, 'Paris, BN Ms. lat. 8846 and the Eadwine Psalter', in Gibson, Heslop, and Pfaff (eds.), *The Eadwine Psalter*, pp. 186–91.

[61] If the initial was executed largely in the ink of the main text, and was executed before the text (as it often was), it is likely that the scribe was the artist of the initial. It is much easier to suppose that the scribe began his task by writing the first letter of his text, than that another hand altogether was asked to supply the first letter only, that the scribe would have then to work around.

[62] See Alexander, 'Aesthetic principles', p. 149.

[63] See D. Gaborit-Chopin, *La décoration des manuscripts à Saint-Martial de Limoges et en Limousin du IXe au XIIe siècle*, Paris-Geneva, 1969, pp. 53–4.

[64] C.R. Dodwell, *Painting in Europe 800–1200*, Harmondsworth, 1971, pp. 78–82.

tells us,[65] and Wulfstan's master Earnwiq was also a scribe and an illuminator.[66] If we take the example of Paris 8824, the illustrations in the text block of this manuscript are monochrome; they reflect their text closely, and they were executed contemporaneously with the script, with the absolute co-operation of the scribe, who shortly after they stopped tried to find another way of filling the spaces in the text block. Whether the scribe executed the now excised full-page colour illustration we cannot say, but it is clear that he was responsible for those that survive in the body of the text. The reason that Dodwell found no colophons by artists in manuscripts might therefore have been that writing a text often meant illustrating it as well,[67] the colophon of Wulfwinus in Paris 8824, on fol. 186r is a case in point.[68] In the Harley Psalter too, artist D was scribe 2, artist E was the rubricator, and Eadui Basan was an artist himself, even if he did not contribute to the illustrating of Harley. The apparent conflicts of artist and scribe seen in Harley were conflicts of technique in the difficult business of planning the illustrated page, and not only conflicts of personality between the artists and scribe 1, and we should see the Harley Psalter's layout in the light of the practical problems involved in planning the illustrated page.

The illustrations in Harley could only be executed before the text because they could be placed by reference to the Utrecht exemplar. Once it was decided that the illustrating was to be done before the writing, the makers of the Harley Psalter had little practical option but to follow the Utrecht Psalter's layout, especially once the Utrecht Psalter was unbound, and they were working on different parts of the book simultaneously. However, it is extraordinary that the artists did illustrate before the scribes wrote. It is an apparently impractical answer to the practical problem of closely integrating text with illustration. It was a difficult enough operation for the scribes to work their text around the illustrations, but that they should have to do this using Caroline minuscule in a format dictated by a different type of script was even more troublesome. It would have been far more sensible if the scribes had always been in charge of the manuscript. To explain why the Utrecht layout was followed so closely in the first five quires, we should explain why the illustrations were drawn before the text was written.

Clearly the difference between the Utrechtian layout of quire 9 and the very different one of quire 10 is in some way linked to the fact that the text was written before the illustrations were drawn. The scribes were in a rather different position to that of the artists. Scribe 1 found the Utrecht layout preserved in Harley by the artists extremely difficult to handle. We have no hard evidence that scribe 1 ever looked at the Utrecht Psalter, and, in contrast to scribe D2, he never followed its layout; all he did in quires 1–4 was to try to come to terms with the ruling pattern that he found predetermined for him by the artists in Harley. Scribe 1 worked contemporaneously with artists who had

[65] W. Stubbs (ed.), *Memorials of St Dunstan*, Rolls Series, London, 1874, '*Vita sancti Dunstani auctore Osberno*', pp. 53–161, p. 79.

[66] R.R. Darlington (ed.), *William of Malmesbury, Vita sancti Wulfstani*, London, 1928, p. 54.

[67] But in the Bury Psalter, there is, most unusually an inscription by an artist. See R. Kahsnitz, *Der Werdener Psalter in Berlin*, Düsseldorf, 1979, p. 220. I am grateful to Michael Gullick for calling this to my attention. An alternative reading is to be found in J.J.G. Alexander, *Medieval Illuminators and their Methods of Work*, Yale, 1992, p. 10.

[68] It reads *Hoc psalterii carmen inclyti regis david sacer dei Wulfwinus, id est cognomento cada, manu sua conscripsit. Quicumque legerit scriptum, animae suae expetiat uotum.*

the Utrecht Psalter to hand. There is absolutely no reason why we should suppose that scribe 1 did not follow the Utrecht Psalter because it was not available to him. Although he could have planned the folios of Harley in the same way as the artists did, following Utrecht, he did not need the Utrecht layout to space his text in advance of the artists' illustrations, and he did not find it useful. It was because the Utrecht layout was only followed because it was useful in the construction of Harley, that both scribe 1 and Eadui were free to alter it. To account for the difference in layout between Harley and Utrecht in these quires, we need to explain why the script was written before the illustrations were drawn.

To sum up, the question we have to answer to account for the difference in layout between the quires ruled by the artists and the quires ruled by the scribes is not why the artists did adhere to that in Utrecht, nor why the scribes did not. This is quite clear: the artists soon had to, scribes 1 and Eadui Basan did not want to. To explain the different technical approaches to the task of making the new manuscript (for that is what they are) we have to account for two major oddities. The first is why the illustrations were ever executed before the text in the first five quires when it led to working procedures that resulted in such problems in integrating text and illustration. The second is why, having started out on this procedure, it was decided to overturn it at the beginning of quire 10. It is these questions that I intend to tackle in the next two sections.

The meaning of the illustrated page: BL Harley Ms. 2506 and the Harley Psalter

It is tempting to think of the placing of illustrations as prescribed by the text in the construction of a codex, and the meaning of illustrations as dependent upon the text in a codex. When we describe manuscripts in catalogues we describe first their textual content and then their decoration. While this is useful, as the above analysis has shown it does not necessarily reflect production procedure. But more importantly, it does not necessarily reflect how the manuscript was conceived by those that made it. Certainly in some manuscripts, the illustrations were considered just as important to the meaning of the codex as the text itself. To demonstrate this I shall discuss the illustrated section of a computus manuscript, BL Harley Ms. 2506, probably written at Fleury and illustrated by an Anglo-Saxon artist about the year 1000.[69]

Fols. 36r–48v of Harley 2506 contain Cicero's verse translation of Aratus of Soli's *Phaenomena*,[70] accompanied by part of a star catalogue known as the *De signis caeli*,

[69] Temple, *Anglo-Saxon Mss.*, cat. 42; see also Saxl and Meier, *Catalogue 3*, pp. 157–60; ; also McGurk *et al.*, *Anglo-Saxon Illustrated Miscellany*, pp. 67–78, and illustrations on plates x–xvii. The origin of the manuscript, and the making of the illustrated section, are discussed in more detail in Noel, 'BL Harley Mss. 2506 and 603', pp. 9–69; also M. Mostert, *The Library of Fleury: A Provisional List of Manuscripts*, Hilversum, 1989, p. 107 and bibliography.

[70] J. Soubiran (ed.), *Cicéron: Aratea, Fragments poétiques*, Paris, 1972, pp. 157–234; see also the introduction, pp. 106–52.

falsely attributed to Bede,[71] and illustrations of the constellations referred to in the two texts. Both texts are written in Caroline minuscule by the same scribe,[72] the Cicero in a brown ink, the Pseudo-Bede in a red. The Cicero text is clearly derived through BL Harley Ms. 647, a Carolingian astrological manuscript created over a number of decades in the ninth century,[73] and at St Augustine's Canterbury by the late tenth,[74] with which it has in common a distinctive selection of texts, variant readings of those texts, and details in the iconography of its illustrations. Other illustrated English relatives of this text are BL Cotton Ms. Tiberius B.v, and BL Cotton Ms. Tiberius C.i.[75] Harley 2506 is distinctive in that, of all the Cicero manuscripts, it is the only one that has extracts from the *De signis caeli* as *scholia*. This text in Harley 2506 has much in common with that in two manuscripts in particular: Paris, BN Ms. Lat. 5543,[76] a mid ninth-century computus manuscript from Fleury, and Paris, BN Ms. Lat. 5239,[77] a mid tenth-century manuscript from Limoges. The Pseudo-Bede text has been edited by Antonio Dell'Era, and Paris 5239 was one of the manuscripts upon which he based his edition.[78] Paris 5543, not included in that edition, shares a number of distinctive variants with it.[79] The iconographic relationship between the two manuscripts, long recognised,[80] is

[71] A. Dell'Era (ed.), 'Una rielaborazione dell'Arato latino', *Studi Medievali*, Ser. 3, 20.1, 1979, pp. 269–301. See the introduction for the early Carolingian origin of the text, which advances the research of C.W. Jones, *Bedae Pseudepigrapha: Scientific Writings Falsely Attributed to Bede*, Oxford, 1939, p. 87.

[72] I am grateful to Dr Michelle Brown for her opinion on this point.

[73] Described in Saxl and Meier, *Catalogue 3*, pp. 149–51. See also W.R. Koehler and F. Mütherich, *Die Karolingischen Miniaturen, IV. Die Hofschule Kaiser Lothars*, Berlin, 1971, pp. 102–3, and plates 62–74.

[74] A St Augustine's scribe added to the text – see T.A.M Bishop, 'Notes on Cambridge Manuscripts Part IV: Manuscripts connected with St Augustine's Canterbury', *Transactions of the Cambridge Bibliographical Society*, 2.4, 1957, pp. 323–36, at p. 326.

[75] P. McGurk, in McGurk *et al.*, *Anglo-Saxon Illustrated Miscellany*, pp. 67–78 is an indispensable guide to this group of astrological texts. BL Cotton Ms. Tiberius B.v is reproduced in facsimile and the illustrations to Tiberius C.i are to be found side by side with those of Harley 647 and 2506 on Plates X–XVII. For a few variant emphases on the relationship between these manuscripts see Noel, 'BL Harley Mss. 2506 and 603', pp. 9–69. See also G. Kerscher, 'Quadriga Temporum. Studien zur Sol-Ikonographie in mittelalterlichen Handschriften und in der Architekturdekoration (mit einem Exkurs zum Codex 146 der Stiftsbibliothek Göttweig)', *Mitteilungen des Kunsthistorischen Institutes in Florenz*, 32, 1988, pp. 1–76, esp. 34–49.

[76] *Catologus codicum manuscriptorum Bibliothecae Regiae Pars Tertia*, 4, Paris, 1744, pp. 129–30. For the provenance of this manuscript see M. Mostert, *Library of Fleury*, pp. 207–8, for the date see C. Samaran and R. Marichal, *Catalogue des manuscrits en écriture latine, portant des indications de date, de lieu ou de copiste*, vol. 2, Paris, 1962, p. 275; see also L. Delisle, *Le Cabinet des manuscrits de la Bibliothèque impériale [nationale]*, 3 vols., Paris 1868–91, vol. 3, pp. 255–6, and Plate XXVI n. 4.

[77] *Catologus codicum manuscriptorum Bibliothecae Regiae*, 4, p. 58. For the date and origin of this manuscript see J. Porcher, *L'Art roman à Saint-Martial de Limoges*, 1950, pp. 50–1.

[78] Dell'Era, 'Una rielaborazione', pp. 282–96.

[79] The following examples are taken from those entries covered by the Pseudo-Bede text in Harley 2506; Hercules: *In sinistro genu I, in eadem tibia I.* [om] (Dell'Era, 'Una rielaborazione', p. 284, ch.iv, line 3) / Deltoton: *stellas* (*ibid.*, p. 289, ch.xx line 1 Consensus omnium – '*stellam*') / Aquarius: *habet in capite stellas II obscuras* (*ibid.*, p. 291, ch.xxv line 1 Consensus omnium – '*obscuras II*') / Orion: *Splendidior est* (*ibid.*, p. 292, ch.xxx line 2 Consensus omnium – '*est splendidior*') / Syrius: *XVI* (*ibid.*, p. 293, ch.xxxi line 6 Consensus omnium – '*xvii*') / Eridanus: *esse* [om] (*ibid.*, p. 294, ch.xxxv line 6) / Piscis: *Usque ad piscis* [om] (*ibid.*, p. 294, ch.xxxvi line 1) *ceteris esse* (*ibid.*, p. 294, ch.xxxvi line 4 Consensus omnium – '*esse ceteris*') / Ara: *dicitur* (*ibid.*, p. 294, ch.xxxvii line 1 Consensus omnium – '*accipitur*') and *autem* [om] (*ibid.*, p. 294, ch.xxxvii line 4).

[80] R.W. Scheller, *A Survey of Medieval Model Books*, Haarlem, 1963, pp. 57–61. See also Gaborit-Chopin, 'Les Dessins d'Adémar', pp. 186–91; also P. McGurk, 'Germanici Caesaris Aratea cum scholiis: a new illustrated witness from Wales', *Cylchgrawn Llyfrgell Genedlaethol Cymru (National Library of Wales Journal)*, 18, 1973, pp. 197–216; also Noel, 'BL Harley Mss. 2506 and 603', pp. 42–52.

complemented by a textual one, and the text of Harley is also related to them.[81]

In terms of its page layout, Harley 2506 is a genuine conflation of two different illustrated traditions. The text is laid out in two columns, with thirty-three lines ruled for each page. The columns are of very different dimensions. The wider column measures *c.* 121 mm, the narrower *c.* 51 mm. On the recto of each page the wider column, containing the verses of Cicero and the illustrations, is on the left; the narrower, containing the Pseudo-Bede catalogue, *De signis caeli*, is on the right. On the verso this relationship is, naturally enough, reversed. In some ways the Pseudo-Bede text seems to be the slave of the Cicero, which dominated the layout of the book, and determined the parameters of the constellations referred to. Preserved only as a fragment, the Cicero text covered far fewer constellations than did the Pseudo-Bede, and as a result many of the constellations normally covered by the Pseudo-Bede text are omitted.[82] Despite this impression of servility, the layout of Harley 2506 was rethought for the Pseudo-Bede text, and, in contrast to other Cicero manuscripts, where each constellation has a page to itself, in Harley 2506 two constellations are frequently depicted on the same folio: for example, Orion and Syrius are both depicted on fol. 41r, Argo and Cetus on fol. 42r, and Centaur and Hydra on fol. 44r.[83] The Pseudo-Bede text simply was not long enough to create a satisfactory mise-en-page if the layout of the manuscript was to adhere to that seen in other Cicero manuscripts. By altering the placement of the Cicero text, and by frequently depicting more than one illustration on each folio, an entirely different and immensely satisfactory new layout was conceived in which both texts and illustrations happily combine to produce well-balanced pages. By frequently illustrating more than one constellation per page, Harley 2506 is in fact adhering more to the layout of Pseudo-Bede texts, such as Paris 5239. The closely knit nature of the interaction between the illustrations and the two texts in Harley 2506 is nowhere more clearly seen than in the admirable page opening on fols. 42v–43r,

[81] Using Dell'Era's edition of the text, Harley 2506 shares three distinctive variants with both 5543 and 5239. These are Deltoton: *stellas* (Dell'Era, 'Una rielaborazione', p. 289, ch.xx line 1 Consensus omnium – '*stellam*') / Aquarius: *habet in capite stellas II obscuras* (*ibid.*, p. 291, ch.xxv line 1 Consensus omnium – '*obscuras II*') / Ara: *autem* [om] (*ibid.*, p. 294, ch.xxxvii line 40). It shares one with 5543 alone, Centaur: *XXXVI* (*ibid.*, p. 295, ch.xxxviii line 12 Consensus omnium – '*xxxiii*'). It shares three with 5239 alone, Pisces: *ad occasum III* [om] (*ibid.*, p. 289, ch.xxi line 2) and *XXXVI[II]* (*ibid.*, p. 289, ch.xxi line 3 Consensus omnium – '*xxxix*') / Hydra: *vertice* (*ibid.*, p. 295, ch.xxxix line 3 Consensus omnium – '*cervice*'). There are only two variants in Harley 2506 that can be paralleled in other texts and not in 5543 and 5239: with Amiens, Bibliothèque Municipale Ms. 222. it shares Cygnus: *I magnam* (*ibid.*, p. 290, ch.xxiv line 3 Consensus omnium – '*magnam i*'); and with Schaffhausen, Ministerialbibliothek Ms. 61 it shares Orion: *XVIII* (*ibid.*, p. 292, ch.xxx line 4 Consensus omnium – '*xvii*'). There are some significant readings not paralleled in any edited text: Piscis: *habet ad aquilonem stellas III* (*ibid.*, p. 289, ch.xxi line 2 Consensus omnium – '*habet stellas ad aquilonem iii*') / lepus: *pedibus* [om] (*ibid.*, p. 293, ch.xxxii line 2) / Ara: *quod* (*ibid.*, p. 294, ch.xxxvii line 1 Consensus omnium – '*qui*') / *obscurior* (*ibid.*, p. 294, ch.xxxvii line 2 Consensus omnium – '*obtunsior*') / Centaur: *signavimus* (*ibid.*, p. 295, ch.xxxviii line 8 Consensus omnium – '*significavimus*') and *pede ipso* (*ibid.*, p. 295, ch.xxxviii line 11 Consensus omnium – '*ipso pede*').

[82] The constellations usually covered by the Pseudo-Bede, and not included in the Cicero, are Ursa Maior, Ursa Minor, Draco, Hercules, Corona, Serpentarius, Scorpio, Bootes, Virgo, Gemini, Cancer, Leo, Auriga, Taurus, Cepheus, Cassiopeia, Andromeda and Equus.

[83] There are a very few exceptions: in Göttweig, Stiftsbibliothek Ms. 146, a manuscript also related to Harley 647 (for which see Kerscher, 'Quadriga Temporum', *passim*), probably independently of its Anglo-Saxon derivatives, Lepus and Argo are both found on fol. 24r, and Piscis and Ara on fol. 25v; in Harley 647 Sagitta appears twice, once on fol. 6v on its own, and once on fol. 7r with Aquila. Tiberius C.i copies this layout, but leaves the bow without the 'Sagitta' on fol. 26r.

illustrating Eridanus and Piscis (fig. 79). Following iconography unique to the Cicero tradition, the water from the Urn of Eridanus runs across the page into the mouth of Piscis.[84] In both Harley 647, fol. 10v, and Cotton Tiberius B.v, fol. 41v, there is no Cicero text at the top of the page, but rather the verses corresponding to the two illustrations, which are of different lengths, are written below. By writing the text to Cetus at the top of the verso, six lines long, and by beginning the text to Eridanus on line 18, the scribe ensured that six lines of the Eridanus text were placed on the recto illustrating Piscis, thus mirroring the Cetus text, and that the sixteen lines of the Piscis text reached the bottom of the page, pictorially matching the Eridanus text on the verso opposite. It is a neat solution, surprisingly complex in its ramifications: it meant for example that Cetus had to be placed at the bottom of the preceding recto, and that, in turn, the text to Argo had to be placed half way up this page, whilst still leaving enough room for the illustration of this constellation at the top. It is no coincidence that compared to the comparatively simple illustration of Lepus, the brilliant depictions of Argo and Cetus have little room. The ruling pattern was constructed for a new combination of texts, and the planning of the manuscript was in fact admirably suited to its task: the wider column gives enough space for the Cicero verses to be displayed, and the narrower column is wide enough to take account of the *De signis caeli*.

The formal relationship between the two texts is complemented by their content: while the Cicero text locates the constellations in relation to one another giving a number of astrological details in the process, the Pseudo-Bede text keeps astrological information to a minimum, and gives an account of the placing of the stars within each constellation. The images are the linchpin of this relationship. The texts discuss the constellations in very different ways, and they relate to each other by bringing different information to bear on the same images. The images therefore have a privileged status in the conception of the manuscript.

The artist of Harley 2506 continued the integration of these two traditions into the iconography of the manuscript. We have seen that in the Eridanus-Piscis illustration, Harley 2506 conforms to the Cicero tradition. The constellation of Capricorn demonstrates that Harley 2506 is also related in its iconography to Paris 5543 and Paris 5239. In this constellation the Harley manuscript differs markedly from those in the Cicero tradition: in the latter the body of the constellation does not have a twist; in the former it turns right round itself, before falling away again. This twist is by no means distinctive, though in many manuscripts there is more than one. However, a feature which shows a direct connection with the Paris Pseudo-Bede Catalogues is the band around the body of the constellation from which lengths of hair emanate like fire, in Paris 5543 on fol. 166v, in Paris 5239 on fol. 221v. We can see how all three images are developments from the form of Capricorn as it is seen on fol. 50v of the Leiden Germanicus, Leiden, UL Vossianus Ms. Q. 79,[85] but they are nonetheless clearly a distinct, though related, species. Harley is closer to Paris 5239 in that the band is lower down the body, but unlike it in that Capricorn has only two horns, and not four. The

[84] Cotton Tiberius C.i and Göttweig, Stiftsbibliothek Ms. 146 depict Eridanus on a recto, and Piscis on a verso, and so the relationship between the two is lost. [85] See above, chapter 3, p. 148, n. 108.

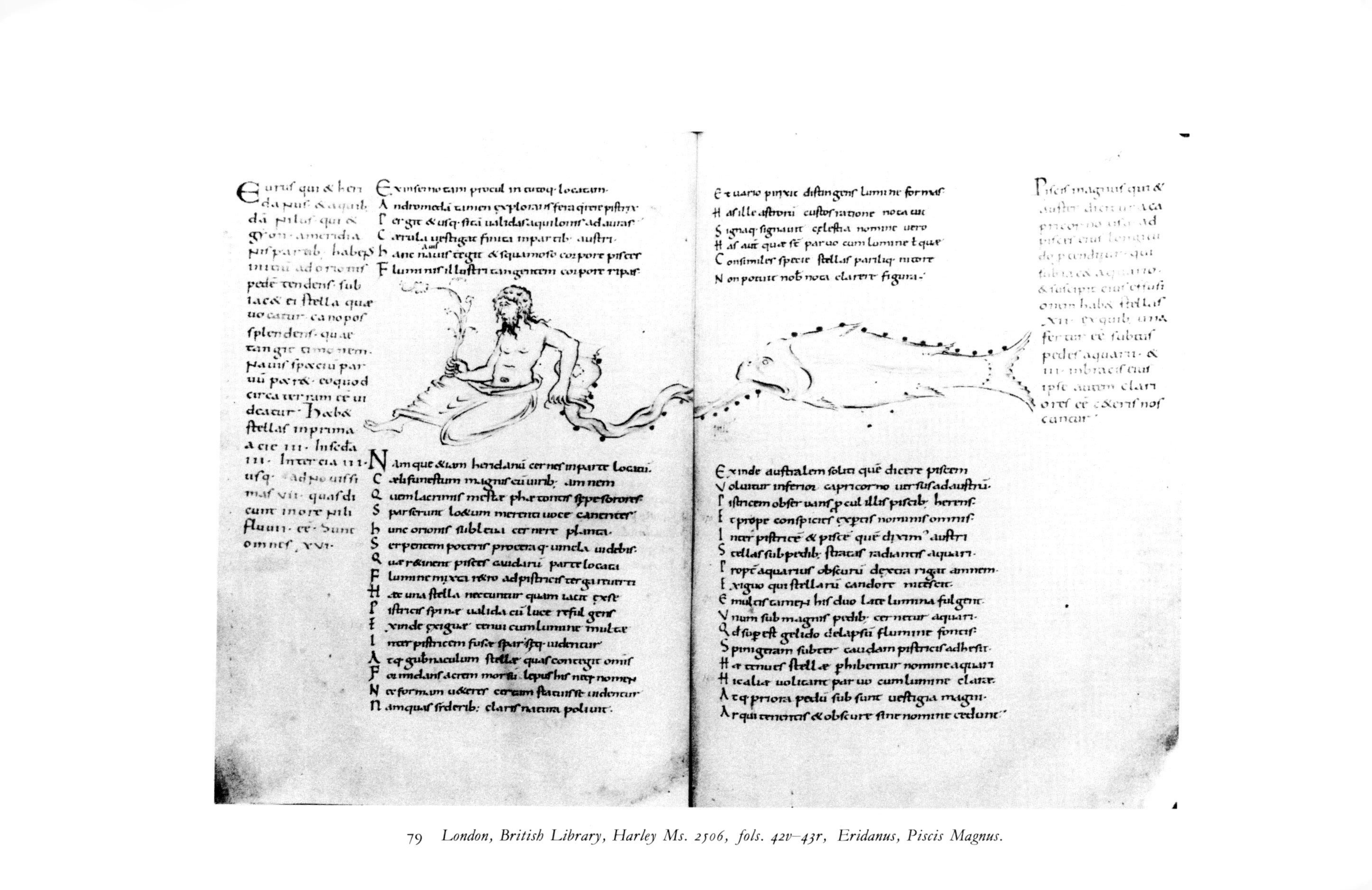

79 *London, British Library, Harley Ms. 2506, fols. 42v–43r, Eridanus, Piscis Magnus.*

figure of Orion on fol. 39r of Tiberius B.v is a development of the iconography seen on fol. 8r of Harley 647, and it is similar to the same figure on fol. 27v of Tiberius C.i. In Harley 2506, on fol. 41r, this constellation is strikingly different, and much closer to that of Paris 5543, fol. 168r (compare figs. 80, 81 and 82): in both manuscripts Orion is seen in profile facing the left; his sword is held horizontally out to the right, and just as in Paris 5543 it punctures the picture frame, so in Harley 2506 it punctures the text block. The scabbard of Orion in the Catalogue is held by a cord around the shoulder, while in Harley 2506 it is apparently attached to the waist. In both the Catalogues and in Harley 2506, the cloak of the constellation is joined at the shoulder by a buckle, and the form of the drape in Harley 2506 looks closer to that in Paris 5239, fol. 222v, than to that in Paris 5543. Indeed the images of Orion's cloak in both Paris 5239 and Harley 2506 look like ill-understood rationalisations of the cord and drape seen in Paris 5543, although that in Harley 2506 is much more imaginatively re-employed.[86] These parallels are sufficient to demonstrate that the synthesis of the Cicero exemplar and the Pseudo-Bede exemplar in Harley 2506 is reflected not just in the planning of the manuscript and in its layout, but also in the iconography of its illustrations. Moreover, since the parallels between the volumes are both textual and iconographic, the artist looked to the same manuscripts for his iconography as the scribe did for his texts. There is a pattern behind the iconographic variants in Harley 2506.[87] In this sense we should see the illustrations as being as much variants from the Pseudo-Bede exemplar, as they are variants from the Cicero. The illustrations to Aries, Pisces, Perseus, Aquarius, Sagitta, Syrius, and Antecanis are as close to the Pseudo-Bede as they are to the Cicero; the illustrations to Capricorn, Orion, and Argo are closer to the Pseudo-Bede; Eridanus-Piscis, Hydra, and Centaur, are clearly closer to the Cicero. Indeed this conflation even extended to the placing of the stars on the bodies of the constellation.[88]

All the elements within Harley 2506 are equally weighted, and they complement each other formally, textually, and iconographically. From disparate sources, an entirely new illustrated text of the constellations has been created; this text was not created through empirical observation, but by questioning the sometimes conflicting illustrated textual traditions, and attempting to harmonise and conflate them in the illustrations. The images were integral and essential to the conception of the text as a whole, and not merely decoration appendaged.

This analysis of Harley 2506 demonstrates that images could play an important role in the conception of a text. Making a book frequently did not involve writing a text and then decorating it; rather it involved conceiving what kind of volume was wanted, and then a consideration of how to execute it. The makers of Harley 2506, like the maker of Paris, BN Ms. Lat. 8824, started from scratch when it came to planning their page

[86] The illustration of Orion in Harley 2506 has implications for our understanding of the sources for the astrological section of the so-called 'Model Book of Adémar of Chabannes', Leiden, UL Vossianus Ms. Oct. xv. It is closer to the illustration of Orion in Adémar's book than that to either of the two Paris Catalogues; see Noel, 'BL Harley Mss. 2506 and 603', esp. pp. 46–8.

[87] For details see Noel, 'BL Harley Mss. 2506 and 603', pp. 27–53.

[88] See Noel, 'BL Harley Mss. 2506 and 603', pp. 53–7.

80 *London, British Library, Harley Ms. 2506, fol. 41r, Orion, Syrius.*

82 *Paris, Bibliothèque Nationale, Ms. Lat. 5239, fol. 222v, Orion, Syrius.*

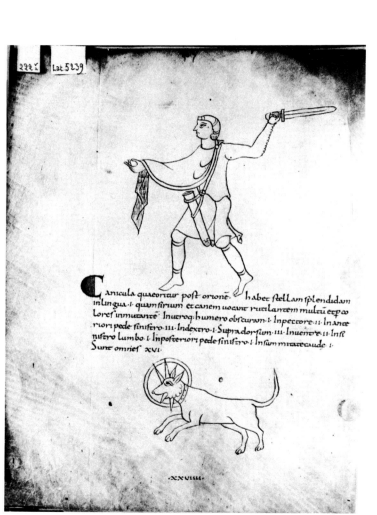

81 *Paris, Bibliotèque Nationale, Ms. Lat. 5543, fols. 167v–168r: Aquila, Delphinus, Oricn.*

layout. The makers of Harley 603 did not, but we can nonetheless deduce the assumptions by which they worked.

As we have seen, the techniques seen in the quires ruled by artists are in stark contrast to those normally employed in making manuscripts in the early eleventh century.[89] But there are at least two manuscripts with very similar construction techniques to those of Harley 603. In BL Cotton Ms. Claudius B.iv, as Clemoes has demonstrated, the artist pricked the parchment, was responsible for some of the ruling, and started his illustrations before the scribe wrote.[90] The same is true of the Prudentius manuscript, BL Add. Ms. 24199.[91] It is hard to see what practical advantage there was in the artists working before the scribes. It is a fruitful question to ask why they were employed; the scribes and artists clearly had reasons. I suggest that we are not witnessing a practical phenomenon, but a conceptual one. These books were seen not as texts illustrated, but as illustrated books with text. Bearing in mind how exceptional it was to have such an extended pictorial cycle, and how much more labour went into the illustrating than into the writing, this is not surprising. The construction techniques of these books may have been made possible by the fact that models were being used, but they were employed because the pictures were at least as important as the text to the makers of the volume. But it is a measure of the illustrative nature of the Harley programme that such techniques were employed for it. Here, the working procedures stand much more obviously counter to reason than they do in the Prudentius manuscript, and in the Hexateuch. It was not because the Utrecht layout and images were to be followed with precision. Rather, it is an indication that the text was a secondary consideration – it was written afterwards, and its placing was dictated by artistic concerns. It is only when we see the making of the manuscript as primarily an illustrative exercise, that the working procedures employed in the first five quires make any sense.

In glossed texts, the main text was normally written before gloss; the order in which the manuscript was executed is a good indication of the importance of the text over the gloss, and a reflection of the fact that formally the text was positioned in relation to the gloss.[92] The illustrative nature of the Harley Psalter programme might strike the reader as odd, since its images gain their meaning from the text, indeed they were literal evocations of it. But the way that the volume was constructed has more to do with the relationship between the book and its makers than it has to do with the relationship between image and text. I said at the beginning of this section that it is tempting to think of the placing of illustrations as prescribed by the text in the construction of a codex, and the meaning of illustrations as dependent upon the text in a codex. In Harley we

[89] See above, chapter 1, pp. 28–9.

[90] Clemoes, in Clemoes and Dodwell, Hexateuch, pp. 53–8. McGurk, *Anglo-Saxon Illustrated Miscellany*, p. 34, n. 9, states that Clemoes considered the illustrations in both the Claudius manuscript and Cambridge, Corpus Christi College, Ms. 23, to have been illustrated after the text; he quotes from Clemoes and Dodwell, *Hexateuch*, p. 58, n. 1, and the quotation refers specifically only to the Cambridge manuscript.

[91] See above, chapter 1, p. 29, and n. 6.

[92] See the comments of N. P. Stork, *Through a Gloss Darkly: Aldhelm's Riddles in the British Library Ms. Royal 12.C.xxiii*, Toronto, 1990 pp. 70–1. The point has also been stressed for the twelfth-century glossed books of the bible in C.R.F. de Hamel, *Glossed Books of the Bible and the Origins of the Paris Booktrade*, Bury St Edmunds, 1984, p. 18.

should think of the illustrations not only as determining the placing of the text, but as determining its content, and the nature of D2's illustrative programme, derived from Utrecht, and Gallican in character, as instrumental in determining his adherence to the text that went with them.

The Harley Psalter is a book of Psalms, and the illustrated section of Harley 2506 is a guide to the constellations, but neither can be defined solely by the texts that they contain. Harley is a truly extraordinary book of Psalms, with an eccentric text, and in which the images played the more important role. As far as the makers of Harley 603 were concerned, the manuscript was envisaged not as a copy of the Utrecht Psalter, but as a 'picture book', for which the Utrecht Psalter provided an excellent model. The makers of the volume could not have had these priorities if the illustrations were not integral to the reasons for its manufacture, and therefore to the concerns of its reader. In this sense, however much the images gain their meaning from the text, the book as a whole gains its meaning from its illustrations. And this again brings us to the brink of the next chapter, and how this manuscript would have been read.

Solutions to conflicting concerns: the development of the Harley Psalter

The Harley Psalter is a restless specimen of manuscript production, and it certainly appears all the more restless because its principal exemplar survives. That is why we can characterise the work of the artists and scribes so precisely, and why the consequences of scribe 1 taking over in quire 10 appear to us to be so dramatic. Clearly there is something to explain: we can be sure that the manuscript did not end up looking as it was originally intended to look. It is easy to see the manuscript as evolving naturally. But evolution is a process of natural selection, not choice. The manuscript developed because the scribes and artists made choices and decisions. To understand the experimental nature of the Harley Psalter, we need to understand what motivated the artists and scribes to change their techniques of production during the course of its making.

The Harley Psalter was meant to be beautiful, and it was meant to be finished. When the aesthetic qualities of the various quires of Harley are considered in relation to the time that they took to execute, the diverse experiments conducted in the manuscript by the scribes and artists concerned make much more sense, and a context can be supplied for scribe 1's controlling influence in quire 10. The battle to make the Harley Psalter can be sketched out.

(1) The campaign opened with the work of artist A. He was concerned to adapt the exemplar greatly, to use a wide colour range, and to integrate text and illustration to a far greater extent than is apparent in the Utrecht exemplar. However, a gradual transformation in artist A's techniques can be discerned: in the later folios of quire 1 and the early folios of quire 2 he could execute his work more quickly because he ceased to adapt the illustrations, he gave up the attempt to integrate them with the

text, he used a far smaller range of colours, and he started to miss many iconographic details. The scribe followed the artist, but he did not try to stretch his text to tie in with the illustrations.

(2) That increased speed of production was not only the result of the development seen in the work of artist A but also the motive for it, is indicated by what appears to be the most radical decision in the production of the manuscript – the decision made at the beginning of quire 2 of Harley to disbind the Utrecht Psalter so that artists could work on the volume simultaneously. It was, not surprisingly, thought impractical for one artist alone to work through the manuscript, continually adapting the layout of his exemplar as he went, and the decision to speed up production was taken at the earliest opportunity.

(3) Quire 9 was executed after quire 1 had been started, simultaneously with quires 2, 3, and 4. We see an attempt by one man to integrate text and illustration in full colour. However the solution was very different from that seen in quire 1, because it was done with techniques that were conducive to following the Utrecht Psalter much more closely. The artist-scribe D2 came to his own eccentric solution, and followed the Utrecht Gallican text word for word.

(4) The character of the work in quires 2, 3 and 4 is very different to the laborious procedures employed in quires 1 and 9. Artists B and C used techniques that were less labour intensive than those employed in the early work of artist A or by artist D2. Taking the later work of artist A as their example, in these quires we see greater adherence to the Utrecht exemplar, in terms of the amount of colour used in the illustrations, as well as their iconography. Technically, it was a simpler, and therefore less time-consuming task. This led to formal problems which became increasingly manifest. By adhering more to the Utrecht Psalter artists A, B and C were giving up aspects of the manufacture of the book that were highly prized at the start of the campaign. This is so much the case that, decades later, artist G felt it necessary to embellish these illustrations in precisely these respects.

(5) Having finished quire 4, Scribe 1 took over the writing of the text from D2 at fol. 54r/a/24. Eventually he found a solution of his own to integrating text and illustration, quite as pictorially satisfactory as that which he had worked out with artist A at the beginning of quire 1. In the second half of quire 9 physical harmony between the minuscule Roman text and the illustrations was finally almost perfected in a format dictated by the Utrecht Psalter. But it must have been a laborious process compared to that in quire 4.

(6) The success of the last few folios of quire 9 indicates that the working procedure employed in quire 10 was not the result of dissatisfaction with the appearance of the manuscript. Rather it should be interpreted as an indication that, despite the disbinding of the exemplar, work on Harley was not progressing swiftly enough, and another decision had to be made to make progress more quickly. As far as scribe 1 was concerned, it was much easier for him to rule quires, write his text, and leave the artist to fill in the spaces in between. The ruling pattern was simpler,

spacing the text did not present so many difficulties, and it was easier for the illustrations to tie in with the text, than it was for the text to tie in with the illustrations. The scribe must have been delighted to have persuaded his colleagues of this solution, because it was born directly of his frustration. He had never been adept at following the layout prescribed by the artists, and it is possible to see his disregard for the layout of Utrecht as a wilful exercise of his new found control over production. Certainly he did not plan his folios very well. However, it is also possible to see artist F's illustrations as symptomatic of the same restlessness in the production of the manuscript, and not just as a response to scribe 1's layout; after Psalm 121 Utrecht's illustrations become increasingly complex, and F's illustrations were certainly much simpler to execute.[93]

(7) Scribes 1 and D2 and artists A–F probably worked within months of each other. Yet one hundred years later the manuscript was still unfinished. The great change in the pace of manuscript production seems to have been heralded by the work of artist E. Artist E's illustrations are, strictly speaking, an extravagance, unnecessary to the functioning of the book as a Psalter in which every Psalm is illustrated. At this point, the concerted effort to finish the manuscript floundered, and only details were added to quires 1–4 and 9–11 by artists E, I, and J.[94]

(8) Although Eadui's work in Harley is altogether more substantial and purposeful than that of artist E, his approach to the problems created by the production of Harley was also time consuming and leisurely. His technique was by far the most satisfactory of all those employed in the making of Harley. Like scribe 1, he too considered it easier for the artist to alter his illustration space than for the scribe to lengthen or compress his text. However, he was far less wilful in his response to the problems posed by Utrecht: he allowed the artists to adhere more faithfully to its iconography than artist F could, and he did not leave any blank spaces at the bottom of pages. Eadui's procedure is best interpreted as an innovative synthesis of the techniques employed by the other rulers of the manuscript: lead point was the answer to ruling on both sides of the folio leaving the illustration spaces unscored, and it was sensible for the scribe to write before the artist drew. But this technique was not employed by someone impatient to finish the project, and this is further indicated by the fact that he spent part of his time on the manuscript correcting the work of scribe 1, rather than completing the text of the volume. Much the same can be said of the character of the contribution of artist G who followed him. He was concerned to beautify the Psalter further by adding a large number of details to the work of other artists, and this he did in preference to the obvious task before him – that of completing the unillustrated section.

93 See Backhouse, 'Making', p. 99.

94 Backhouse 'Making', p. 99 suggests that the initials and rubrics were added to give the manuscript a superficial appearance of completion quickly. But, if my hypothesis for the sequence of manuscript production is correct (see above, chapter 3), then this would not be the case. The manuscript could never have been considered remotely complete.

(9) The urgency with which work began on Harley eventually disappeared completely. A further attempt to complete the book was started only decades later, by artist H, but it was unsuccessful. There is some circumstantial evidence to suggest that even the text of the manuscript was never finished. Although a number of Psalters surviving from Anglo-Saxon England are clearly incomplete because of damage, this may well not have been the case with Harley. With the sequence of manuscript production as I have reconstructed it, the first quarter was started just before the third quarter, which was finished before the second quarter (Eadui's section) was begun. Since the second quarter was never finished, it is possible that the last section of the manuscript was never started.

Chronologically speaking, the campaign to make the Harley Psalter can be divided into two main phases, a fast phase (artists A, B, C, and F, scribe 1, and artist-scribe D2), and a much slower one (artist-scribe E, artists I, J, G and H, and Eadui Basan). These phases do not correspond to the extent to which the manuscript deviated from the Utrecht exemplar, and there is no neat equation between speed of production and distance from the model. The leisurely pace with which artist A began the project led to a greater deviation from Utrecht than the apparent haste seen in quire 2. The opposite effect can also be seen: in quires 10 and 11 the speed of production coincided with a distancing from the exemplar, while in Eadui's quires we return to a more sympathetic appraisal of Utrecht. The changing pace with which the Harley Psalter was made did not determine its appearance therefore, but it was one factor in determining the techniques that its scribes and artists employed, and perhaps the deciding factor that made the scribes and artists move from one technique to another.

We cannot assume that the speed with which the early part of the manuscript was made was the result of some urgent necessity such as an impending deadline. Disbinding a manuscript should be seen as a well-understood technique in the monastic scriptorium, rather than as a dramatic operation performed on a revered manuscript. It was only sensible for the scribes to take control of production from quire 10, and not a sign of a collapse under pressure; indeed artist F, like artist D2 before him, still had a wide colour range. The increased speed of production can be interpreted as a sign of impatience on the part of the members of the scriptorium and their overseer. It is not, after all, the deviation of artist F that is difficult to explain. Instead, there is another problem entirely, and that is the apparently desultory nature of progress after he finished working. It is clear that the Harley Psalter was not finished for the person or people for whom it was started, and that following an attempt to expedite the production of the manuscript there were long periods of neglect, punctuated by sporadic interest. As the analysis of the external evidence for the origin and dates of the Harley Psalter has shown, a heavy burden of proof rests upon those who wish to find the motives behind the slow down in the production of the manuscript. Moreover, so many *de luxe* manuscripts are unfinished that we cannot assume that the horsemen of the Apocalypse, that ride so freely across the Anglo-Saxon Chronicle, were responsible for it.

Conclusion to chapter 4

Any one decision in the making of the Harley Psalter had many causes, and that is why it is useful to look at the making of the manuscript from different angles. But all the decisions that were made were only possible because of certain underlying assumptions. If, as I have argued, the illustrations of the Harley Psalter were not just integral to the meaning of the volume, but its *raison d'être*, if its images were not designed to be copies of those in the Utrecht Psalter, but rather to be visual realisations of a selection of verses of the Psalm text, and if the layout of the Harley Psalter could change in the light of practical problems encountered in the course of production, then we can regard the developing character of the manuscript as the result of a series of very different but nonetheless related experiments, born of practical experience, conducted by a number of people, starting from a particular premise. This premise lies in the reason for the making of the manuscript. We can be sure that the artists and scribes of the Harley Psalter were making the manuscript in response to a requirement that they tried to meet, and that there is therefore a connection between the appearance of the book and its intended reader. The purpose of the next chapter is to understand how the Harley Psalter would have been read, and who would have wanted it.

5

Reading the Utrecht and Harley Psalters c. 1000 – c. 1150

Any one book could have many different functions, and many different readers. As Orderic Vitalis relates it, Queen Emma, wife of King Aethelred, had a large Psalter, decorated with various pictures, which she gave to her brother, Robert, the archbishop of Rouen.[1] The archbishop's son William carried it off from his father's chamber, and gave it to his wife Hawise, 'whom he sought to please in all things'. Through the offices of Robert de Grandmesnil, Hawise's son by her first husband, the community of St Evroul acquired the volume shortly after 1050. Robert had just become a monk at St Evroul, and was later to become its abbot. In Orderic's day it was still used almost daily by the choir of the community as they chanted the Psalms. While Queen Emma might have used her Psalter in her private devotions, the archbishop of Rouen's son seems to have used it as a love token, and the monks of St Evroul used it in the liturgy. In large part, the way that a book is used depends upon who is using it.[2] This is of fundamental importance, because the Utrecht Psalter was used by members of the Christ Church community even though it was not designed to be used by them, and because, while we cannot assume that the Harley Psalter was designed to be used by them either, they did use it. The first part of this chapter is concerned with how Utrecht and Harley were read at Christ Church.

An important difference between the Utrecht Psalter and the Harley Psalter around *c.* 1020 is that while the Utrecht Psalter was an inherited object from Carolingian Francia, the Harley Psalter was designed for a specific reason, relevant to a recipient in the early eleventh century. If the way that Harley is used depends in large part on who uses it, it was only made at all, and it only looks as it does, because someone specifically asked for a manuscript like Utrecht. The patron of Harley may have had completely different reasons for wanting an extensively illustrated Psalter from those of the Carolingian patron of Utrecht. To understand why the Harley Psalter was made, we should explore not how it was used, but how it was intended to be used, and who intended to use it. This is the purpose of the second part of this chapter.

There is a common thread to the two parts of the chapter, and this lies in the

[1] M. Chibnall (ed.), *The Ecclesiastical History of Orderic Vitalis (Book III)*, vol. 2, Oxford, 1963, pp. 41–2.

[2] One only has to compare the approaches to Harley 603 by present-day scholars to realise that this is as true today as it was then.

characteristics of Utrecht and Harley. There were intrinsic limitations on how they could be used, irrespective of the user. The perception of these limitations is helpful in determining who might have wanted Harley and for what purpose.

The Utrecht and Harley Psalters at Christ Church

The character of religious life at Christ Church at the time that Harley was started is elusive: it is difficult to determine both the extent to which the community was reformed in the tenth century, and the process by which reform was achieved.[3] The earliest date we have for concrete evidence of a monk there is that provided by the Anglo-Saxon Chronicle; the entry for 1020 records that on 13 November, Aethelnoth, a monk, who was dean at Christ Church, was consecrated bishop, with his see at Christ Church.[4] Nonetheless, Dunstan's successors as archbishop until the time of Aethelnoth were all abbots of reformed monasteries earlier in their careers,[5] and the image of the monks presenting the Rule to St Benedict in BL Arundel Ms. 155 presupposes a community that aspired to the life prescribed by St Benedict, even if it had not been entirely achieved, before 1023. Whether secular clerks were absorbed, expelled or killed, they had disappeared by the third decade of the eleventh century at the latest.[6] When we have evidence that the Utrecht Psalter was at Christ Church, the community was becoming Benedictine in character, if it had not already become so. The circumstances by which Utrecht came to Christ Church are not known; it may have been a gift unasked for. But in determining how Utrecht could have been read in the community, we can better understand how Harley would have been used, even if it was made for use outside it.

A magnificent manuscript though it is, Utrecht was not used in the performance of the liturgy at Christ Church.[7] Its imagery had no specific liturgical role, and the Gallican version of the Psalter was inappropriate in a Christ Church context. The priority in the production of Harley was its illustrations, and it seems most unlikely that Harley was designed to perform a liturgical function that Utrecht itself could not. Of course, much of the apparatus associated with liturgical usage might not be present simply because the manuscript was never finished. That would explain why there are no hymns, canticles, nor litany, and possibly why there is no calendar. But the character of the surviving text is not liturgical. For example, in BL Arundel Ms. 155 the division into nocturns of sixes is marked regularly by initials. In Harley the only initials to receive special attention are those to Psalms 1, 51, 101, and 119, and these are ill-related to each other, all of them were executed after the work of artist A–E, and scribes 1–D2 had been

[3] See the account in Brooks, *The Church of Canterbury*, pp. 250–87. If the Bosworth Psalter, BL Add. Ms. 37517, is a St Augustine's manuscript (see above, Introduction, p. 3, and n. 13) we are deprived of the main source of our knowledge of the liturgical regime before Harley was made, and we have to rely on BL Arundel Ms. 155.

[4] Brooks, *The Church of Canterbury*, p. 256. [5] Ibid., p. 279. [6] Ibid., pp. 255–61.

[7] H. Gneuss, 'Liturgical books in Anglo-Saxon England and their Old English terminology', in M. Lapidge and H. Gneuss (eds.), *Learning and Literature in Anglo-Saxon England: Studies presented to Peter Clemoes on the occasion of his Sixty-Fifth Birthday*, Cambridge 1985, pp. 91–142, at pp. 114–15 gives a summary of the characteristics of liturgical Psalters.

completed, and the initial to Psalm 101 was a replacement for an initial that laid no emphasis on Psalm 101. Psalm 119 reflects the importance placed on Psalm 119 in the monastic office, but the others reflect the old non-liturgical division into three 'fifties'. They are all conventionally employed in manuscripts of different functions to help the reader negotiate his text, and are not indicative of the function that the text was supposed to perform. There are Psalm divisions to Harley's text but, as we have seen, the planning for them was also erratic: scribe D2 did not leave room for any; scribe 1 left room for only one; the rubricator only executed one of them; the rest were probably the work of Eadui Basan, who wrote them when he corrected the text of scribe 1.[8] Finally, as it was actually manufactured Harley was useless as a liturgical text, even if it had been completed: the uncorrected Gallican intrusion of scribe D2 compromised it completely.

Nor could Utrecht have been used in the classroom. The Latin glosses in 'classroom books', for example Arator's *De actibus apostolorum*, Prosper's *Epigrammata* and Prudentius' *Psychomachia*, had many functions, and could have been used in different ways, but most are lexical, grammatical, and syntactical aids that could help the student negotiate his Latin text.[9] The vernacular too was used for the purposes of teaching.[10] Psalters were sometimes provided with Latin apparatus, sometimes with a vernacular gloss that provided word for word translations, and sometimes both.[11] But the images of Utrecht do not provide a pictorial translation of the Latin in the way that these glossed Psalters could provide a translation, nor do they provide syntactical and grammatical clarification. In the illustration to Psalm 38, for example, there is a spider's web above a rich man, but this does not indicate in itself that the rich man's soul will curl up like a spider's web.[12] The illustrations in Utrecht cannot act as an apparatus to explain the text, the illustrations do not help the reader gain literate skills, and the Harley Psalter cannot have been made to perform that function, whether inside the community or outside it.

Books normally cited as classroom books could also have been used for private reading.[13] Indeed it is hard to explain the function of images in Prudentius manuscripts

[8] See above, Introduction, p. 25.

[9] I refer the reader to the following studies of manuscripts with latin glosses in late Anglo-Saxon England: A.G. Rigg and G.R. Wieland, 'A Canterbury classbook of the mid-eleventh century (the 'Cambridge Songs' manuscript)', *Anglo-Saxon England*, 4, 1975, pp. 113–30; M. Lapidge, 'The study of Latin texts in late Anglo-Saxon England [I]', in N. Brooks (ed.), *Latin and the Vernacular Languages in Early Medieval Britain*, Leicester, 1982, pp. 99–140; G. Wieland, *The Latin Glosses on Arator and Prudentius in Cambridge University Library, Ms. Gg.5.35*, Toronto, 1983; G. Wieland, 'The glossed manuscript: classbook or library book?', *Anglo-Saxon England*, 14, 1985, pp. 153–73; G. Wieland, 'The Anglo-Saxon manuscripts of Prudentius'; N.P. Stork, *Through a Gloss Darkly*. See also Keynes, *Anglo-Saxon Mss. in Trinity*, cats. 14 and 15.

[10] See D.A. Bullough, 'The educational tradition in England from Alfred to Aelfric: teaching *utriusque linguae*', *Settimane di Studio del Centro Italiano di Studi sull'Alto Medioevo*, 17, 1972, pp. 453–94, esp. pp. 480ff. See also R. Page, 'The study of Latin texts in late Anglo-Saxon England [II]', in N. Brooks (ed.), *Latin and the Vernacular Languages in Early Medieval Britain*, Leicester, 1982, pp. 141–65.

[11] For continuous glosses to the Psalter see C. and K. Sisam, *The Salisbury Psalter*, esp. pp. 52–75; see also Gneuss, *Hymnar und Hymnen*, esp. pp. 194–201, for the *Expositio Hymnorum*, and the grammatical and Psalter manuscript contexts in which it is found. See also P. P. O'Neill, 'Latin learning at Winchester in the early eleventh century: the evidence of the Lambeth Psalter', *Anglo-Saxon England*, 20, 1991, pp. 143–66.

[12] See above, chapter 1, p. 38.

[13] See the comments of M. Lapidge, 'The study of Latin texts [I]', pp. 99–140, esp. pp. 126–7. At Fleury, a monk was given a book a year to read, but the state of the evidence does not permit that assumption to be made for the Christ Church community.

in the classroom, and they seem to have been expendable.[14] However, in private reading, the *Psychomachia* would not have been used as a teaching manual, but as a literary text. Here the images could have had a role. But only when knowledge of the text, or the ability to read, is assumed can illustrations be seen as Wieland sees them – as glosses, as interpretations of the text, but in a different medium.[15] Exactly the same is true of Utrecht and Harley. They too could work as glosses: it is just that, as McKitterick has pointed out with reference to Utrecht, you had to know the text to read the illustrations, and not vice versa.[16]

Books in religious communities were stored in book chests, *armaria*, which could contain volumes relating to particular purposes.[17] Liturgical books could be kept separately from classroom books and books for private reading. Although Psalters appear in all three contexts in Anglo-Saxon England,[18] if Utrecht was read at all, it could only have been read in private reading. In practice, it would not have fitted comfortably into any of the *armaria*: it was probably too highly prized for its imagery, and too curious and splendid to be used as private reading material by members of the community.[19] The Harley Psalter might have been made as a new, readable, and usable version. But this is to anticipate. After considering how Utrecht could have been used, and before considering where the Harley Psalter was designed to be used, we can pause. We know that the Utrecht Psalter was used in the scriptorium by those that made Harley, and Harley provides excellent evidence for how they read its illustrations.

The evidence that I have presented in the preceding chapters would suggest that the makers of Harley employed the text of the psalms, studied those in Utrecht, as well as those in other manuscripts, and drew inspiration from their contemporary environment, when they were constructing their literally illustrated Psalter. It may be significant that the figure plucking a quill from a goose on fol. 59v in the illustration to Psalm 116, a short Psalm praising the Lord, is a monk preparing to do his work in the scriptorium. The artists and scribes were in all probability members of the Christ Church community, and may have regarded the making of Harley as a spiritual activity, and a meditative process.[20] We cannot know how many people had access to the Harley Psalter in the scriptorium. But there is no need to think that those who did gain access to it read the book in any other way than the artists and scribes who left their mark upon it. They would have studied the text of the Psalms in the same way, and made the same connections between the imagery in the manuscript and that of the world around them. The artists of the Harley Psalter provide us with an insight into how the Psalmist's imagery was interpreted at Christ Church.

[14] See Wieland, *Arator and Prudentius*, pp. 161–3. [15] Ibid., p. 7.

[16] R. McKitterick, 'Text and image in the Carolingian world', in R. McKitterick (ed.), *The Uses of Literacy in Early Mediaeval Europe*, Cambridge, 1990, pp. 297–318, at p. 311.

[17] M. Lapidge, 'Surviving booklists from Anglo-Saxon England', in M. Lapidge and H. Gneuss (eds.), *Learning and Literature in Anglo-Saxon England: Studies presented to Peter Clemoes on the occasion of his Sixty-Fifth Birthday*, Cambridge, 1985, pp. 33–89, esp. at pp. 34–5.

[18] Lapidge, 'Booklists', pp. 35–6 and the lists there referred to.

[19] On pre-Conquest libraries see D.N. Dumville, 'English libraries before 1066: use and abuse of the manuscript evidence', in M.W. Herren (ed.), *Insular Latin Studies*, Toronto, 1981, pp. 153–78, esp. pp. 164–7.

[20] I am indebted to Dr Sarah Foot for suggesting to me that the work of the Harley artists might be seen in this way.

One of the great skills exhibited by the Harley artists was their articulation of the literal sense of the Psalter text in visual form, often over and above that seen in Utrecht itself. The images of Utrecht may have been particularly admired because they concentrate so much on this aspect of textual elucidation, rather than on exegetical comment; certainly there was little enough of the latter in the Christ Church library.[21] A parallel for this emphasis can be seen in the word-for-word translations of the vernacular gloss to the Psalter. The Christ Church reader would have concentrated on the literal sense of the Latin from the time that he started to learn it: in the classroom it was his greatest concern, and he looked for equivalents to the words of his text in the lexical glosses.[22] There is no need necessarily to think that he gave up this habit in private reading, where the learning process would have been transformed into a contemplative one, and where he may have been using similar books to those that he used in the classroom.[23] In the context of the scriptorium, it certainly became a creative one: artist B's spider's web demonstrates acute sensibility to the literal sense of the Psalms at the most detailed level. The Psalms were a suitable text for private study, and their pictorial realisation in Utrecht was of a type to which readers would have responded.

However, the appeal of the images in Utrecht and Harley was not confined to their literal interpretation of the Psalms. They could not but be appreciated, in addition, for the miraculous pictorial way in which this was done. In the illustrations we see an exotic world:[24] domed tempiettos, a Roman lot machine,[25] a lion fountain springing from an aqueduct,[26] Hercules,[27] and a classical conqueror.[28] Artist F too, employed an architectural and formal vocabulary largely drawn from the Utrecht Psalter. That Utrecht's imagery was admired quite outside the context of providing visual formulae to illustrate textual themes is indicated by the popularity of its architectural devices employed in other contexts. For example, its architecture was re-employed in the frames of the Evangelists of the Arenberg Gospels, New York, Pierpont Morgan Library, M. 869, the drawing of the temple in BL Royal Ms. 15.A.xvi, and Harley's Utrecht-inspired architecture was used as a model for the artist who depicted the Siege of Canterbury in the stained glass of the cathedral.[29]

Just as the illustrations were used by artists as models for images in different contexts, so they could be interpreted by them with considerable freedom. For example, Henderson has noted that on page 79 of Oxford, University College, Ms. 165, the twelfth-century artist of Bede's Life of St Cuthbert drew a well-head to refer

[21] Brooks, *The Church of Canterbury*, pp. 275–6. For a wider context see H. Gneuss, 'Anglo-Saxon libraries from the Conversion to the Benedictine reform', *Settimane di Studio del Centro Italiano di Studi sull'Alto Medioevo*, 32, 1984, pp. 643–88, esp pp. 680ff. Compare the reading material available at Cluny in the mid-eleventh century in R.W. Southern, *The Making of the Middle Ages*, London, 1953, p. 189.

[22] See Wieland, *Arator and Prudentius*, p. 191

[23] See particularly the comments of O'Neill, 'Lambeth Psalter', pp. 162–3.

[24] See in particular G.D.S. Henderson, 'Emulation and invention in Carolingian art', in R. McKitterick (ed.), *Carolingian culture: emulation and innovation*, Cambridge, 1994, pp. 248–73, esp. pp. 263–7.

[25] In the illustration to Psalm 21 on fol. 12r.

[26] In the illustration to Psalm 25 on fol. 14v.

[27] In the illustration to Psalm 18 on fol. 10v.

[28] In the illustration to Psalm 23 on fol. 13v.

[29] See above, chapter 3, pp. 141–142, p. 147, and n. 99.

to the Roman fountain beside which Cuthbert had his spiritual warning of the death of King Ecgfrith, and that this contrasts with the antique qualities of the fountain on fol. 14v of Utrecht.[30] The Life of Cuthbert was also written in verse and in prose in BL Harley Ms. 1117 at Christ Church in the early eleventh century, perhaps in part by artist-scribe D2.[31] If the scribes of this text had tried to imagine what Cuthbert's Roman fountain looked like, the one in the Utrecht Psalter might have matched their expectations. We cannot know that they interpreted this fountain as Roman, but it certainly contrasted markedly with their own at Christ Church in the twelfth century: the topographically accurate *fons in comiterio laicorum* in the large waterworks drawing on fol. 284v of the Eadwine Psalter is rather like that in the drawing from the life of St Cuthbert.[32] Connections with contemporary ritual would also have been made. Harris noted that the depiction of the Maundy ceremony in artist F's illustration to Psalm 127 on fol. 66v, where three poor men are having their feet washed by a cowled figure, alludes to the *Regularis Concordia*.[33] The *Regularis Concordia* instructs that the Maundy should be given daily to three poor men, and that their feet should be washed, dried and kissed; this image was part of the daily lives of the members of the community.[34] Parallels could also have been drawn with other imagery. As well as alluding to the text of Psalm 13, the image of *insipiens* treading on a crumpled figure in Psalm 52 on fol. 29r of Harley,[35] would be understood as a foolish variant on one of the most influential of all the Utrecht Psalter's images – the Lord's footstool in the illustration to Psalm 109.[36] As the text requires, the Lord's footstool consists of his squashed enemies. This image could not but have been understood as the fool's footstool. As well as illustrating the text, the man being stoned in the illustration to Psalm 52 of the Harley Psalter would have been understood as St Alphege, and the man sawn in half in the illustration to Psalm 13 as Isaiah. Harley and Utrecht may literally illustrate the text, but connections would inevitably have been made with historical and biblical events, with pictures, poetry and with contemporary life.

The most difficult image to interpret in Harley, and possibly the most crucial, is that of the Trinity on fol. 1r of the manuscript, by artist I, which acts as a frontispiece to the

[30] G. Henderson, *Early Medieval*, Harmondsworth, 1972, pp. 118–19, and fig. 73, and pp. 140–1, and fig. 92.

[31] Bishop, 'Notes VII', p. 421, arts. 4 and 15; but see above, chapter 3, p. 136, n.27.

[32] The so-called 'waterworks drawings', are discussed in detail by F. Woodman in Gibson, Heslop, and Pfaff (eds.), *The Eadwine Psalter*, pp. 168–77. See also fig. 43.

[33] Harris, 'Marginal drawings', pp. 553–4.

[34] See Duffey, 'Inventive group', pp. 130–2. She is right to link this depiction with the *Regularis Concordia*, ch. x.62, where three men are stipulated, rather than with the Rule of St Benedict, Chapter 53, where no number is given. Whether the ceremony refers to the Maundy Thursday ceremony itself (*Regularis Concordia*, ch.IV.40), as she suggests, is much less clear; the ceremony is similar on Maundy Thursday, except for the fact that money is given out at the abbot's discretion. In Harley, a crowned figure distributes money to the poor to the right. Duffey, 'Inventive group', pp. 134–5, suggests that this is early evidence for royal participation in the distribution of Maundy coins. To my eye, the crowned figure is walking in the ways of the Lord, as required by verse 1, and he is the same crowned figure who just above is eating the labour of his hands, whose wife is like a fruitful vine, and whose children are like olive plants, as required by verses 2 and 3. He seems to be King David.

[35] See above, chapter 2, p. 118.

[36] E.H. Kantorowicz, 'The Quinity of Winchester', *The Art Bulletin*, 29, 1947, pp. 73–85, *passim*, discusses the iconographic use of the illustration to Psalm 109 in the Utrecht Psalter by later artists and sculptors.

entire volume (fig. 83).[37] But if we cannot know under what specific circumstances it was placed there, we can begin to appreciate how it would have been understood by those that saw it in the scriptorium. Fol. 1r of the Utrecht manuscript is blank, and this must have appeared eccentric in Anglo-Saxon England, where there are normally a number of prefatory prayers in front of the Psalter text proper. It has been suggested that it was this prefatory material that gave rise to the interest in prefatory illustrated cycles to the Psalter.[38] The Trinity illustration is Harley's only prefatory material. Although it is possible that originally there was another quire at the beginning of the manuscript, there is no evidence for this in the physical make-up of the book, and it seems more likely that, at the start of a project that was never finished, fol. 1 of the Utrecht Psalter was designed to be fol. 1 of the Harley. Bearing in mind the pictorial emphasis of the entire programme, this illustration may have been designed to take the place of, rather than supplement, prefatory texts.[39] A fruitful parallel for it is the prefatory prayer (on fol. 11v) opposite the *Beatus* page of BL Arundel Ms. 155, which invokes the name of the Holy Trinity to receive the consecrated Psalms of the sinner.[40] The intimate character of this prayer is echoed in Harley's illustration, and there can be few more appropriate images to put the Psalms in their broadest possible devotional context. The relevance of the Trinity illustration to a English monastic audience in particular was probably self-evident. For example, the *Regularis Concordia* stipulated that every time a monk rose in the night for the work of God, he should sign himself with the cross and invoke the Holy Trinity.[41]

It is easy to be led astray in making such parallels precisely because the viewer of images, in contrast to the reader of a gloss, is left to make his own comparisons. This was ever the danger. For Theodulf of Orleans, for example, writing in *c.* 794, although a picture was painted to convey the true memory of historical events, it sometimes inclined the mind to think falseness instead of truth.[42] Theodulf's censure demonstrates

[37] It cannot be linked to a supposed dedication of Christ Church to the Trinity in 990, as has been proposed in Hasler, 'Zu zwei Darstellungen', p. 320. Brooks, *The Church of Canterbury*, pp. 54–5 notes that the testimony of the thirteenth-century *Historia Anglicana* of Bartholomew Cotton that in the year 990 *dedicata est sancti ecclesia Trinitatis Cantuariensis*, cannot be trusted. Holy Trinity was the dedication of Lanfranc's Norman cathedral built in the decade after the fire of 1067, and is found in charters and official documents after that time, and the dedication to the Trinity is not found in any pre-Conquest record; in the eleventh century the Saxon Cathedral is always *ecclesia sancti Salvatoris* or *ecclesia Christi*. Hasler's evidence rests on a document he refers to in F. Harmer, *Anglo-Saxon Writs*, Manchester, 1952, p. 181, n.3, which refers to the *monachi Sancte Trinitatis*, but this turns out to be none other than the *Domesday Monachorum*, written after the death of Lanfranc, and therefore after his dedication of Christ Church to the Trinity, and therefore of no consequence as evidence for a pre-Conquest dedication to the Trinity.

[38] K. Haney, *The Winchester Psalter, an Iconographic Study*, Leicester, 1986, p. 47 and forward.

[39] There are many possible literary sources for the image. See Hasler, 'Zu zwei Darstellungen', pp. 324–30; F. Wormald, 'Late Anglo-Saxon art: some questions and suggestions', in M. Meiss (ed.), *Studies in Western Art: Acts of the Twentieth International Congress of the History of Art*, Princeton, 1963, pp. 19–26, reprinted in F. Wormald, *Collected Writings I*, pp. 105–10, at pp. 106–8. He states that the Trinity is 'making the World'. See also Kantorowicz, 'Quinity', pp. 84–5, and Henderson, 'Idiosyncrasy', p. 243.

[40] The text of this prayer is in Haney, *Winchester Psalter*, p. 50.

[41] Symons (ed.), *Regularis Concordia*, Ch.1.14: '*Ideoque omni tempore nocturnis horis cum ad opus diuinum de lectulo surrexerit frater, primum sibi signum sanctae crucis imprimat per sanctae trinitatis inuocationem.*'

[42] H. Bastgen (ed.), *Libri Carolini*, Monumenta Germaniae Historica, Concilia, vol. 2 Supplementum, 1924, bk 1, ch. 2, p. 13. For the attitude of Theodulf and his contemporaries to images see R. McKitterick, 'Text and image', esp. pp. 297–301.

83 *The Harley Psalter, fol. 1r. The Trinity, by I.*

that the interpretation of images outside their texts was done just as much in the Middle Ages as it is done today. In fact it could not but be done, and it has been argued that it was much more a mediaeval habit of mind than a modern one.[43] But it was a habit of mind that was better exercised through images than through texts, and some readers might have preferred pictures to written glosses for this reason: while commentary glosses provided interpretation, the images of Utrecht and Harley invited it.

We should understand the Harley Psalter as being read by, as well as designed by, members of the Christ Church community who knew the Psalms well. The visual conundrums of Harley and Utrecht would have been satisfactory outlets for the intellectual curiosity of private readers at the community, as much as the riddles of Aldhelm and Tatwine.[44] As in the riddles, where the answers are given, curiosity was not expended so much in trying to understand the conceit, verbal or visual, as in appreciating its construction. It is in a similar spirit that artist H appreciated artist A's construction in the illustration to Psalm 13. Utrecht's images suited the private reader at Christ Church, and the images of Harley seem tailor-made for them. We have evidence that they were studied for over a hundred years. The monks of Christ Church might not have feasted on the illustrative subtleties of Utrecht and Harley in private, but they did in the scriptorium.

Whether Harley was made for use inside the community or outside it, it was either designed as a coffee-table book, or for close scrutiny in the light of the Psalms; it was made either for viewing independently of the text, or for someone who would study the illustrations with it. As we have seen, the images could be interpreted without a knowledge of the text, but only if the text is known already can they become visual interpretations of the words and phrases of the text itself in the eyes of the viewer. The ladder of literacy in the Middle Ages had many rungs, but the images in Harley do not help you climb it. Rather, they allow you to enjoy being near the top of it. With this in mind we can approach the patron of the volume.

The intended reader of the Harley Psalter

As Bishop has shown, Harley is one of a number of manuscripts that are the work of Christ Church scribes writing in Style II Anglo-Caroline minuscule at the turn of the millennium.[45] The period of greatest activity may not have been very prolonged, since many of the scribes found in the surviving manuscripts participated together in one book, Cambridge, Trinity College, Ms. B.4.27. Although unillustrated, it is quite as ambitious a programme in its way as Harley 603.[46] Many of these texts were made for

43 See T.A. Heslop, '"Brief in words"', *passim*. 44 Brooks, *The Church of Canterbury*, p. 276.

45 Bishop, 'Notes VII', *passim*.

46 See Bishop, 'Notes VII', pp. 416–17, and Keynes, *Anglo-Saxon Mss. in Trinity*, cat. 14. An article on this manuscript is in preparation by Linda Brownrigg.

the routine needs of the community.[47] The only function that the Harley Psalter could have served in such a context is as a private reading text. It is tempting to draw a further parallel with manuscripts made for the Christ Church library: like many of them, Harley is greatly indebted to a continental exemplar.[48] Presumably these exemplars were used, not just because they were available, but because they were considered pertinent to readers of manuscripts at Christ Church around the year 1000. The responsibility for choosing which manuscripts were to be used as exemplars for these library books probably lay with one man. At Fleury, a house with close English connections, this person was the *armarius*: master of the archives, schoolmaster, and librarian, he was responsible for ensuring that the scriptorium had all that it needed to keep the schoolroom supplied with the texts that it required.[49] The scale of operations at Fleury was probably larger than at Christ Church, and this may have necessitated a degree of delegation that was not needed in the Anglo-Saxon community, where the choosing of books to be copied, the borrowing of them from other centres,[50] the co-operation of the scribes,[51] and possibly decisions such as the arrangement of the vellum,[52] may all have been the work of one man. But we cannot doubt that one man was in overall control of the scriptorium. It was this man who was in charge of the project and, if Harley was meant to be confined within the walls of the community, we can regard him as responsible for the book.

The literal interpretation of the Psalms in visual form found in Utrecht fitted the intellectual and artistic milieu at Christ Church well, and it helps us to understand how the manuscript would have been appreciated. Nonetheless, we cannot assume that Harley was made to disseminate the Utrecht Psalter's imagery in the Christ Church Library, and to determine how Utrecht was appreciated by the monks of Christ Church is not necessarily to account for their laborious task of making a similar manuscript. There may have been a demand for two such illustrated Psalters in one community, but two might have been wanted precisely because they were needed in different places. If Utrecht was on loan to Christ Church so that it could be used as an exemplar, then we can interpret Harley as the community's own version of a Psalter with literal illustrations. But it is equally possible, theoretically speaking, that Utrecht was Christ Church's manuscript, and Harley was made for use elsewhere.

Moreover, Harley is unlikely to have been intended as a library book for ordinary

47 Brooks, *The Church of Canterbury*, pp. 266–78. 48 See Lapidge, 'The study of Latin texts', esp. p. 125.

49 See M. Mostert, *The Library of Fleury, A Provisional List of Manuscripts*, Hilversum, 1989, esp at pp. 24–7. The details of the *armarius* are given in the *Consuetudines Floriacenses Antiquiores* of Thierry of Amorbach, edited by A. Davril and L. Donnat, *Corpus Consuetudinum Monasticarum*, VII.3, Sieburg, 1984, pp. 7–60, at pp. 16–17.

50 Many books came from St Augustine's, see Bishop, 'Notes VII', pp. 417–18. Presumably most were returned. The Christ Church community would have been lucky to get away with keeping the Utrecht Psalter if it had been lent on that basis.

51 See the remarks by Bishop, 'Notes VII', p. 416–17, on Trinity College Cambridge Ms. B.4.27.

52 Bishop, 'Notes VII', p. 420, uses the abrupt change of policy in the arrangement of vellum, from the insular arrangement to the continental arrangement, to suppose that it was the decision of one man who changed his mind. However, see above, chapter 3, p. 136.

members of a religious community. The scale of the project is probably too ambitious to allow for such a context. Heslop has plausibly suggested that many *de luxe* manuscripts were commissioned from scriptoria by King Cnut and Queen Emma, and designed to be diplomatic gifts.[53] This manuscript falls outside the normal character of the volumes used in Heslop's analysis, but Psalters, as well as Gospel books, were used as diplomatic gifts.[54] St Wulfstan's master at Worcester, Earnwig, wrote a Psalter, 'of which the principal letters were fashioned in gold'. This was given to Queen Emma, and subsequently sent by King Cnut as a diplomatic gift to the continent. Later still, Bishop Aldred, acting as a legate for Edward the Confessor, received it back in Cologne from someone in the circle of Emperor Henry III 'either out of reverence for him or because he was the legate of such a great king'.[55] Like the Psalter that Queen Emma gave to her brother,[56] Harley is a large Psalter decorated with various pictures, and it could well have been undertaken by the community for goodwill or financial gain.[57] Psalters were used as prayer books by the laity, as well as by ecclesiastics.

Theoretically, there is an endless list of potential patrons for the Harley Psalter. This list has been fully exploited by Hasler, who suggested that the Harley Psalter was started for one King, and finished for another. He considered that the manuscript was begun as a copy of the Utrecht Psalter for Aethelred the Unready, because its imagery was appropriate for a Christian king surrounded by an iniquitous foe.[58] However there are no iconographical pointers intruded into the cycle to suggest such a connection. Possible reasons to employ Utrecht iconography 'wholesale' are many and various: its imagery had a widespread and enduring fascination for at least two hundred years in England alone, and we must assume that it was used in the Eadwine and Paris Psalters for altogether different reasons. A good case might be made for a particular patron wanting a version of the Utrecht Psalter, but there will always be many other potential patrons who would have wanted it just as much, and several who would have been in the position to pay for it. It is to differences between Utrecht and Harley that we must look for a patron.

The depiction of the winged bowman, *Aegelmund*, in the illustration to Psalm 119 of Harley, on fol. 64r, provoked Hasler to suggest that there had been a change of patron.[59] The image, he maintained, was in fact an allusion to King Cnut. The manuscript was unfinished on Aethelred's death, and it became a present, given by archbishop Aethelnoth to the king. But if connections found by Hasler between Cnut and the depiction of Aegelmund in the illustration to Psalm 119 are valid, they are in astonishing contrast to the overt depictions of royalty in other Anglo-Saxon manuscripts.[60]

[53] Heslop, 'Cnut and Emma', *passim*.

[54] Athelstan gave many of his books away: for the Athelstan Psalter see Keynes, 'King Athelstan's Books', esp. pp. 147–53. [55] R.R. Darlington (ed.), *Vita S. Wulfstani*, p. 5 and pp. 15–16. [56] See above, p. 188.

[57] See M. Lapidge, 'Artistic and literary patronage in Anglo-Saxon England', *Settimane di Studio del Centro Italiano di Studi sull'Alto Medioevo*, 39, 1992, pp. 137–91, at pp. 143–5.

[58] Hasler, 'Zu zwei Darstellungen', pp. 321–2. [59] Ibid., pp. 330–8.

[60] Ibid., pp. 334–8. For thoughts on '*Aegelmund*', see also de Gray Birch, *Utrecht Psalter*, p. 115, and Duffey, 'Inventive group', pp. 123–6, who, in a detailed and more balanced analysis than that of Hasler, notes that the name was added to the manuscript at the same time that the wings were added to the figure, perhaps in an attempt to clarify its rather ambivalent position, and tentatively links it to the name of Aethelnoth, the

Whoever Aegelmund is, he is rather hidden away, and unprepossessing as a potential recipient of the volume; his genesis was as a spare part, created by the conflation of imagery of the Harley Psalter and the Odbert/Bury tradition.[61]

If Harley were designed for a member of the laity, then the way that it would have been used would have depended on who it was for. But, if it was to be used for close scrutiny in the light of the text, then it is possible that it could have had a specific effect on the reader that it is unlikely to have had within a religious community; it might have helped him or her to remember the Psalms. Memorising the Psalms was of course crucial in a monastic community, and the Rule of St Benedict instructs reading and study of the Psalms,[62] and stipulates that the Psalter should be recited once a week in the liturgy.[63] But this requirement would have been met by memorising the word read, spoken, or sung, and not the words visualised. The genesis of Utrecht's illustrations may owe something to medieval memory techniques, as Carruthers argues,[64] but they are unlikely to have impinged upon more usual methods of learning the Psalter in such an environment. However, the situation may have been altogether different outside the cloister. Here the illustrations may have been designed to encourage the reader to become more familiar with the Psalter text. If they succeeded in this role, then they would have had the effect of making that person remember at least individual verses through the images, and this is the case whether the images were designed specifically for memorising or not.

But in fact, it is not to the laity that we should look for our patron.[65] What few indicators we have suggest that we should return to a monastic context for Harley.[66] We have seen that reference was made to the *Regularis Concordia* in artist F's work,[67] and Duffey has noted that a monastic context for the manuscript is provided by the illustration to Psalm 132 on fol. 68v. To illustrate verse 1 *quam bonum et quam iucundum est habitare fratres in unum*, artist F has depicted a congregation of cowled figures within an aedicule, grouped around a chalice.

By far the best evidence for a patron for the manuscript is the archbishop in the *Beatus*

archbishop of Canterbury, who, as is noted below, has a reasonable claim to the manuscript. An example of a less iconographically and onomastically contorted reference to Cnut is to be found on fol. 6r of BL Stowe Ms. 944 (Temple, *Anglo-Saxon Mss.*, cat. 78, ill. 244). Other clearly royal figures are Athelstan on fol. 1v of Cambridge, Corpus Christi College, Ms. 183 (Temple, *Anglo-Saxon Mss.*, cat. 6, ill. 29), and Edgar on fol. 2v of BL Cotton Ms. Vespasian A.viii (Temple, *Anglo-Saxon Mss.*, cat. 16, ill. 84).

[61] See above, chapter 4, pp. 154–6.

[62] R. Hanslik (ed.), 'Benedicti Regula', *Corpus Scriptorum Ecclesiaticorum Latinorum*, 75, 1960, ch. 48, p. 117.

[63] Ibid., ch. 18, p. 73. In addition, in the *Regularis Concordia* it is stipulated that the Psalter should be recited in its entirety on Maundy Thursday, Good Friday, and Holy Saturday (see T. Symons (ed.), *Regularis Concordia*, Edinburgh, 1953, ch. IV, 40).

[64] M. Carruthers, *The Book of Memory: A Study of Memory in Medieval Culture*, Cambridge, 1990, pp. 226–7.

[65] Attempts to link it to the political events of the early eleventh century have been universally unconvincing. Duffey, 'Inventive group', pp. 111–12, is correct to connect the image illustrating Psalm 112 verse 6 with contemporary adoption rites and to the image of Samuel in the Bury Psalter. But she is probably incorrect (pp.163–4) to link it to King Cnut's offspring. He did not need to adopt anybody.

[66] Hasler 'Zu zwei Darstellungen', pp. 320–1, considered the absence of liturgical apparatus to be an indication that the manuscript was made for a layperson, and not for a monastic foundation. However there are other reasons than the liturgical for a community having an illustrated Psalter. He also argues, on pp. 320–1, that the manuscript cannot have been meant for the Christ Church community because of the version of the Psalter employed. However, BL Arundel Ms. 155, closely contemporary in date, was made for the Christ Church community, and this too was a Roman Psalter.

[67] See above, p. 193.

initial of artist I, on fol. 2r. The archbishop, wearing his pallium, is prostrate before the Lord who is cross-nimbed and holding a book in his left hand and surrounded by a mandorla topped with a cross.[68] The archbishop is holding on to a banderole, uninscribed, which appears from the Lord's left hand. He is squeezed uncomfortably into the lower bow of the initial, which is otherwise occupied by foliage, and the Lord helps to form the upright of the letter. Obviously he was involved with the manuscript in some way, either as a donor or as a recipient, but he appears at an unsettlingly late stage in the production of the manuscript, after artist F had finished working. He is a second *Beatus uir*, executed after the *Beatus uir* in the full-page illustration.

We can match the meagre evidence of the iconography with the way that the manuscript could be used. There are two fundamentally different ways in which the Harley Psalter could have been used. As we have seen, the images do not help bridge the gap between literate and illiterate contemplation of the volume. If the manuscript was designed for use by someone not interested in the textual nature of its illustrations, if it had been designed to be used as a beautiful version of the fascinating Utrecht Psalter, as a 'coffee-table book' perhaps, but certainly as a closed book, then my explanations for the deviation from the exemplar of scribe 1 and artist F would be excuses for something unacceptable. The Harley Psalter would, after all, have been a facsimile of the Utrecht Psalter gone wrong. But if the Harley Psalter was designed to be used by someone who wanted to study the illustrations with a knowledge of the Psalms, if that was the motive behind the making of Harley, then we would have a motive for using the Utrecht Psalter as an exemplar, and while deviation from it would still need to be explained, it would not need to be excused; the illustrations of artist F could perform the same role as those of artist D2. The advantage of the latter alternative is that it not only helps to explain the great attraction of the exemplar, it also accounts for the literate character of the deviations from it. The artists of Harley were never asked to make a facsimile of Utrecht; they were asked to make a manuscript similar to Utrecht, but one which was yet better suited to an eleventh-century reader's appreciation of a selection of Psalm verses in visual form. This is where the Harley Psalter is consistent, and the manufacture of the Harley Psalter therefore only makes sense if we understand the manuscript as a book designed to be used in this way. Harley provides evidence that its patron did not see the Utrecht Psalter as a book merely to be treasured and looked at, but rather that he saw its potential for the basis of a book that he could use, and the illustrations of which he could read. Both manuscripts could only perform such a role at all if the text was known before the illustrations were 'read'. The priority of the image-making over the writing of the text in the Anglo-Saxon manuscript therefore has to be less an indication that the text was unimportant, than that the Psalms were so familiar to its intended reader, as well as to its makers, that they could be taken as read.[69]

[68] George Henderson has suggested to me that the cross may owe something to the form of seals, which have a cross at their apex preceding the inscription. Perhaps the design is an adaptation of a seal with a standing figure. That a pictorial parallel of an inscribed image is a possibility is also suggested by the cross at the beginning of the inscription of the painter around the painter depicted in the *Beatus* initial of the Bury St Edmunds Psalter (see above, chapter 4, p. 173, n. 67). However, this cross is not at the apex of the roundel surrounding this figure.

Harley is not alone in being a *de luxe* manuscript started at the beginning of the eleventh century that was designed for literate study rather than for casual perusal. A parallel can be drawn with the illustrated Prudentius manuscript, Cambridge, Corpus Christi College, Ms. 23. We know that a late antique exemplar ultimately lay behind the many illustrated versions of Prudentius' *Psychomachia* produced in Anglo-Saxon England.[70] The details of the stemma are obscure, but Corpus 23 retains its large late antique square format.[71] Moreover, if it preserved the dimensions of its ultimate exemplar, this might explain why the lines of script only occupy two-thirds of the width of the ruled space, while the illustrations fill it: originally the script would have been written in spacious rustic capitals filling the length of the ruled space.[72] The formats of both Harley and Corpus 23 result from the fact that greatly admired manuscripts were used as exemplars, which were employed for a particular purpose. The use of exemplars in this way might take the manuscripts out of a monastic library context, but there is no need to think that, because they are grander than such books, they could not be studied by a grander person in a similar way.[73]

The Harley Psalter was certainly an appropriate present for an archbishop and, as we have seen, archbishops owned grand psalters.[74] If the archbishop was the intended reader of the manuscript there would be no need to draw a sharp contrast between *de luxe* manuscripts made as diplomatic gifts, and reading material for the private study of monks. Any of Dunstan's successors would have been an appropriate recipient of the volume, and since, until Aethelnoth, all of them had been abbots of reformed houses, they would have fully appreciated the deliberately literate nature of the imagery within it. Backhouse may well be right in supposing that the Psalter was begun as a present for Aethelnoth by a grateful community.[75] Had Aethelnoth ever received the manuscript he might not have read the manuscript very differently from a member of the community. On the other hand, if he had already travelled to Rome to receive the pallium, he might have made the connection between the images in the Utrecht Psalter and the buildings that he saw on his travels.

The Harley Psalter was designed for someone who wanted a lavishly illustrated manuscript, and who wanted one with a picture of an archbishop in it; for someone who knew the Utrecht Psalter, and who wanted a manuscript similar to it; for someone who probably already knew the Psalter text, and who certainly intended to read the images in this version of it. It seems more likely than not that it was the archbishop himself who would have been frustrated that the Harley Psalter was never finished. However, the future literate use of the manuscript might have been assured precisely because this was the case. The lesson of Orderic Vitalis's tale, of St Wulfstan's experience, and of the

[69] See above, chapter 4, pp. 182–183.

[70] See R. Stettiner, *Die illustrierten Prudentius-Handschriften*, Berlin, 1895; H. Woodruff, *The Illustrated Manuscripts of Prudentius*, Harvard, 1930; and G. Wieland, 'The Anglo-Saxon manuscripts of Prudentius', *passim*.

[71] The manuscript measures 290 mm by 365 mm; its lower margin is *c.* 65, its upper *c.* 30, its outer *c.* 80; its inner *c.* 20.

[72] Some corroboration for this kite has kindly been supplied by Tim Graham, who has demonstrated to me that the word division of the scribe is eccentric. This might be the result of following a text written in Rustic capitals, without spacing between words.

[73] For a different interpretation see the comments of Lapidge, 'Artistic and literary patronage', at pp. 145–7.

[74] See above, p. 188, and Introduction, p. 1. [75] Backhouse, 'Making', pp. 108–10.

inscription in the Stockholm *Codex Aureus*, is that there was no telling where a *de luxe* manuscript could end up. If Harley had ever fallen into the hands of someone who didn't know the Psalms, or who was not prepared to read them, then the result would have been curiously tragic: the very essence of so much of the artistic creativity in the manuscript would have gone unappreciated. The manuscript was not useless because it was never finished; on the contrary, its use was thereby assured, and we have the evidence of the later artists of the manuscript to prove it. The archbishop may have been frustrated, but the student who wants to know how Psalm illustrations were read, how styles of art and script developed, and how books were made, need not be.

Conclusion

The Harley Psalter was designed to be used in a certain way, and this intended use was a formative influence on its appearance. This can be illustrated through a convenient comparison, provided by the Eadwine Psalter.[1] In Eadwine, the Psalter texts were not mixed but separated and placed side by side, and the illustrations were added afterwards. The glosses accompanying the texts provide, amongst other things, instant access to patristic exegesis. In the first few Psalm illustrations of this manuscript, there are signs of visual exegesis intruded into the literalism of Utrecht's images.[2] However, in interpreting the Psalms, as in making the book, the important relationships are not between images and text, but between texts. After the first few folios, the illustrations seem not to have been executed with a spirit of intellectual endeavour, and it is difficult to 'read' them in that spirit. As Heslop says of Eadwine's illustrations,

> The prime motive was simply to incorporate the most elaborate Psalter illustrations available in order to increase the readers' awareness that this Psalter had the best of everything.[3]

Harley and Eadwine were designed to perform different functions in different intellectual climates, and this is responsible for their very different approaches to the Utrecht Psalter. This is why it is so misleading to call either manuscript a 'copy' of the Utrecht Psalter. The readers of Eadwine would have considered Harley inadequate to the task of elucidating the Psalter, and its artists show very little sign of understanding the interests of those in Harley. Perhaps the inadequacies of Harley were perceived, and gave rise to the Eadwine project. But if Harley was inadequate to the requirements of a mid-twelfth century student of the Psalms, then Eadwine's illustrations might well not have matched the expectations of a student of them in the eleventh century.[4]

Today the Utrecht Psalter's images are wanted for fundamentally different reasons

[1] For the Eadwine Psalter, see Gibson, Heslop, and Pfaff (eds.), *The Eadwine Psalter*, *passim*.

[2] See Heslop, in Gibson, Pfaff and Heslop (eds.), *The Eadwine Psalter*, pp. 43–9, esp. at p. 45, where he states that the principal illuminator 'adjoins a visual gloss to the Utrecht pictures in the same way that the scribes added commentary to the Psalter text'.

[3] Ibid., p. 52.

[4] The Eadwine Psalter was not above criticism a few decades later. Paris 8846 adopts the textual apparatus of Eadwine, but the illustrations are reinterpreted with a wholly fresh vigour: choices were made between the alternatives offered by Eadwine and Utrecht in the light of many other factors, but the text itself was frequently the determining one. The intent of the artists of Paris 8846 was to take the best from their forebears, and improve upon them.

again. One of these is so that they can be compared with Harley's. Indeed, the Harley Psalter is now hardly ever used except in conjunction with the Utrecht Psalter. But in the eleventh century, Harley was designed to be used on its own, independently from the Carolingian manuscript that inspired so much of its imagery. The role that Harley was designed to perform, as an illustrated Psalter manuscript designed for literate appreciation, was not incompatible with departures from Utrecht's images, and adherence to the Utrecht Psalter and departure from it are both symptomatic of the way it was designed to be used. Distinctions drawn today between 'copy' and 'interpretation', and between the reliance on 'tradition' on the one hand, and the intrusion of 'innovation' on the other, are not helpful in this context: exemplars were employed for reasons that were appropriate to the culture that transmitted them, and they could be interpreted freely when required.[5]

This interpretation of the way that Harley was intended to be used has implications for how we should understand the task of the artists and scribes of the manuscript. They were not remaking an old manuscript, but making a new one, and rather than analyse the techniques of the artists of Harley by the extent to which they were conducive to making a facsimile of Utrecht, we should set them in the context of the creation of new books in the early eleventh century.

Although the works of Ker and Bishop are seminal texts for the student of Anglo-Saxon book production,[6] most of their material was not illustrated, and neither scholar set out to investigate the role of the artist in the production of manuscripts. As a result, the general supposition that the decoration of manuscripts was normally executed after the text has been left unchallenged in discussions of manuscript production in the late Anglo-Saxon period. Indeed, the one attempt to deal in a concerted manner with the technique of production of Anglo-Saxon manuscripts reinforced this view. Dodwell based his study on the illustrated Hexateuch, BL Cotton Ms. Claudius B.iv, but extended it to include the Harley Psalter. He came to the conclusion that gatherings were handed first to the scribes, who wrote out the text, and then later the artists inserted the illustrations, and that this was the case whether or not the illustrations were derived from earlier models.[7] This is not a scriptorium context that fits well with my analysis.

Clemoes's masterly discussion of the making of the illustrated Hexateuch threw into doubt the secure picture of scriptorium practice painted by Dodwell.[8] Subsequently there have been a number of detailed studies of individual books which have demonstrated that the relationship between scribe and artist did not conform to a set

[5] The distinction is particularly unhelpful when 'tradition' and 'innovation', are not just seen as different, but are actually set in opposition to each other. See C.R. Dodwell, *Anglo-Saxon Art: A New Perspective*, Manchester, 1982, p. 171. He writes of the Harley Psalter as a copy of the Utrecht Psalter, and goes on to state 'Against this must be set the tendency of other artists to interpret the events of history in terms of their own day.'

[6] Ker, *Catalogue*; Bishop, *Caroline Minuscule*.

[7] C.R. Dodwell, 'Techniques', pp. 653–4. This contradicts his interpretation of fols. 1–27v and 50–57v of the Harley Psalter given in Dodwell, *Canterbury School*, p. 3, where he writes 'it is of interest to see that these drawings were actually copied into the book before the text, for one can clearly see where the ink of the script overlays the lines of the drawings'. Actually, such incidents are few, and anything but clear, which may account for the change in his point of view.

[8] Clemoes, in Clemoes and Dodwell, *Hexateuch*, pp. 53–8.

procedure.[9] My analysis would indicate that the issue is frequently not one of scribe versus artist at all, although that is how it manifests itself on the page, for the reason that scribes were artists, and artists were scribes. In Harley, the gatherings were illustrated before they were written, it was the illustrations that determined where the text would go; and the importance of the illustrations was such that they determined the production of the manuscript as a whole. That this working procedure was overturned is not an indication that Harley was to be a fundamentally different book, but merely that practical problems in its making had to be taken into account. In all its eccentricity, the Harley Psalter is a good example of *de luxe* Anglo-Saxon book production.

The student of the Harley Psalter is in the privileged position of examining a manuscript for which the principal exemplar survives, and can trace how the artists adhered to it, and deviated from it, in great detail. But other Anglo-Saxon manuscripts had models that were used in similar ways, and distinctions between tradition and innovation are equally anachronistic when imposed upon them. A distinction has been made between the innovative creativity seen in the illustrated Hexateuch, and the wholesale copying seen in the illustrated miscellany, BL Cotton Ms. Tiberius B.v.[10] Such a distinction is blurred by a number of factors in the actual manufacture of these two manuscripts. The miscellany was not copied wholesale. To take the astrological section alone, its nearest iconographic relative is BL Cotton Ms. Tiberius C.i., which, like the ultimate exemplar of both manuscripts, BL Harley Ms. 647, has scholia taken from Hyginus, *De astronomia*, within the body of its constellations.[11] Unlike these, the Miscellany has scholia taken from the Revised Aratus Latinus, not the Hyginus text, and these surround fully painted depictions of the constellations, not ones 'fleshed out' by their scholia.[12] The Hexateuch, for its part, is related to earlier cycles, as noted by Henderson, and Weitzmann and Kessler.[13] Moreover the manuscript itself is closely derived from an earlier Anglo-Saxon model, and the degree of adherence can be gauged by noting that its production techniques, in terms of how the manuscript was planned, are so very similar to those quires of the Harley Psalter that were 'ruled by artists'. As far as the artists of BL Cotton Ms. Claudius B.iv are concerned, their task was probably not dissimilar to that of the artists of the Harley Psalter, or the various artists of the illustrated *Psychomachia* manuscripts. Tracing iconographic models is challenging for today's iconographers precisely because artists found them easy to adapt as well as useful to employ in making new creations for contemporary readers. There is a complementary relationship between the act of following and the act of inventing, and we should only expect an absolute reliance on tradition when invention was not needed

[9] See P. J. Lucas, 'Ms. Junius 11 and Malmesbury (I)', *Scriptorium*, 34, 1980, pp. 197–220, E.C. Teviotdale, 'The making of the Cotton Troper', in C. Hicks (ed.), *Harlaxton Medieval Studies II: England in the Eleventh Century*, Stamford, 1992, pp. 301–16, McGurk, *Anglo-Saxon Illustrated Miscellany*, pp. 34–5, and Heslop, 'Cnut and Emma', esp. pp. 167–8, and 188–195. [10] Gameson, 'Decorative tradition', p. 75.

[11] See Noel, 'BL Harley Mss. 2506 and 603', pp. 29–40.

[12] See McGurk, *Anglo-Saxon Illustrated Miscellany*, pp. 67–78.

[13] See G.D.S. Henderson, 'Late-antique influence on some English Mediaeval illustrations of Genesis', *Journal of the Warburg and Courtauld Institutes*, 25, 1962, pp. 172–98, and now K. Weitzmann and H. Kessler, *The illustrations in the manuscripts of the Septuagint 1: Genesis*, Princeton, 1986, esp. at p. 25, where they state that Aelfric's Paraphrase is a rather conservative member of the Cotton Genesis Tradition.

for the manuscript to have a contemporary relevance. Pictorial tradition was not threatened by innovation, nor distinct from it; pictorial continuity was the product of pictorial experiments, and reliant upon them.[14]

Finally, we can, as far as possible, apportion responsibility for the pictorial experiments conducted in Harley Psalter. Making the manuscript was a technical process that involved counting and measuring, disbinding one of the exemplars, and possibly tracing it. It also involved reading its images in the light of the text, transcribing at least one other text, and studying a manuscript similar to the Bury Psalter. While the artists and scribes might have been told what type of book was wanted, the actual execution of Harley, in the scriptorium, was the concern of the scribes and artists themselves. A patron might not have had the skill, even if he had had the time and the will, to oversee the development of the project in all its particulars. Moreover, he would have given up waiting for his book by the time that artist G started work, while it continued to be a source of interest to the Christ Church community long after he had died. In the execution of such a complex manuscript there was plenty of room for artistic and scribal personality to show itself. The responsibility for the very different characteristics of the various parts of Harley, for the iconographic subtleties created, and for the planning solutions devised, rests firmly with Eadui and his colleagues.

[14] For the Carolingian period see Henderson, 'Emulation and invention', esp. p. 271.

APPENDIX I

The Harley Psalter: a tabulated description

KEY

A	Artist A	I	Artist I
1	Scribe 1	J	Artist J
B	Artist B	Eadui	the scribe Eadui Basan
C	Artist C	G	Artist G
D2	Artist-scribe D2	H	Artist H
F	Artist F		
E	Artist-scribe E		

Square brackets indicate illustrations that do not head the individual Psalm texts. Lower case letters refer to later additions to illustrations by other artists.

N.B. This description draws on the conclusions of my analysis. Note in particular that it incorporates my reconstruction of quires 7 and 8, and therefore fols. 46 and 47 are placed in quire 8, and not in their present position at the end of quire 7.

QUIRE ONE

Fol.	Hair/ Flesh	Psalm Space	Ruling	Text	Illustrations	Tituli	Initials
1r	Hair	Trinity			[I]		
1v	Flesh	1	A		A		
2r	Hair	2	A	1	Ag	E	I, J
2v	Flesh	3,4	A	1	A,A	E	J
3r	Hair	5	A	1	Ag	E	J
3v	Flesh	6	A	1	A	E	J
4r	Hair	7	A	1	Ag	E	J
4v	Flesh	8	A	1	Ag	E	J
5r	Flesh	9	A	1	A	E	J
5v	Hair		A	1			
6r	Flesh	10	A	1	Ag	E	J
6v	Hair	11	A	1	A	E	J
7r	Flesh	12	A	1	Ag	E	J
7v	Hair	13	A	1	Ag	E	J
8r	Flesh	14,15	A	1	Ag,Ag	E	J
8v	Hair	16	A	1	Age	E	J

QUIRE TWO

Fol.	Hair/Flesh	Psalm Space	Ruling	Text	Illustrations	Tituli	Initials
9r	Hair	17	A	1	Ag	E	J
9v	Flesh		A	1		E	J
10r	Hair		A	1			
10v	Flesh	18	A		[E]*,Ag		
11r	Hair	19	A	1	Age	E	J
11v	Flesh	20	A	1	Ag	E	J
12r	Hair	21	B	1	Bg	E	J
12v	Flesh		B	1		E	J
13r	Hair	22	C	1	C	E	J
13v	Flesh	23	C	1	Cg	E	J
14r	Flesh	24	C	1	Cg	E	J
14v	Hair	25	C	1	Cg	E	J
15r	Flesh	26	B	1	Be	E	J
15v	Hair	27	I	1	E	E	J
16r	Flesh	28	A	1	Ag	E	J
16v	Hair	29	A	1	Ag	E	J
17r	Flesh	30	B	1	Bg	E	J
17v	Hair		B	1	[G]		

*This is a sketch, partially erased.

QUIRE THREE

Fol.	Hair/Flesh	Psalm Space	Ruling	Text	Illustrations	Tituli	Initials
18r	Hair	31	B	1	Bg	E	J
18v	Flesh	32	B	1	Bg	E	J
19r	Flesh	33	B	1	Bg	E	J
19v	Hair	34	B	1	Bg	E	J

QUIRE FOUR

Fol.	Hair/Flesh	Psalm Space	Ruling	Text	Illustrations	Tituli	Initials
20r	Hair		B	1			
20v	Flesh	35	B	1	Bg	E	J
21r	Hair	36	B	1	Bg	E	J
21v	Flesh		B	1			
22r	Hair	37	B	1	Bg	E	J
22v	Flesh	38	B	1	Bg	E	J
23r	Hair	39	B	1	Bg		
23v	Flesh		B	1	E	J	
24r	Flesh	40	B	1	Bg	E	J
24v	Hair	41	B	1	Bg	E	J
25r	Flesh	42,43	B	1	B,Bg	E	J
25v	Hair		B	1	[E]	E	J
26r	Flesh	44	B	1	B	E	J
26v	Hair	45	B	1	B		
27r	Flesh	46	B	1	Bg	E	J
27v	Hair	47	B	1	Bg	E	J

QUIRE FIVE

Fol.	Hair/Flesh	Psalm Space	Ruling	Text	Illustrations	Tituli	Initials
28r	Hair	48	Eadui	Eadui	G	Eadui	G
28v	Flesh	49	Eadui	Eadui	G	Eadui	
LEAF WANTING							
29r	Hair	52	Eadui	Eadui	H	Eadui	H,
29v	Flesh	53	Eadui	Eadui	H	Eadui	H
30r	Flesh	54	Eadui	Eadui	H	Eadui	
30v	Hair	55	Eadui	Eadui	H	Eadui	
31r	Hair	56	Eadui	Eadui	H	Eadui	
31v	Flesh	57	Eadui	Eadui	H	Eadui	H
32r	Flesh	58	Eadui	Eadui	H	Eadui	
32v	Hair	59	Eadui	Eadui	H	Eadui	
33r	Hair	60,61	Eadui	Eadui	H,H	Eadui	
33v	Flesh	62	Eadui	Eadui	H	Eadui	
LEAF WANTING							

QUIRE SIX

Fol.	Hair/Flesh	Psalm Space	Ruling	Text	Illustrations	Tituli	Initials
34r	Hair	65	Eadui	Eadui	H	Eadui	
34v	Flesh	66	Eadui	Eadui	H*	Eadui	
35r	Flesh	67	Eadui	Eadui	H*	Eadui	
35v	Hair		Eadui	Eadui			
36r	Hair	68	Eadui	Eadui		Eadui	
36v	Flesh		Eadui	Eadui			
37r	Flesh	69,70	Eadui	Eadui		Eadui	
37v	Hair		Eadui	Eadui		Eadui	
38r	Hair	71	Eadui	Eadui		Eadui	
38v	Flesh	72	Eadui	Eadui		Eadui	
39r	Flesh	73	Eadui	Eadui			
39v	Hair		Eadui	Eadui		Eadui	
40r	Hair	74,75	Eadui	Eadui		Eadui	
40v	Flesh	76	Eadui	Eadui		Eadui	
41r	Flesh	space	Eadui	Eadui			
41v	Hair	77	Eadui	Eadui		Eadui	

*These two illustrations are faint underdrawings only

QUIRE SEVEN

Fol.	Hair/Flesh	Psalm Space	Ruling	Text	Illustrations	Tituli	Initials
42r	Hair		Eadui	Eadui			
42v	Flesh		Eadui	Eadui			
43r	Flesh	78	Eadui	Eadui			
43v	Hair	79	Eadui	Eadui		Eadui	
44r	Hair	80	Eadui	Eadui		Eadui	
44v	Flesh	81	Eadui	Eadui		Eadui	
45r	Flesh	82	Eadui	Eadui		Eadui	
45v	Hair	83	Eadui	Eadui		Eadui	
FOUR LEAVES WANTING							

QUIRE EIGHT

Fol.	Hair/Flesh	Psalm Space	Ruling	Text	Illustrations	Tituli	Initials
46r	Hair	90	Eadui	Eadui		Eadui	
46v	Flesh	91	Eadui	Eadui		Eadui	
47r	Flesh	92	Eadui	Eadui		Eadui	
47v	Hair	93	Eadui	Eadui		Eadui	
48r	Hair	94	Eadui	Eadui		Eadui	
48v	Flesh	95	Eadui	Eadui		Eadui	
49r	Flesh	96	Eadui	Eadui		Eadui	
49v	Hair	97	Eadui	Eadui		Eadui	
LEAF WANTING							

QUIRE NINE

Fol.	Hair/Flesh	Psalm Space	Ruling	Text	Illustrations	Tituli	Initials
50r	Hair	101	D2	D2	D2	D2	D2,I
50v	Flesh		D2	D2			
51r	Hair	102	D2	D2	D2g	D2	D2
51v	Flesh	103	D2	D2	D2g	D2	D2
52r	Hair		D2	D2			
52v	Flesh	104	D2	D2	D2	D2	D2
53r	Hair		D2	D2	[E]		
53v	Flesh	105	D2	D2	D2	D2	D2
54r	Flesh		D2	D2,1			
54v	Hair	106	D2	1	D2g	E	J
55r	Flesh		D2	1			
55v	Hair	107	D2	1	D2	E	J
56r	Flesh	108	D2	1	D2	E	J
56v	Hair	109	D2	1	D2g		
57r	Flesh	110	D2	1	D2g	E	J
57v	Hair	111	D2	1	D2g	E	J

QUIRE TEN

Fol.	Hair/Flesh	Psalm Space	Ruling	Text	Illustrations	Tituli	Initials
58r	Hair	112,113	1	1	F,F	E	J
58v	Flesh		1	1	[E]	E	J
59r	Flesh	114,115	1	1	Fg,Fg	E	J
59v	Hair	115,116	1	1	F,F	E	J
60r	Hair	117	1	1	F	E	J
60v	Flesh	118	1	1	F		
61r	Flesh		1	1	[E]	E	J
61v	Hair		1	1	[E]	E	J
62r	Hair		1	1		E	J
62v	Flesh		1	1	[E]	E	J
63r	Flesh		1	1		E	J
63v	Hair		1	1		E	J
64r	Hair	119	1	1	Fg	E	J
64v	Flesh	120,121	1	1	F,F	E	J
65r	Flesh	122	1	1	F	E	J
65v	Hair	123,124	1	1	F,F	E	J

QUIRE ELEVEN

Fol.	Hair/Flesh	Psalm Space	Ruling	Text	Illustrations	Tituli	Initials
66r	Hair	125	1	1	F	E	J
66v	Flesh	126,127	1	1	F,F	E	J
67r	Flesh	128	1	1	F[E]	E	J
67v	Hair	129,130	1	1	F,F	E	J
68r	Hair	131	1	1	F	E	J
68v	Flesh	132,133	1	1	F,F	E	J
69r	Flesh	134	1	1	Fc	E	J
69v	Hair	135	1	1	F	E	J
70r	Hair	136	1	1	F[E]	E	J
70v	Flesh	137	1	1	F[E]	E	J
71r	Flesh	138	1	1	F	E	J
71v	Hair	139	1	1	F	E	J
72r	Hair	140	1	1	F	E	J
72v	Flesh	141	1	1	F[E]	E	J
73r	Flesh	142	1	1	F	E	J
73v	Hair	143	1	1	Fe	E	J

APPENDIX 2

The Utrecht and Harley Psalters: parallel collations

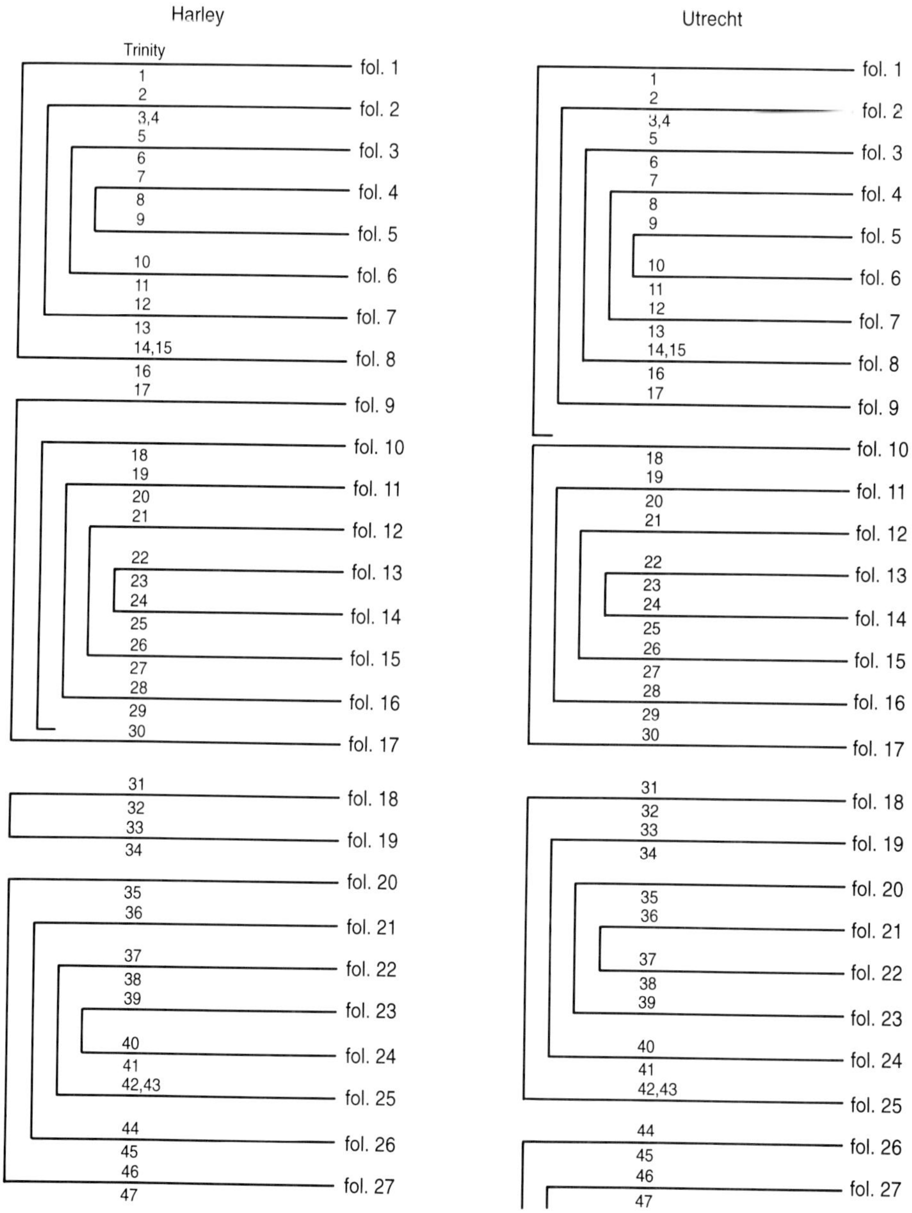

Harley

Trinity
fol. 1
1
2
fol. 2
3,4
5
fol. 3
6
7
fol. 4
8
9
fol. 5
10
fol. 6
11
12
fol. 7
13
14,15
fol. 8
16
17
fol. 9
fol. 10
18
19
fol. 11
20
21
fol. 12
22
fol. 13
23
24
fol. 14
25
26
fol. 15
27
28
fol. 16
29
30
fol. 17
31
fol. 18
32
33
fol. 19
34
fol. 20
35
36
fol. 21
37
fol. 22
38
39
fol. 23
40
fol. 24
41
42,43
fol. 25
44
fol. 26
45
46
fol. 27
47

Utrecht

fol. 1
1
2
fol. 2
3,4
5
fol. 3
6
7
fol. 4
8
9
fol. 5
10
fol. 6
11
12
fol. 7
13
14,15
fol. 8
16
17
fol. 9
fol. 10
18
19
fol. 11
20
21
fol. 12
22
fol. 13
23
24
fol. 14
25
26
fol. 15
27
28
fol. 16
29
30
fol. 17
31
fol. 18
32
33
fol. 19
34
fol. 20
35
36
fol. 21
37
fol. 22
38
39
fol. 23
40
fol. 24
41
42,43
fol. 25
44
fol. 26
45
46
fol. 27
47

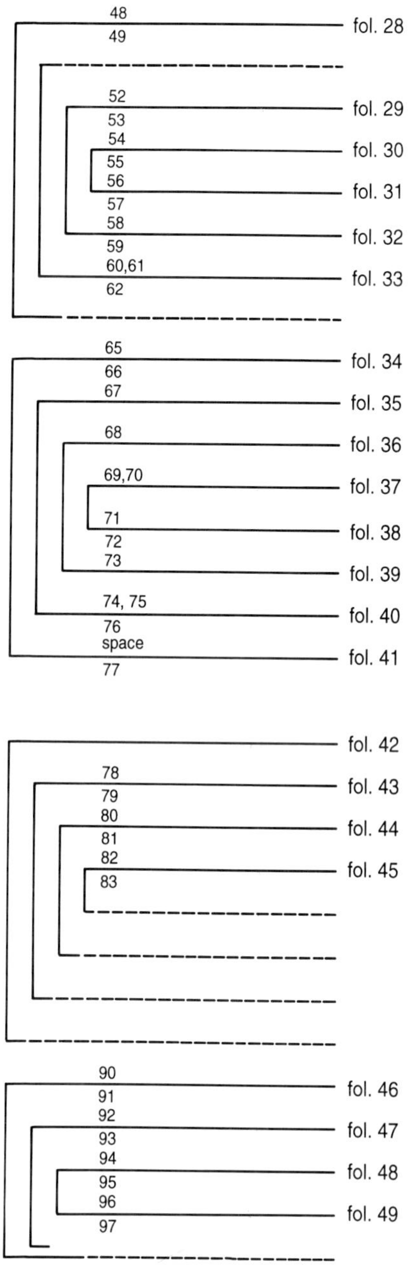

48
49 fol. 28
52
53 fol. 29
54
55 fol. 30
56
57 fol. 31
58
59 fol. 32
60,61
62 fol. 33
65
66 fol. 34
67 fol. 35
68 fol. 36
69,70 fol. 37
71
72 fol. 38
73 fol. 39
74, 75
76 fol. 40
space
77 fol. 41
fol. 42
78
79 fol. 43
80
81 fol. 44
82
83 fol. 45
90
91 fol. 46
92
93 fol. 47
94
95 fol. 48
96
97 fol. 49

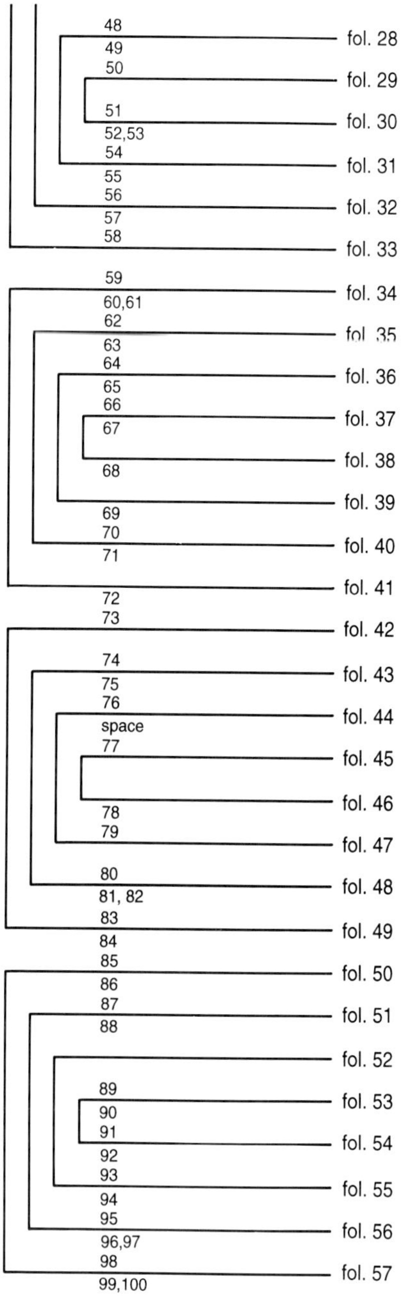

48
49 fol. 28
50 fol. 29
51
52,53 fol. 30
54
55 fol. 31
56
57 fol. 32
58 fol. 33
59
60,61 fol. 34
62
63 fol. 35
64
65 fol. 36
66
67 fol. 37
68 fol. 38
69 fol. 39
70
71 fol. 40
72 fol. 41
73 fol. 42
74
75 fol. 43
76
space fol. 44
77 fol. 45
78 fol. 46
79 fol. 47
80
81, 82 fol. 48
83
84 fol. 49
85
86 fol. 50
87
88 fol. 51
fol. 52
89
90 fol. 53
91
92 fol. 54
93
94 fol. 55
95
96,97 fol. 56
98
99,100 fol. 57

101
fol. 50
102
fol. 51
103
fol. 52
104
fol. 53
105
fol. 54
106
fol. 55
107
108
fol. 56
109
110
fol. 57
111
112,113
fol. 58
114,115
fol. 59
115,116
117
fol. 60
118
fol. 61
fol. 62
fol. 63
119
fol. 64
120,121
122
fol. 65
123,124
125
fol. 66
126,127
128
fol. 67
129,130
131
fol. 68
132,133
134
fol. 69
135
136
fol. 70
137
138
fol. 71
139
140
fol. 72
141
142
fol. 73
143

101
fol. 58
102
fol. 59
103
fol. 60
104
fol. 61
105
fol. 62
106
fol. 63
107
108
fol. 64
109
110
fol. 65
111
112,113
fol. 66
114,115
fol. 67
116,117
fol. 68
118
fol. 69
fol. 70
fol. 71
119
120,121
fol. 72
122,123
124,125
fol. 73
126,127
128
fol. 74
129,130
131
fol. 75
132,133
134
fol. 76
135
136
fol. 77
137
138
fol. 73
139
140
fol. 79
141,142
143
fol. 80
144
fol. 81
145,146
147
fol. 82
148
149,150
fol. 83
Cant. Isaiah
Cant. Hezekiah
fol. 84
Cant. Hannah
Cant. Moses 1
fol. 85
Cant. Habakkuk
Cant. Moses 2
fol. 86
fol. 87
Cant. of 3 Hebrews
Te Deum
fol. 88
Cant. Zacharias
Magnificat
fol. 89
Cant. Simeon
Gloria in Excelsis
Pater Noster
Sybolum Apostolorum
fol. 90
Fides Catholica
fol. 91
Psalm 151
fol. 92

Select bibliography

Alexander, J. J. G., 'Some aesthetic principles in the use of colour in Anglo-Saxon art', *Anglo-Saxon England*, 4, 1975, pp. 145–54.

Insular manuscripts 6th to the 9th Century, *A Survey of Manuscripts Illuminated in the British Isles*, vol. 1, 1978.

Medieval Illuminators and their Methods of Work, Yale, 1992.

Alexander, J. J. G. and C. M. Kauffmann, *English Illuminated Manuscripts 700–1500*. Catalogue of the Exhibition at the Royal Library of Albert 1, 29 Sept. – 10 Nov., Brussels, 1973.

Aratea, Faksimile Verlag, Luzern, 1989, with a commentary volume by B. Bischoff, B. Eastwood, T. Klein, F. Mütherich, and P. Obbema.

Arnold, T. (ed.), *Memorials of Bury St Edmunds Abbey*, vol. 1, Rolls Series, London, 1890.

Avril, F. and P. D. Stirnemann, *Bibliothèque Nationale, Département des Manuscrits: Manuscrits enluminés d'origine insulaire vii*[e]*–xx*[e] *siècle*, Paris, 1987.

Backhouse, J. M., 'The making of the Harley Psalter', *British Library Journal*, 10.2, 1984, pp. 97–113.

Backhouse, J. M., D. H. Turner, and L. Webster (eds.), *The Golden Age of Anglo-Saxon Art 966–1066*, Exhib. cat., London, 1984.

Barker, N. (ed.), *The York Gospels*, Roxburghe Club, London, 1986.

Bastgen, H. (ed.), *Libri Carolini*, Monumenta Germaniae Historica, Concilia, vol. 2 Supplementum, 1924.

Beckwith, J., *Ivory Carvings in Early Medieval England*, London, 1972.

Benson, G. R. and D. T. Tselos, 'New light on the origin of the Utrecht Psalter', *The Art Bulletin*, 13, 1931, pp. 13–79.

Bischoff, B., *Latin Palaeography: Antiquity and the Middle Ages*, trans. D. O. Cróinín and D. Ganz, Cambridge, 1990.

Bischoff, B. and W. Koehler, 'Un' edizione illustrata degli annali Ravennati del Basso Impero', *Studi Romagnoli*, 3, 1952, pp. 1–17.

Bishop, E. and F. Gasquet, *The Bosworth Psalter*, London, 1908.

Bishop, T. A. M., 'Notes on Cambridge Manuscripts Part IV: Mss. connected with St Augustine's Canterbury', *Transactions of the Cambridge Bibliographical Society*, 2.4, 1957, pp. 323–36.

'Notes on Cambridge Manuscripts Part V: Mss. connected with St Augustine's Canterbury, continued', *Transactions of the Cambridge Bibliographical Society*, 3.1, 1959, pp. 93–5.

'Notes on Cambridge Manuscripts, Part VII: The Early Minuscule of Christ Church Canterbury', *Transactions of the Cambridge Bibliographical Society*, 3.5, 1963, pp. 413–23.

English Caroline Minuscule, Oxford, 1971.

Boutemy, A., 'Two obituaries of Christ Church, Canterbury', *The English Historical Review*, 50, 1935, pp. 292–9.

'Un monument capital de l'enluminure anglo-saxonne: le Ms. 11 de Boulogne-sur-mer', *Cahiers de Civilisation Médiévale*, 1, 1958, pp. 179–82.

British Museum, *A Catalogue of the Harleian Manuscripts in the British Museum*, 4 vols., by H. Wanley, D. Casley. W. Hocker, and others. Revised by R. Nares, H. Ellis and T.H. Horne, 1808–12.

Brooks, N., *The Early History of the Church of Canterbury*, Leicester, 1984.

Brown, M. P., *Anglo-Saxon Manuscripts*, London, 1991.

'The role of the wax tablet in medieval literacy: a reconsideration in the light of a recent find from York', *British Library Journal*, 20.1, 1994, pp. 1–16.

Understanding Illuminated Manuscripts: A Guide to Technical Terms, London, 1994.

Brown, T. J., *A Palaeographer's View: The Selected Writings of Julian Brown*, J. Bately, M. P. Brown, and J. Roberts (eds.), London, 1993.

Brownrigg, L. L., 'Manuscripts containing English decoration 871–1066, catalogued and illustrated: a review', *Anglo-Saxon England*, 7, 1978, pp. 239–66.

Bruyne, D. de, 'Le Problème du Psautier Romain', *Revue Bénédictine*, 42, 1930, pp. 101–26.

Bullough, D. A., 'The educational tradition in England from Alfred to Aelfric: teaching *utriusque linguae*', *Settimane di Studio del Centro Italiano di Studi sull'Alto Medioevo*, 17, 1972, pp. 453–94.

Carruthers, M., *The Book of Memory: A Study of Memory in Medieval Culture*, Cambridge, 1990.

Carver, M. O. H., 'Contemporary artefacts illustrated in late Saxon manuscripts', *Archaeologia*, 108, 1986, pp. 117–45.

Catologus codicum manuscriptorum Bibliothecae Regiae Pars Tertia, 4, Paris, 1744.

Caviness, M. H., *The Early Stained Glass of Canterbury Cathedral c. 1175–1220*, Princeton, 1977.

'Conflicts between *Regnum* and *Sacerdotium* as reflected in a Canterbury Psalter of ca. 1215', *The Art Bulletin*, 61, 1979, pp. 38–58.

Corpus Vitrearum Medii Aevii. Great Britain Volume II: Christ Church Cathedral Canterbury, London, 1981.

Chaplais, P., 'The Anglo-Saxon chancery: from the diploma to the writ', *Journal of the Society of Archivists*, 3, 1966, pp. 160–76.

Review of D. N. Dumville, *English Script and Monastic History: Studies in Benedictinism AD. 950–1030*, Woodbridge, 1993, in *Journal of the Society of Archivists*, 16, 1995, pp. 105–7.

Chibnall, M. (ed.), *The Ecclesiastical History of Orderic Vitalis*, vol. 2, Oxford, 1969.

Clemoes, P. and C. R. Dodwell, *The Old English Illustrated Hexateuch*, Early English Manuscripts in Facsimile XVIII, Copenhagen, 1974.

Colgrave, B. (ed.), *The Paris Psalter*, Early English Manuscripts in Facsimile, VIII, Copenhagen, 1958.

Darlington, R. R. (ed.), *Vita S. Wulfstani*, London, 1928.

Davril, A. and L. Donnat (ed.), *Consuetudines Floriacenses Antiquiores: Corpus Consuetudinum Monasticarum*, VII.3, Sieburg, 1984, pp. 7–60.

Delisle, L., *Le Cabinet des manuscrits de la Bibliothèque impériale [nationale]*, 3 vols., Paris, 1868–91.

Dell'Era, A. (ed.), 'Una rielaborazione dell'Arato latino', *Studi Medievali*, Ser. 3, 20.1, 1979, pp. 269–301.

Deshman, R. 'The Leofric Missal and tenth-century English art', *Anglo-Saxon England*, 6, 1977, pp. 145–73.

'*Benedictus Monarcha et Monachus*. Early Medieval ruler theology and the Anglo-Saxon reform', *Frühmittelalterliche Studien*, 22, 1988, pp. 204–40.

DeWald, E. T., *The Illustrations of the Utrecht Psalter*, Princeton, 1932.

Dodwell, C. R., *The Canterbury School of Illumination 1066–1200*, Cambridge, 1954.

Painting in Europe 800–1200, Harmondsworth, 1971.

'Techniques of manuscript painting in Anglo-Saxon manuscripts', *Settimane di Studio del Centro Italiano di Studi sull'Alto Medioevo*, 18, 1971, pp. 643–62.

Anglo-Saxon Art: A New Perspective, Manchester, 1982.

'The final copy of the Utrecht Psalter and its relationship with the Utrecht and Eadwine Psalters', *Scriptorium*, 44.1, 1990, pp. 21–53.

The Pictorial Arts of the West, Yale, 1992.

(ed.) *Theophilus. De Diversis Artibus*, Oxford, 1986.

Duffey, J. E., 'The inventive group of illustrations in the Harley Psalter (British Museum Ms. Harley 603)', unpublished D.Phil. thesis, University of California, Berkeley, 1977.

Dufrenne, S., 'Les copies anglaises du Psautier d'Utrecht', *Scriptorium*, 18, 1964, pp. 185–97.

Les illustrations du Psautier d'Utrecht, Sources et apport carolingien, Paris, 1978.

Dumville, D. N., 'English libraries before 1066: use and abuse of the manuscript evidence', in M. W. Herren (ed.), *Insular Latin Studies*, Toronto, 1981, pp. 153–78.

English Caroline Script and Monastic History: Studies in Benedictinism, A.D. 950–1030, Woodbridge, 1993.

Engelbregt, J. H. A., *Het Utrechts Psalterium. Een eeuw wetenschappelijke bestudering (1860–1960)*, Utrecht, 1965.

Gaborit-Chopin, D., 'Les Dessins d'Adémar de Chabannes', *Bulletin Archéologique du Comité des travaux historiques et scientifiques*, Nouv. Ser. 3, 1967, pp. 163–225.

La décoration des manuscripts à Saint-Martial de Limoges et en Limousin du IXe au XIIe siècle, Paris-Geneva, 1969.

Gaehde, J. E., 'The draughtsmen of the Utrecht Psalter', in K. Bierbrauer, P.K. Klein, and W. Sauerländer (eds.), *Studien zur mittelalterlichen Kunst 800–1250, Festschrift für Florentine Mütherich zum 70. Geburtstag*, Munich, 1985, pp. 49–52.

Gameson, G., 'The Anglo-Saxon artists of the Harley (603) Psalter', *Journal of the British Archaeological Association*, 143, 1990, pp. 29–48.

'English manuscript art in the mid-eleventh century: the decorative tradition', *The Antiquaries Journal*, 71, 1990, pp. 64–122.

'Manuscript art at Christ Church, Canterbury, in the generation after St Dunstan' in N. Ramsay, M. Sparks and T. Tatton-Brown (eds.), *St Dunstan: His Life, Times and Cult*, Woodbridge, 1992, pp. 187–220.

'The Romanesque artist of the Harley Psalter', in P. Beal and J. Griffiths (ed.), *English Manuscript Studies 1100–1700*, 4, 1993, pp. 24–61.

Gibson, M. T., 'Who designed the Eadwine Psalter?', in S. Macready and F. H. Thompson (eds.), *Art and Patronage in the English Romanesque*, London, 1986, pp. 71–6.

Gibson, M. T., T. A. Heslop, and R. W. Pfaff (eds.), *The Eadwine Psalter: Text, Image, and Monastic Culture in Twelfth-Century Canterbury*, Modern Humanities Research Association, vol. 14, London, 1992.

Gifford, D. J., 'Iconographical notes towards a definition of the medieval fool', *Journal of the Warburg and Courtauld Institutes*, 37, 1974, pp. 336–42.

Gneuss, H., *Hymnar und Hymnen im englischen Mittelalter. Studien zur Überlieferung, Glossierung und Übersetzung lateinischer Hymnen in England mit einer Textausgabe der lateinisch-altenglischen Expositio Hymnorum*, Tübingen, 1968.

'Anglo-Saxon libraries from the Conversion to the Benedictine reform', *Settimane di Studio del Centro Italiano di Studi sull'Alto Medioevo*, 32, 1984, pp. 643–88.

'Liturgical books in Anglo-Saxon England and their Old English terminology', in M. Lapidge and H. Gneuss (eds.), *Learning and Literature in Anglo-Saxon England: Studies presented to Peter Clemoes on the occasion of his Sixty-Fifth Birthday*, Cambridge, 1985, pp. 91–142.

Gray Birch, W. de,*The History, Art and Palaeography of the Manuscript Styled the Utrecht Psalter*, London, 1876.

Gumbert, J. P., 'The sizes of manuscripts: some statistics and notes' in A.R.A. Croiset van Uchelen (ed.), *Hellinga: Festschrift/Feestbundel/Mélanges*, Amsterdam, 1980, pp. 277–88.

Hamel, C. R. F. de, *Glossed Books of the Bible and the Origins of the Paris Booktrade*, Bury St Edmund's, 1984.

Haney, K., *The Winchester Psalter, an Iconographic Study*, Leicester, 1986.

Hanslik, R. (ed.), 'Benedicti Regula', *Corpus Scriptorum Ecclesiasticorum Latinorum*, 75, 1960.

Harmer, F., *Anglo-Saxon Writs*, Manchester, 1952.

Harris, R. M., 'The marginal drawings of the Bury St Edmunds Psalter (Rome, Vatican Library Ms. Reg. lat. 12)', unpublished D.Phil. thesis, Princeton University, 1960.

'An illustration in an Anglo-Saxon Psalter in Paris', *Journal of the Warburg and Courtauld Institutes*, 26, 1963, pp. 255–63.

Hasler, R., 'Zu zwei Darstellungen aus der ältesten Kopie des Utrecht–Psalters, British Library, Codex Harleianus 603', *Zeitschrift für Kunstgeschichte*, 44, 1981, pp. 317–39.

Heimann, A., 'Three illustrations from the Bury St Edmunds Psalter and their prototypes. Notes on the iconography of some Anglo-Saxon drawings', *Journal of the Warburg and Courtauld Institutes*, 29, 1966, pp. 39–59.

'The last copy of the Utrecht Psalter', *The Year 1200: A Symposium*, The Metropolitan Museum of Art, New York, 1975, pp. 313–38.

'Notes unpublished', Warburg Institute, London.

Henderson, G. D. S., 'Late-antique influence on some English Mediaeval illustrations of Genesis', *Journal of the Warburg and Courtauld Institutes*, 25, 1962, pp. 172–98.

Early Medieval, Harmondsworth, 1972.

'The idiosyncrasy of late Anglo-Saxon religious imagery', in C. Hicks (ed.), *Harlaxton Medieval Studies II: England in the Eleventh Century*, Stamford, 1992, pp. 239–49.

'Emulation and invention in Carolingian art', in R. McKitterick (ed.), *Carolingian culture: emulation and innovation*, Cambridge, 1994, pp. 248–73.

Herbert, J. A., *Illuminated Manuscripts*, London, 1911.

Heslop, T. A., 'The Romanesque seal of Worcester Cathedral', *British Archaeological Association Conference Transactions*, 1, Worcester Cathedral, 1978, pp. 71–9.

"Brief in words, but heavy in the weight of its mysteries", *Art History*, 9, 1986, pp. 1–11.

'The production of *de luxe* manuscripts and the patronage of King Cnut and Queen Emma', *Anglo-Saxon England*, 19, 1990, pp. 151–95.

Review of D. N. Dumville, *English Caroline Script and Monastic History: Studies in Benedictinism, A.D. 950–1030*, Woodbridge, 1993, in *Journal of Theological Studies*, 45, 1994, pp. 378–81.

Higgit, J., 'Glastonbury, Dunstan, monasticism and manuscripts', *Art History*, 2, 1979, pp. 275–90.

Homburger, O., *Die Anfänge der Malschule von Winchester im X. Jahrhundert*, Leipzig, 1912.

James, M. R., *The Ancient Libraries of Canterbury and Dover*, Cambridge, 1903.

(ed.), *The Canterbury Psalter*, London, 1935.

Jones, C. W., *Bedae Pseudepigrapha: Scientific Writings Falsely Attributed to Bede*, Oxford, 1939.

Jordan, L., 'Demonic elements in Anglo-Saxon iconography' in P. Szarmach (ed.), *Sources of*

Anglo-Saxon Culture, Kalamazoo, 1986, pp. 283–317.

Kahsnitz, R., *Der Werdener Psalter in Berlin*, Düsseldorf, 1979.

Kantorowicz, E. H., 'The Quinity of Winchester', *The Art Bulletin*, 29, 1947, pp. 73–85.

Kauffmann, C. M., *Romanesque Manuscripts 1066–1200, A Survey of Manuscripts Illuminated in the British Isles*, vol. 3, London, 1975.

Kelleher, C., 'Illumination at St-Bertin at St-Omer under the abbacy of Odbert', unpublished D.Phil thesis, University of London, 1968, pp. 292–310.

Kendrick, T. D., *Late Saxon and Viking Art*, London, 1949.

Ker, N. R., 'Membra Disiecta', *British Museum Quarterly*, 12, 1938, pp. 130–5.

Catalogue of Manuscripts Containing Anglo-Saxon, Oxford, 1957.

English Manuscripts in the Century after the Norman Conquest, Oxford, 1960.

Kerscher, G., 'Quadriga Temporum. Studien zur Sol–Ikonographie in mittelalterlichen Handschriften und in der Architekturdekoration (mit einem Exkurs zum Codex 146 der Stiftsbibliothek Göttweig)', *Mitteilungen des Kunsthistorischen Institutes in Florenz*, 32, 1988, pp. 1–76.

Keynes, S., *The Diplomas of King Aethelred 'The Unready' 976–1016: A Study in their use as Historical Evidence*, Cambridge, 1980.

'King Athelstan's books', in M. Lapidge and H. Gneuss (eds.), *Learning and Literature in Anglo-Saxon England*, Cambridge, 1985, pp. 143–201.

Facsimiles of Anglo-Saxon Charters, London, 1991.

Anglo-Saxon manuscripts and other items of related interest in the library of Trinity College, Cambridge, Old English Newsletter *Subsidia*, vol. 18, 1992.

Kiff, J., 'Images of War: illustrations of warfare in early eleventh-century England', *Anglo-Norman Studies*, 7, 1985, pp. 177–194.

Knowles, D., *The Monastic Order in England*, 2nd edn, Cambridge 1966.

Koehler, W. R. and F. Mütherich, *Die Karolingischen Miniaturen, IV. Die Hofschule Kaiser Lothars*, Berlin, 1971.

Korhammer, P. M., 'The origin of the Bosworth Psalter', *Anglo-Saxon England*, 2, 1973, pp. 173–87.

Lampe, G. W. H. (ed.), *The Cambridge History of the Bible Vol. 2: The West from the Fathers to the Reformation*, Cambridge, 1969.

Lapidge, M., 'The study of Latin texts in late Anglo-Saxon England [1]', in N. Brooks (ed.), *Latin and the Vernacular Languages in Early Medieval Britain*, Leicester, 1982, pp. 99–140.

'Surviving booklists from Anglo-Saxon England', in M. Lapidge and H. Gneuss (eds.), *Learning and Literature in Anglo-Saxon England: Studies presented to Peter Clemoes on the occasion of his Sixty-Fifth Birthday*, Cambridge, 1985, pp. 33–89.

'Artistic and literary patronage in Anglo-Saxon England', *Settimane di Studio del Centro Italiano di Studi sull'Alto Medioevo*, 39, 1992, pp. 137–191.

Leroquais, V., *Les psautiers manuscrits latins des bibliothèques publiques de France*, 3 Vols, Mâcon, 1940–41.

Lobrichon, G., 'Le Psautier d'Otbert', in J. Vezin and J-H. Martin (eds.), *Mise en page et mise en texte du livre manuscrit*, Paris, 1990, pp. 175–8.

Lucas, P. J., 'Ms. Junius 11 and Malmesbury (1)', *Scriptorium*, 34, 1980, pp. 197–220.

Makothakat, J. M., *The Bosworth Psalter: A Critical Edition*, unpublished D.Phil. thesis, University of Ottawa, 1972.

McGurk, P., '*Germanici Caesaris Aratea cum scholiis*: A new illustrated witness from Wales', *Cylchgrawn Llyfrgell Genedlaethol Cymru (National Library of Wales Journal)*, 18, 1973, pp. 197–216.

McGurk, P., D. N. Dumville, M. R. Godden, and Ann Knock (eds.), *An Eleventh-Century Anglo-Saxon Illustrated Miscellany (British Library Cotton Tiberius B.V, Part 1)*, Early English Manuscripts in Facsimile XXI, Copenhagen, 1983.

McKitterick, R., 'Carolingian book production: some problems', *The Library*, 6th Series, 12, 1990, pp. 1–33.

'Text and image', in R. McKitterick (ed.), *The Uses of Literacy in Early Mediaeval Europe*, Cambridge, 1990.

Morgan, N., *Early Gothic Manuscripts (1): 1190–1250. A Survey of Manuscripts Illuminated in the British Isles*, Vol. 4, London, 1982.

Mostert, M., *The Library of Fleury: A Provisional List of Manuscripts*, Hilversum, 1989.

Noel, W. G., 'The making of BL Harley Mss. 2506 and 603', unpublished Ph.D. dissertation, Cambridge, 1993.

'The division of work in the Harley Psalter', in Linda L. Brownrigg (ed.), *Making the Medieval Book: Techniques of Production*, Los Altos Hills, 1995, pp. 1–15.

'A Prototype for the Bury Psalter', in A. Gransden (ed.), *British Archaeological Association Conference Transactions*. Bury St Edmunds, forthcoming.

Ohlgren, T. H., *Anglo-Saxon Textual Illustration*, Kalamazoo, 1992.

Omont, H., *Psautier illustré (XIIIe S.). Reproduction des 107 miniatures du manuscrit latin 8846 de la Bibliothèque Nationale*, Paris, 1906.

O'Neill, P. P., 'Latin learning at Winchester in the early eleventh century: the evidence of the Lambeth Psalter', *Anglo-Saxon England*, 20, 1991, pp. 143–66.

Orchard, N. A., 'The Bosworth Psalter and the St Augustine's Missal', in R. Sharpe (ed.), *Canterbury and the Norman Conquest*, 1995, forthcoming.

Ortenberg, V., *The English Church and the Continent in the Tenth and Eleventh Centuries*, Oxford, 1992.

Pächt, O., C. R. Dodwell, and F. Wormald, *The St Albans Psalter (Albani Psalter)*, London, 1960.

Page, R., 'The study of Latin texts in late Anglo-Saxon England [II]', in N. Brooks (ed.), *Latin and the Vernacular Languages in Early Medieval Britain*, Leicester, 1982, pp. 141–65.

Panofsky, D., 'The textual basis of the Utrecht Psalter illustrations', *The Art Bulletin*, 25, 1943, pp. 50–8.

Pfaff, R. W., 'Eadui Basan: Scriptorum Princeps?', in C. Hicks (ed.), *Harlaxton Medieval Studies II: England in the Eleventh Century*, Stamford, 1992, pp. 267–83.

Porcher, J., *L'Art roman à Saint-Martial de Limoges*, 1950.

Rand, E. K., *A Survey of the Manuscripts of Tours*, 2 vols, Studies in the Script of Tours I, Cambridge, Massachusetts, 1929.

Rand, E. K. and L. W. Jones, *The Earliest Book of Tours, with Supplementary Descriptions of Other Manuscripts of Tours*, Studies in the Script of Tours II, Cambridge, Massachusetts, 1934.

Randall, R. H., 'An eleventh-century ivory pectoral cross', *Journal of the Warburg and Courtauld Institutes*, 25, 1962, pp. 159–71.

Raw, B. C., 'The construction of Oxford, Bodleian Library, Junius 11', *Anglo-Saxon England*, 13, 1984, pp. 187–207.

Anglo-Saxon Crucifixion Iconography and the Art of the Monastic Revival, Cambridge, 1990.

Rella, F. A., 'Continental manuscripts acquired for English centers in the tenth and early eleventh centuries: a preliminary checklist', *Anglia*, 98, 1980, pp. 107–16.

Rensch Erbes, R., 'The development of the medieval harp: a re-examination of the Utrecht Psalter and its progeny', *Gesta*, 11.2, 1972, pp. 27–36.

Rickert, M., *Painting in Britain: The Middle Ages*, Harmondsworth, 1954.

Rigg, A. G. and G. R. Wieland, 'A Canterbury classbook of the mid-eleventh century (the 'Cambridge Songs' manuscript)', *Anglo-Saxon England*, 4, 1975, pp. 113–30.

Rosenthal, J. E., 'The historiated canon tables of the Arenberg Gospels', unpublished D.Phil.

thesis, Columbia University 1974.

'The unique architectural settings of the Arenberg Evangelists', in K. Bierbrauer, P.K. Klein, and W. Sauerländer (eds.), *Studien zur mittelalterlichen Kunst 800–1250, Festschrift fur Florentine Mütherich zum 70. Geburtstag*, Munich, 1985, pp. 145–53.

Samaran, C. and R. Marichal, *Catalogue des manuscrits en écriture latine, portant des indications de date, de lieu ou de copiste*, vol.2, Paris, 1962.

Sawyer, P. H., *Anglo-Saxon Charters, An Annotated List and Bibliography*, Royal Historical Society Guides and Handbooks 8, London, 1968.

Sanders, W. B. (ed.), *Facsimiles of Anglo-Saxon Manuscripts*, 3 vols., Southampton, 1878–84.

Saxl, F. and H. Meier, *Catalogue of Astrological and Mythological Illuminated Manuscripts of the Latin Middle Ages III: Manuscripts in English Libraries*, 2 vols., ed. H. Bober, London, 1953.

Schapiro, M., 'The image of the disappearing Christ: the ascension in English art around the year 1000', *Gazette des Beaux-Arts*, 6th ser. 23, 1943, pp. 135–52.

Scheller, R. W., *A Survey of Medieval Model Books*, Haarlem, 1963.

Sisam, C. and K., *The Salisbury Psalter*, Early English Text Society, 242, 1959, pp. 47–52.

Soubiran, J. (ed.), *Cicéron: Aratea, Fragments poétiques*, Paris, 1972.

Southern, R. W., *The Making of the Middle Ages*, London, 1953.

The Life of St Anselm by Eadmer, Oxford, 1963.

Stenton, F. M., *Anglo-Saxon England*, 3rd edn, Oxford, 1971.

Stettiner, R., *Die illustrierten Prudentius-Handschriften*, Berlin, 1895.

Stevenson, W. H., *Asser's Life of King Alfred*, Oxford, 1904.

Stork, N. P., *Through a Gloss Darkly: Aldhelm's Riddles in the British Library Ms. Royal 12.C.xxiii*, Toronto, 1990.

Stubbs, W. (ed.), *Memorials of St Dunstan*, Rolls Series, London, 1874.

Swarzenski, H., 'Unknown Bible pictures by W. de Brailes', *Journal of the Walters Art Gallery*, 1, 1938, pp. 65–9.

Symons, T. (ed.), *Regularis Concordia*, Edinburgh, 1953.

Talbot Rice, D., *English Art 871–1100*, Oxford, 1952.

Temple, E., *Anglo-Saxon Manuscripts 900–1066. A Survey of Manuscripts Illuminated in the British Isles*, vol. 2, London, 1976.

Teviotdale, E. C., 'The making of the Cotton Troper', in C. Hicks (ed.), *Harlaxton Medieval Studies II: England in the Eleventh Century*, Stamford, 1992, pp. 301–16.

Thompson, E. M., *The New Palaeographical Society Facsimiles of Ancient Manuscripts*, 2nd series, London, 1903–30.

Thomson, R. M., 'The library of Bury St Edmunds Abbey in the eleventh and twelfth centuries', *Speculum*, 47, 1972, pp. 617–45.

Manuscripts from St Albans Abbey, 1066–1235, 2 vols., Bury St Edmunds, 1982.

Toubert, H., 'L'illustration dans les colonnes du texte', in J. Vezin and J. H. Martin (eds.), *Mise en page et mise en texte du livre manuscrit*, Paris, 1990.

Tselos, D., *The Sources of the Utrecht Psalter Miniatures*, Minneapolis, 1955.

'English manuscript illumination and the Utrecht Psalter', *The Art Bulletin*, 41, 1959, pp. 137–49.

'Defensive addenda to the problem of the Utrecht Psalter', *The Art Bulletin*, 49, 1967, pp. 334–49.

Utrecht Psalter, A collotype facsimile, 2 vols., The Palaeographical Society, 1874.

Codices Selecti Phototypice Impressi, 75, Graz, 1982–4, with a commentary volume, including a bibliography, by K. Van der Horst and J. H. A. Engelbregt.

Vaccari, A., 'I Salteri di s. Girolamo e di s. Agostino', *Scritti di erudizione e di filologia*, 1, Rome,

1952, pp. 207–55.

Vezin, J., 'Manuscrits des dixième et onzième siècles copiés en Angleterre en minuscule caroline et conservés à la Bibliothèque national de Paris, in *Humanisme actif. Mélanges d'art et de littérature offerts à Julien Cain*, 2 vols., Paris, 1968, vol. 2, pp. 283–96.

'La réalisation matérielle des manuscrits latins pendant la haut Moyen Âge', *Codicologica*, 2, 1978, pp. 15–51.

Weber, R. (ed.), 'Le Psautier Romain et les autres anciens Psautiers latins', *Collectanea Biblica Latina*, 10.2, 1953.

Weber, R. and B. Fischer (eds.), *Biblia Sacra: Iuxta Vulgatam Versionem*, 2 vols., Stuttgart, 1969.

Weitzmann, K. and H. Kessler, *The Illustrations in the Manuscripts of the Septuagint 1: Genesis*, Princeton, 1986.

Whitelock, Dorothy (ed.), *Anglo-Saxon Wills*, Cambridge, 1930.

Wieland, G. R., *The Canterbury Hymnal*, Pontifical Institute of Medieval Studies, Toronto, 1982.

The Latin Glosses on Arator and Prudentius in Cambridge University Library, Ms. Gg.5.35, Toronto, 1983.

'The glossed manuscript: classbook or library book?', *Anglo-Saxon England*, 14, 1985, pp. 153–73.

'The Anglo-Saxon manuscripts of Prudentius *Psychomachia*', *Anglo-Saxon England*, 16, 1987, pp. 213–321.

Wilmart, A., 'The Prayers of the Bury Psalter', *The Downside Review*, 48, 1930, pp. 198–216.

Codices Reginenses Latini, 1, Vatican, 1937.

Woodruff, H., *The Illustrated Manuscripts of Prudentius*, Harvard, 1930.

Wormald, F., *English Kalendars Before AD 1100*, Henry Bradshaw Society, vol. 72, 1934.

English Drawings of the Tenth and Eleventh Centuries, London, 1952.

The Utrecht Psalter, Utrecht, 1953.

'Late Anglo-Saxon art: some questions and suggestions', in M. Meiss (ed.), *Studies in Western Art: Acts of the Twentieth International Congress of the History of Art*, Princeton, 1963, pp. 19–26.

Wright, C. E. and R. C., *The Diary of Humphrey Wanley 1715–1726*, 2 vols., London, 1966.

Wright, D. H., *The Vespasian Psalter: British Museum, Cotton Vespasian A.I*, Early English Manuscripts in Facsimile xiv, Copenhagen, 1967.

Yapp, W. B., 'The birds of English manuscripts', *Journal of Medieval History*, 5, 1979, pp. 315–48.

Zarnecki, G. *et al.*, *English Romanesque Art 1066–1200*, (Exhib. Cat.), London, 1984.

Index of Psalm iconography

Index of manuscripts

General index